Davi

Manchester University Press

BRIAN MCFARLANE, NEIL SINYARD *series editors*
ALLEN EYLES, PHILIP FRENCH, SUE HARPER,
TIM PULLEINE, JEFFREY RICHARDS, TOM RYALL
series advisers

already published

Lindsay Anderson: Cinema authorship JOHN IZOD, KARL MAGEE, KATHRYN MACKENZIE, ISABELLE GOURDIN-SANGOUARD

Anthony Asquith TOM RYALL

Richard Attenborough SALLY DUX

Roy Ward Baker GEOFF MAYER

Sydney Box ANDREW SPICER

Jack Clayton NEIL SINYARD

Lance Comfort BRIAN MCFARLANE

Terence Davies WENDY EVERETT

Terence Fisher PETER HUTCHINGS

Terry Gilliam PETER MARKS

Derek Jarman ROWLAND WYMER

Launder and Gilliat BRUCE BABINGTON

Mike Leigh TONY WHITEHEAD

Richard Lester NEIL SINYARD

Joseph Losey COLIN GARDNER

Carol Reed PETER WILLIAM EVANS

Michael Reeves BENJAMIN HALLIGAN

Karel Reisz COLIN GARDNER

Tony Richardson ROBERT SHAIL

J. Lee Thompson STEVE CHIBNALL

Michael Winterbottom BRIAN MCFARLANE and DEANE WILLIAMS

David Lean

MELANIE WILLIAMS

Manchester University Press

Copyright © Melanie Williams 2014

The right of Melanie Williams to be identified as the author of this work has been asserted by her in accordance with the Copyright, Designs and Patents Act 1988.

Published by Manchester University Press
Altrincham Street, Manchester M1 7JA, UK
www.manchesteruniversitypress.co.uk

British Library Cataloguing-in-Publication Data
A catalogue record for this book is available from the British Library

ISBN 978 1 5261 1681 9 *paperback*

First published by Manchester University Press in hardback 2014

This edition first published 2017

The publisher has no responsibility for the persistence or accuracy of URLs for any external or third-party internet websites referred to in this book, and does not guarantee that any content on such websites is, or will remain, accurate or appropriate.

Typeset in Scala with Meta display by
Koinonia, Manchester
Printed in Great Britain by
TJ International Ltd, Padstow

Contents

LIST OF PLATES — *page* vii
SERIES EDITORS' FOREWORD — ix
ACKNOWLEDGEMENTS — xi

1 Introduction — 1

2 Cutting and Coward: David Lean's early career and *In Which We Serve* (1942), *This Happy Breed* (1944) and *Blithe Spirit* (1945) — 15

3 Nineteenth-century blues: *Great Expectations* (1946), *Oliver Twist* (1948), *Madeleine* (1950) and *Hobson's Choice* (1954) — 40

4 Women in love: *Brief Encounter* (1945), *The Passionate Friends* (1949) and *Summer Madness* (1955) — 84

5 Men of vision: *The Sound Barrier* (1952), *The Bridge on the River Kwai* (1957) and *Lawrence of Arabia* (1962) — 133

6 Feminising the epic: *Doctor Zhivago* (1965), *Ryan's Daughter* (1970) and *A Passage to India* (1984) — 175

FILMOGRAPHY AS DIRECTOR — 246
BIBLIOGRAPHY — 253
INDEX — 262

List of plates

1. Flashbacks from home: Shorty (John Mills) remembers his wedding to Freda (Kay Walsh) in *In Which We Serve* (Two Cities Films, 1942) — page 22
2. A domestic still life: Frank (Robert Newton), Sylvia (Alison Leggatt) and Ethel (Celia Johnson) listen to the radio announcement of the death of George V in *This Happy Breed* (Two Cities Films, 1944) — 29
3. Ghostly first wife Elvira (Kay Hammond) comes between Charles (Rex Harrison) and second wife Ruth (Constance Cummings) in *Blithe Spirit* (Cineguild-Two Cities Films, 1945) — 34
4. Miss Havisham (Martita Hunt) and Estella (Jean Simmons) conspire to break the heart of Pip (Anthony Wager) in *Great Expectations* (Cineguild, 1946) — 46
5. Nineteenth-century noir: Sikes (Robert Newton), Fagin (Alec Guinness) and Nancy (Kay Walsh) argue over the fate of Oliver (John Howard Davies) in *Oliver Twist* (Cineguild, 1948) — 57
6. Woman as enigma: Ann Todd as the eponymous heroine at the end of *Madeleine* (Cineguild, 1950) — 70
7. Father versus daughter: Hobson (Charles Laughton) clashes with Maggie (Brenda de Banzie) in *Hobson's Choice* (London Films in Association with British Lion, 1954) — 75
8. Sweet sorrow: Laura (Celia Johnson) and Alec (Trevor Howard) say goodbye in *Brief Encounter* (Cineguild, 1945) — 98
9. The love triangle of *The Passionate Friends* (Cineguild, 1949): Mary (Ann Todd), Howard (Claude Rains) and Stephen (Trevor Howard) — 108
10. Jane (Katharine Hepburn) and her camera in *Summer Madness* (Lopert Films/London Films, 1955) — 119
11. Ridgefield (Ralph Richardson) seduces Tony (Nigel Patrick) with a model of the new Prometheus in *The Sound Barrier* (London Films, 1952) — 138

viii LIST OF PLATES

12 Nearer the end than the beginning: Nicholson (Alec Guinness) and Saito (Sessue Hayakawa) at sundown in *The Bridge on the River Kwai* (Horizon Pictures, Columbia, 1957) 150
13 T. E. Lawrence (Peter O'Toole) surveys his new white robes in *Lawrence of Arabia* (Horizon Films, Columbia, 1962) 158
14 Zhivago (Omar Sharif) and Lara (Julie Christie) seek refuge from revolution in *Doctor Zhivago* (Carlo Ponti/MGM, 1965) 198
15 The voluptuous quality of an erotic thought: Rose (Sarah Miles) among the lilies in *Ryan's Daughter* (Faraway Productions, MGM, 1970) 216
16 A life-changing moment of physical contact: Aziz (Victor Banerjee) offers his hand to Adela (Judy Davis) as they climb up to the Marabar caves in *A Passage to India* (G. W. Films, John Heyman, Edwards Sands, Home Box Office 1984) 230

Series editors' foreword

The aim of this series is to present in lively, authoritative volumes a guide to those film-makers who have made British cinema a rewarding but still under-researched branch of world cinema. The intention is to provide books which are up-to-date in terms of information and critical approach, but not bound to any one theoretical methodology. Though all books in the series will have certain elements in common – comprehensive filmographies, annotated bibliographies, appropriate illustration – the actual critical tools employed will be the responsibility of the individual authors.

Nevertheless, an important recurring element will be a concern for how the oeuvre of each film-maker does or does not fit certain critical and industrial contexts, as well as for the wider social contexts which helped to shape not just that particular film-maker but the course of British cinema at large.

Although the series is director-orientated, the editors believe that reference to a variety of stances and contexts is more likely to reconceptualise and reappraise the phenomenon of British cinema as a complex, shifting field of production. All the texts in the series will engage in detailed discussion of major works of the film-makers involved, but they all consider as well the importance of other key collaborators, of studio organisation, of audience reception, of recurring themes and structures: all those other aspects which go towards the construction of a national cinema.

The series explores and charts a field which is more than ripe for serious excavation. The acknowledged leaders of the field will be reappraised; just as important, though, will be the bringing to light of those who have not so far received any serious attention. They are all part of the very rich texture of British cinema, and it will be the work of this series to give them all their due.

Acknowledgements

Firstly, I would like to thank the David Lean Foundation for their stalwart support and financial assistance during the long gestation of this book; likewise, the staff of Manchester University Press have been outstanding in their patience and sensitivity, particularly Matthew Frost. The series editors deserve my enormous thanks for giving the book the go-ahead and sticking with it. I would like to thank Neil Sinyard in particular for his unending encouragement, kindness, and good advice. As Feisal says in *Lawrence of Arabia*: 'what I owe you is beyond evaluation'.

I wish to thank my former colleagues at the University of Hull and my current colleagues at the University of East Anglia for their kind words and deeds (especially coffee and cake appointments) which have kept me going over some tough years, with extra thanks for support in the project's late stages going to Eylem Atakav and Su Holmes. The University of St Andrews, Queen Mary, University of London, Manchester Metropolitan University and BFI Southbank enabled me to try out my ideas at research seminars, conferences and discussion panels. The BFI library and BFI Special Collections have been indispensable sources of key research materials, both units being peopled by helpful and generous staff; ditto the University of Reading's Special Collections (UoR Spec Coll) and the East Anglian Film Archive. Thanks also to Steve Chibnall for providing the book's cover image and Studio Canal for permitting its use.

All newspaper and magazine reviews referred to, unless otherwise indicated, are taken from BFI library microfiches (and therefore don't have individual references in the Bibliography).

I would like to dedicate this book to my friends and my family, those who are still here and those who have passed on. I think my mum would have been very proud of this book; I really wish she was here to read it. I hope one day my wonderful daughter will; she owes her name to a David Lean heroine, after all. And to my husband Matthew Bailey, for his love, thoughtfulness, fun, hours of extra childcare, square meals, tea, sympathy, sparkling conversation, inspired suggestions and editorial shrewdness, for everything really: thank you from the bottom of my heart.

ial establishment of the auteur theory in Anglo-American critical circles.
Introduction

When the critic Graham Fuller interviewed David Lean in 1985, his opening observation was that the director's films were 'not everyone's cup of tea.'[1] Leaving aside the apposite Englishness of the metaphor, prompting recollection of all the cups of tea that punctuate Lean's masterpiece *Brief Encounter* (1945), Fuller was quite right to detect a certain degree of critical ambivalence towards the work of David Lean. On one hand, Lean had an incredibly high standing in the industry and retained that reputation even during his long fallow period in the 1970s and early 1980s. 'A rule of mine is this', said William Goldman in 1983: 'there are always three hot directors and one of them is always David Lean.'[2] Many of his films had been regarded as cinematic touchstones by his contemporaries, directors such as George Cukor, Billy Wilder and William Wyler, and continued to be highly influential among the next generation of filmmakers, with Steven Spielberg in particular crediting Lean with inspiring him to become a director. But while Lean had the admiration of his peers, a brace of Oscars and other awards, and could boast impressive box-office figures for many of his films, critical acclaim was often much harder to come by. As one journalist remarked in 1985: 'The curious thing about Sir David Lean is that everyone likes him except the critics.'[3] This imbalance of opinion was very clearly demonstrated by the 2002 results of *Sight and Sound*'s ten-yearly poll of the greatest films of all time. Lean enjoyed an extremely strong position in the list based solely on directors' opinions: in their estimation, *Lawrence of Arabia* (1962) was the fourth greatest film and Lean the joint-ninth greatest director of all time. By contrast, in the equivalent lists compiled from the votes of critics, Lean and his films were absolutely nowhere to be seen.[4]

David Lean's lesser reputation among critics is a legacy of the initial establishment of the auteur theory in Anglo-American critical circles. In Andrew Sarris's founding text of English-speaking auteurism, *The American Cinema*, Lean was placed under the pejorative heading of 'less than meets the eye', a deliberately iconoclastic grouping into which Sarris decanted all the directors whose industry veneration he felt belied their essential emptiness of vision (admittedly Lean was in very good company there, next to the likes of John Huston, Elia Kazan, Carol Reed, and his admirers Billy Wilder and William Wyler).[5] A few years earlier, the first issue of the influential British-based magazine *Movie* had included an infamous directorial histogram and editorial which denigrated British cinema for its 'lack of what we would consider as talent'.[6] David Lean was no exception to this general rule, placed in the category 'competent or ambitious' (an ambiguous pairing) with his most recent film *The Bridge on the River Kwai* (1957) specifically singled out for exemplifying the bogus formula for the 'quality' picture.[7] It is instructive to compare Lean's reputation at this time with another British director who certainly *was* the object of auteurist adoration, Alfred Hitchcock. Whereas Hitchcock's British work was characterised by the auteur critics as preliminary practice for a talent that reached full fruition within the Hollywood studio system, by comparison Lean's early British work was generally seen as the highpoint of his career before it was swallowed up by overblown international epics.[8] As Robert Horton points out, 'Lean's critical profile suffered from the timing' of the auteurist moment; just at the point when 'Hitchcock needed championing, Lean was busy winning Oscars'[9] for his epic films, and appeared to be critically invulnerable. However, on a personal level, this was far from the truth. Lean was profoundly affected by critical disdain for his work, still able to quote word for word a slighting review from twenty years before. 'The critics are the intellectuals. I'm always frightened of intellectuals',[10] he admitted in 1984, referring back to long-standing feelings of intellectual inferiority compounded by having been overshadowed at school by his academically gifted younger brother Edward. For that reason, when critics disapproved of a film, their judgement had a particular force: 'There it is written down – *The Times* says so, the *Daily Telegraph* says so, the *Daily Mail* says so, all shades of opinion – and it *must* be true.'[11] Lean's worst fears were realised by the excoriating reviews he received for *Ryan's Daughter* (1970) and the blow they dealt to his confidence was a strong contributory factor in his fourteen-year absence from the screen thereafter.

With the respectful and celebratory reception of Lean's final film, *A Passage to India* (1984) – 'An old master's new triumph'[12] announced the cover of *Time* magazine – and the 'chorus of awe-struck hosannas'[13] that greeted the 1989 restoration of *Lawrence of Arabia*, it might appear that the critical battle had been won, and that Lean's advocates now outnumbered his detractors. No longer would the director be disparaged as 'safely schematic, blandly middlebrow and British, the sort of artist for whom knighthoods in the arts were invented'.[14] Even those who had, in Kevin Jackson's words, 'lavish[ed] praise on his early British films – particularly the Dickens adaptations – the better to disdain his international epics'[15], would have to revise their opinion of Lean's later achievements in the light of the reappraisal of *Lawrence*. Up to a point this is true, and the publication in the mid-1990s of Kevin Brownlow's brilliant and definitive biography of David Lean certainly helped to consolidate the growing sense that he was a filmmaker worth taking seriously.[16] Even so, there still remain notable pockets of that critical ambivalence towards his work detected by Fuller. There was a striking example in *Sight and Sound*'s coverage of David Lean's centenary in 2008, for instance. A series of articles on Lean as film editor, on his representation of empire and on the restoration of his films was prefaced with a short introduction by the magazine's editor Nick James in which he acknowledges that *Sight and Sound* had been 'routinely dismissive' of Lean's work in the past and goes on to explain:

> If that seems absurd in retrospect, then we must yet acknowledge that Lean's films are more complex in their craftsmanship than in their conception. That he made enduringly gripping and entertaining films is because he believed in a critically unfashionable kind of total cinema, one in which every moment counts towards the primacy of thrilling the audience ... that's what he was: a hugely successful populist director with no Boswell on hand to raise his reputation, as Truffaut did with Hitchcock. We're not aiming to laud Lean in quite that way here, but we do want to give him his due.[17]

Somewhat damning Lean with faint praise, James admits the popularity and stylistic verve of Lean's films but still insists that technical craft outpaced conceptual complexity, echoing critiques first made back in the 1960s. The tone suggests that obligation rather than enthusiasm may have driven the editorial decision to devote space to the director, culminating in the final statement on giving Lean no more than 'his due', declining any suggestion that they might 'laud' him – even on the occasion of his centenary.

In contrast, this book aims to give Lean his due *and* laud him; indeed, it would be impossible for me to do the former without doing the latter. David Lean remains one of the outstanding directors of British as well as world cinema, and thus an essential addition to a book series dedicated to British filmmakers. As Peter Hutchings has noted, scholarship on British cinema has exhibited a tendency 'to shy away from making evaluative judgements', to claim the significance of particular texts on the grounds that they are 'interesting' rather than because they are 'good'.[18] There is very cogent reasoning behind the valorisation of 'the interesting' as equally worthy of attention as 'the good' and a retreat from a purely evaluative agenda of film studies in favour of more pluralistic concerns. However, Hutchings suggests that 'despite all the new work being done on British film, evaluative claims are not being made nearly enough'[19], an argument with which I fully concur. So while this book gives full consideration to the many ways in which Lean's body of work is interesting, it also aims to demonstrate the ways in which it 'deploys the resources of cinema in an imaginative, intelligent and distinctive manner';[20] in short, why these are also good films. To argue that David Lean made good films might seem to be pushing at an open door. But, as I've shown, the fact remains that Lean still occupies a strangely subaltern position within British film's critical culture. It is telling, for example, that this is the first full-length study of all the director's films to originate from a British author and press, nearly all previous scholarly overviews of that kind having come from the United States. What the journalist Hollis Alpert observed in 1965 still seems surprisingly true: that Lean is somehow 'less honoured in his own country than anywhere else'.[21] Yet his films offer one of the most triumphantly affirmative and convincing answers I can think of to Peter Wollen's question to British cinema scholars, 'Which are the films that really count, the ones we wouldn't mind seeing again and again? ... The British cinema that interests me is a cinema which produces great films – films which are masterpieces.'[22]

The original auteurist grounds for dismissing Lean frequently rested on his perceived impersonality as a filmmaker, a criticism which perplexed Lean: 'they tell me that I am not a personal filmmaker. I don't know what they mean by this. Everything goes through me from script to final print, and nothing is done which is not a part of me.'[23] The archival materials available attest to his full involvement in all aspects of his films, with notes pertaining to every single stage of production from the initial germ of an idea right through to the tiniest of final editorial tweaks. Sometimes this attention to infinitesimal detail was presented as the cornerstone of Lean's achievement, as with George Stevens Jr's quotation from Dickens – 'Genius is the infinite capacity for taking pains' – at the gala presentation of Lean's American Film Institute lifetime achievement award. However, the director's total commitment to the film in hand could equally be presented in a negative light as suffocatingly perfectionist, 'like being made to build the Taj Mahal out of toothpicks'[24] as Robert Mitchum memorably remarked. This is the David Lean of the icy stare and the long impenetrable silence, of whom a technician on *Kwai* allegedly complained: 'The bloody perfectionist!

INTRODUCTION 5

He shot thirty seconds of film a day and then sat on a rock and stared at his goddamn bridge!'[25] Some of those kinds of stories are undoubtedly apocryphal exaggerations but Lean's commitment once a film was under way was indeed absolute and all-encompassing: one of his collaborators described him as having 'no peripheral vision'.[26] While working for him on *Doctor Zhivago* (1965), Rod Steiger even wondered aloud 'just how much of that man is alive when he is not working'.[27] As far back as *The Passionate Friends* in 1949, Lean was being described as a fanatical filmmaker with 'celluloid instead of blood in his veins',[28] simultaneously suggesting cinematic prowess but also possibly an unfeeling approach to his craft, technically exacting but essentially cold. And yet Lean spoke of his attachment to his films as 'entirely emotional' and likened choosing a project to 'falling in love'.[29] His question to fledgling directors seeking his guidance was never a practical one but the more creatively inclined 'do you dream?',[30] and he described his own 'dream-like imagination' when envisaging scenes for a film.[31] What emerged from Lean's daydreaming was a definite vision for his films: 'it's as if I've got an imaginary negative in my mind, and when I get on the set, I try to make a positive which will match that negative.'[32]

This book aims to give full and balanced credit to Lean's collaborators for the achievements of the films, particularly key figures like his fellow Cineguild members Anthony Havelock-Allan and Ronald Neame in his earlier career, and in later years, producer Sam Spiegel, composer Maurice Jarre and – particularly – writer Robert Bolt, as well as the many actors who contributed memorable and moving performances to his films.[33] There is not as much space in this book as I would like to devote to the invaluable contributions made to Lean's films by other production staff, from outstanding cinematographers like Guy Green, Freddie Young and Jack Hildyard and production designers John Bryan and John Box, to stalwart continuity supervisors Maggie Unsworth and Barbara Cole or someone as indefinable and indispensable as Lean's property master, location scout and all-round fixer Eddie Fowlie. But at the same time, my account of the films is still underpinned by the belief that David Lean was the central guiding intelligence behind each of his films. This is true even of his collaborative debut with Noël Coward, *In Which We Serve* (1942); that the film works in cinematic terms is largely down to Lean's script guidance, co-direction and editorial expertise. Although Lean took very seriously the advice Noël Coward gave him to 'always come out of a different hole' and never do the same thing twice, Lean's body of work actually has more than enough aesthetic and narratological continuity to satisfy the most avowed auteurist. Moreover, Lean's position on the authorial role of the director converged to a remarkable degree with the auteur theory. Even back in 1947, Lean was arguing that the 'best films are generally those that have the stamp of one man's personality'.[34] A later comment echoed Alexandre Astruc's auteurist notion of the *camera-stylo* (camera-pen): 'What is directing? It's trying to use a lot of people and some very heavy apparatus, and give it all the lightness of a pen while you are writing.'[35] And Lean's status as the man in charge of the machinery, the one with the central controlling vision, was absolutely self-evident on set, according to his former cinematographer Nicolas Roeg: 'If the Martians landed they would not have needed to say "Take me to your leader". They would have picked David out from the crowd immediately.'[36]

My approach to Lean's work deploys methodologies and sources associated with film history, consulting archival documentation relating to the production, marketing and original critical reception of the films. But this is combined with close analytical attention to those films, not only in terms of narrative structure and characterisation but also *mise en scène*, camera framing and movement, lighting, colour, editing and soundtrack. Lean, like many other filmmakers before him and since, advocated the primacy of the visual in the medium, stating categorically that 'moments you remember in movies are not often dialogue. They are images – pictures with music and sound that move you.'[37] As we have seen, Lean was absolutely meticulous in his construction of the flow of images, working to the 'imaginary negative' in his mind's eye, and thus his films repay equally meticulous scrutiny of their textual properties. In writing about Lean's films in this book, I am engaged in the activity of *ekphrasis*, using the written word to invoke a visual medium, offering what Adrian Martin has described as film criticism's 'secondary elaboration, after the primary elaboration of the film-work itself ... re-describing what has already been etched onto the screen'.[38] But the act of re-description is never neutral and, Martin observes, has the potential to act in an 'alchemical, transformative' way upon the film text, enabling new ways of understanding it.[39] My *ekphrastic* endeavour in this book is 'to evoke for a reader that lost object ... to bring the film into imaginative being for the reader, so that she views it in the process of reading. In reading, she becomes a film viewer.'[40] Through that process of evocation, of drawing out particular features of Lean's films and positing potential interpretations, I hope to demonstrate fully their outstanding cinematic achievement. Although there is no small irony in using V. F. Perkins, author of the famously slighting *Movie* editorial about British cinema mentioned earlier, as a touchstone for an analysis of David Lean's work, Perkins's defence of this model of film writing is both inspirational and indispensable:

No intra-textual interpretation ever is or could be a proof. More often, it is a description of aspects of the film with suggested understandings of some of the ways they are patterned. Rhetoric is involved in developing the description so that it evokes a sense of how, seen in this way, the film may affect us, or so that it invites participation in the pleasure of discovering this way in which various of the film's features hang together.[41]

I hope to give Lean his interpretive due, showing how his films demonstrate precisely that sense of aesthetic coherence alluded to by Perkins, and to build a persuasive case for David Lean as someone more than worthy of being lauded.

Lean's directing career spanned major industrial changes from the 1940s through to the 1980s, and took him from modest British studio production to Hollywood-financed widescreen blockbusters. Those series of very different filmmaking contexts – from working under the aegis of J. Arthur Rank's generously laissez-faire Independent Producers, then moving to Alexander Korda's London Films with a cohort of fellow refugees from Independent Producers after its curtailment by John Davis, to later setting up big-budget epics with Sam Spiegel and Columbia, then Carlo Ponti and MGM, and so on – obviously played a strong role in determining the content and style of each of the productions. However, despite the undeniable changes in Lean's filmmaking attendant on very different industrial contexts, I contend that there are clear continuities observable from his earliest films to his last. The unmistakable recurrence of certain motifs, themes, situations, character types, and visual and aural tropes in films spanning the five decades of Lean's directorial career belies the idea of a total split between his early and late films, as suggested in Sue Harper and Vincent Porter's statement that Lean's later work 'bears no visual relation to the films he made before 1955'.[42] and that from *Kwai* onwards 'the demands of Sam Spiegel and the epic genre overcame any claims to visual authorship'.[43] I beg to differ from this viewpoint. Is it pure coincidence that the last words of *Kwai*'s fanatical visionary Colonel Nicholson – 'what have I done?' – are identical to those of another half-mad fanatic, Miss Havisham, from one of Lean's earlier films, *Great Expectations* (1946)? The image of a man's hand placed on the woman's shoulder from *Brief Encounter* returns in his much later work *Ryan's Daughter*, a repetition across the decades which Robert Horton finds 'uncannily moving. It's less the work of a cool technician than a physical memory.'[44] There are other correspondences between Lean's films across the separations of time and genre: the reverberation of the word 'home', sometimes comforting but more often tinged with disappointment;[45] and, connected to this, the recurrent return to aspects of the

British Empire, from the Wembley exhibition visited by the family in *This Happy Breed* (1944) through to the Raj depicted in *A Passage to India*. In Richard Dyer's work on whiteness, his shorthand phrase to denote white identity – 'strangled vowels and rigid salutes'[46] – maps perfectly onto the worlds of *Brief Encounter*, *Kwai* and *Lawrence*, as well as many other Lean films, suggesting the director's inadvertent but no less profound entanglement with the representation of whiteness.

One central recurring theme of Lean's work is illuminated by an intriguing literary reference which appears in *The Passionate Friends*. The films shows its former lovers Mary and Stephen thumbing through old books on his shelves before stopping to read the epigraph of one particularly cherished volume. 'God gave to every people a cup of clay', Mary reads, and then Stephen completes the sentence, 'and from this cup they drink their life'. Although never acknowledged in the film, this Native American proverb was used to preface Ruth Benedict's pioneering work of anthropology, *Patterns of Culture* (1934). It's unclear whether the reference to Benedict's work was the invention of Eric Ambler and Ronald Neame in their original draft screenplay for *The Passionate Friends* or an addition made by Stanley Haynes and David Lean in their heavily revised version, but Benedict's ideas certainly have a special resonance in relation to Lean's work. Her investigation into different 'primitive' societies is structured around a comparison of those tribes who embrace an ethos of restraint and tribes who embrace frenzy and abandon. Benedict draws on Nietzsche's distinction between the Dionysian and the Apollonian as a means of characterising 'two diametrically opposed ways of arriving at the value of existence':

> The Dionysian pursues them through 'the annihilation of the ordinary bounds and limits of existence'; he seeks to attain in his most valued moments escape from the boundaries imposed upon him by his five senses, to break through into another order of experience ... he values the illuminations of frenzy. The Apollonian distrusts all of this, and has often little idea of the nature of such experiences. He keeps the middle of the road, stays within the known map, does not meddle with disruptive psychological states.[47]

This dyad perfectly encapsulates the struggles undergone by a number of Lean's heroes and heroines, torn between sticking to the routes offered by known maps or trying to embrace other orders of experience which promise perfect fulfilment but frequently shade into madness. I think it's fair to surmise from biographical evidence from various sources that this conflict between the Dionysian and the Apollonian was deeply felt by David Lean himself, whose austere Quaker upbringing clashed with his wayward libidinous impulses, civilized respectability

INTRODUCTION 9

coming up against what Lean memorably described as 'the "animal" which is only a little way under all our skins, which can be very exciting but very dangerous'.[48] Producer Anthony Havelock-Allan remarked that he had 'never seen a man who was in more of a subconscious dilemma between his sensuality and his strict sense of morality'.[49] His second wife Kay Walsh saw him as 'a disturbed, split man', while Cineguild associate Ronald Neame suggested that beneath Lean's cool guarded surface, there was indeed 'a battle royal going on'.[50] Likewise, Omar Sharif characterised Lean as a divided soul, 'a human being as Anglo-Saxon as they come and as romantically oriental as ever I have known'.[51] His planned but never made project about *HMS Bounty* may have represented the ultimate expression of his inner conflict with 'Captain Bligh, the rigid disciplinarian, and Mr Christian, the man of feeling who embraces the sybaritic life' symbolising 'the two sides of David', according to his friend and admirer John Boorman.[52] 'A very emotional man', his biographer Kevin Brownlow observed of him, 'but being English I take a lot of care to cover it up', Lean added.[53] But the traces of that division and repression are writ large in his films.

The conflict between Apollonian and Dionysian in Lean's films is often expressed via a focus on 'repressed sexuality', and, as Steven Organ observes, 'Lean's repressed protagonists were mostly women'.[54] The feminine angle of much of Lean's work has seldom been fully acknowledged even though, as Alain Silver and James Ursini point out, six of Lean's sixteen films – *Brief Encounter, The Passionate Friends, Madeleine* (1950), *Summer Madness* (1955; US title *Summertime*), *Ryan's Daughter* and *A Passage to India* – have 'preeminent female protagonists',[55] and a good deal more also feature women in key roles: from *This Happy Breed*'s Ethel and Queenie through to *Doctor Zhivago*'s Lara. In a sense, the all-male worlds of *Kwai* and *Lawrence* are anomalous in Lean's career, although they have come to be seen as representative of his work, because of the higher critical profile those films have enjoyed in comparison with some of Lean's more female-focussed pictures: indeed, when Judy Davis was cast in *A Passage to India* she expressed doubts about Lean's ability to direct women precisely because his reputation was so strongly tied up with those two male-dominated epic war films.[56] One of the major objectives of this book is to bring into sharper focus the other side of Lean's filmmaking, the more female-centred films, in order to redress this imbalance in perception. My study prioritises questions of gender in relation to Lean's work, marking a departure from previous studies of its kind. It deliberately foregrounds films which have tended to occupy a more marginal position within Lean's oeuvre, arguing for their significance not only on the grounds that they're 'interesting' but also because they're 'good'. For instance, it is my contention that *Summer Madness* is a film of equal emotional power and visual complexity, albeit in a very different register, to the much better-known and more widely celebrated *Lawrence of Arabia*. Therefore my analysis gives both films equal space and explores them in equal depth (if anything, slightly weighted in the former's favour to counteract the usual bias in attention towards the latter).

David Lean has been characterised as a director of highly romantic disposition whose films offer a vision of 'the romantic sensibility attempting to reach beyond the restraints and constrictions of everyday life'.[57] He once quoted with approval William Wyler's contention 'I don't see why anything shouldn't be told through a love story',[58] and Lean's male-centred adventure films are arguably just as much love stories as his more female-oriented romances; indeed, Michael Anderegg observes how 'in Lean's hands, adventure and romance are very much the same thing', both centred on someone trying to 'break through the barriers of conventional thought and feeling, of morality and custom ... to some higher, more intense, deeply felt existence'.[59] But that common ambition is expressed via very different routes depending on genre and gender, and has very different outcomes for male and female protagonists. As mentioned earlier, the final words of Miss Havisham and Colonel Nicholson are identical and both characters orchestrate grand but tragically flawed schemes to make their mark on the world. But Miss Havisham is defined by her hermitage, shut up in a cobwebbed interior space, not seeing the sun for decades, whereas Nicholson, although similarly psychologically hampered, is burnt by the sun and driven mad by it, his own dreams of immortality bound up with the megalomania of imperial endeavour, of being a protagonist on the world stage. There are other crucial differences of gender at play here: while Nicholson's fanaticism revolves around the *construction* of a lasting monument, the bridge, Havisham's revolves around *destruction*, using her ward Estella to break men's hearts. Male characters in Lean's work are often granted a degree of visionary insight through their romantic obsession (before their eventual and inevitable descent), but the female characters who share the same impulses generally remain passionate but frustrated, driven to sabotage or self-destruction, rather than grand action on an epic scale. Laura in *Brief Encounter* can only daydream that the coppiced willows at the level crossing are palm trees, remaining all the while in her fireside armchair and conjuring up her affair through flashback. The epic hero, T. E. Lawrence, sees the palm trees for real while traversing the vast expanses of the desert. But both are romantics whose aspirations are ultimately thwarted and who must endure unhappy homecomings.

INTRODUCTION   11

The structure of this book is based on part-chronological, part-thematic groupings of David Lean's films. After this general introduction, chapter two deals with Lean's early career, covering his entry into the film industry and flourishing formative years as an editor, honing skills he would continue to apply through his filmmaking career, and his official entry into direction in collaboration with Noël Coward on the war film *In Which We Serve*, an incredibly prestigious and successful directorial debut. The chapter goes on to cover all of Lean's subsequent films in association with Coward (with the exception of *Brief Encounter*, which is dealt with in chapter four instead) and details the formation of David Lean into a major British directorial talent.

Chapter three examines Lean's four forays into the nineteenth century, encompassing his two Dickens adaptations, *Great Expectations* and *Oliver Twist* (1948), as well as his two later Victorian dramas, both centred on rebellious females, the 'true crime' tale *Madeleine* and the comedy *Hobson's Choice* (1954). By grouping these four films together rather than placing the Dickens films in their own separate subcategory and examining them exclusively through the lens of adaptation studies, various continuities in Lean's representation of the nineteenth century become apparent. Each film presents a vivid instance of the twentieth century in the process of 'inventing the Victorians';[60] put together, the quartet of films show how perceptions began to change during the pivotal postwar years, with Lean's films both contributing to and reflecting those changes.

The remaining three chapters are centred on gender, beginning with chapter four, which focusses on a trio of films about women in love, *Brief Encounter*, *The Passionate Friends* and *Summer Madness*. The latter two films are probably among the least well known of Lean's films and the most deserving of reclamation and celebration as fascinating investigations into female subjectivity, rendered with astonishing visual panache and total emotional commitment. There is also, I argue, evidence for a large degree of authorial identification with their lovelorn heroines: David Thomson is absolutely right when he says that in *Brief Encounter* 'Lean has dug up his own buried soul in the name of a woman's picture'.[61] Chapter five then moves onto ground more readily associated with the director, with three films centred on male visionaries, *The Sound Barrier* (1952), *The Bridge on the River Kwai* and *Lawrence of Arabia*. These latter two films also consolidated Lean's total transformation from parochial British to epic international filmmaker; although the process had actually begun with *Summer Madness*, the director's first transatlantic coproduction. The sixth and final chapter looks at the three concluding productions of Lean's career, *Doctor Zhivago*, *Ryan's Daughter* and *A*

Passage to India, examining them in the light of a growing tension in Lean's career between epic form and intimate subject matter. Critical responses to those films often perceived a mismatch between monumental style and small-scale stories which reached its apotheosis in the animosity expressed towards *Ryan's Daughter*.

The opposition of later international and early British films, of big versus small, undoubtedly defines Lean's career and his reputation. But Lean himself sidestepped its significance by insisting that 'emotions not spectacle make a picture big',[62] so a 'small' film like *Brief Encounter* could potentially be as 'big' as a blockbuster like *Zhivago*. Such dissolution of the usual boundaries between the different stages of his career is refreshing and prompts new ways of thinking about his films beyond the customary pre-and-post-epic divide. In this respect, it corresponds perfectly with the overarching aim of this book, which is to propose new perspectives on the work of David Lean and offer a fuller and more varied appreciation of his manifold achievements as a filmmaker. In so doing, the study makes interventions in wider academic debates around authorship, gender, genre and aesthetics in relation to the British cinema and transnational cinema of British cultural inheritance of which Lean was such a remarkable exponent.

Notes

1 Graham Fuller and Nicholas Kent, 'Return Passage: Interview with David Lean', *Stills*, March 1985, p. 34.
2 William Goldman in 1983, quoted in Sandra Lean with Barry Chattington, *David Lean: An Intimate Portrait* (London: Universe, 2001), p. 44.
3 Peter Waymark, 'Portents of an Indian Summer', *The Times*, 16 March 1985.
4 *Lawrence* had dropped to 48th position in the 2012 directors' poll, perhaps indicating a fall in his fortunes as a key influence on filmmakers. However, Lean still has definite advocates among younger directors, particularly Joe Wright (2007's *Atonement*, 2012's *Anna Karenina*). When the poll was first conducted in 1952, Lean's *Brief Encounter* managed to attain joint tenth place, the first and last time to date any of his films occupied a position of significant esteem among critics in this invaluable litmus test of critical preferences.
5 Andrew Sarris, *The American Cinema: Directors and Directions 1929–1968* (New York: E. P. Dutton, 1968).
6 *Movie*, May 1962, p. 8.
7 Ibid. Further on this difference in opinion between directors and critics as to Lean's worth, *Movie* critic Ian Cameron once ruefully commented that 'on confronting many of the film-makers I most admire, I invariably find that the film-makers *they* most admire are Messers. Lean and Fellini whose work I cannot abide.' Quoted in Alain Silver and James Ursini, *David Lean and His Films* (Los Angeles: Silman-James Press, 1992), p. 9.
8 Incidentally, Lean is on record stating his admiration for Hitchcock, stating that the shower scene in *Psycho* (1960) is very good 'but the three minutes before

INTRODUCTION 13

  it, when nothing happens, they're *brilliant*'. Steven M. Silverman, *David Lean* (London: Andre Deutsch, 1998), p. 136.
9 Robert Horton, 'Jungle Fever: A David Lean Joint', *Film Comment*, September/October 1991, p. 14.
10 Lean interviewed by Jay Cocks in 1984 anthologised in Steven Organ (ed.), *David Lean: Interviews* (Jackson: University of Mississippi Press, 2009), p. 59.
11 Fuller and Kent, 'Return Passage', p. 36.
12 *Time*, 31 December 1984.
13 J. Hoberman, *Village Voice*, 14 February 1989, p. 57.
14 Brian Case, *Time Out*, 12 April 1989.
15 Kevin Jackson, *Lawrence of Arabia* (London: BFI, 2007), p. 9.
16 Kevin Brownlow, *David Lean* (London: Faber, 1997).
17 Nick James, 'David Lean', *Sight and Sound*, July 2008, p. 38.
18 Peter Hutchings, *Dracula* (London: I. B. Tauris, 2003), p. 3.
19 Ibid., p. 4.
20 Ibid.
21 Quoted in Organ (ed.), *David Lean: Interviews*, p. 13.
22 Peter Wollen, 'Riff-Raff Realism', *Sight and Sound*, April 1998, p. 22. Wollen's essay was also cited in Neil Sinyard's book in this series on Jack Clayton, in a discussion which anticipates Hutchings in its recognition of how 'in the invaluable re-evaluation of the British cinema which has taken place over the last two decades, the aesthetic case has been tentatively handled.' Neil Sinyard, *Jack Clayton* (Manchester: Manchester University Press, 2000), p. 17.
23 Gerald Pratley, *The Cinema of David Lean* (London: Tantivy: 1974), p. 21.
24 Quoted in Brownlow, *David Lean*, p. 559.
25 Quoted in Silverman, *David Lean*, p. 123.
26 Ernest Day, 'A Passage to India', *American Cinematographer*, March 1985, p. 59.
27 Interview by Jay Cocks in Organ (ed.), *David Lean: Interviews*, p. 65.
28 *The Passionate Friends* pressbook, BFI Library.
29 Lean interviewed by Robert Stewart 1965 in Organ (ed.), *David Lean: Interviews*, p. 22.
30 Lean with Chattington, *David Lean*, p. 50.
31 Interviewed by Stewart in Organ (ed.), *David Lean: Interviews*, p. 24.
32 Ibid.
33 Who, asked producer Michael Balcon in 1951, 'can entirely separate the names of David Lean, Ronald Neame and Anthony Havelock-Allan?' He added, however, 'I think neither of the other members of the triumvirate would quarrel with my guess that Lean was the leading member.' 'Ten Years of British Films', *Films in 1951: A Special Publication on British Films and Film-Makers for the Festival of Britain* (London: BFI, 1951), p. 37.
34 David Lean, 'The Film Director', in Oswell Blakeston (ed.), *Working for the Films* (London: Focal, 1947), p. 36.
35 Quoted in George Stevens Jr. (ed.), *Conversations with the Great Moviemakers of Hollywood's Golden Age* (New York: Knopf, 2006), p. 425. A variation also appears in another interview: 'Can you think of any art that isn't one person's vision? Making a movie is using a vast piece of machinery like a crane to draw a fine line. One person must control the machinery.' Lean quoted in Aljean Harmetz, 'David Lean films a famed novel', *New York Times*, 7 December 1984, p. 21.
36 Adrian Turner, *The Making of David Lean's Lawrence of Arabia* (London: Dragon's World, 1994), p. 143.
37 Quoted in Lean with Chattington, *David Lean*, p. 6.
38 Adrian Martin, 'Incursions', in Alex Clayton and Andrew Klevan (eds.), *The Language and Style of Film Criticism* (London: Routledge, 2011), p. 56.

39 Ibid., p. 57.
40 Lesley Stern and George Kouvaros (eds.) *Falling for You: Essays on Cinema and Performance* (Sydney: Power Publications, 1999), p. 7.
41 V. F. Perkins, 'Must we say what they mean? Film criticism and interpretation', *Movie*, Vol. 34, No. 5, 1990, p. 4.
42 Sue Harper and Vincent Porter, *British Cinema of the 1950s: The Decline of Deference* (Oxford: Oxford University Press, 2003), p. 311.
43 Ibid., p. 212.
44 Horton, 'Jungle Fever', p. 15.
45 See Neil Sinyard, 'David Lean: home and the concept of Englishness', unpublished paper, 1998.
46 Richard Dyer, *White* (London: Routledge, 1997), p. 10.
47 Ruth Benedict, *Patterns of Culture* (Boston: Houghton Mifflin, 1934), p. 79.
48 Interviewed by Joseph Gelmis in 1970 in Organ (ed.), *David Lean: Interviews*, p. 44.
49 Anthony Havelock-Allan quoted in Brownlow, *David Lean*, p. 217.
50 Kay Walsh quoted in Brownlow, *David Lean*, p. 111. Ronald Neame in 1946, quoted ibid., p. 217.
51 Quoted in Lean with Chattington, *David Lean*, p. 9.
52 John Boorman, *Adventures of a Suburban Boy* (London: Faber, 2003), p. 299.
53 Brownlow, *David Lean*, p. xv.
54 Steven Organ, 'Introduction' in Organ (ed.), *David Lean: Interviews*, p. x.
55 Silver and Ursini, *David Lean and His Films*, p. 3.
56 Brownlow, *David Lean*, p. 673.
57 Steven Ross, 'In Defence of David Lean', *Take One*, July/August 1972, p. 10.
58 Lean interviewed by David Ehrenstein in 1984 in Organ (ed.), *David Lean: Interviews*, p. 74.
59 Michael Anderegg, *David Lean* (Boston: Twayne, 1985), p. xiii.
60 To borrow Matthew Sweet's useful phrase from his book of the same name, *Inventing the Victorians* (London: Faber, 2001).
61 David Thomson, 'Unhealed wounds', *Guardian* (Review section), 10 May 2008, p. 13.
62 Quoted in Lean with Chattington, *David Lean*, p. 6.

Cutting and Coward: David Lean's early career and *In Which We Serve* (1942), *This Happy Breed* (1944) and *Blithe Spirit* (1945)

2

David Lean might well have had an undistinguished career in accountancy, a profession for which he had absolutely no aptitude, had it not been for the intervention of his aunt Edith. Visiting the family one day, she remarked: 'I look around David's room and I don't see any accountancy books. All I see are film magazines. Why doesn't he go in for films?'[1] This idea had never occurred to his parents before, but once the seed was planted, it quickly took root. This was in spite of the family's deep-seated suspicion of cinema due in large part to their Quaker faith and in its inbuilt antipathy to 'music, colour and ornamentation'.[2] Lean had not been allowed to visit the cinema until he was fourteen years old, although as a child he had heard about the movies from his family's charlady Mrs Egerton, who would entertain him by imitating Charlie Chaplin. The first film he saw for himself was *The Hound of the Baskervilles* (1922) and the teenager was instantly hooked. He became a regular picturegoer thereafter, often visiting magnificent picture palaces like the Tivoli on the Strand after his dull day job in the city adding up figures. 'If you knew what the London suburbs were like, you will understand', Lean told an interviewer years later; 'it was very, very grey, and the movies were a journey into another world.'[3] Rex Ingram's *Mare Nostrum* (1926) was a favourite and the film that made him realise 'there was somebody behind the cameras. Somebody was actually *guiding* it.'[4] The visual storytelling of silent movies appealed strongly to a boy more comfortable with pictures than words. David Lean had been regarded as the dunce of his family, 'alarmingly backward'[5], especially in comparison with his prodigious younger brother Edward. However, the present of a Box Brownie camera when he was twelve years old revealed David Lean's previously unsuspected aptitude for photography. 'That camera became my great friend', Lean said years later, and he remained a keen photographer all his life.[6]

After the young man had forsaken accountancy following aunt

Edith's inspired observation, luckily Lean's father was able to find his son a very junior entry-level job at British Gaumont studios, where the nineteen-year-old immediately flourished. He worked in all departments and in all areas of production, fetching and carrying and even being a junior 'wardrobe mistress' before finding his metier in the cutting room. Lean had entered the industry just at the point where the new cinematographic quota act was coming into force, reversing years of terminal decline in British film production. Suddenly, studios were experiencing a boom and working incessantly to meet the demands of the quota. This sometimes had a deleterious effect on film quality – for many years, the 'quota quickie' was a byword for British film at its worst – but it also enabled a great number of fledgling filmmakers to get started in the industry, including Lean. The early years of his career also coincided with the transition to sound, and he honed his editing skills further while working first for Gaumont Sound News and later British Movietone News, cutting newsreels and sometimes also providing voiceover narration.[7] He learned how to work to tight deadlines, quickly assembling raw footage into sharp stimulating sequences. Lean moved back into features while loaned to British and Dominions, working under the tutelage of Merrill White, formerly Ernst Lubitsch's chief cutter. Lean's work on the Elisabeth Bergner vehicle *Escape Me Never* (1935) brought him increasing recognition as an editor, particularly for its emotive crosscutting between the hero's moment of triumph and the heroine's tragic collapse. He began to build up a reputation in the industry as a 'film doctor' and was able to negotiate an impressive fee for his services: 'They used to send for me if a film was in trouble, if it was too long and needed cutting, or if it was loose and they didn't know what to do with it.'[8]

Not long afterwards, Lean also made his very first moves into the realm of film direction, albeit un-credited. Gene Philips describes *Pygmalion* (1938) as the 'first film on which David Lean acted unofficially as a co-director',[9] and years later in a private letter, Lean paid tribute to 'the generosity of Tony Asquith' enabling him 'to poke my nose into the directorial field for the first time'.[10] Lean conceived the film's two key montage sequences, detailing Eliza Doolittle's exhausting vocal coaching at the hands of Professor Henry Higgins and her triumphant makeover into a fair lady. He even made up the film's memorable concluding line, 'Eliza, bring me my slippers'.[11] A further George Bernard Shaw adaptation on which Lean worked extensively, *Major Barbara* (1941), was credited solely to Gabriel Pascal, disguising the vital contribution Lean made via his whispered on-set guidance to Pascal.[12] The same year on *49th Parallel* (1941), Michael Powell admitted that he gave Lean editorial 'carte blanche. I had been saved by some good editors but never on this scale.' With Powell's endorsement, Lean organised the filming of additional material in order to insert extra shots, and Powell would later acclaim him as the 'best editor I ever worked with – or should I say *for*?'[13]

Given Lean's position as a 'star cutter'[14] at the absolute pinnacle of British editing, and his emergent directorial career, it is unsurprising that he was one of the first names suggested to Noël Coward when the playwright was looking for a first-class technician to assist him on his filmmaking debut. Although the invitation to work on *In Which We Serve* would mark the official credited beginning of Lean's career as a director, Lean never forgot his grounding in cutting. He would go on to supervise the editing of all his films and gave himself an official credit for it on his final film, *A Passage to India*. Cutting was so important to Lean that some actors felt that all the travails of production were mere preamble for the part of the process that he truly cherished. Trevor Howard thought him 'really only in love with celluloid and his movieola. He doesn't really like actors.'[15] Lean concurred to a certain extent – 'I'm really still an editor at heart'[16] – and spoke lovingly of the job's cloistered pleasures: 'It's so peaceful. The film. A movieola. A pair of scissors and a quiet room with no pressures.'[17] But the cutting room was also the place where his ultimate vision for a film – the negative in his head – began to take shape.

The art of making clean cuts seemed to become a guiding principle in Lean's personal as well as his professional life, explaining his ability to amputate emotional connections to the past in what appeared to be a totally ruthless manner: 'You see, you must cut. Anything that is finished is finished. You must just pretend people aren't there. Once you've made that decision, you've just got to cut people out of your life.'[18]

In Which We Serve (1942)

The opening credits for *In Which We Serve*, and the story behind them, raise pertinent questions about this particular film as a product of Lean's authorship. The film is billed as 'Noël Coward's *In Which We Serve*' and the primary authorial presence throughout the credits is undoubtedly Coward who dominates as producer, co-director, composer and lead actor (in the role of Captain Kinross). As Mark Glancy has observed, Coward's polymath status bore some resemblance to Orson Welles, with notable similarities between Welles's famous 'carte-blanche' contract at RKO and the unprecedented freedom Del Giudice's company Two Cities offered Coward for his own filmmaking debut.[19] Kevin Brownlow notes another Wellesian correspondence: the cinematographer Ronald Neame sharing the same frame as the directorial credit, just as Welles had with Gregg Toland on *Citizen Kane*.[20] However, this only came about after rather fractious negotiations in which Coward's initial attempt to claim sole directorial credit was followed by the idea of a compromise credit of 'produced, directed, written and photographed by Noël Coward, David Lean and Ronald Neame', which was then changed again to its final version when Lean threatened to retreat to the cutting room if his work on set was not directly acknowledged, perhaps still smarting from a lack of credit on previous productions.[21] Lean and Neame had managed to attain a better level of accreditation than might have been expected but nothing summed up the paternalistic power dynamic of the project quite so well as Coward dubbing himself 'Daddy' and 'Father' and his three protégés Lean, Neame and producer Anthony Havelock-Allan his 'little darlings'.[22]

Another significant authorial presence in *In Which We Serve* is Lord Louis Mountbatten who inspired the film with his recounting over dinner with Coward the story of the sinking of his own ship *HMS Kelly* in the Battle of Crete. 'Absolutely heart-breaking and so magnificent. He told the whole saga without frills and with a sincerity that was very moving', wrote Coward in his diary.[23] Mountbatten would go on to play an extensive advisory role on the production as well as being a powerful fixer able to 'cut through many strings of red tape and set many wheels turning', according to Coward.[24] He had been instrumental in setting up the King and Queen's visit to the set in April 1942, imbuing the production with an aura of royal assent and giving Coward a 'trump card that he was able to play' in negotiations.[25] This kind of support from on high was all the more vital to *In Which We Serve* in order to counteract the objections of the Ministry of Information (MOI). The Head of the MOI's Film Division, Jack Beddington, judged the film to be 'exceedingly bad propaganda for the Navy',[26] not least 'because a ship was sunk in it'.[27] Coward also had to contend with animosity from the Beaverbrook press, which was determined to represent him (in coded homophobic language) as an insincere playboy not fit to wear naval uniform even in a fictional capacity. They had decried in similar fashion Coward's brief appointment as special emissary to the US: 'Coward is not the man for the job. His flippant England – Cocktails, Countesses, Caviare – has gone. A man of the people more in tune with the new mood of Britain would be a better proposition.'[28] During the production of *In Which We Serve*, Coward received a summons to appear in court for breaking currency regulations, accruing more negative publicity. Despite his ambassadorial activities and tireless work for ENSA, Coward remained a contentious figure during wartime. He wrote the definitive song of defiance against the blitz, 'London Pride' (later used on the soundtrack of *This Happy Breed*), but also composed the controversial satirical song 'Don't Let's Be Beastly to the Germans', which was banned by the BBC for its supposedly seditious sentiments.

Although *In Which We Serve* would go on to be an enormous domestic and international success, magnanimously praised by MOI officials and Beaverbrook papers alike, there is strong evidence for considerable public ambivalence towards Noël Coward. In Mass-Observation's November 1943 directive on favourite films, *In Which We Serve* attained top position (likewise, in *Kine Weekly*'s annual round up of box-office hits it was only surpassed by *Random Harvest*[29]). However, many Mass-Observation respondents suggested that their admiration for *In Which We Serve* was in spite of rather than due to Noël Coward. Although one young bombardier proclaimed him 'a genius',[30] criticism of Coward was actually far more common, particularly his performance in the leading role: 'Noël Coward I disliked profoundly'; film 'outstanding' but 'Noël Coward was a little too much to the fore'; 'Noël Coward spoiled it. I was never once was able to forget that I was watching Noël Coward, an actor, and not a naval officer'; 'his frequent "draw nearer men" little talks gave me a pain'; 'too much of Noël Coward and his pep talks'.[31] One of the most intriguing comments on the film came from a 36–year-old female stenographer: 'I have a small snob fear about confessing that I thought this was extremely good, because one or two of my brainier friends thought it was rather bad. Nevertheless, I was extraordinarily moved by it.'[32] A similar ambivalence is evident in the review of the film in the leftist specialist journal *Documentary News Letter*, which simultaneously acknowledges its lack of democratising impulses – 'nowhere is there any suggestion that the present war represents a revolution not only in thinking but in class relationships' – while still deeming it 'exceptionally sincere and deeply moving'[33] in spite of their ideological misgivings.

Unlike other war films with a more proletarian emphasis, *In Which We Serve* makes no bones about its hierarchical, non-meritocratic worldview. While many looked forward to the forging of a postwar New Jerusalem, Coward stated his suspicion and fear of even the mildest social revolution in his diary entry for 28 July 1941, during the filming of *In Which We Serve*: 'Wondering what it [the war] will do to all of us. Obviously foolish to expect life to be as it was. I dread the almost inevitable class ructions in this country.'[34] Swimming against this political tide, Coward proselytises the harmony and strength that comes from everyone knowing their place and occupying it correctly, which in the case of *In Which We Serve* also corresponds with the regime of naval discipline. The community of the destroyer hinges on authority but it is benign authority resulting in 'a happy and an efficient ship'. It is generous rather than cruelly punitive, proved by the cautioning rather than court-marshalling of the nervous young stoker who deserts his post under fire (Richard Attenborough). Coward described his film as 'a naval *Cavalcade*',[35] suggesting similar aspirations towards patriotic national allegory. 'This is the story of a ship' states the opening narration but *In Which We Serve* is also the story of a country. As Gavin Lambert suggests, the Royal Navy destroyer HMS Torrin functions as 'the ship of England'[36] with *Cavalcade*'s above and below stairs turned into above and below decks, a visually perfect synecdoche of British class hierarchy in action.

However, *In Which We Serve* is distinct from other patrician visions of war in its equal attention to each stratum of society. As Anthony Aldgate and Jeffrey Richards point out, unlike its predecessors *Convoy* (1940) and *Ships With Wings* (1941), *In Which We Serve*'s other ranks are not presented merely as 'cheerful "gorblimey" cockney stereotypes'[37] but characters as rounded and complex as those in the upper echelons. Coward later stated that 'it was essential to the accuracy of the picture that the lower deck and fo'c'sle should be represented as accurately as the quarterdeck, the bridge and the ward-room',[38] and this is borne out in the film's balanced tripartite focus on upper-middle-class Captain Kinross, played by Coward, lower-middle-class Chief Petty Officer Walter Hardy (Bernard Miles) and working-class Ordinary Seaman Shorty Blake (John Mills). At the top of the hierarchy, Neil Rattigan observes, 'Kinross's authority is natural and naturalized'.[39] Dying men insist on speaking to their Captain before they can slip away. Shorty Blake possesses the working-class virtue of cheerful resilience and, as Gill Plain points out, was a character 'designed both to embody and speak for a significant dimension of the nation'.[40] The character who occupies the middle territory, Hardy, is presented as the most comic of the three, awkward but doggedly insistent on making his Christmas speech, and singing along with laughable gusto at a variety theatre. But the scene in which this uxorious husband discovers his wife has died is played sincerely as low-key tragedy. In the middle of writing a letter to his 'dear wife', Shorty breaks the news. 'Oh, I see. Thanks son, I'm very much obliged' is Hardy's heartbreakingly polite response while the true depth of his feelings are suggested by his private moment on deck crumpling up his unfinished letter and throwing it into the sea. Dignified emotional restraint is not the exclusive preserve of the upper classes.

It is fitting that the film's title includes the group pronoun 'we' because it hinges on group consensus and common purpose across the classes. All the men aboard ship are visually and aurally linked at crucial moments: their massed efforts to stock the newly commissioned ship; representatives from all ranks listening to Chamberlain's broadcast announcing war; ditto the seamen moved by the bravery of the soldiers they've rescued at Dunkirk; and most importantly, their group mobilisation in battle presented via rapid montage. We see the ship created by a group of men working together, showcased in the documentary-inflected opening montage, which was shot at the Newcastle shipyards. Her final demise is witnessed and mourned by another group of men, her surviving crew all clinging onto a life-raft. This last image, as Aldgate and Richards suggest, offers 'a powerful and irresistible metaphor for class levelling: differences in background matter very little when they are up to their necks in seawater and oil'.[41] The only outsider is the Richard Attenborough character, singled out in close-up as he loses his nerve and abandons his post, the camerawork thus underlining his separation from his shipmates. We later see him wander along a shadowy dockside, totally isolated in his ignominy, with the camera adopting a *noir*-style canted angle as he goes off to get drunk alone. His shame is only exonerated when he can re-join the group.

The film's primary means of suggesting the connections between men of all classes is through its intermingling of their memories. A series of flashbacks transport the viewer into the men's recollections of life aboard ship but also back at home. Often a flashback begins as one character's memory and ends as though it is the recollection of another, but this is not so much careless attribution than it is a deliberate blending, an expression of their collective identity conveyed through shared memory. *In Which We Serve* emphasises the coincidental correspondences between sailors of all ranks, such as shared honeymoon destinations or the practice of making a speech at Christmas, revealing their underlying unity. Lean initiated the film's extensive use of flashback, advising Coward to see Orson Welles's pioneering recent film *Citizen Kane* (1941) for inspiration when trying to compress his overlong first screenplay.[42] Just like Welles, Coward uses flashback to bring the past vividly into the present but he also uses it to place the sailors' domestic lives right at the heart of the drama. The film's first flashback begins with Kinross engulfed by water as the *Torrin* capsizes, his thoughts returning to first setting up his cabin in the newly commissioned ship. Particular prominence is given to his placement of wedding and family photographs, and in the next part of the flashback we see a reunion with his wife Alix (Celia Johnson) and their children back at his home. Likewise, when Shorty is hit by overhead bombardment, his mind goes back to his first meeting with his future wife, Freda (Plate 1),

1 Flashbacks from home: Shorty (John Mills) remembers his wedding to Freda (Kay Walsh) in *In Which We Serve* (1942)

and then to an expressionistically shot memory of their wedding day that shows the bride walking slowly towards the camera in a hail of confetti.

Through its flashbacks of home, *In Which We Serve* extends its 'story of a ship' beyond those who sail in her, suggesting a wider ideal of national service which encompasses naval wives and families. Milton's proverbial line 'They also serve who only stand and wait' is echoed in the film's poster tagline eulogising both 'the men who sail – and the women who wait!' Because of its 'melancholy yet magnificent tributes to woman's silent part in the boundless fracas', *Kine Weekly* trumpeted *In Which We Serve*'s 'tremendous feminine angle', concluding: 'There has never been a more comprehensive, a more emotionally stimulating, a more thrilling war film or a greater woman's picture than this'.[43] This splitting of the film's generic and gender address – it is both war film *and* woman's picture – is intriguing given the film's habitual placement in the canon of British war films.[44] Although Mountbatten's recounting of the *Kelly*'s sinking provided Coward's primary inspiration, he seems to have been powerfully inspired by a moment of home front courage that he witnessed on Plymouth Hoe, mentioned in both diary and letters around the same time the film was taking shape:

The behaviour of the people in the midst of such appalling devastation was beyond praise and beyond gallantry. They were genuinely cheerful and philosophic and I never heard anyone even grumble. In the evenings between 7.30 and 9.30 there is a band on the front and the whole of the town, or what is left of it, come out and dance in the sunlight. The girls put on their bright coloured frocks and dance with the sailors and marine and soldiers.[45]

In total war, civilians are also combatants – the home is another front – and *In Which We Serve* strongly celebrates women's bravery in its air-raid sequences showing three generations of women, knitting or sewing and trying to keep their nerve but nonetheless betraying their fear through tense over-polite exchanges which eventually collapse into bickering. The film's first flashback eloquently conveys the anxiety of being a waiting wife through Celia Johnson's slight hesitation with the cocktail shaker as she asks her husband about why his ship is being commissioned in a hurry, expecting the worse (imminent war) but concealing her fear by keeping her back to him. All the while we are granted special access to her troubled expression and the effort she must put into suppressing it. Wanting to keep the home fires burning for her husband Walter will be the cause of Kath Hardy's (Joyce Carey) death in the Blitz, but while she's alive she tutors her niece Freda (Kay Walsh) in how to cope with separation from loved ones, putting a maternal arm round her as they depart from their husbands at the quayside.

However, the ultimate statement of the sacrifices inherent in this way of life comes with Alix's impromptu Christmas day speech warning a young naval fiancée about what awaits her, supposedly drawn from the real words of Coward's friend Mrs Bertie Packer on how she 'knew and accepted her husband's ship as his "grey mistress" – a rival she could never conquer but one she came to love'.[46] In the film, the speech is beautifully performed by Johnson, who moves convincingly from festive jocularity into being surprised by the sudden unexpected depth of her emotions:

> Wherever she goes there is always in her life a permanent and undefeated rival. Her husband's ship. Whether it be a battleship or a sloop, a submarine or a destroyer, it holds first place in his heart, it comes before wife, home, children, everything. Some of us try to fight this and get badly mauled in the process. Others, like myself, resign themselves to the inevitable. That is what you will have to do, my poor Maureen. That is what we all have to do if we want any peace of mind at all. Ladies and Gentlemen, I give you my rival – it is extraordinary that anyone could be so fond and so proud of their most implacable enemy – this ship – God Bless this ship and all who sail in her.

The camera stays fixed on her face throughout, declining the option to use cutaways to show the reactions of others at the table; we only hear them as noises off. The unwavering focus makes it a privileged moment, unusually candid and revelatory in a film in which strong emotion is continually being pushed down and resisted. Decades later, recalling the speech and Celia Johnson's performance of it still had the power to bring David Lean close to tears.[47]

Just as seamen across classes are linked by their shared sense of duty and love of their ship, there is also a parallel cross-class community of women, linked by their forbearance under extreme pressure. After the *Torrin*'s sinking, the dreaded official telegram home is first shown arriving at the home of Shorty's mum (Kathleen Harrison), his wife Freda and their baby. The mother is terror-stricken but then cries with relief upon learning that Shorty is alive ('It's alright, he's safe! He's all right, my boy's all right!') and the film makes good use of the potency of cheap music by having 'If you were the only girl in the world' (Shorty and Freda's theme song) playing on a barrel organ on the street outside. The same situation is then immediately repeated with Alix – the telegram on the maid's tray jutting rudely into the frame – whose reaction is the same as the other women; to cry and hug her children. The techniques of intercutting and flashback are used here and elsewhere in *In Which We Serve* not to create contradiction and uncertainty, as in *Kane*, but to set out a vision of continuity and coherence, across time, space, class and sex: not one man's fractured ego but a nation brought together and made whole.

It may be tempting to view *In Which We Serve* in the light of countless pastiches of its kind of film, lampooning the exhortation to 'keep a stiff upper lip, old boy' (a real line from the film) and the white cliffs of Dover as a backdrop for scenes of exemplary courage. British cinema had never quite recovered from the film's impact, Lindsay Anderson argued, and this was to its great detriment.[48] To modern eyes, the final scene in which Coward's Captain bids farewell to and shakes the hand of each one of his surviving crew might tread the giddy line midway between sincerity and self-parody. But at the same time it is hard to disagree with Pudovkin's often-quoted estimation of its achievement: 'You can see the face of England in it. The scene in which the captain, taking leave, shakes the hand of a whole file of his compatriots, and each conducts himself as though he were like no one but himself, and yet at the same time all are like each other, will remain long in memory.'[49] His goodbyes said, Captain Kinross is left alone. The deep-focus shot of the vacated custom warehouse after the men's departure is eloquent in its emptiness. But, *In Which We Serve* insists, life goes on, the navy endures, and new ships are launched; the script calls for an abundant montage of them as the film ends: 'minelayers, sloops, destroyers, trawlers, aircraft carriers, submarines, cruisers, tugs, converted liners, MTBs and battleships'.[50] Despite its initially rocky relationship with official channels of propaganda, *In Which We Serve* ended up being a vital vehicle for boosting national pride. It was, and perhaps remains, the 'definitive film tribute to the Royal Navy',[51] a film which made one Mass-Observation respondent 'feel I would die for the Senior Service – and I'm hanged if I would die for any other employer'.[52] But it also demonstrated a new-found confidence and skill in British filmmaking, an early indication of the wartime renaissance in the national cinema that would enable its films to speak beyond parochial boundaries. After watching *In Which We Serve*, a young Russian film worker Vera Kolodyaznaya described the film as 'a hymn to human nobility, staunchness, friendship and love':[53] fine testimony to the success of Lean's first fully credited foray into direction.

This Happy Breed (1944)

The moments that dwell on ordinary domesticity in *In Which We Serve* would be expanded to occupy the entirety of Lean's next film, *This Happy Breed*, an adaptation of Noël Coward's play about a lower-middle-class London family, the Gibbonses. Just how self-consciously *This Happy Breed* positioned its family saga as national allegory is indicated by its marketing taglines: 'You'll find you know the Gibbonses ... meet them every day ... they are British ... they are you'; 'Here is the spirit of England ... the reason England **is** ... the story of an English family ... **your** family.'[54] Just how successful this portrait of the nation then was with its intended audience is proven by its elevated position in the *Kine Weekly* annual box-office review for 1944, where it was not only the top British money-maker that year but second most popular of all films, beaten only by *For Whom the Bell Tolls*. *This Happy Breed* was one of a number of texts of the period that seemed to quench a widespread thirst for national self-explication. On radio and in print, writers like J. B. Priestley and George Orwell mused over the meaning of Englishness, echoing the anthropological project of Mass-Observation. Meanwhile, there appeared 'a spate of books analysing and investigating England and the English; books with titles like *The English People*, *The Character of England* and *God's Englishman*'.[55] With films such as *This Happy Breed*, as well as 1943's *Millions Like Us* and *The Demi-Paradise* appearing on British screens, suggested critic William

Whitebait, 'we shall no longer be able to keep up any pretence of not knowing ourselves'.[56]

The reason for *This Happy Breed*'s success, according to C. A. Lejeune, was female word-of-mouth: 'Women in fish queues, fruit queues, cake queues, bus queues and queues for queues have passed the word to each other over their baskets.' Lejeune also describes receiving an unprecedented number of appreciative letters from people who 'felt impelled to sit down and write some sort of ordered account of their impressions' of the film:

> For one astonished moment this strange film has made artists of them all. One man speaks with a kind of flame about a smoky evening sky over the roofs of Clapham. Another refers to the solid sense of family. A third comments on the nice use of Coward's London Pride as background music. A flying Officer in the Balkan air force writes that he has seen the film on three consecutive nights with an enthusiastic audience of dominion and allied troops, who 'were seeing England, the real England, for the first time.'[57]

Despite its narrative stopping in 1939 before the outbreak of war, its implicit propaganda value during wartime is clear: we fight to preserve this way of life. *This Happy Breed* boosts morale by proposing the existence of an indomitable national ethos embodied by its people, a representative family who can 'survive wars, zeppelins, Heinkels, the Kaiser, strikes, political upheavals, despairs, jubilations – the same as YOU'.[58] In J. P. Mayer's research into cinema preferences, he quotes a 24-year-old typist who brackets *This Happy Breed* alongside *In Which We Serve* as 'the two BEST British films ever made', her reason being that 'these people were us'.[59]

Coward's *This Happy Breed* owed much to his earlier hit play, 1931's *Cavalcade*. But instead of following two families from 1899 to 1930 as in *Cavalcade*, *This Happy Breed* traces the fortunes of a single family between 1919 and 1939, years bookended by war but also the period of the family's occupation of No. 17 Sycamore Road, Clapham. Both play and film of *This Happy Breed* begin and end with the family moving house, and just as *In Which We Serve* had been the story of a ship, *This Happy Breed* offered 'the story of a house' possessing the same ability to represent an entire nation in microcosm as had *HMS Torrin*. One significant difference from *Cavalcade* came in *This Happy Breed*'s class focus, with the earlier play's Marryot and Bridges families being upper and working class respectively, whereas the Gibbons family fall between these categories as solidly lower middle class. Frank (Robert Newton) works for a travel agency and is married to Ethel (Celia Johnson), and they have three children, Reg (John Blythe), Queenie (Kay Walsh) and

Vi (Eileen Erskine). Completing the family group are Ethel's mother Mrs Flint (Amy Veness), Frank's spinster sister Sylvia (Alison Leggatt) and Percy the cat. Their twenty years at No. 17 cover personal milestones such as weddings, births and family Christmases but also the impact of wider social changes and historical events, from the Wembley Empire Exhibition of 1924, the General Strike of 1926, the abdication crisis and even the arrival of the talking pictures. *Cavalcade* had ended on a note of ambiguous patriotism, concluding with flashing frenzied images of contemporary chaos. The play's final scene boldly interspersed 1920s nightclub revelry with hospitalised shellshock sufferers, connecting them as products of postwar malaise. The accompanying soundtrack blended Coward's song 'Twentieth Century Blues' with a mounting crescendo of steam rivets and aeroplane propellers, the sounds of the machine age. Finally, the tumult subsided into silence and darkness before the stage directions requested the gradual illumination of a Union Jack, the sole point of light on the otherwise dark stage, with the play ending as the cast sing 'God Save the King'. No such apocalyptic stagecraft makes an appearance in *This Happy Breed*, play or film, and its sense of patriotic celebration is much less fragile or contingent than in the previous play. Written in 1939, though not performed until 1942, *This Happy Breed* inevitably had a greater duty towards public morale as the country went to war again. Unlike the traumatised war veterans featured in *Cavalcade*, Frank Gibbons seems remarkably unaffected by his wartime experiences to the extent of cheerfully taking up a postwar job running tours of the Great War battlefields. His former comrade Bob (Stanley Holloway) is similarly unclouded by grief about their experiences in the trenches, and the pair happily attend regimental dinners and victory parades together. In place of *Cavalcade*'s suggestion of an irreparable tear in the historical fabric, on trauma and crisis, *This Happy Breed* centres on continuity and repetition.

The film opens with a lofty establishing shot of the London cityscape (shot from a Battersea gasometer) before dissolving to a shot over the rooftops and gardens of a suburban Clapham street, then finally entering one particular house through the window, moving slowly downstairs to the front door which is about to be opened by its new occupants, the Gibbons family. Ronald Neame's fluid camerawork was described as 'pure Orson Welles in its dash and functionalism'[60] but it also anticipates Terence Davies's much later exploration of empty but emotionally meaningful domestic space. Using colour photography to depict such an unapologetically ordinary setting was highly unusual at the time, and Neame took great pains to avoid Technicolor's tendency towards sparkling brightness by using 'shades of gray and brown to "dirty down" the sets and costumes' so he could 'light the picture so that everything looked drabber than normal'.[61] The careful attention to detail in the film's *mise en scène* was praised by several critics: C. A. Lejeune noticed 'the dirty rim left in the bathtub',[62] while Richard Winnington eulogised 'the fading wallpaper as the years mount, the grease mark by the door handle, the pictures on the wall, the chime of the clock'.[63] But in its quasi-fetishistic insistence on carefully chosen historically accurate objects – like Sylvia's bottle of Wincarnis tonic wine, the antimacassars on the armchairs, the Christmas decorations adorning the house in 1925 or even the tea things lying untouched on the table when Frank and Ethel receive dreadful news – *This Happy Breed* enacts a voyeuristic proto-heritage aesthetic, according to Andrew Higson, in which the national past 'exists as an exotic, compelling, fascinating spectacle'.[64] The idea of the petit-bourgeois home being subject to a near-anthropological gaze links with the objections raised against Coward's *de haut en bas* patronage of his protagonists; a criticism he strongly refuted, citing his own upbringing in the suburbs of Clapham and Battersea. Sheridan Morley even describes Coward's play as 'a throwback to his original South London childhood'[65] and Coward had played the paterfamilias Frank Gibbons on stage, albeit doused in hardly-in-character Chanel No. 5.[66] Coward wrote sincerely of the importance of 'twisted sentimental roots, stretching a long way down and a long way back, too deep to be unearthed by intelligence or pacific reason or even contempt, there, embedded for life.'[67] But his vision achieved its fullest expression, according to the *Times* reviewer, through cinematic rather than theatrical means: Lean's direction and Neame's photography were able to turn 'a brilliant piece of reporting from the outside into something observed and treasured from within'.[68]

This Happy Breed hinges on a rejection or suspicion of politics. The table collapses when Frank tries to propose a toast to Ramsay MacDonald, and there's a slight irony in Bob's designation of Stanley Baldwin as 'a face you can trust'. Nonetheless its ideological stance in relation to the events of the interwar years is clear. The General Strike of 1926 is presented as a national trauma, with lingering shots of abandoned steel works and empty railway lines presented in eerie silence, while Frank and Bob's voluntary bus-driving is enthusiastically endorsed as the correct course of action in 'keeping the country steady'. The socialist rhetoric of Reg's friend Sam (Guy Verney) is belittled as the product of an adolescent phase, and indeed the 'red agitator' is later 'cuddled into a pink pet' by his girlfriend and later wife Vi.[69] All forms of political hysteria are criticised, from the wildly rapturous reception of Chamberlain from Munich in 1938 to the Mosley-esque British fascist declaiming from Speaker's Corner in Hyde Park, whose anti-Semitic diatribe is undercut by Ethel's decision to move on in favour of a cup of tea. The phlegmatic refusal to get carried away by anything has its less attractive aspects: as Edgar Anstley suggested, the Gibbonses 'reveal sterling qualities but these are generally the attributes of uncomplaining packhorses than inhabitants of this other Eden'.[70] However, the domestic quietude of the drama possesses its own poetic force. The brief tableau dealing with the death of George V is a case in point; shots of the radio aerials suspended over the Clapham rooftops, indicating the growth of the mass media, are accompanied by the solemn second movement of Beethoven's seventh symphony. This gives way to a beautifully composed tripartite shot of Sylvia reading, Frank mending a clock and Ethel ironing, presented in a subdued palette of grey-blues and browns (Plate 2). The music ceases and the thump of the flat iron briefly stills, as each of them pauses from their activities to listen to the news that the king is 'moving towards death'. Potential fears surrounding modernity and the creation of an 'Admass' society are abated through the evocation here of a very traditional form of popular British monarchism; hence the rupture in that continuity caused by the abdication. Although Coward was not permitted to refer to the crisis as directly as he had

2 A domestic still life: Frank (Robert Newton), Sylvia (Alison Leggatt) and Ethel (Celia Johnson) listen to the radio announcement of the death of George V in *This Happy Breed* (1944)

hoped in either play or film, it is succinctly alluded to by a calendar of Edward VIII being thrown into the dustbin.

The episode detailing the old king's death presents the family like a still life, and the notion of stasis is important in a broader political sense. *This Happy Breed* is a deeply conservative text, enacting what John Lahr describes as an 'almost feudal vision of social inertia'[71] whose primary mouthpiece is Frank Gibbons. One Christmas day, when he and Ethel escape into the kitchen to get away from Sylvia's tuneless singing in the parlour, Frank elaborates his gradualist credo:

> Oh, there's something to be said for it [socialism], there's always something to be said for everything. But where they go wrong is trying to get things done too quickly and we don't like doing things quickly in this country. It's like gardening, somebody once said we was a nation of gardeners, and they weren't far wrong. We like planting things and watching them grow and looking out for changes in the weather. What works in other countries won't work in this one. We've got our own way of settling things; it may be a bit slow and it may be a bit dull, but it suits us all right and always will.

Here the English love of gardening, also noted by Orwell, is pressed into the service of ideology, used as a metaphor for the superiority of slow incremental growth over sudden violent upheaval. As he explains elsewhere, social systems are not at the root of unhappiness; the blame lies with 'good old human nature' which can't be changed by any social revolution.

The play of *This Happy Breed* ended with a further lengthy speech covering similar ground but in more bullish terms, with Frank addressing his infant grandson Frankie in his pram, a kind of right-wing precedent for *A Diary for Timothy* (1946), similarly using a baby as the pretext for addressing the country's future. It was because of that final speech that Robert Donat, Coward's first choice to play Frank in the film, rejected the role, writing to Coward 'I don't believe in the things that Frank believes in. He's human and loveable until he tries to justify himself and his kind.'[72] Ironically, the speech was then cut in the adaptation to film (despite Coward's wishes) and its ultimate superfluity is proved by the fact that the things made ploddingly explicit in the speech – 'we know what we belong to, where we come from, and where we're going. We may not know it with our brains, but we know it with our roots' – resonate all the more in the film for being left implicit and unsaid.

Just as steadiness is valued politically in *This Happy Breed*, this quality is equally valued in terms of gender identity exemplified by its enduring central couple, Frank and Ethel Gibbons. Frank is the benevolent patriarch who embodies common sense, occasionally a little drunk but never truly wayward, while Ethel demonstrates forbearance throughout, occasionally tired and snappy but an icon of maternal resilience. Their greatest trial comes when they lose their son Reg in a car accident. The scene in which they are informed of his death has the bad news being broken to them off screen while the camera stays in the unchanged parlour still set out for tea, while the radio that Reg had bought for his parents merrily blares out dance music until Ethel returns to switch it off. The camera tracks away from the bereaved parents in a state of shock. A fade to black suggests the passing of time and when we fade back up on the couple they are only a few years older but prematurely aged and worn by grief. But still they endure and continue.

While the respectable married woman is celebrated, in the shape of Ethel and her like-minded daughter Vi, the single woman is a much more problematic figure in the film. The widowed Mrs Flint is engaged in constant conflict with hypochondriac spinster Aunt Sylvia, who eventually finds solace in unconventional spiritualist faith and female friendship. The two women's antagonistic exchanges and secret alliances, hilariously performed by Amy Veness and Alison Leggatt, are one of the film's chief glories. However, perhaps the most interesting female characterisation in *This Happy Breed* is the dissatisfied daughter Queenie, the manicurist with a regal name to match her upwardly mobile aspirations, who by her own admission is 'not like Vi' and wants to 'look different from all the others'. There is an interesting parallel between Sam's socialism, and his critique of the iniquities of the British class system, and Queenie's own refusal to know her place and be thankful, both being dismissed as symptoms of arrested development. But while Sam rapidly becomes a respectable petit-bourgeois citizen upon marriage to Vi, Queenie's hunger for a different way of life is less easily quelled. She turns down boy-next-door Billy's Christmas day proposal with an eloquent speech that takes place just before Frank's meditation on gardening, and in some way acts as its ideological counterpoint:

> I want too much – I'm always thinking about the kind of things I want and they wouldn't be the kind of things you'd want me to want ... I'll tell you something awful. I hate living here, I hate living in a house that's exactly like hundreds of other houses. I hate coming home from work on the tube. I hate washing up and helping Mum darn Dad's socks and listening to Aunt Syl keeping on about how ill she is all the time, and what's more I know why I hate it, it's because it's all so common. There! I suppose you'll think I'm getting above myself and perhaps I am, but I can't help it.

Conveying a fierce sense of being torn apart by guilt and conflicted desires – as Silver and Ursini suggest, 'her dissatisfactions are heartfelt and her fears ring true'[73] – this moment animates the flipside of the social acquiescence celebrated throughout. It may even, through the conviction of Kay Walsh's performance, not to mention her red-headed Technicolor radiance, provide a vivid oppositional point of identification. Michael Anderegg argues that Queenie's rebellion 'opens up a discussion of the place of women in the bourgeois family with such intensity that Coward's text no longer succeeds in containing the disturbance it has posed'.[74] And of course she is just the first in a long line of Lean heroines 'whose primary characteristic is an unfocussed but powerful yearning for something more, something different, something better'.[75] Not content merely to look upon parades, films and other spectacles, Queenie wants to be part of the action, demonstrated by her enthusiastic and skilful performance of the new Charleston dance in which she 'takes pleasure in being the object of the gaze'.[76] The film's original promotional trailer used shots taken from these sequences to single her out as the girl 'who liked having a good time', with all the risqué connotations that phrase has. Her partner in that dance has the foreign-sounding surname Alliado, and may be the married man with whom she runs away to France, rejecting suburban respectability in favour of continental romance. As Philip Hoare remarks, although Noël Coward was a proficient social climber himself, he 'was not about to encourage further social acrobatics'[77] of the kind Queenie attempts. Her attempt at a life beyond the confines of England eventually fails. She returns to the fold, fulfilling what the pressbook calls 'her natural destiny of becoming the bride of Billy', although there are subtle hints that what constitutes woman's natural destiny might be changing: Amelia Earhart's solo Atlantic flight features prominently on the front of Mrs Flint's newspaper. Kay Walsh strongly identified with her character's rebellious streak but not with her return to her family: 'I would never have given in, never have gone back home.'[78] But it is significant that Queenie is never presented as a totally chastened woman, and the film's dialogue alludes to her ongoing spikiness even once she becomes a mother, with Ethel complaining 'you'd think nobody'd ever had a baby before, all the fuss we've had this last month'.

Queenie is the necessary grit in the oyster to prevent *This Happy Breed*'s vision of English family life from becoming overly sentimental or stolid, but she also functions as the character who points out the limitations and exclusions of the suburban 'demi-paradise' the film depicts. However, the constancy and affection in her mother and father's relationship is what the film chooses to end on. In place of Frank's hectoring speech, the film of *This Happy Breed* bows out on Frank and Ethel's touching badinage: his soppy endearment 'I don't mind how many flats we move into or where we go or what we do, as long as I've got you' followed by her gentle rebuke 'Don't talk so silly'. The very last shots repeat in reverse the opening of the film, pulling back out of the empty house and back over the London cityscape of which the Gibbonses have been a small but symbolically rich part. Coward's song 'London Pride' plays over the film's last moments, underlining his authorial imprimatur. But the contribution made by David Lean, Ronald Neame and Anthony Havelock-Allan was being increasingly recognised by critics like Richard Winngton, who offered unstinting praise for 'the three young men who made the picture' and who collectively offered 'a confirmation and a hope for those who believe in British cinema'.[79]

Blithe Spirit (1945)

David Lean's third film in association with Noël Coward marked a new direction, perhaps following Coward's advice to Lean to 'always come out of another hole'. Having hitherto cleaved to Coward's more homely side, *Blithe Spirit* would be the closest Lean came to the playwright's world of upper-crust wit and sophistication: the Molyneux-clad, cocktail-shaking classes represented in *Private Lives* and *Design for Living*. The debonair hero of *Blithe Spirit*, Charles Condomine (Rex Harrison), is a successful novelist married to his second wife Ruth (Constance Cummings), the couple inhabiting what Coward describes as a 'charming country house'. But this affluent and slightly smug milieu is disturbed by a sudden eruption of the supernatural when Charles's deceased first wife Elvira (Kay Hammond) materialises at a séance keen to make mischief and reacquaint herself with her former husband (Plate 3).

Much of the play's humour derives from its refusal to dramatise death in portentous terms, tackling it through brittle witticism instead. The fad for spiritualism is beautifully sent up via the dotty medium Madame Arcati (Margaret Rutherford), just as it had been satirised in *This Happy Breed* through Aunt Sylvia. All the same, Coward actually credited his ability to write the play in just five days to an 'almost psychic gift'[80] of his own, suggesting a more open-minded attitude to matters occult than mere dismissal. The play's form may have been farcical fantasy, 'very gay, superficial comedy' in Coward's own estimation,[81] but its origins lay in the darkest realities of wartime Britain. It was written and premiered during the Blitz, and its first audience had to walk across planks laid over the rubble to enter the theatre, while a programme note from that production suggested its mood of defiance: 'If an air raid warning be received ... those desiring to leave the theatre may do so but

3 Ghostly first wife Elvira (Kay Hammond) comes between Charles (Rex Harrison) and second wife Ruth (Constance Cummings) in *Blithe Spirit* (1945)

the performance will continue.'[82] Although Graham Greene thought the play's humorous treatment of death 'a weary exhibition of bad taste',[83] one might equally see it as a triumphant rebuttal of mortality, sublimating Coward's 'fear and rage' into 'mockery'.[84]

The play's enormous transatlantic success, holding the record for longest-running play in the West End prior to *The Mousetrap* as well as enjoying a long Broadway run, made it a valuable property for Cineguild and yet Lean seems to have been less than blithe about undertaking this particular assignment. His 'strong prejudice against upper-class frivolity', according to Anthony Havelock-Allan,[85] and discomfort with directing comedy was most likely exacerbated by the fact that the piece offered limited scope for directorial reinvention. As C. A. Lejeune reported from her visit to the set: 'little could be valuably done with the script, Mr Lean tells us, except break up the dialogue here and there and add a fresh line or two to get the actors from spot to spot.'[86] But this belies the cinematic creativity that Lean and his team brought to bear on the screen adaptation: the mobile camera that follows the maid Edith around the house at double speed in the opening sequences, succinctly introducing us to the domestic setting; the use of subjective camera from Madame Arcati's point-of-view as she approaches the table in a trance; the slow track into a close-up of Edith's face as she falls under hypnosis; the neat montage of Arcati's increasingly bizarre attempts at exorcism; and, most striking of all, the languid camera movement which pulls away from the reunited Elvira and Charles, the latter enjoying the soothing surrogate touch of a cool breeze though his hair and perhaps other ghostly sensual delights. The shot finally settles on the couple's reflection in the hallway mirror, apparently confirming her objective reality – she can't be a figment of the imagination if she actually appears in the mirror – and yet her weird yellow-green glow renders her conspicuously unreal. Creating a plausible ghost posed one of the film's biggest technical challenges. Kay Hammond's distinctive pallid make-up (offset by her scarlet lips and nails) and floaty chiffon costuming do some of the work, helped by occasional use of a wind machine and some hidden wire work, along with Ronald Neame's use of a ghostly green light created by 'two "brutes" [the strong light required for colour photography], fitted with green filters and shutters ... when she passed behind other people, an electrician would close the shutters on one lamp while another electrician opened those on the second.'[87]

The film also makes effective comic use of the specifically filmic device of viewing the same scene from different perspectives, alternately with and without ghost, a 'double joke' which, Dilys Powell suggested, made 'modest use of the camera's power to lie'.[88] It supports the humour of Condomine's anger being aimed at Elvira but mistakenly answered by Ruth. Apart from the genuinely poignant moment in which Charles and Elvira pledge their continuing love while Irving Berlin's haunting song 'Always' plays in the background, the reappearance of Elvira is played strictly for laughs. The comedy has sometimes been viewed as rather misogynist in tone, presenting Charles entrapped in a 'nightmare of female suffocation'.[89] He describes himself as 'hag-ridden', and certainly his two wives' final remarks as they are exorcised are either reproachful nagging or spiteful reminders of adulterous liaisons. No wonder Charles appears more content when both of them are dead and gone, chiming with one review of Coward's original play which suggested that *Blithe Spirit* hinged upon the 'possibly ungallant and certainly facile implication that wives present only one problem to the well-regulated masculine mind: how they are to be got rid of'.[90] However, Charles does not have the upper hand as he does in the play, in which he escapes unscathed: in the film, his wives have the last laugh, fatally tampering with his brakes and forcing them to join him in a truly eternal triangle.[91]

The film's pressbook for its US release suggested the staging of a 'battle of the sexes' event as a publicity stunt, reflecting the conflict running throughout *Blithe Spirit* between male rationality, represented by Charles, which finds itself continually disturbed and undermined by female spirituality, represented by the ghost of Elvira (and later of Ruth as well), the genuinely psychic maid Edith, and the inimitable force of nature Madame Arcati. *Kine Weekly* remarked of Margaret Rutherford's bravura performance in the role, 'This is the fat part and she certainly does seize her chances!'[92] The first twenty minutes of the film, devoted to the preparation and enactment of the séance, belong to Rutherford more than anyone else, including the ostensible leads (to their consternation: 'what he did to me was unforgivable', Rex Harrison later complained of Lean[93]). Although the *New Statesman*'s William Whitebait would characterise Rutherford's Arcati grotesquely as 'a tough old biking, cussing, grimacing, hand-clapping baboon of an Englishwoman',[94] the actress plays her as a holy innocent, eccentric in appearance but definitely her own woman, taking equal sensual pleasure in ovaltine or dry martinis, committed to her craft and acerbic about those who casually criticise it: 'You should think, Dr Bradman, but I fear you don't – at least, not profoundly enough.'

Blithe Spirit was not particularly beloved by Lean or by Coward. The latter's reaction to the film, according to Ronald Neame, was to suggest that they had 'fucked up the best thing I've ever written'.[95] As Sarah Street argues, it continues to be marginalised in discussions of Lean's work despite capturing effectively Coward's trademark offhand wit as well as being a tour de force of technique.[96] Lean's direction was praised in reviews for being unobtrusive and for having the ability to 'tide over the boring passages'.[97] But this would be damningly faint praise to an ever more confident director growing frustrated with living in Coward's shadow. If, as *Time* magazine proclaimed, *Blithe Spirit* was '99.9% Noel Coward'[98] then the remaining 0.1 per cent was becoming an increasingly claustrophobic space to inhabit. One more film, arguably the finest achievement of their four-film association, was still to come later that year: *Brief Encounter* (discussed in chapter four). Then the partnership that had got Lean's directorial career started would be permanently dissolved and he would move into new territory with his Cineguild colleagues.

Notes

1 Silverman, *David Lean*, p. 24.
2 Brownlow, *David Lean*, p. 742.
3 Lean interviewed by David Ehrenstein in 1984 in Organ (ed.), *David Lean: Interviews*, p. 67.
4 Silverman, *David Lean*, p. 22.

5 Brownlow, *David Lean*, p. 14.
6 Silverman, *David Lean*, p. 20.
7 For more on Lean's period at Movietone News, see Linda Kaye, 'David Lean and the Newsreels', unpublished paper, available at www.sllf.qmul.ac.uk/filmstudies/davidlean/index.html (accessed 23 July 2010).
8 Silverman, *David Lean*, p. 28.
9 Gene D. Phillips, *Beyond the Epic: The Life and Films of David Lean* (Lexington: University of Kentucky Press, 2006), p. 30.
10 Letter dated 12 November 1964. UoR Spec Coll.
11 Phillips, *Beyond the Epic*, p. 33.
12 Ibid.
13 Ibid., p. 46.
14 Silverman, *David Lean*, p. 29.
15 Quoted in Pratley, *The Cinema of David Lean*, p. 15.
16 Ibid., p. 28.
17 A 1956 interview with Lean quoted in Anderegg, *David Lean*, p. 3.
18 Lean with Chattington, *David Lean*, p. 12.
19 Mark Glancy, 'David Lean and Noël Coward: *In Which We Serve* and Authorship', paper presented at the David Lean centenary conference, Queen Mary, University of London, July 2008.
20 Brownlow, *David Lean*, p. 155.
21 Ibid. Perhaps Anthony Havelock-Allan came off worst in the end, getting only a minor associate producer credit when, according to Brownlow, 'the film was really produced by [him]'. Interesting also that the impetus for Lean's stand seems to have come from the urging of his wife Kay Walsh, whose off-screen assertiveness stands in ironic counterpoint to her on-screen role of Freda, the very model of biddable femininity.
22 Ronald Neame, *Straight from the Horse's Mouth* (Lanham MD: Scarecrow, 2003), p. 59, p. 64.
23 Graham Payn and Sheridan Morley (eds.), *The Noël Coward Diaries* (London: Weidenfeld & Nicolson, 1982), p. 7.
24 Noël Coward, *Future Indefinite* (London: Bloomsbury Methuen, 2004), p. 208.
25 Sheridan Morley, *Noël Coward* (London: Haus Publishing, 2005), p. 86.
26 Anthony Aldgate and Jeffrey Richards, *Britain Can Take It: The British Cinema in the Second World War*, 2nd edition (Edinburgh: Edinburgh University Press, 1994), p. 199.
27 Payn and Morley (eds.), *The Noël Coward Diaries*, p. 14. There is a complete and magnanimous turnaround once the film is released though, with Beddington and Brendan Bracken congratulating him and asking him to make its army equivalent. See Aldgate and Richards, *Britain Can Take It*, pp. 204–5.
28 Quoted in Coward, *Future Indefinite*, p. 397. Coward got his revenge on Beaverbrook's papers in the film, dwelling at length on the *Express*'s misjudgement of international politics – their headline 'No War This Year' – now discarded and floating in dirty water. This is another link to *Citizen Kane* and its mockery of a press baron's hubris in stating unequivocally 'you can take my word for it, there'll be no war.'
29 *Kine Weekly*, 13 January 1944, p. 16.
30 Jeffrey Richards and Dorothy Sheridan (eds.), *Mass-Observation at the Movies* (London: Routledge, 1987), p. 238.
31 Ibid., pp. 225, 228, 233, 241, 247, 257.
32 Ibid., p. 267.
33 *Documentary News Letter*, Vol. 3, No. 10, October 1942, p. 143.
34 Payn and Morley (eds.), *The Noël Coward Diaries*, p. 16.

35 Quoted in Morley, *Noël Coward*, p. 86.
36 In Stephen Frears's documentary *Typically British: A Personal History of British Cinema* (1995).
37 Aldgate and Richards, *Britain Can Take It*, p. 336.
38 Coward, *Future Indefinite*, p. 426.
39 Neil Rattigan, *This Is England: British Film and the People's War, 1939–1945* (Madison NJ: Fairleigh Dickinson University Press, 2001), p. 85.
40 Gill Plain, *John Mills and British Cinema* (Edinburgh: Edinburgh University Press, 2006), p. 58.
41 James Chapman, *The British at War: Cinema, State and Propaganda, 1939–1945* (London: I. B. Tauris, 2000), p. 186.
42 Brownlow, *David Lean*, p. 154. See also Neame, *Straight from the Horse's Mouth*, p. 58.
43 *Kine Weekly*, 1 October 1942, p. 28.
44 Women's fashions featured prominently in the US pressbook for the film – 'Simplicity marks styles worn by British women' – which noted Alix's tweed suit and brimmed hat for travelling: 'even her dress up clothes have a fine restrained air ... she wears a crepe frock of simple lines, the only trimming a band of beaded ornamentation around the neckline'. Freda's stylish 'beret and reefer' were also noted.
45 Barry Day (ed.), *The Letters of Noël Coward* (London: Methuen, 2007), pp. 436–7. Letter dated 18 July 1941. Also diary entry, 11 July 1941: watching servicemen and 'gaily dressed' girls dancing on Plymouth Hoe: 'A sight so infinitely touching, not that it was consciously brave, but because it was so ordinary and unexhibitionist.' Payn and Morley (eds.), *The Noël Coward Diaries*, p. 8.
46 Philip Hoare, *Noël Coward: A Biography* (London: Sinclair-Stevenson, 1995), p. 324.
47 Silverman, *David Lean*, p. 45.
48 Anderson's essay 'Get Out and Push!' quoted in Anderegg, *David Lean*, p. 11.
49 *Documentary News Letter*, May 1944, p. 2.
50 *In Which We Serve* final treatment dated 10 Dec 1941, p. 77. DL/1/1, BFI Spec Coll.
51 Chapman, *The British at War*, p. 184.
52 Richards and Sheridan (eds.), *Mass-Observation at the Movies*, p. 276.
53 *Manchester Guardian*, 3 June 1944.
54 *This Happy Breed* pressbook, BFI Library. It added in a note to exhibitors: 'Work up in preliminary press matter the idea that family life is the backbone of this country.'
55 Aldgate and Richards, *Britain Can Take It*, p. 46.
56 *New Statesman*, 27 May 1944.
57 C. A. Lejeune, *Observer*, 27 August 1944. She calls it 'a film that finds in a house in a row the symbol of the nation'.
58 *This Happy Breed* pressbook, BFI Library.
59 J. P. Mayer, *British Cinemas and their Audiences* (London: Dennis Dobson, 1948), p. 214.
60 Undated *Observer* article quoted in Hoare, *Noël Coward*, p. 337.
61 Neame, *Straight from the Horse's Mouth*, p. 77.
62 Quoted in Hoare, *Noël Coward*, p. 337.
63 Richard Winnington, *News Chronicle*, 27 May 1944.
64 Andrew Higson, *Waving the Flag: Constructing a National Cinema in Britain* (Oxford: Clarendon, 1995), p. 262.
65 Morley, *Noël Coward*, pp. 82–3.
66 Hoare, *Noël Coward*, p. 335.
67 Noël Coward, *Present Indicative* (London: Heinemann, 1937), p. 131.

68 *The Times*, 24 May 1944.
69 C. A. Lejeune, *Observer*, 28 May 1944.
70 Edgar Anstley, *Spectator*, 2 June 1944, p. 499.
71 John Lahr, *Coward the Playwright* (London: Methuen, 1982), p. 105.
72 Day (ed.), *The Letters of Noël Coward*, p. 504.
73 Silver and Ursini, *David Lean and His Films*, p. 18.
74 Anderegg, *David Lean*, p. 15.
75 Ibid., p. 17.
76 Higson, *Waving the Flag*, p. 260.
77 Hoare, *Noël Coward*, p. 302.
78 Quoted in Brian McFarlane, *An Autobiography of British Cinema* (London: Methuen, 1997), p. 595.
79 *News Chronicle*, 27 May 1944.
80 Noël Coward, 'Introduction', *The Collected Plays of Noël Coward*, Vol. 5 (London: Heinemann, 1958), p. xxxii.
81 Hoare, *Noël Coward*, p. 319.
82 Frances Gray, *Noël Coward* (Basingstoke: Macmillan, 1987), p. 177.
83 Quoted in Morley, *Noël Coward*, p. 81.
84 Lahr, *Coward the Playwright*, p. 115.
85 Brownlow, *David Lean*, p. 183.
86 C. A. Lejeune, *Observer*, 27 February 1944.
87 Neame, *Straight from the Horse's Mouth*, p. 81.
88 Dilys Powell, *Sunday Times*, 8 April 1945.
89 Lahr, *Coward the Playwright*, p. 128.
90 Quoted in Morley, *Noël Coward*, p. 82.
91 Havelock-Allan suggested a further problem with their adaptation, in that Charles was too young and his second wife more attractive than his first, thus throwing its humorous premise off balance. Brownlow, *David Lean*, p. 185.
92 *Kine Weekly*, 12 April 1945, p. 31.
93 Quoted in *The Times*, T2 section, 6 July 2006, p. 20.
94 William Whitebait, *New Statesman*, 7 April 1945.
95 Neame, *Straight from the Horse's Mouth*, p. 82.
96 Sarah Street, '"In Blushing Technicolor": Colour in *Blithe Spirit*', *Journal of British Cinema and Television*, Vol. 7, No. 1, 2010, p. 36.
97 William Whitebait, *New Statesman*, 7 April 1945.
98 *Time*, 10 April 1945.

Nineteenth-century blues: *Great Expectations* (1946), *Oliver Twist* (1948), *Madeleine* (1950) and *Hobson's Choice* (1954)

3

It has become customary to look at David Lean's two consecutive Dickens adaptations together, often in semi-isolation from his other work around this time. *Great Expectations* (1946) and *Oliver Twist* (1948) offer a clearly demarcated sub-section of the director's career – his Dickens period – and moreover one with considerable prestige. Both films are regarded as exemplary film versions of classic novels and have been frequently used as examples for discussing the pros and cons of literary adaptation. However, as a number of scholars have noted, the terms of this discussion can be quite restrictive, frequently 'bedevilled by the fidelity issue'.[1] Although, as Sarah Cardwell argues, 'a considerable proportion of the filmic text' may not be 'explicable in terms of the source book',[2] the mechanics of transposing page to screen have nearly always dominated discussions of film adaptations, in spite of what Robert Stam calls the 'ongoing whirl of intertextual reference and transformation' that *all* texts inhabit, whether they are direct adaptations or not.[3] Although adaptation offers an important explanatory framework through which to view certain films, there may be other equally productive contexts in which to place them. Christine Geraghty suggests that more emphasis should be placed on evaluating adaptations *as films*, not just as versions of books or plays. Although 'associations generated by its relationship with its source' are very important to a screen adaptation, 'generic associations from other films also accompany it on the screen' and these ought to be properly acknowledged, Geraghty argues.[4] This certainly applies to Lean's Dickens films, which could be just as usefully analysed in relation to 1940s film noir or other costume dramas made around the same period as they could be analysed in terms of transpositions of Dickens.

In that spirit, I have chosen to place Lean's two Dickens films alongside his two other films set in the nineteenth century: the melodrama *Madeleine* (1950), set in the 1850s, and the comedy *Hobson's Choice* (1954), set in the 1880s. This broadens the scope of my discussion both socially and geographically. Lean's two Dickens films depict London and the South of England but *Madeleine* and *Hobson's Choice* add the very different nineteenth-century worlds of bourgeois Glasgow and lower-middle-class Salford. The upwardly mobile social progress of boys in *Great Expectations* and *Oliver Twist* is counterbalanced by the emphasis on determined young women in the other two films. Compiled thus, the four films constitute a kind of nineteenth-century quartet, offering different versions of the (at that time) still recent past. Going beyond adaptation studies into the wider realm of 'inventing the Victorians' provides an original and useful framework through which to discuss the Dickens films. After all, Charles Dickens was famed as a unique literary genius but he was also, arguably, *the* author of his age. 'In the very structure of his work', argues Peter Ackroyd, 'it is possible to recognise the force and elaboration of the nineteenth century.'[5] Indeed, as historian John Gardiner observes, '"Dickensian" seems almost at times to come before "Victorian". Asked about the workhouse, our thoughts are bound to fly before long to *Oliver Twist*; asked about Victorian London generally, Dickens becomes virtually inescapable.'[6] As an eminent Victorian, he helped to define the age in which he lived, both during that age itself and in the years subsequently.

Lean's four nineteenth-century films span a time when perceptions of the Victorian were changing in Britain. Throughout the twentieth century, the Victorian period (1837–1901) was continually reinvented in a variety of guises for diverse ideological purposes. As with any epoch, the years of Victoria's reign were fashioned according to the requirements of any given historical moment but their dominant role in the twentieth century was as modernity's 'other'. For Matthew Sweet, the Victorians are 'the people against whom we have defined ourselves. We are who we are because we are not the Victorians.'[7] These sentiments seem to have been even truer of the first years of the twentieth century. The autobiographical writings of Samuel Butler and Edmund Gosse raged against the Victorian patriarch, and Lytton Strachey's 1918 book *Eminent Victorians* presented a series of profoundly iconoclastic character studies of heroes of the age such as Florence Nightingale and General Gordon. Strachey's revolutionary work had a remarkable impact on the reputation of the Victorians and, as historian Miles Taylor suggests, if Victorians 'remained in the public memory at all in the years immediately following 1918 it was as the subject of satire, irony and detachment'.[8] By 1934, the OED was using 'Victorian' as a synonym for 'prudish, strict; old-fashioned, out-dated'.[9]

And yet even during the 1920s, the decade seen as 'the zenith of what we might call anti-Victorianism',[10] there were small pockets of affection and admiration for them including a cult of Victoriana among Oxford aesthetes and Bright Young Things. In Evelyn Waugh's *Brideshead Revisited*, Sebastian Flyte's college rooms are whimsically decorated with outré Victorian kitsch: 'a strange jumble of objects – a harmonium in a gothic case, an elephant's foot waste-paper basket, a dome of wax fruit'.[11] The attractions of the Victorian past were obvious; given the circumstances of 'our own unpleasant century', Basil Willey noted, 'many are tempted to take flight into the nineteenth as into a promised land'.[12] The Victorians' most significant advocate at this time was the historian G. M. Young, whose book *Victorian England: Portrait of an Age* (1936) helped to counteract some of the Strachey-ite extremities of anti-Victorianism.[13] Not long after the publication of Young's book came a more populist indicator of pro-Victorianism, the box-office success of Herbert Wilcox's two Queen Victoria biopics, *Victoria the Great* (1937) and *Sixty Glorious Years* (1938). Although, Miles Taylor suggests, 'up until the 1940s, the negative verdict of the Bloomsbury generation on the Victorians remained powerful',[14] change was beginning to happen. 'The Age of Recrimination', characterised by 'disdain and contempt', was becoming 'The Age of Evaluation', with historians Kelly Boyd and Rohan McWilliam marking the tipping point somewhere around 1945,[15] just as the first of Lean's four forays into the nineteenth century, *Great Expectations*, entered pre-production.

All four of Lean's nineteenth-century films appeared during a period in which perceptions of the Victorian were in a greater state of flux than they had been for some time. On the one hand, it was a period defined by hypocrisy and patriarchal oppression as well as widespread squalor and poverty against which the postwar welfare state defined itself. On other hand, it provided 'a kind of refuge in an age that had not witnessed the mass destruction of the twentieth century',[16] an era of charm and allure. By 1948, the Victorians were being taken seriously again, with the BBC commissioning a major radio series in that year, broadcast over four months, whose aim was to 'examine the assumptions of the Victorian Age, appraise its ideas, and reassess its controversies in the belief that such an examination will shed light on the urgent issues of today'.[17] However, the Festival of Britain in 1951 marked the key transitional moment in the Victorians' rehabilitation, according to Asa Briggs, with its deliberate celebratory echoes of the Great Exhibition of 1851.[18] Whereas gothicism had been the keynote of many Victorian-themed films of a few years before, now the tone became more festive, with commemorative biopics of Florence Nightingale in 1951 and Gilbert and Sullivan in 1953 as well as a version of Dickens's jolliest novel, *The Pickwick Papers*, appearing on British cinema screens in 1952. In the fledgling medium of television, the BBC started its celebration of Victorian Music Hall *The Good Old Days* in 1953, a series that would run until 1983. A re-evaluation of the Victorians, taking into account good points as well as bad, was well under way by the 1950s, and towards the end of the decade one of its most reviled features, its architecture, would come under the protection of the Victorian Society, founded with the aim of halting the seemingly unstoppable demolition of Victorian buildings.

Perceptions of the Victorians would change again in the 1960s and the decades beyond it. But the late 1940s and early 1950s were to prove a particularly formative moment of reappraisal to which Lean's four variations on the theme of 'nineteenth-century blues' (to adapt the title of Noël Coward's song from *Cavalcade*) made a significant contribution.

Great Expectations (1946)

Great Expectations opens on a shot of a book, the Charles Dickens novel on which the film is based; a commonplace strategy for beginning a screen adaptation of a respected work of literature. On the soundtrack, we hear a voiceover narrator (John Mills, who plays the adult Pip in the film) reading aloud exactly the same famous introductory words displayed on the first page. Both these details announce and underline the film's fidelity to its source text, that this will be 'a film of the book'. However, the pages of the book are then ruffled and blown over by a gust of wind which not only acts as a bridging motif to what we see next – a dissolve to young Pip running across similarly windswept marshlands – but also disrupts the fixity of the literary source. When the pages are acted upon by the sensual force of the wind, reading the words is no longer possible and thus the viewer is propelled into the film proper. This short introductory sequence seems to me to be a perfect microcosm of *Great Expectations*'s position as a literary adaptation: simultaneously faithful *and* free-spirited, happy to disturb textual stasis as it sees fit but still grounding itself in the world of the source book. For many scholars, Lean's *Great Expectations* occupies near totemic status as ideal adaptation. For the editors of the essay collection *Screening the Novel*, it is the sole transposition of a novel 'universally admitted to be a great film' and they state unambiguously that 'wherever you look you will find this film acclaimed'.[19] It is fitting that an adaptation of Dickens occupies this hallowed territory, echoing the idea that he was a uniquely proto-cinematic writer (brilliantly set out in Eisenstein's essay, 'Dickens, Griffith and the Film Today').[20] Throughout Dickens's novels, there are moments of striking optical intensity that seem to anticipate film;

indeed, Dickens makes a point about the primacy of the visual in *Great Expectations* when Pip describes how a moment of extreme emotional duress 'presented pictures to me, and not mere words. In the excited and exalted state of my brain, I could not think of a place without seeing it, or of persons without seeing them. It is impossible to over-state the vividness of these images.'[21] While writing his novels, Dickens said that his characters appeared to him as physically present manifestations verging on the hallucinogenic.[22] Given the centrality of the pictoral to Dickens's creative practice, it is unsurprising that his works were some of the earliest texts selected for cinematic adaptation and continue to be popular choices for dramatisation.

Although much admired, Lean's *Great Expectations* is by no means a slavishly close adaptation. It omits altogether the character of Orlick, Pip's dark *doppelgänger*, minimises the significance of Biddy, and truncates the narrative details of Mrs Joe's illness and death. But, in Brian McFarlane's reckoning, the film manages to achieve something far more elusive than mere fidelity of incident, which is to harness 'a visual stylistic verve' equivalent to the source novel's 'peculiar rhetorical powers'.[23] One example of this is the startling first encounter between young Pip (Anthony Wager) and the escaped convict Magwitch (Finlay Currie) which achieves its impact from the imaginative deployment of cinematic technique. The scene is set with the atmospheric location photography by Guy Green of the Medway marshes, subtly augmented by the special effect of a carefully superimposed matte cloud. The frame's strong horizontal lines – sky, water, earth – are bisected by the verticals of the lone running boy and a gibbet creaking in the wind. When Pip reaches his destination, we see and hear the canopy of trees creaking in the wind over the churchyard as Pip approaches his parents' gravestone. Lean's stated aim in this sequence was to evoke 'the world as it seemed to Pip when his imagination was distorted with fear'.[24] This culminates in the shock of Magwitch's first appearance on screen, a justly celebrated moment of cinematic ambush. The sideways movement of the quick panning shot which follows Pip running scared from screen right to screen left (after he's been spooked by a gnarled tree trunk that resembles a frightening human face) is abruptly halted when Pip unexpectedly runs up against something to be truly scared of: the imposing man-mountain who threatens him with 'keep still you little devil or I'll cut your throat!'

Pip's point-of-view is the determining factor in the presentation of much of what follows: the memorable gothic terror of Magwitch's warning that 'your heart and liver'll be torn out and roasted and ate', Freda Jackson's whip-wielding turn as his cruel surrogate mother, Mrs

Joe, going 'on the rampage', and even the cows in the field who seem to stand in judgement on him as he runs to deliver stolen 'victuals' to the escaped convict. The extremity of the situations and the indelible impression they make on the child's mind is the keynote here. Furthermore, the film is already establishing different moral behaviours to which the adult Pip might ascribe: the snobbery and cruelty of Mrs Joe and her friend Mr Pumblechook, compared to the honour demonstrated by Magwitch when he takes responsibility for the theft from Mrs Joe's cupboard to protect the boy, or the compassion expressed by Joe Gargery (Bernard Miles), after Magwitch is recaptured on the mudflats, for a 'poor miserable fellow creature' being bundled back into captivity.

Pip's education in the strange ways of the adult world continues a year later, when he is summoned to 'play' at the mansion of the wealthy eccentric Miss Havisham (Martita Hunt). If the first appearance of the convict Magwitch hinged on shock, then the first appearance of Havisham offers a more slow burning introduction to a character, but equally unforgettable. Pip pushes open the heavy wooden door to her room as first the room, opulent but cobwebbed and dishevelled, and then Miss Havisham herself, in much the same state, are gradually revealed. 'Let me look at you', she instructs Pip, and the camera tracks forward to mimic his slow walk towards her, but it also permits us a closer look at this extraordinary broken-hearted woman who since Pip's birth 'has never seen the sun'. A close-up of her heavily cobwebbed Bible and hairbrush untouched for many years on the dressing table compounds the eerie stasis of the scene.[25]

Of course, just prior to this encounter, there had already occurred Pip's equally fateful first meeting with another incomprehensible female who will mark him for life: the young Estella (Jean Simmons), Miss Havisham's adopted child and protégée (Plate 4). Estella first appears at a high window, confidently checking the identity of the visitor – 'What name?' 'Quite right' –and when she comes down to admit Pip into the house we are granted our first proper view of her. She approaches him swinging a bunch of keys (the same nonchalant gesture as the young waitress in *Brief Encounter*), the breeze blowing through her hair, dressed in a pinafore and knickerbockers that seem a little too juvenile for her, an over-grown Alice. As she opens the gate and lets him in, the film provides its first close-up of her face, radiant and (apparently) totally self-possessed. The obvious attractions of the beautiful teenage Jean Simmons are allied with the character's arrogant sense of superiority over Pip, which begin with harsh entreaties ('Don't loiter, boy'; Simmons enunciates the word 'boy' with delicious contempt) and soon reach a crescendo of aristocratic disdain: 'Look at his boots', 'What coarse hands', 'You stupid clumsy labouring boy!' As Alison Light suggests, the novel *Great Expectations* is very astute on 'the connection between bullying and deference in English society', or 'the "metaphysics" of ill-treatment, what comes of being made to feel inferior',[26] and this applies equally to the film. Pip's class-motivated cringing is all the more painful because of its entanglement with burgeoning pubescent sexual attraction. When pressed by Miss Havisham, Pip admits that he finds Estella 'very proud' and 'very insulting' but also 'very pretty', and it's this potent and highly eroticised combination that bewitches him, a view shared by many male viewers of *Great Expectations* according to Peter Lennon's retrospective analysis: 'every red-blooded schoolboy in England experienced that delicious sense of helpless happiness associated with being alone in the spooky dark with Jean Simmons.'[27]

The film goes on to explore this sense of erotic enslavement and masochistic attraction in some depth, although with greater piquancy in the scenes featuring Simmons's young Estella than the adult Estella (a more sedate Valerie Hobson). Estella's behaviour during Pip's boyhood visits to Satis House is confusingly polarised: she slaps him and calls him a 'coarse little monster', then the next time she sees him she invites an embrace ('You may kiss me if you like. Now you are to go home'). Later, the film provides a pertly perfect summary of their

4 Miss Havisham (Martita Hunt) and Estella (Jean Simmons) conspire to break the heart of Pip (Anthony Wager) in *Great Expectations* (1946)

relationship: her virulent hiss of 'I hate you' as she escorts him from the house followed by adult Pip's explanatory voiceover: 'My admiration of her knew no bounds.' Lean's chief rule for literary adaptation was to 'Choose what you want to do in the novel and do it proud'[28] and it seems that one of his main interests in *Great Expectations* was this perverse psychosexual dynamic around Pip and Estella, incubated and encouraged by Miss Havisham, and Lean and his collaborators certainly do it proud. Indeed, for the critic Richard Winnington, the twin glories of the film were the performances from Martita Hunt and Jean Simmons, who both possessed an 'inimitable cachet and revive most potently the lost dreams of the book'.[29] For a number of other contemporary reviewers, they outshone even Finlay Currie's Magwitch, and certainly marginalised the ostensible hero of the piece, John Mills's Pip. Indeed, Lean admitted to Mills when persuading him to play the role that he would be 'a coat hanger for all the wonderful garments that will be hung on you'.[30]

Just as with Yuri Zhivago twenty years later, Pip functions as a character to whom things happen rather than a strong narrative dynamo in his own right (the staging of Pip's witnessing of a hanging from a high window is remarkably similar to Zhivago's witnessing of the massacre from a balcony in the later film). A certain ambiguity and uncertainty in his characterisation seems appropriate for someone whose motivations and desires are inscrutable even to himself, as Dickens has Pip recognise with hindsight: 'What I wanted, who can say? How can *I* say, when I never knew?'[31] However, the perceived weakening of Pip's characterisation from page to screen presents problems for literary scholar Grahame Smith. For him, the loss of Orlick fatally weakens Pip's characterisation, a problem compounded by the film's alleged dodging of 'Pip's ownership of Magwitch, not merely at the personal level but as part of Dickens's understanding of class relationships in Victorian Britain'. He continues, damningly: 'any adaptation that fails to grasp it, or is unable to enact it filmically, is doomed to ultimate failure'.[32] However, I would contend that Lean does find an eloquent cinematic means to depict Pip as an owned consciousness, imprinted with others' wishes and commands; especially Miss Havisham's manipulation of his feelings towards Estella. 'Love her', Havisham instructs Pip, gripping his arm and intoning the words like a curse, and he obeys unquestioningly. Although Pip possesses the retrospective narrative voiceover, at several strategic points the soundtrack is taken over by the voices of others echoing in Pip's head and determining his behaviour. This first occurs when Pip returns home from London after assuming his 'great expectations', and the inner voices of Joe and his new wife Biddy (Eileen Erskine) anticipating his visit home give way to those of Miss Havisham and finally Estella stating unequivocally 'Gentlemen stay at the Blue Boar', urging him away from the comforts of his old life and towards the more illusionary goal of being a gentleman. Towards the end of the film, as he mounts the staircase at Satis House one last time, Pip hears many voices from his past, and follows Estella's orders to the letter even as an adult: 'Don't loiter, boy', 'Come along boy, take your hat off', 'This door, boy'.

Earlier in the film, there had been a pun on the double meaning of 'at home' – the social gathering hosted by Pip and Herbert and a sense of comfort and ease with one's position and surroundings – but when Pip has his breakdown on the busy urban streets after Magwitch's death, his London home offers no refuge. The remarkable short sequence begins with Pip being jostled by the crowds, the lone figure moving forwards through a mass of people and traffic moving in opposing directions (a device Lean borrowed from King Vidor's *The Big Parade* (1925) and used again in *Zhivago*. The sound of the streets begins to echo, and an insistent high-pitched violin begins to dominate the soundtrack, while rapidly rotating white lights strobe over the shot. Pip's point of view is presented as warped and distorted as he enters his house, past the nameplate on his door, up into his bedroom, finally collapsing on the bed as the film itself appears to break down, ceding to the void of a black screen (presaging the presentation of a character's breakdown in Powell and Pressburger's *Black Narcissus* (1947) the following year). This is the collapse of a man who no longer has an assured identity, in spite of his fine clothes and a smart nameplate outside his London address.

Pip's mistaken belief that Miss Havisham was his benefactor has been overturned by the revelation that it was Magwitch all along, and that Pip's gentlemanly pursuits have been bankrolled by a former criminal (the moment of Magwitch's return is a masterpiece of gothic melodrama to match his first appearance, reappearing suddenly in Pip's doorway on a stormy night, cloaked, muffled, in shabby stovepipe hat and eye patch). Now Pip has overcome his initial disgust and grown fond of his true benefactor, Magwitch dies in the condemned cell after re-capture and re-trial, but in the knowledge that his little daughter has grown up to be a lady. In a typically Dickensian contrived narrative coincidence she is in fact revealed to be Estella. Pip had also been partly complicit in the earlier death of Miss Havisham, his slamming of the door dislodging the flaming coal from the fire which then ignites her paper-dry wedding dress. Both architects of Pip's great expectations are dead (at his hand?) while Estella is unhappily married to Bentley Drummle. All that is left for Pip is a return to his lowly origins back at Joe Gargery's forge. After Pip's physical and mental collapse, the film slowly fades back up on a new subjective shot: Joe's face over the bed, and the sound of birdsong on the soundtrack. Pip is back 'home' at last: 'You're home. I brought you home, dear old Pip, old chap.' But whether he is 'at home' is another question.

Grahame Smith also critiques the film's lack of what he feels to be the requisite 'heightened comic exaggeration' in relation to characters like Wemmick.[33] Lean perhaps has less facility for comic Dickens than for gothic Dickens (or less interest in it), and the brief scene featuring Wemmick's deaf 'aged P' who enjoys vigorous nodding from his guests feels like a Pickwickian infiltration from a different kind of Dickens film. However, there is a comic edge to many of the film's bruising social encounters, from Pip's excessive politeness when threatened with evisceration by Magwitch, to Estella's sheer horridness to her playmate, and also via characters such as Joe Gargery and Herbert Pocket (played brilliantly as both man and boy by Alec Guinness and John Forrest respectively). They each represent key staging posts in Pip's development, and his interactions with them are played as sharp comedies of social embarrassment, from Herbert's gentle tutorials in table manners to Joe's discomfort when he comes to visit Pip's London abode. A character like Francis L. Sullivan's lawyer Jaggers also treads a line between humour and horror (he is, after all, a man who decorates his office with death masks and nooses). His 'Put the case' speech to Pip is concise plot exposition (there are a lot of complicated narrative threads to untangle) that also doubles as sharp social critique about the fate of the poor, and his motivation to rescue 'one pretty little child out of the heap' – in other words, Estella and her adoption by Miss Havisham. It is all the sharper through being expressed in once-removed hypotheticals; a grammatical form that distances the speaker from the emotive content of his speech and pretends to be mere hypothesis rather than confession. Although Smith claims that Dickens's social criticism is blunted in Lean's film of *Great Expectations* – as opposed to Lean's *Oliver Twist* which he judges a far more successful transposition – moments like Jaggers's speech, and the earlier panning shot across the criminals in the dock being sentenced to hanging – both old and young, male and female, black and white, trembling and numb, all of them wretched – give eloquent voice to the brutal social wrongs of the Victorian period.[34]

If, as John Gardiner suggests, Dickens's *Great Expectations* was dealing with a question exercising many Victorians – 'was a gentleman bred or born?'[35] – the appreciation of the novel since then has hinged on slightly different questions of class. In the immediate postwar period in which Lean's Dickens adaptations appeared, Raphael Samuel noted, the films played a powerful role 'not only as landmarks of British *film noir*, but also for fixing a notion of the Victorian as a time of oppression and fear. They represented a social democratic as well as a Gothic imagination, the summit of some three decades of modernist revolt.'[36] The nineteenth century was being retrospectively constructed as the period against which the 'New Jerusalem' would define itself. The 'five giant evils' identified by the Beveridge Report of 1942, blueprint for the postwar welfare state, were characterised in explicitly Victorian terms; squalor, ignorance, want, idleness, disease (two of Beveridge's evils, 'ignorance' and 'want', even shared the names of emblematic figures from Dickens's *A Christmas Carol*). In this atmosphere of postwar anti-Victorianism, the conclusion of Lean's *Great Expectations* has a particular significance. Pip's final posthumous confrontation with Miss Havisham and her legacy, and his declaration that he has 'come back to let in the sunlight' as he rips down the multiple layers of curtains and blinds, acts as a powerful visual metaphor for rejecting, or to use Pip's own word, defying, the legacy of the Victorian era.[37] As Pip insists to Estella, who is fast becoming another Havisham walled up in Satis House, 'It's a dead house. Nothing can live here'; it offers 'nothing but dust and decay!' Initially, Estella clings to the certainties of the past – 'This is the house where I grew up. It's part of me, it's my home' – but is finally persuaded by the beams of sunlight and Pip's declaration of love to abandon the house and all that it represents. It's startlingly different from Noël Coward's insistence on tradition and continuity as guiding principles, as extolled in *In Which We Serve* and *This Happy Breed*. The reprisal of the film's title over the image of Pip and Estella exiting the grounds of Satis House together hand in hand imbues the phrase 'great expectations' with new meanings relating to their future together, free from the dead hand of the past, two working-class children made good in adulthood albeit after long and tortuous personal journeys. As Samuel argued of this ending, 'it does not seem fanciful to align it to the social-democratic vision of 1945, a dream of light and space'.[38] It links up with Labour's 1945 manifesto, prior to their postwar landslide victory, being entitled 'Let Us Face the Future'.

Finding the right ending for *Great Expectations* presented Dickens with problems, and he famously revised the last chapter on the advice of his friend, fellow novelist Edward Bulwer Lytton. Dickens created a reunion between Pip and Estella to replace his more downbeat original conclusion, which had insisted Pip would remain unmarried and the only positive result of his legacy would be to assist Herbert in finding a position. As Claire Tomalin notes, such an ending would have compounded the non-triumphalism of the text, making Pip's story 'one of failure, failure to understand what is happening to him, failure to win the girl he loves, failure to save his benefactor, failure to make anything of himself'.[39] But even in its adjusted version, the ending of the novel remains a hesitant, tentative reconciliation of Pip and Estella, ending on Pip's words (after the pair have agreed to stay as 'friends apart') that he 'saw no shadow of another parting from her'.[40] Lean's film version builds on that ending, and more decisively suggests the formation of a romantic couple, but it also speaks to the contemporary need for heroism rather than failure to be the parting sentiment of a film defying Victorian 'dust and decay'.

Raphael Samuel praised the likes of Lean's *Great Expectations* and *Oliver Twist* for their bracing refusal to become mired in painstaking historical reconstruction. This was in contrast with what he saw as the 'contrived authenticities' of the 1980s heritage cycle, 'in which the past is not a dead weight to be thrown off but a heritage to preserve'.[41] However, when one consults the publicity and marketing materials relating to *Great Expectations*, a rather more complicated attitude to their historical subject matter emerges. Although one press release issued by Cineguild insisted that 'No diminuendo in the tempo has been allowed to creep in by any insistence on authenticity', it nonetheless places great store by its historical authenticity and literary fidelity, stating that 'accuracy and detail have been the keynotes of all Cineguild productions, and no greater care has been taken than with their latest film *Great Expectations* to ensure a faithful reproduction of the scenes depicted in Charles Dickens' famous novel'.[42] To support these credentials, it cites the praise received from the Honorary Secretary of the Dickens Fellowship after he'd seen the rushes and makes much of Cineguild's efforts to secure exactly the right kind of paddle steamer for the climactic scenes of Magwitch's attempted escape, having found an original ship giving pleasure trips in Weymouth and then sailing it round to the Medway to restore it for location filming.[43] This is hardly the past as dead weight, and its ethos of painstaking reconstruction actually anticipates the priorities of heritage film.

Costume is another arena in which discourses of period authenticity and fashionable modernity awkwardly coexist. A Cineguild press release dated 8 October 1945 emphasises the great care taken over *Great Expectations*'s costuming: 'To present truthfully such productions, not only must the minute detail of costume and décor be in keeping with the subject, but the all-important questions of fabric and design must be studied and adhered to.' But this attention to detail should be applied more broadly to British filmmaking, not just costume drama, in the hope of 'present[ing] to the world the authentic English atmosphere, whether contemporary or of an historical nature'.[44] This could have obvious trade benefits, as a later press release for the film suggested: 'British fabrics and British films can be of great help to one another in establishing the export drive – the films will act as a shop-window for the fabrics, and the fabrics, especially designed as they now will be, will enhance the films.' It continues: '*Great Expectations* will thus be acting as a ambassador for British manufacturers in every country in which it is shown – a shop-window in which Britain can show the world just what she can do in the sphere of fashion when the restrictions of austerity are removed.'[45] The material culture of the film thus simultaneously points back to the past *and* forward to the future. Cineguild entertained hopes that the film's nineteenth-century costumes could influence current female fashions: '*Great Expectations* is expected to have a very decided influence on fashions when it is shown in the autumn. Already leading couturiers have expressed considerable interest in the beautiful clothes which have been designed for the film and their application to modern fashion trends', possibly pre-empting the corseted and full-skirted New Look of 1947.[46] Perfumier Goya even created a special 'Great Expectations' eau de toilette inspired by Valerie Hobson, while designer Sammy produced a ladies' scarf with 'the motif of a nineteenth-century stage coach with the film title rolling from the wheels in the form of a cloud of dust. Characters from the film are drawn around this centre panel.'[47]

This evidence of a more eclectic approach to the past, potentially as worthy of enjoyment and appropriation as it is of repudiation, problematises the idea that *Great Expectations* is totally dominated by a 'nightmare vision of the Victorian ... thoroughly in line with the progressive consensus of the time'.[48] Instead the film offers, at least if its publicity paratexts are taken into account, substantial nostalgia for the previous century, with its pressbook even suggesting that exhibitors 'create a Dickensian atmosphere in your town' and 'revive memories of 19th century transport' by using a stage coach for a street stunt: 'An original idea – why not arrange for your copy of the film to be collected at the station by the coach?'[49] *Great Expectations*'s conspicuous success at the box-office, featuring in the *Kine Weekly* top money-makers of 1947 and even rivalling such hit films as *The Wicked Lady* and *The Bells of St Mary's* at some cinemas,[50] may have owed much to its Janus-faced attitude to the previous century, looking back not only in anger but also in a strange kind of semi-celebration.

Oliver Twist (1948)

If Lean's *Great Expectations* offered an occasionally ambivalent approach to the previous century, then his *Oliver Twist* is far more pronounced in its evocation of darkness and danger, as befits a book written in a spirit of impassioned social protest. Although only Dickens's second novel, *Oliver Twist*'s enormous popularity (its readers included Queen Victoria herself) secured his foremost status, in Peter Ackroyd's words, as a 'novelist of topical and even propagandist intent': 'What a thing it is to have power', Dickens reflected after experiencing the impact his novel had made not only as a work of literature but also as an intervention in debates on the poor law and the fate of orphaned children.[51] Lean later said of his two Dickens adaptations that he aimed 'to recapture my impressions on first reading the two stories. I imagined *Great Expectations* as a fairy tale, just not quite true, and *Oliver Twist* as a grimly realistic study of what poverty was like at that time.'[52] One thing that the two films shared though was an insistence on prioritising dramatic intensity over slavish fidelity, choosing in the latter film to excise completely the character of Rose Maylie, a paragon of female virtue who had been Dickens's tribute to his recently deceased young sister-in-law. For critic Grahame Smith, this editorial decision works in the film's favour, unlike the cutting of Orlick in Lean's previous Dickens film, and actually enhanced *Oliver Twist*'s narrative by removing 'an indulgence in escapist sentimentality on the part of a still inexperienced writer',[53] symptomatic of some of Dickens's shortcomings in female representation.[54]

However, the cutting of one key female character from page to screen was accompanied by the addition of a new one, or at least one who had not been directly represented in Dickens's novel. Lean's *Oliver Twist* opens on Oliver's mother, heavily pregnant, struggling to find somewhere to give birth to her child. Beginning with the mother had been Kay Walsh's suggestion, partly in recollection of a haunting film sequence she remembered from her childhood in which a lone girl sank down into a ditch with her shawl pulled around her.[55] Lean seized upon this idea and created an unforgettable opening sequence which postpones all dialogue until six minutes into the film, corresponding with his overarching belief according to the film's pressbook 'that the primary purpose of a film is to tell a story visually'.[56] The pretty but dishevelled expectant mother makes her way across desolate moorland. Her slow hesitant progress is intercut with shots of gnarled branches and jagged thorns, visual metaphors for her labour pains.[57] She is caught in the middle of a violent storm and, as Silver and Ursini note, her 'knifing pain is equated with a white sheet of lightning' flashing across the screen.[58] The camera tilts on its axis to indicate the sudden onset of a contraction – and the young woman clings to a tree to withstand the sharp pain – returning back to an un-canted shot as it releases its grip on her body; a brilliant visualisation of bodily sensation. The film's composer Arnold Bax also improvised a memorably discordant motif to underline her agonies.[59] She finally reaches her destination – a building high on a hill – and is granted access through the high barred gates. At this point, the film reveals what this building is via an upward tilt of the camera and a flash of lightning which illuminates the words on the gate: 'Parish Workhouse'. Then, over an image of the moon in the dark sky, we hear a baby's cry. The mother is fatally weakened but strains to see her child lying next to her, her face the image of maternal pride and love. She is able to proffer a single kiss on the child's forehead (the only one Oliver will experience until he meets Mrs Bedwin years later) before she falls back, dead. Ironically, the very first words in the film actually indicate an ending: the doctor's confirmation that 'it's all over'. The doctor notes the child's illegitimacy ('The old story. No wedding ring, I see', failing to notice a far more significant piece of jewellery around the mother's neck) and the baby is duly taken away by a nurse to join the other unfortunate orphans who inhabit the workhouse. The shots that follow showcase John Bryan's brilliant and visually eloquent set design, one of the splendours of the film, and show the infant Oliver dwarfed by the imposing and miserable environs the nurse carries him through, ironically decorated with placards encouraging Christian gratitude for his lot: God is Good, God is Just, God is Love, God is Life. The satiric tone will continue later with the juxtapositions between the pompous workhouse board's insistence that they're providing 'a regular place of entertainment' and the sudden cut to the inmates' hard labour in the washroom, or the board pleading poverty whilst laying on for themselves a lavish dinner of juicy poultry and heaped roast potatoes. But for now, the film relies upon Dickens's own words to convey the desperation of Oliver's situation, making its first direct reference to the text (unlike the book's immediate appearance in *Great Expectations*) with a title card quoting the novel: 'Oliver Twist cried lustily. If he had known that he was to grow up under the tender mercies of the Beadle and the Matron, he would have cried even louder.'

From the shots of the helpless baby in these initial sequence to the later scenes depicting Oliver's experiences of life within and beyond the workhouse, the keynote is the terrifying vulnerability of this 'pretty little child' who, unlike Estella, isn't saved from the heap, or at least not until much later in the story. Most famously, this includes the scene in which Oliver (John Howard Davies), having picked the short straw, has to ask for more. The shot composition is all the more powerful from being arranged in deep perspective, with Oliver slowly approaching from near vanishing point at the back of the room, past long benches full of his expectant peers, and towards the threatening quivering stick held in the immediate foreground, representing punitive authority ready to attack the lone ragged child. Oliver is set to work as child labourer, scrubbing floors (our first sight of the character beyond his infancy), picking oakum, or working for the undertaker Sowerberry and being made to sleep in the coffin workshop. Here is he tormented by the taunts of 'workhouse' and aspersions against his mother from Noah Claypole and the other gruesome members of the Sowerberry household (including 16-year-old Diana Dors as Noah's sycophantic girlfriend Charlotte), and eventually flees for London with his few meagre positions rolled into a handkerchief.

His move from the country to the town may initially appear to be a liberatory one: we shift from the cramped angular interiors of workhouse and undertakers to the open road and the lively bustle of the capital. The Artful Dodger (Anthony Newley) offers friendship, or appears to (his first sighting of Oliver is rather more sinister in appearance, like an animal sighting its prey), and leads him through an increasingly vertiginous cityscape – like 'passing through a human rabbit-warren'[60] according to the film's script – before reaching Fagin's den. Fagin (Alec Guinness) is undoubtedly a dark and manipulative character, the ersatz father to a family of boy thieves, but he can also be humorous and ingratiating. His pantomime of a rich gentleman waiting to have his pocket picked, accompanied by Bax's jocular music, is the first thing that elicits an actual laugh from Oliver (Lean and Alec Guinness did some impromptu comedy to get genuine laughter from John Howard Davies[61]). However, Fagin is a false friend in comparison with Oliver's later benefactor Mr Brownlow (Henry Stephenson). Brownlow rescues the boy after he faints in the dock while accused of theft and his attitude contrasts with the brutality or indifference of most adults towards the boy's fate (represented by the subjective shot of Oliver being punched in the face by a grown man whose fist smashes into the camera lens – he later boasts 'I cut my knuckles against his face' – or the feverish close-ups on Oliver's face as he is about to faint, totally ignored by the magistrate and court officials). Mr Brownlow takes Oliver home with him to recover from his illness and injuries. Here the boy experiences genuine kindness for the first time from his benefactor and the housekeeper Mrs Bedwin (Amy Veness), and the spontaneous embrace he offers her when he wakes in his nice clean bed to see her watching over him is extremely moving.

In its concern for the destiny of a vulnerable child, Lean's *Oliver Twist* faithfully replicated its literary source (Plate 5). But it also corresponded to contemporary postwar anxieties about children. As Christine Geraghty has noted, 'children are everywhere' in British films of this period,[62] including the two Dickens adaptations undertaken by Lean. The boy protagonists of his films fit perfectly into the blueprint Geraghty identifies of a 'pre-teenage, slight, fair boy' often with 'blond hair and pale skin' whose imperilment drives the narrative of a number of postwar films, including *The Fallen Idol* (1948), *The Magnet* (1950), *The Yellow Balloon* (1952) and *Hunted* (1952).[63] As discussed earlier in relation to *Great Expectations*, the postwar welfare state often constructed the Victorian period as its 'other' against which modern humanitarian advances could be measured. The pressbook for *Oliver Twist* certainly encouraged such comparisons of past and present, encouraging exhibitors to invite their 'local child welfare organisation' to see the film: 'Their comments on conditions in those days, together with details of who orphan children are looked after today would make interesting press material.'[64] One press release even presented the disparity between children then and children now as slightly problematic when it came to casting the film: 'As Ronald Neame said despairingly, what with the government's free milk and free lunches and cod-liver-oil and orange juice, the present generation of British boys are about as tough and healthy-looking a lot of youngsters as anyone could imagine.'[65] Despite complaints from some quarters that Cineguild were staying in the past rather than engaging with current conditions (and being compared unfavourably to Italian neo-realism[66]), *Oliver Twist*, like its Dickensian predecessor, was mediating contemporary concerns through period drama. Its status as a text of austerity was marked not only by details of its production (the film's smoke and smog had to be created by smoke bombs and burnt rice paper in order to avoid wasting coal[67]) but also in its cross-reference to highly relevant issues of the immediate postwar years such as orphaned children, unmarried motherhood, and commonplace criminality courtesy of the black market.[68] One Cineguild press release headlined 'Dickens knew all about spivs' drew explicit parallels between dodgy dealing of the nineteenth and twentieth centuries: 'several of the extras in the Smithfield Market sequences of Cineguild's *Oliver Twist* were called upon to play the 19th century equivalent of that ubiquitous modern type, the spiv: for in Dickens' days, the barrow-boys were a recognised, if not beloved, feature of London life, selling fruit and vegetables to the passing crowds at doubtless excessive prices. Even in those more colourful days, these gentlemen were remarkable for their flashy clothes and gaudy neckware.'[69] Another linked Victorian criminal slang used in the film, 'flash talk', with its present-day spiv equivalents.[70]

5 Nineteenth-century noir: Sikes (Robert Newton), Fagin (Alec Guinness) and Nancy (Kay Walsh) argue over the fate of Oliver (John Howard Davies) in *Oliver Twist* (1948)

However, in another area of acute connection with contemporary social concerns, Lean's *Oliver Twist* appears to have been blissfully or perhaps wilfully ignorant. Its presentation of Fagin as, to quote the script, 'a VERY OLD SHRIVELLED JEW, whose villainous looking and repulsive face is obscured by a quantity of matted red hair'[71] is faithful to both Dickens's and the original illustrator Cruikshank's vision of the character. But it was also inseparable from representations of the predatory Jew that had proliferated in the virulently anti-Semitic culture of Nazism. As *Life* magazine pointed out in 1949, 'between Dickens and director Lean, history had interposed the ghosts of six million murdered Jews and the spectre of genocide'.[72] To blithely maintain fidelity to that aspect of the source text in spite of recent history was, as Al McKee suggests in his account of the *Oliver Twist* anti-Semitism scandal, 'a startling example of artistic tunnel vision'.[73] The film's presentation of Fagin would go on to cause offence and controversy not only in Britain and the USA, where the film was heavily criticised and cut, and had its release delayed for two years – Lean thought the cuts made the film look more anti-Semitic by removing all Fagin's humorous scenes – but also in Berlin, where the prospect of a screening prompted violent demonstrations. Jewish protestors forced their way into the Kurbel cinema in the

British sector of Berlin and stopped its performance, and the association 'Victims of Fascism' released the following statement: 'it is the responsibility of British military government to decide whether to encourage anti-Semitism and racial discrimination by showing the film'.[74] A Berlin critic concurred with this viewpoint, questioning the wisdom of showing the film 'in a country where the anti-Semitic plague has caused such terrible destruction, and where the germs of the disease are still active'.[75] Clearly the setting of the film in the past and its adherence to Dickens's original text proved no protection at all, and instead Lean's *Oliver Twist* ended up occupying a highly divisive position in urgent debates about anti-Semitism, a fact that still colours its reputation.

One of the challenges in adapting this particular novel, Lean reflected in the pressbook for *Oliver Twist*, was 'making fantastic larger-than-life characters fit into a starkly real setting'.[76] The big personalities of key dramatis personae would also feature as a selling point in the film's poster campaign, which picked out Bill Sikes, Fagin, The Artful Dodger and Nancy on their own individual posters, anticipating the identical publicity campaign for *Trainspotting* (1996) nearly fifty years later. However, as Raphael Samuel points out, 'Nancy was the leading character in the stage version of *Oliver Twist* and her murder by Bill Sikes the accepted dramatic climax'[77], a suitably Manichean and melodramatic battle between innocence and evil. In Dickens's readings from his work, Nancy's death also became the most celebrated set-piece of his entire repertoire, and the exhausting physical effort of bringing it to violent life for audiences night after night may well have contributed to the author's premature death. Dickens saw the death of Nancy as one of his most powerful legacies – 'I wanted to leave behind me the recollection of something very passionate and dramatic', he said[78] – and Lean's film certainly stays faithful to that aim. The film's murder scene is a masterpiece of horrific insinuation which alludes to the brutal attack taking place but never shows its full extent, focussing instead on the reaction of Bill Sikes's dog and leaving the spectator to speculate as to the full horror of what the dog is trying to escape. As the shooting script describes it:

> NANCY weakly raises her hands in a last plea for mercy. He lifts the club and –
> the DOG runs into Picture and starts tearing at the foot of the door like a dog at a rabbit hole. It looks round and then resumes its efforts to get out, more terrified than before.[79]

Equally powerful are the sequences which detail the aftermath of Nancy's murder. Her undiscovered body lies on the floor just where she fell, and Sikes piles bedclothes over her trying ineffectually to cover up his crime. A shot of the dog, still trembling, returns us briefly to the memory of the same creature's terror the night before. There are shots of Nancy's lifeless arm and her paltry little cluster of prettifying trinkets and 'the frail flowers on her dresser',[80], terrible reminders of her vulnerable humanity that prompt her murderer's growing remorse. An increasingly disturbed Sikes hallucinates Nancy's face, alive again, in another extreme close-up and canted shot, followed by a close-up of Fagin, and then re-imagines the bludgeoning but with Fagin taking Nancy's place. Later, the clock will chime past the hour of her appointment with Brownlow while we remain in this static interior, a murder scene waiting to be discovered. In these grim expressionistic moments, Lean's *Oliver Twist* comes closest to McKee's designation of the film, echoed by Samuel and many other critics, as 'Victorian film noir';[81] here again it demonstrates a resolutely contemporary mode of expression in spite of its period trappings.

Kay Walsh 'greatly disliked' her own performance as Nancy[82] but it is arguably a near-impossible role to play. Claire Tomalin, Dickens's biographer, felt that the character, despite Dickens's best efforts, was 'the chief failure of the book ... he makes her behave like an actress in a bad play: she tears her hair and clothes, writhes, wrings her hands, sinks to her knees ... and is loaded with false theatrical speeches.'[83] One of these moments makes it into the film – Nancy's attack on Fagin, which helps to explain her shift in allegiance from the gang to helpless young Oliver – and Walsh's playing of the scene does suggest a hysterical outpouring of long-suppressed grievances against the man responsible for her exploitation ('I've thieved for you since I was a child', 'the cold wet dirty streets are my home ... day and night, day and night!') ending with a psychosomatic faint which is unusually filmed in slow motion. Walsh's Nancy is not the lovelorn 'tart with a heart' figure of Lionel Bart and Carol Reed's *Oliver!* (1968) but someone far more spiky and damaged whose sudden unexpected impulse towards goodness will be the weakness that ultimately results in her demise.

Nancy's death acts as the catalyst for the film's denouement, signalled by a montage of 'wanted' posters put up for Sikes, Fagin and Monks in her name. As they are captured one by one by the agents of the law, a torch-wielding mob gathers around Fagin's den. As with *Madeleine* and then *Ryan's Daughter*, the onlookers who jeer and enjoy the spectacle of retribution are treated ambivalently. Fagin's question, 'What right have you to butcher me?', is one that has resonance beyond this film alone. Unlike Dickens, Lean and his collaborators do not dwell on Fagin's ultimate fate and there is no equivalent to the chapter 'The Jew's last night alive' with its famous Cruickshank illustration of a fearful Fagin in the condemned cell. Instead, the film's focus shifts to Bill Sikes and Oliver up on the roof trying to evade capture before Sikes is shot and the rope around him becomes a noose in a wonderfully shot and edited moment of cinema, as Kevin Brownlow describes: 'Sikes falls, the rope streams through shot and the focus-puller adjusts the lens so that when the rope suddenly goes taut we know only too well the reason why.'[84] This trio of deaths – Nancy's, Fagin's and Sikes's – enable Oliver to escape and to be rescued from a life of degradation. After the oppressive gloom of the workhouse and then Fagin's world, Oliver is finally rendered to his 'true home', the perfectly symmetrical white stuccoed house of Mr Brownlow, shot in brilliant daylight and recalling Ruskin's definition of home as 'the place of Peace; the shelter, not only from all injury, but from all terror, doubt and division'.[85]

The sudden predominance of white at the end of *Oliver Twist* is visually startling given the darkness which predominates for the majority of the film, echoing the ripping down of the blinds to let in the bright sun at the end of *Great Expectations*. Through Guy Green's chiaroscuro cinematography, the only objects to have had lustre up to that point are jewellery, coins (like the Artful Dodger's 'pieces of silver' for informing on Nancy) and the shiny spoils of a burglary. And Oliver himself, with his shining blond hair and pale skin, a boy who is also 'stolen property', taken from his rightful family and lost in the criminal underworld. Dickens wanted to show, through Oliver, 'the principle of Good surviving through every adverse circumstance'[86] but as many critics of Dickens have argued, the writer is disproportionately fixated on the accidentally displaced angelic (middle-class) child, reflecting his own trauma at being a child labourer in a blacking factory, an experience he would continually revisit and rework in his fiction. Gerald Pratley is not the first critic to describe the story's ending as 'a selfish one, happiness for Oliver, but no thought for the boys who are left behind'.[87] But the ending is not simplistically upbeat. Oliver's eventual escape is highly contingent, only being rescued from the heap (like Estella) because of the unusual intervention of an individual philanthropist. The darkness and misery of what the boy has to endure before that rescue takes place still resonate beyond his happy ending. In its gothic images of poverty and degradation, Lean's *Oliver Twist* made powerful propaganda for embracing the progressive postwar politics of the welfare state and dissociating British society as far as possible from the dark days of the nineteenth century.

Madeleine (1950)

Of Lean's four films set in the nineteenth century, *Madeleine* is arguably the film most directly concerned with anatomising the spirit of the Victorian age. It begins with a present-day framing device in which we are introduced first to contemporary Glasgow and then to the house in Blytheswood Square where the story will take place, one of a number of 'solid, well-built Victorian houses' which managed to survive the wartime bombing. The film seems fascinated by the simultaneous proximity and distance of the Victorians; of course, in 1950 the Victorian age was not that long ago. As the film's pressbook pointed out, Madeleine Hamilton Smith, the heroine of the story, 'really existed, loved and suffered, almost within living memory'.[88] The house she lived in still stood unchanged, a marker of the continuing presence of the nineteenth century well into the twentieth. And yet the moral and social world Madeleine inhabited is characterised as strange, mysterious, and vanished. Using the 1857 murder case as its basis, *Madeleine* deliberately excavates the hidden depths and dark secrets of the Victorians. A respectable middle-class young woman, Madeleine Smith was accused of murdering her ex-lover Emile L'Angelier by administering arsenic after their affair had broken off and he had threatened to blackmail her with their sexually candid private correspondence. Smith had purchased arsenic but claimed it was for cosmetic purposes. She was charged with L'Angelier's murder, but the jury's final verdict was one peculiar to Scottish law: not proven. In the end, as the film's narration says, Madeleine Smith walked from the courtroom 'neither guilty nor not guilty'; free but without her name being cleared. The trial was a sensation in the Victorian press, and her case continues to provoke fascination and re-investigation to this day.[89] As Mary S. Hartman points out, the story 'had everything: an attractive and socially prominent defendant, illicit sexual adventure, poisoning, and shocking behaviour all round'.[90]

The case's specific historical moment was also important. The 1850s was Britain's 'age of equipoise', and, for historian G. M. Young at least, the decade which 'of all decades in our history, a wise man would choose ... to be young in'.[91] Britain, alone among its major European peers, had escaped revolution in the tumultuous year of 1848. The Great Exhibition of 1851 and Paxton's Crystal Palace had demonstrated British pre-eminence on a grand scale and, as Asa Briggs suggests, even the growing cognisance of 'dangerous times ahead on the Continent did not go far enough in 1851 to disturb the mood of self-satisfaction.'[92] But that hubris would be dented as the decade wore on, not least by the publication in 1859 of two books with revolutionary implications;

John Stuart Mill's *On Liberty* and Charles Darwin's *On the Origin of Species*. When it came to women, the decorous feminine ideal of the 'angel in the house', first voiced in Coventry Patmore's poem of 1854, still held sway. But the revelations from the Madeleine Smith case of 1857 would call into question received wisdom about women's inherent sexual modesty and virtue. As *The Saturday Review* reported at the time, the most shocking dimension of the case was the insight it offered into 'what may be going on in the inmost core of all that is apparently pure and respectable'.[93] Madeleine Smith was to all outward appearances a virtuous and attractive young woman, an angel-in-the-house in waiting, but appearances were highly deceptive. Even if she had not committed murder, it was clear from her letters that she had enjoyed pre-marital sex with L'Angelier, almost as heinous a crime in the culture of that period. Smith became an object of horrified contemplation, but seasoned with a pinch of erotic excitement at this bewitching femme fatale, as indicated by one male court observer's remarks: 'her smile was ravishing ... I was compelled again and again to look upon her, so magnetic were her eyes.'[94] This repressed world of sex and violence that would become familiar via twentieth-century historiography as the domain of 'the other Victorians'.[95] Despite the appearance of equipoise, dark and troubling undercurrents created ripples on the surface in mid-nineteenth-century Britain.

Given Cineguild's success with several stories set in the previous century, it is perhaps unsurprising that they should return to this territory for another production. However, the impetus for the company's film version of the Madeleine Smith story actually came from Ann Todd, whom Lean had recently married after meeting during production on *The Passionate Friends* (discussed in chapter four). Todd had appeared in a play based on the Smith case, *The Rest is Silence*, a few years earlier and suggested to her new husband that it could make a good film. In lieu of any better ideas at that moment, Lean agreed. Lean's associate Norman Spencer noticed 'a new element' creeping into Cineguild after Lean and Todd's marriage 'because Ann understandably wanted pictures that gave her an opportunity to star'[96] and the producer Anthony Havelock-Allan later intimated that Todd believed 'she would be leading lady in all his films from then on', while the British press also increasingly envisaged the husband and wife as 'a glamorous team'.[97] The production ended up being deeply problematic for Lean, dogged by strikes and a myriad of technical difficulties as well as personal struggles, especially between husband and wife, and he would later describe *Madeleine* as 'miserable' and 'the worst film I ever made', lacking in warmth and narrative engagement because 'I had no particular feelings for anybody in the picture and as far as movies are concerned that is pretty well fatal'.[98] Many critics who reviewed the film in 1950 agreed with Lean's low estimation of it, with the disappointed *News Chronicle* reviewer lamenting: 'Hardly anywhere in this film are there signs of the imagination and artistry we have learned to expect from this director, and much of the action is desperately slow.'[99] Even those who praised the film still found it wanting in comparison with Lean's previous work: one reviewer deemed it the 'best picture of week' but 'not what I expected from the man who gave us *Brief Encounter* and nobly re-created Dickens'.[100] Another supplied a back-handed compliment about its technical prowess, calling it 'a brilliant job of movie making but a disappointing movie'.[101]

Some of this critical disquiet centred on the film's refusal to take a clear position on Madeleine Smith's guilt. Instead, *Madeleine* maintains the ambiguity of the court's 'not proven' verdict, presenting a range of visual evidence that supports the cases for both the prosecution and the defence. The maintenance of mystery is also foregrounded in the film's publicity campaign, with giant question marks superimposed over images of the main characters, and a series of urgent questions posed in the accompanying text: 'Did he know she loved another?', 'Why did she buy arsenic?', 'Was his love too demanding?', 'Is she a Lucretia Borgia? Or is she only a boarding-school miss?', culminating in the most central question of all, 'Guilty... or not guilty?'[102] What *Madeleine* loses in narrative clarity by refusing to decide one way or the other as to its heroine's guilt, it gains in narrative intrigue. As Michael Anderegg argues, it is 'both an ambiguous film and a film about ambiguity'.[103] It has the effect of turning Ann Todd's central performance into a code that we attempt to decipher, looking for signs of guilt or innocence. She delicately sings 'Je ne suis q'une faible femme' (I am but a feeble woman) but is she more steely and self-possessed than she seems? Just as with Todd's previous film with Lean, *The Passionate Friends*, *Madeleine* offered another interrogation of female inscrutability and mystery, made all the more piquant because director and star were husband and wife at the time; a productive parallel might be drawn with Orson Welles's investigation of a similarly blonde and implacable Rita Hayworth in *The Lady from Shanghai* (1947). It may be that the problems Lean faced in bringing the story to the screen and his increasing estrangement from Todd only augmented that aura of fascinating ambiguity the film possesses, making it one of his most rich and resonant female-focussed films despite his own misgivings about it.

Once the film's contemporary framing has been swiftly established, *Madeleine* goes straight back in time to the 1850s, and the story begins *in media res* with Madeleine and Emile L'Angelier (Ivan Desny) already conducting their secret affair. Indeed, as soon as the Smith family are shown into their new house on Blytheswood Square, Madeleine seeks out its lower depths, finding the most convenient places to communicate with Emile and allow him access. Later that evening, she plays the dutiful daughter, snuffing out all the household lights before she goes to bed, but the waltz tune on the soundtrack and the restless swishing movements of her crinoline skirt indicates that this might be more than mere domestic diligence on her part. As she retreats downstairs and applies scent at her dressing table, she hears Emile's approaching footsteps and hears the knocking of his cane against the railings, their secret signal. The sense of excitement that characterises their illicit love affair continues in the next scene as Madeleine and Emile embrace outside in the rain. The subterranean shadowy setting for their kiss strongly recalls the embrace in the underpass in *Brief Encounter*, as does its furtive quality. Emile's hand traces Madeleine's corseted upper body and the camera accentuates its eroticism by following his movement in a downward tilt. Madeleine offers reassurances to Emile that their love will soon be socially ratified rather than conducted in secret, once Emile is introduced to her father and they can marry. However, her dual nature is already apparent in small but significant symbolic details. This scene marks the first appearance of Madeleine's signature hairstyle, which she will wear throughout her romance with Emile. Its combination of smooth face-framing locks with an almost invisible but very ruffled V of curls right at the back of her head speaks volumes about Madeleine's ability to contain clandestine excitement within a serene exterior.[104]

The antagonist at this stage of the film is Madeleine's 'papa', played by Leslie Banks as an archetypal stiff and unyielding Victorian patriarch, intertextual cousin to tyrants like Charles Laughton in *The Barretts of Wimpole Street* (1934), Robert Newton in *Hatter's Castle* (1941) and Mervyn Johns in *Pink String and Sealing Wax* (1945). While Madeleine is positioned at his feet, helping him put on his shiny black boots, he informs her 'it is time that you were married'. Despite his daughter's reluctance, Madeleine's father has given permission for William Minnoch (Norman Wooland) to court her, and he warns Madeleine that she 'will incur my gravest displeasure' should the suit be discouraged. At such a moment, the film makes very plain her lack of room for manoeuvre. It seems the only form of rebellion available to her is the secret pursuit of her love affair without her father's knowledge or consent. When the family relocate to their country retreat in Rhu, Emile secretly follows. As Madeleine reads aloud to her family, she struggles to contain her excitement when she hears the steamer's horn in the distance announcing her lover's arrival.

The couple's secret tryst later that night is one of the most distinctive set pieces in the film as, up on the hillside, they hear music from the village ceilidh down below and join in the dance from a distance. As with the wedding scene in *Ryan's Daughter* years later, 'natural' peasant sexuality is juxtaposed with a more restrained couple removed from the fray. *Madeleine* cuts between the whirling whooping joyous dancers below and the more awkward movements first of Madeleine and then of Emile, who seems reluctant to dance despite Madeleine's request in his own language, 'danse avec moi'. Our attention is drawn to one particular couple at the ceilidh, whose dancing becomes increasingly frenzied and passionate. Meanwhile Madeleine grabs Emile's cane and throws it into the bracken to stop it impeding their dancing, an action which angers Emile; the cane not only announces his status as a gentleman but is an obvious symbol of phallic power.[105] However, Madeleine's aggressive act becomes the catalyst for her seduction of Emile. She evades his grasp, runs away from him and falls onto the ground, looking back up over her shoulder at Emile standing above her. The cutaway to the couple below, hurriedly leaving the hall to continue their dancing in private, makes clear by implication the parallel action taking place on the hillside above. When we return to Emile and Madeleine again, it is to see Emile retrieving Madeleine's discarded white shawl, synecdoche for a larger casting-off of restraint.

Madeleine's sexual knowledge is evident in her next exchange with her father over Minnoch's courtship. The father expresses annoyance that it is taking so long for an engagement to be announced and Madeleine asks, in mock-innocence, if she should 'bring him to the boil, Papa?', the film having shown her do much the same to Emile. Papa upbraids her for being 'both vulgar and flippant' but she has merely voiced the unsayable truth about what lies behind the elaborate mannered rituals of Victorian courtship. However, *Madeleine* will not go on to be a simple love story, pitting passionate rebellion against patriarchal obstruction, idealising the star-crossed lovers. Indeed, it soon becomes clear that Emile is just as much Madeleine's antagonist as her papa. Emile's insistence on an introduction to her father becomes more pressing, making Madeleine's reluctance to comply with his wishes all the more obvious. He speaks words for her to repeat to her father – 'we wish to be married' – but as the camera tightens in on a tracking shot of her distressed face, and the score provides a shrill insistent high violin, it is clear that what

Emile offers Madeleine is another trap. It is not the snowy weather that 'oppresses' her, as she claims, but rather her lover.

When, in a last-ditch romantic gesture, Madeleine offers to elope with Emile and he refuses, the extent of his social climbing becomes apparent. By comparison, the previously spurned Minnoch now looks attractive, offering not only romantic commitment but also status, respectability and paternal approval. She encourages his advances at a society ball, where there are highland reels being danced but in a much more sedate, bowdlerised manner than back in Rhu, as if to indicate the taming of illicit passion within conjugal restraint. To seal their engagement, Minnoch gives Madeleine his ring with a crossbow crest, which she mistakes for an anchor, indicating her desire for security and, as Silver and Ursini suggest, 'the refuge of a relationship free of anxiety'.[106] But Emile will refuse to be dismissed, maintaining a covert presence at the margins of her new life, whether looking down on her dancing with Minnoch at the ball or lurking outside her basement window while she excitedly tries on a hat for her new trousseau. He is the return of Madeleine's repressed: infatuation, sexual desire, rash promises and proclamations of love made in writing.

Emile forces entry to her house to confront her about her new engagement and reminds her 'you made yourself my wife' while she still insists 'I cannot tell Papa'. The confrontation ends with Madeleine falling at Emile's feet, just as she had on the hills at Rhu. This time the atmosphere is much bleaker but the intent seems similar, with a desperate sexual bargaining taking place in order to buy Emile's silence. 'I will do anything', she pleads as the camera ranges over her supine body and her strangely wanton facial expression. Once again, they kiss and Emile's abandoned cane rolls noisily across the flagstone floor, a covert allusion to orgasm.[107] As one reviewer noted, this crash of the cane seemed 'almost to initiate the sharply-struck bell at the Apothecary's shop',[108] noticing the clever use of a sound bridge to cover the edit between the two scenes. But there is more at stake than the usual desire for mere editorial smoothness. Everything that happens after this point will be as a result of that decisive confrontation between Madeleine and Emile. The loud bell that accompanies Madeleine's entry into the druggist to request arsenic signals the start of the next section of the film: the presentation of evidence for and against Madeleine as murderess.

Madeleine's possession of arsenic is never in question in the film. Although her first request for poison is refused by the druggist, she is successful in getting it on a subsequent occasion. She lies about its usage, claiming it is to kill a rat in the cellar (perhaps a private joke to herself) but admits to her sister that this is just a little white lie so she

NINETEENTH-CENTURY BLUES 67

can procure it for cosmetic purposes. Just like the rosewater she buys alongside it, arsenic enables another kind of 'white lie', the feminine deception of a perfect pale complexion. Madeleine is also shown using it for this very purpose, washing her hands with it in a basin, but the film reminds us of its lethal potential by the prominent cutaways to its skull and crossbones label and – subtextually – by her younger sister's song, 'Who killed Cock Robin'. Evidence and counter-evidence is built up to both support and demolish the case for Madeleine as a murderer. L'Angelier is a user of laudanum and is shown dissolving white powder into a drink, so perhaps his death was due to a self-administered overdose of that drug. But then Madeleine lingers in the kitchen just before Emile's cocoa is prepared by the maid and the camera lingers over the china cup he puts to his mouth in a manner reminiscent of Alicia's poisoned drink in Hitchcock's *Notorious* (1946). However, Madeleine also drinks a cup poured from the same silver jug and shows no ill effects. The film refuses to account for the hours between 10.30pm and 1am on the night before L'Angelier's death. Madeleine is not shown admitting any visitor but there is a direct cut from her head on the pillow as she lies awake in the middle of the night, Minnoch's engagement ring glowing on the hand held to her cheek, to Emile's head hitting his pillow as he suffers the painful contortions that will end with his death. In each case, possible readings of events in terms of cause and effect are implied but never fully followed through or made explicit.

Emile's death sets in train the events which lead to Madeleine's shaming exposure and eventual trial for murder. Her greatest fear, that her papa should find out about her love affair, is realised when L'Angelier's friend Thuau (Eugene Deckers) visits the family home and requests an audience with her father. This happens just as Madeleine is on the brink of becoming a respectable married woman. Indeed, she is trying on her bridal gown when she is called in by her father to answer to Thuau's allegations. The use of deep focus composition creates a distorted inquisitorial space in which Madeleine is suspended between a dominant father in the foreground and a dangerous stranger in the background. She initially denies knowing Emile but cracks when confronted with the fact of his death, and Todd's acting is superbly subtle here, making full use of what John Orr calls her 'facility for changing look and expression from one shot to the next'.[109] The two wholly incompatible separate spheres of her life, propriety above stairs and deception below, each kept in careful equilibrium up to this point, now collide. As her father declares, in a very striking (and quasi-oedipal, as Orr notes[110]) phrase: 'We are naked.' Another tightly framed deep-focus shot, filmed near ground level, shows Madeleine falling to the floor in supplication, as she had for both father and lover before, desperately pleading 'he did not come, Papa!' But this time her appeal is in vain and the public exposure of her illicit behaviour is inevitable.

The remainder of *Madeleine* adheres to the generic conventions of the courtroom drama, quoting real court records of the Smith trial and following in detail the cases for the prosecution and then for the defence, relying on compelling performances from Barry Jones and Andre Morell respectively. The film firmly establishes Madeleine's vulnerability as a woman on trial for murder, making extensive use of shots suggesting her point of view. Her journey to the court itself is terrifying, presented through a close-up on her face as her vehicle is barracked and beaten by violent crowds outside. C. A. Lejeune described these 'scenes inside the Black Maria, with the waves of sound from the mob outside plotting an almost exact geographical course through the streets' as forcefully impressing 'the dread of ugly hooliganism on the spectator'.[111] They echo similarly uneasy scenes of mob violence in *Oliver Twist* and also point forward to the besieged young women in *Ryan's Daughter* and *A Passage to India*. We share Madeleine's point of view as she waits to mount the steep stairs up to the courtroom framed in an intimidating low-angle shot, as she jumps at the sharp bang the trap door makes as it shuts behind her (an aural suggestion of the fate that might await her on the scaffold) and when she first notices her personal effects bundled up as court exhibits. The trial section of the film is first heralded with the appearance of hellfire preacher John Laurie's banner – 'The wicked shall be destroyed!' – making a furious tirade against the feminine hypocrisy of Madeleine Smith's fine dresses and perfume which mask her inner evil. Although the film by no means presents a coherent feminist case in any way akin to what Matthew Sweet describes as 'academic attempts to reclaim female killers of the nineteenth century as proto-feminist figures whose poisonings and shootings were, in some sense, anti-patriarchal acts',[112] some elements of *Madeleine* do suggest that she is a martyr to Victorianism. The film's pressbook certainly mounts a case for her being 'born out of her time. She had a strange passionate nature, allied to a hard, swift, uncompromising intellect, with an unusually coherent and forceful style of self-expression. Her letters to her lover would have been outstanding today; in the muffled age in which she lived they were a sensation.'[113] The film's reviewers concurred that Madeleine Smith was 'a Victorian rebel',[114] with both *Reynolds News* and the *Daily Herald* comparing her to another famous female nonconformist of the age, Florence Nightingale.[115] For the *New Statesman*'s reviewer, 'her chief claim to sympathy' was that 'mid-century middle-class manners almost compelled her to lead two lives, one for papa upstairs and another for her lover in the maid's bedroom'.[116] Much is at stake in this insistent repudiation of the hypocrisy and prudery of the Victorian age, which is deployed to cast the present moment as far more liberated and enlightened. In that sense 'Madeleine Smith' is a useful comparative fiction for boosting the self-esteem of postwar Britain.

The fact that she is a *woman* on trial creates interesting possibilities for a feminist reading of the film, since *Madeleine* chooses to critique the Victorians through an analysis of what it meant to be a *female* subject of the period's moral structures. The film makes clear that its heroine is being judged and appraised by mostly male observers. The deep-focus photography enables us to see that all the court clerks and reporters in the raked seating behind her are male, with a feminine presence only becoming evident in the public gallery right at the back. The jury members are addressed by the prosecuting lawyer as 'gentlemen!', verbally reinforcing the film's visual evidence that Madeleine is only being tried by a jury of male peers. Her defence rests upon a very feminine deception (the use of arsenic as a cosmetic preparation) that a male expert in the dock deems 'unlikely and highly dangerous'. It is only when the druggist intervenes to the contrary – informing the jurors that, despite its dangers, ladies still request it because 'they've read about it or a friend has told them' – that Madeleine's possession of the poison takes on a less sinister cast. Women jurors might have already known this, of course, and the implications about the gendered nature of supposedly impartial justice are not a million miles away from Marleen Gorris's lacerating feminist film *A Question of Silence* (1982).

Madeleine presents the processes by which Madeleine Smith is turned from a private citizen into an object of public infamy, showing her being studied and sketched by a court artist, and replicating the newspaper headlines about her, most notably the shocking revelation that she entertained her lover in the maid's bedroom, disregarding the proprieties of both sex and class. The media's creation of Madeleine as a notorious woman runs in parallel with the other patriarchal lenses through which the character is viewed. For the prosecution, she represents 'sin and disgrace and degradation' and an un-feminine 'strength of will'. The defence depicts her as a 'poor girl' with a 'sad, strange story'. Neither version of Madeleine is decisively 'proven' right, but both are highly patriarchal visions of the woman. There is little room for Madeleine's own voice here; as she tells Minnoch, she may seem cool and impassive but this is because all she is able to do is 'to sit and listen'.

The one channel of communication within her control is her clothing, and this becomes an important means of self-expression throughout the trial indicated by her apparently disproportionate anxiety about showing

6 Woman as enigma: Ann Todd as the eponymous heroine at the end of *Madeleine* (1950)

an unstitched glove. She covers her face with a dramatic black veil as she first enters the court, and while she awaits the jury's verdict she changes into a new dress, partly as displacement activity but also to present a smart feminine façade to the world. She even comments that her trial provides unrivalled publicity for her dressmaker, and the real Madeleine Smith was written about as much in terms of fashion as much as criminality, the *Spectator* remarking not only on her heinous crime but on her 'perfect self-possession', 'fashionable' clothes and 'most attractive appearance'.[117] As with Lean's other Victorian films, the often contradictory discourses around costume complicate the generally negative view of the period. The period may have been highly restrictive for women (Ann Todd is described as suffering while wearing a corseted dress with 'six stiff petticoats', a fur muff and matching hat) but at the same time the star liked the embroidered nightgowns she wore for the film so much, she requested copies to be made for herself. An article in the film's pressbook, 'Creating clothes for a real Victorian character', has designer Margaret Furse stressing the importance not only of historical accuracy but of psychological accuracy, of knowing both what Madeleine Smith actually wore and 'what Madeleine would have *chosen* to wear'.[118] Costume thus becomes key to making sense of this outwardly opaque character as well as being a vital aspect of the film's visual appeal.

After the court's verdict of 'murder not proven' Madeleine exits the courts to find the previously angry mob outside now cheering her as a folk heroine, proving the volatility of the public mood. The final shots of the film repeat the earlier image of Madeleine on the way to the trial (Plate 6). She is alone in her carriage, removed from the outside world, accompanied only by the presence on the soundtrack of the film's Scottish narrator. He asks the still unanswered question, 'Madeleine Smith, ye have heard the indictment, were ye guilty or not guilty?' Todd's head turns slightly and her gaze meets the spectator's, a last look back at the camera which has spent most of the preceding film carefully scrutinising her actions. She does not answer his question. The half-smile that plays on Todd's lips as the film ends is the closest *Madeleine* comes to stating a definite position on her guilt, but this subtle change in facial expression might be read as relief at being free rather than a coquettish admission of guilt. In the end, the final close-up offers the perpetuation of an enigma rather than its solution and in that respect, it presages the similarly inscrutable final shot of *Lawrence of Arabia*. But whereas Lawrence's face is impossible to read because it is obscured by a dusty windscreen, Madeleine's face is in plain view, not just shot in close-up but with the camera tracking ever closer to her face. But its appearance of candour belies its insistence on mystery. Despite the doubts of the critics, *Madeleine*'s bold decision to maintain its heroine's ambiguity is what endows the film with such power. Lean generally described it as his least successful film but in at least one interview he was able to summarise it in more positive terms: 'very original, very romantic, and not a little sad'.[119]

Hobson's Choice (1954)

There are some intriguing parallels between *Hobson's Choice* and Lean's previous foray into Victoriana, *Madeleine*. Both feature young women who are single-minded, unconventional in their behaviour and in revolt against the strictures of patriarchy exemplified by dominant fathers. But while Madeleine is all enigma, fitting for the heroine of a mystery melodrama, *Hobson's Choice*'s Maggie (Brenda de Banzie) is comically blunt and forthright in attaining her objectives of a loving husband, a thriving business and dominion over her bullying father, Henry Hobson (Charles Laughton). Where *Madeleine* ends with an unanswered question, *Hobson's Choice* closes with an exuberant exclamation, taken verbatim from Harold Brighouse's original play: Will Mossop's (John Mills) astonished but triumphant 'Well, by gum!'

Despite having its 1915 theatrical debut in America, Brighouse's play *Hobson's Choice* played an integral role in the development of the British theatre, a product of the 'Manchester School' that also encompassed work by Allan Monkhouse and Stanley Houghton. These dramatists had been nurtured by Annie Horniman's Manchester Gaiety Theatre and its policy of supporting 'plays by local authors about local life'[120] and have been described as 'the first English dramatists to take provincial life as their subject',[121] setting plays in their native Lancashire, using local dialect, as well as frequently dealing with controversial subject matter, such as the illicit love affairs featured in Monkhouse's *Mary Broome* (1911) and Houghton's *Hindle Wakes* (1910). With their shared emphasis on class conflict enacted in north of England settings, the Manchester School anticipated the 'angry' revolution in British drama and literature that was just around the corner in 1954 when Lean made his film of Brighouse's play. It is a nice irony that one of the sentences Will is made to copy out by Maggie when she is teaching him to read and write is 'There is always room at the top' (a detail from the play also used in the film), inadvertently pre-empting the title of John Braine's groundbreaking novel of provincial revolt *Room at the Top* (1957) and the inaugural film of the British New Wave in 1959. Lean would never be part of that school of British cinema, moving further into internationalism in the late 1950s and early 1960s, but in some respects *Hobson's Choice* is his period-dress equivalent, with its story of class mobility through marrying the boss's daughter. It even features one of the New Wave's stylistic hallmarks, what John Krish called the 'Long Shot of Our Town from That Hill'.[122]

In many ways, a down-to-earth Lancashire comedy seems a far from obvious directorial assignment for David Lean, especially coming directly after the aestheticised aerobatics of *The Sound Barrier* (discussed in chapter five). However *Hobson's Choice* was met with praise in some quarters for its renewed focus on character over spectacle. The *Daily Mail*'s Fred Majdalany felt that the film answered the director's critics 'who have in the past felt that he was happier dealing with action and sophistication than with human beings'.[123] Although Lean was by no means a specialist in comedy, he had handled *Blithe Spirit* effectively, as well as the moments of humour in his other Coward and Dickens adaptations, which seems to have been enough to convince Korda that he would be a safe pair of hands for his newly acquired project. And, after all, Lean's love of cinema had first been kindled by comedy, through Mrs Egerton's Chaplin impersonations. As for the Lancastrian aspect of the play, quite alien to Lean as someone who was 'in every fibre a Southerner',[124] the director seems to have risen to the challenge by immersing himself in character, even beginning to say 'aye' instead of yes in conversation with his co-writer and producer Norman Spencer.[125]

When it came to adapting the play, Spencer and Lean did very little to alter the substance of Brighouse's dialogue and dramatic structure, although they did excise some passages and compress the timeframe. However, they put significant effort into opening it out from its two original settings (Hobson's shop and Mossop's shop), presenting scenes in locations ranging from Will's lowly lodgings to the home of wealthy customer Mrs Hepworth, as well as exteriors in the cobbled streets and alleys of Salford, Peel Park and the banks of the River Irwell (although its 'murk and scum' had to be faked with soap powder[126]). As Dilys Powell was to note, these 'brief excursions' were used so effectively that *Hobson's Choice* managed to suggest 'a complete society, not merely a fraction of a society'.[127] A great deal of credit for the film's authenticity should also go to Art Director Wilfred Shingleton whose period designs were promoted in a Shepperton Studios press release as one of the film's highlights, including 'his emphasised Victoriana in the living quarters behind the shop and his realistic approach to the somewhat sordid basement residence of Mossop and his new wife'.[128] As with *Madeleine*, some use is made of deep-focus photography in *Hobson's Choice* to present both the foreground and background of a scene in pin-sharp detail; there is a lovely example of this when all the shop owners on Hobson's street are preparing to leave their respective businesses to meet at the Moonraker's and we see each man placed within his milieu. Some of the exterior shots on the impeccably recreated 1880 high-street set, with characters walking and talking past a series shopfronts recall similar moments in Welles's period drama *The Magnificent Ambersons* (1942) in which character and historical context are carefully interwoven.

Lean's previous confidence in imbuing theatrical material with cinematic life is clearly in evidence in *Hobson's Choice*. As with *This Happy Breed* and *Blithe Spirit*, a mobile camera glides around interiors, subtly avoiding any sense of the visual stasis that often beleaguers stage adaptations. In the film's near-wordless opening sequences, the camera movement and editing are dynamic and varied, introducing the viewer to the world of Hobson's shop via the large black boot sign swinging above the cobbles in the wind, switching then into the shop's interior with close-up panning shots over the range of footwear on display from ladies' fancy heeled shoes and high-button boots to children's shoes and riding boots (all matched with appropriate musical motifs in Malcolm Arnold's score). The rapid swish-pans to tree branches hitting a window and then to the door suddenly flying open mimic the perspective of someone in the shop (an intruder?) being surprised by unexpected noises. The sinister aspects of the sequence's climatic moment – its silhouetted figure suddenly looming in the doorway, casting a giant shadow on the floorboards – are then beautifully undercut by the first human sound in the film: a belch immediately followed by a quick 'beg pardon'.[129] This is our first sighting (and hearing) of Hobson and it suggests his character in a beautifully succinct fashion: a seemingly threatening figure who turns out to be actually rather comic and bathetic, his little bit of wind not matching up to the gothic tempest that preceded him and had hinted at the arrival of an altogether more terrifying personage.

Malcolm Arnold's memorable score performs a similar role. Chosen for his 'Rabelaisian sense of humour' (and coincidentally his own background as the son of a shoe maker),[130] the composer supplies a wonderfully flatulent brass sound in which slide trombone is the lead instrument for the main theme. The music aptly represents Hobson's noisy bluster (literal and metaphorical wind) but also anticipates the clownish drunken pratfall which will eventually seal his fate. It's a big score to match a big lead performance from Charles Laughton as Hobson. The actor was Lean's preference for the role and was hired in spite of Korda's slight misgivings about reuniting with the quixotic performer who had given him a world-class performance in the first truly international British film *The Private Life of Henry VIII* (1933) – had the casting of Robert Donat as Mossop gone ahead, *Hobson's Choice* would have been a kind of group reunion for that film. The director's admiration for his lead actor, whom he regarded as 'a sort of genius',[131] meant that Laughton was given time and space to experiment with his performance while Lean, in his own words, 'just sat there, on a ninepenny seat in the stalls, just watching'.[132] If anything, he encouraged Laughton to deliver something as barnstorming and bravura as possible. Although this attracted some critical animus for its lack of subtlety, its very performativity chimes with the pomposity of Hobson, playing the role of the sage patriarch at home and 'hail-fellow-well-met' at the pub. Hobson's reluctant ingestion of Maggie's wedding cake, his reaction to dipsomaniac hallucinations (a predatory insect and a giant winking rat, leaning over the bedstead) and, most notably of all, his drunken tiptoeing pursuit of the moon's reflection in the puddles on the street are moments to cherish, unimaginable with another actor. As *Picture Post* suggested in a special laudatory piece on the film, 'It's acting on a grand scale: The Laughton Scale.'[133]

However, the narrative centres on dramatic conflict and this means that Hobson must have a worthy antagonist. That role goes to his eldest daughter, Maggie (Plate 7). Although Hobson rails against his two other daughters, against Will Mossop and even against his drinking pals at one point, his main rivalry is with Maggie. *Hobson's Choice* enacts a 'battle of the sexes', with Hobson's broadsides against the 'uppishness' of 'rebellious females' pitched against Maggie's smart outmanoeuvring of her father on all fronts. In the end the only choice he has is 'Hobson's choice' – in other words, no choice at all. Through its focus on the enmity between father and daughter, it also dealt with generational conflict; Charles Laughton later took the lead in *King Lear* on stage in 1959, but with *Hobson's Choice* he had a dry run as a thwarted patriarch divested of his property by three daughters.

Brenda de Banzie's performance in the role of Maggie was quieter and more self-contained than Laughton's as her father, entirely fitting for their difference in their characters' personalities, and she was singled out for praise by a number of reviewers. For *The Star*'s Robin Nash, de Banzie's Maggie was 'a girl to be reckoned with, shrewd as a proverb, hard-headed as a walking stick, determined as a spring tide' who 'may not be beautiful in the film star sense but ... glows with intelligence and charm'.[34] In the estimation of the *Telegraph*'s Campbell Dixon, the actress even managed 'the feat of making a strong-minded woman attractive'.[35] Maggie embodies the Victorian virtues eulogised by Samuel Smiles – 'self-help, perseverance, duty, thrift, and character'[36] – and there is evidence that she has a sharper business sense than her father in her very first scenes in the film, in which she bamboozles

7 Father versus daughter: Hobson (Charles Laughton) clashes with Maggie (Brenda de Banzie) in *Hobson's Choice* (1954)

Albert Prosser into buying brand new boots when he had only come in for bootlaces. But she recognises that her plan to 'settle her life's course' can only be achieved through an alliance with a man, not as a spinster, and at thirty she is considered 'ripe' and time is running out. Once she has announced her intention to marry, she is unstoppable in the attainment of her objectives, ruthlessly dispatching former fiancées and shrugging off Will Mossop's initial rejection. 'You're my man' she announces in her proposal scene and doesn't stop until she's got him, changed him, made him love her and installed him at the head of the family business. This is a feminised take on Shaw's *Pygmalion*, this time with the woman taking unlikely raw material and transforming it into an ideal man who can pass in polite society, and indeed in its central theme of 'the right of women to determine their own lives', according to E. R. Wood, it follows in the feminist theatrical tradition of 'Ibsen, Shaw and Granville-Barker'.[137] The play, as Kevin Brownlow suggests, was 'a distinctive product of the Suffragist era'[138] while its generic orientation probably enabled it greater licence in depicting a nonconformist woman. Maggie, Silver and Ursini point out, 'is the least sentimental, most aggressive of Lean's heroines; so aggressive, in fact, that she could probably never exist in his work except in a comedy'.[139]

Hobson's Choice parodied the gothic stylings of Lean's Dickens films in its opening sequence, but in its depiction of the relationship between Will and Maggie it seemed to be offering a comic retread of the relationship of Pip and Estella, and the erotic potential of a man being dominated by a woman who is above him – literally, in the case of basement-dwelling Will called up to the shopfloor by Maggie. He cringes in her presence but she offers him the means to fulfil his own 'great expectations', converting him from an illiterate cobbler into a prosperous entrepreneur. As he waits outside his old lodgings while Maggie breaks off his former engagement on his behalf ('Beware the Wrath to Come' warns a nicely timed Salvation Army banner), Will overhears Maggie's stirring rhetoric about what she sees in him and it makes him prouder by the moment, underlined by the crescendo in Arnold's score, but swelling pride and swelling music are both silenced by a sudden smack round the mouth from his angry former landlady. But there will be a later moment of burgeoning pride where no such undercutting occurs, after Will has seen the painted sign outside his new premises with his name on it – all arranged by Maggie – and he walks home through the streets, a close-up of his elated face accompanied by Arnold's soaring music. He has been made into something with her help.

Maggie's proposal to Will is couched in terms that initially resemble a commercial alliance ('you're a business idea in the shape of a man') and she is quick to dismiss the romantic mythology surrounding courtship and marriage, dismissing the former as pointless 'glitter' and insisting on a simple brass ring as a wedding band rather than a gold ring from the jewellers; when one of her sisters protests that it's from their own stock, she reminds her that all wedding rings are from somebody's 'stock', emphasising the hard facts of commerce underpinning wedding expenses. But any assumption that this arrangement derives from pure financial expediency is dispelled as the relationship between Maggie and Will develops into something more than hunter and prey. The ring may be brass but the marriage is not just about 'brass'. Although the *mise en scène* of the church in which their wedding takes place may suggest a sacrificial tabernacle, with long shadows cast by tombstones and a portentous bell tolling in the background, the wedding that takes place within is a genuine match. Back at home, Maggie unsentimentally discards her bouquet in the sink with the dirty dishes from their wedding breakfast but then goes back to save one rose from the debris to press as a keepsake, the first hint of a buried romanticism within the character.

Hobson's Choice seems to suggest a magical exchange of power via sex, centred on its wedding night sequence. Up to a point, the film follows its equivalent in Brighouse's play, which has the reluctant bridegroom trying to stall his guests' departure and finding different ways to procrastinate and postpone his entry into the bedroom to consummate the marriage. An impatient Maggie returns to the kitchen to grab Will by the ear and lead him to bed, using broad comedy to bring down the curtain on the third act with uproarious laughter. Lean's film presents a more delicate take on the comedy of male sexual trepidation. Earlier we had seen Will look terrified as Maggie tested the springs on a secondhand bed at the market and when the time finally comes to test the bed properly, Will is even more hesitant. He takes more time than is strictly necessary poking the fire (an action heavy with ribald symbolism) and undressing, even carefully arranging his bib and cuffs on the mantelpiece like a suit of armour. He doesn't take down his trousers until he has his nightshirt safely on and has to affect nonchalance when Maggie surprises him by opening the door. 'I'm ready', she calls, and Will steels himself for action, turning down the gaslight and entering the bedroom accompanied by music resembling a fanfare for battle, swelling into a full military band march. The door closes and the camera discreetly retreats, tracking back into the now empty parlour and remaining there for a beat before the scene fades to black. Although Norman Spencer retrospectively concluded that his and Lean's revised version of the wedding night had been done 'more elaborately but worse'[140] than Brighouse's original, the critic Jympson Harman regarded it as 'a model of tender comedy for all producers who try to skate around censorship'.[141] It shifts the mood of the consummation of the marriage from pure farce into something gentler, and sets up the shift in the relationship that seems to have taken place by the next morning. This time, Maggie is poking the fire and Will looks upon her admiringly before uttering his characteristic 'By gum!' Now he is empowered to take the initiative in kissing his wife, and is similarly empowered in his business dealings, selling his first pair of bootlaces from his own shop and again saying 'by gum!' Carnal delight and business success are intertwined.

As Will Mossop grows in stature (almost literally, thanks to John Mills's gradual transformation from stooped subterranean boot-hand to someone who can stand straight and square) and his business grows in prosperity, so Hobson shrinks into failure and alcoholism. Maggie has capitalised on the writ for damages he is served by the corn merchant Mr Beenstock, sorted out dowries for her two sisters to marry their desired suitors, stolen her father's best workman and set up a rival business which has stolen all his trade, *and* deprived him of a dependable housekeeper by marrying. He has been outflanked on all counts and is hopelessly vulnerable to the final coup. This depends on Will presenting himself effectively as a man of equal, if not superior, stature to his old boss. He has been coached by Maggie but this represents his greatest challenge. Rather like the heroine Beatie in Arnold Wesker's kitchen-sink play *Roots* (1959), Will finally transcends his careful instruction and pre-learned phrases and finds his own voice, his own eloquence, when forced to speak up and fight his corner: as he confesses afterwards, 'Words came to me mouth that made me jump at me own boldness.'

So *Hobson's Choice* ends with parental tyranny quashed and replaced by an affectionate and companionate marriage of equals and a triumphant fulfilled female; a happy ending to match those of the Dickens adaptations but this time much less marked by the dark shadows that had nearly engulfed Pip and Oliver. Lean's final outright comedy seems an appropriate farewell to the nineteenth century for the director, his move from haunted melodrama to warm humour replicating wider cultural changes afoot in society's feelings about the Victorians during the years 1945–55, and a shift from outright rejection to fond nostalgia.

Notes

1. Brian McFarlane, *Novel to Film: An Introduction to the Theory of Adaptation* (Oxford: Clarendon, 1996), p. 8.
2. Sarah Cardwell, *Adaptation Revisited: Television and the Classic Novel* (Manchester: Manchester University Press, 2002), p. 62.
3. Robert Stam, 'Beyond Fidelity: The Dialogics of Adaptation', in James Naremore (ed.), *Film Adaptation* (London: Athlone Press, 2000), p. 66.
4. Christine Geraghty, *Now a Major Motion Picture: Film Adaptations of Literature and Drama* (Lanham MD: Rowman and Littlefield, 2008), p. 9.
5. Peter Ackroyd, *Introduction to Dickens* (London: Sinclair-Stevenson, 1991), p. 8.
6. John Gardiner, *The Victorians: An Age in Retrospect* (London: Hambledon and London, 2002), p. 179.
7. Sweet, *Inventing the Victorians*, p. 231.
8. Miles Taylor, 'Introduction', in Miles Taylor and Michael Wolff (eds.), *The Victorians since 1901: Histories, Representations and Revisions* (Manchester: Manchester University Press, 2004), p. 2.
9. Cited in Gardiner, *The Victorians*, p. 3.
10. Ibid., p. 21.
11. Evelyn Waugh, *Brideshead Revisited* (London: Penguin, 2000 [1945]), p. 33.
12. Quoted in Asa Briggs, *Victorian People* (Harmondsworth: Penguin, 1990 [1955]), p. 15.
13. Miles Taylor, 'G. M. Young and the Early Victorian Revival', in Taylor and Wolff (eds.), *The Victorians since 1901*, p. 82.
14. Miles Taylor, 'Introduction', in Taylor and Wolff (eds.), *The Victorians since 1901*, p. 6.
15. Kelly Boyd and Rohan McWilliam, 'Introduction: Rethinking the Victorians', in Kelly Boyd and Rohan McWilliam (eds.), *The Victorian Studies Reader* (Abingdon: Routledge, 2007), pp. 6–12.
16. Michelle Hawley, 'Quiller-Couch, the Function of Victorian Literature and Modernism, 1890–1930', in Taylor and Wolff (eds.), *The Victorians since 1901*, p. 59.
17. Quoted in James Thompson, 'The BBC and the Victorians', in Taylor and Wolff (eds.), *The Victorians since 1901*, p. 152.
18. Asa Briggs, *Victorian Things* (Harmondsworth: Penguin, 1990), pp. 12–13.
19. Robert Giddings, Keith Selby and Chris Wensley (eds.), *Screening the Novel: The Theory and Practice of Literary Dramatisation* (Basingstoke: Macmillan, 1990), p. 16. Grahame Smith takes issue with this view, however, in his book *Dickens and the Dream of Cinema* (Manchester: Manchester University Press, 2003), p. 123.
20. Sergei Eisenstein, 'Dickens, Griffith and the Film Today', in *Film Form* (London: Dennis Dobson, 1951), p. 195. More specifically, Dickens played a key role in the emergence of cinema in Britain. Film pioneer Cecil Hepworth's father, a magic lantern lecturer, had a hugely popular slideshow called 'The Footprints of Charles Dickens', and when his son moved into the emergent technology of moving pictures, he made films based on the novels *Oliver Twist* (1912) and *David Copperfield* (1913), the latter being Britain's first eight-reel feature film. Cited in Smith, *Dickens and the Dream of Cinema*, p. 57.
21. Charles Dickens, *Great Expectations* (Harmondsworth: Penguin, 1982 [1861]), p. 438.
22. Ackroyd, *Introduction to Dickens*, p. 11.
23. McFarlane, *Novel to Film*, p. 105.
24. Brownlow, *David Lean*, p. 211.
25. Lean revealed how he and Guy Green used different lenses to make Miss Havisham's room look vast to the child but much smaller to the grown-up Pip. Interview

in 1985 with Lean conducted by Harlan Kennedy, in Organ (ed.), *David Lean: Interviews*, p. 79.
26 Alison Light, 'What larks, Pip', *Guardian* (Review), 21 September 2002, p. 37.
27 *Guardian* (section 2), 12 November 1999, pp. 10–11.
28 Lean interviewed in 1984 by David Ehrenstein in Organ (ed.), *David Lean: Interviews*, p. 72.
29 *News Chronicle*, 11 December 1946.
30 Brownlow, *David Lean*, p. 211.
31 Dickens, *Great Expectations*, p. 135.
32 Smith, *Dickens and the Dream of Cinema*, p. 124.
33 Ibid., p. 123. Raphael Samuel also states his disappointment with Wemmick's castle in *Theatres of Memory Vol. 1* (London: Verso, 1994), p. 419.
34 Stephen Bourne praises for film for its inclusion of black actors in 'Secrets and Lies: Black Histories and British Historical Films', in Claire Monk and Amy Sargeant (eds.), *British Historical Cinema* (London: Routledge, 2002), p. 55.
35 Gardiner, *The Victorians*, p. 11.
36 Samuel, *Theatres of Memory*, p. 402.
37 It's also strongly reminiscent of the moment in *Dracula* when the vampire is exposed to and destroyed by sunlight. Might it also be a sly reference to the longed-for ending of wartime blackout restrictions?
38 Samuel, *Theatres of Memory*, p. 420. After Labour's landslide, Hugh Dalton invoked Edward Carpenter in his diary: 'After the long storm of war, after the short storm of election, we saw sunrise. As we had sung in the shadows, so now in the light. England is risen and the day is here.' Steven Fielding, Peter Thompson and Nick Tiratsoo, *England Arise! The Labour Party and Popular Politics in 1940s Britain* (Manchester: Manchester University Press, 1995), p. 83.
39 Claire Tomalin, *Charles Dickens: A Life* (London: Viking: 2011), p. 314.
40 Dickens, *Great Expectations*, p. 493.
41 Samuel, *Theatres of Memory*, p. 411.
42 Cineguild press release dated July 1946. Microfiche on *Great Expectations*, BFI Library.
43 Ibid.
44 Cineguild press release dated 8 October 1945. Microfiche on *Great Expectations*, BFI Library.
45 Cineguild press release from 1946 (undated). Microfiche on *Great Expectations*, BFI Library.
46 Cineguild press release dated 6 July 1946. Microfiche on *Great Expectations*, BFI Library. The film's costume designer, Sophia Devine, wrote a response to questions from journalist Catherine de la Roche relating to the film's costuming which is illuminating in relation to Victorian crinolines and the New Look. She notes, 'If a "costume" picture is popular and successful it does undoubtedly give modern fashion designers a "new line"', and also writes about ladies protesting at having to put corsets on for the Richmond Hall sequences but then expressing 'their delight on finding how well it made them look and how tiny their waists appeared'. Undated letter, microfiche on *Great Expectations*, BFI Library.
47 *Great Expectations* pressbook, BFI Library.
48 Samuel, *Theatres of Memory*, p. 424.
49 *Great Expectations* pressbook, BFI Library.
50 An article in the *Mirror*, 3 January 1947, discusses the film's success, stating: 'Up and down the country the story is the same. It has played from Dundee down through Yorkshire, from Doncaster to the Medway towns of Rochester and Chatham and right down to Southampton. It has scooped the pool. The one fear in the minds of its British makers – that the idea of a Dickens classic might scare

51 Ackroyd, *Introduction to Dickens*, p. 56. George Bernard Shaw claimed *Little Dorrit* as a more seditious book than *Das Kapital*. Cited in Gardiner, *The Victorians*, p. 164.
52 Pratley, *The Cinema of David Lean*, p. 76.
53 Smith, *Dickens and the Dream of Cinema*, p. 124.
54 As even Dickens's great advocate Peter Ackroyd is forced to admit: 'what do we find in his novels but the constant oscillation between the portrayal of absurd and garrulous (or cold and selfish) women and idealised, virginal young girls?' Ackroyd, *Introduction to Dickens*, p. 23.
55 Brownlow, *David Lean*, pp. 228–9. Kay Walsh also suggested that Estella should be turning into another Havisham for the ending of *Great Expectations*. See Phillips, *Beyond the Epic*, p. 118.
56 *Oliver Twist* pressbook, BFI Library.
57 The shooting script describes a shot silhouetting 'the branch a sharp prickly briar against the clouds. The wind shrieks out.' *Oliver Twist* shooting script dated 12 May 1947, p. 2. DL/3/1, BFI Spec Coll.
58 Silver and Ursini, *David Lean and His Films*, p. 5.
59 Neame, *Straight from the Horse's Mouth*, p. 112.
60 *Oliver Twist* shooting script dated 12 May 1947, p. 40. DL/3/1, BFI Spec Coll.
61 Brownlow, *David Lean*, p. 236. It was also one of the scenes that got cut from the US version of the film, conversely making Fagin less rather than more sympathetic.
62 Christine Geraghty, *British Cinema in the Fifties: Gender, Genre and the 'New Look'* (London: Routledge, 2000), p. 133.
63 Ibid., pp. 141–2.
64 *Oliver Twist* pressbook, BFI Library.
65 Cineguild press release, 8 November 1947. Microfiche on *Oliver Twist*, BFI Library.
66 Brownlow, *David Lean*, p. 227.
67 Cineguild press release, 12 August 1947. Microfiche for *Oliver Twist*, BFI Library.
68 Grahame Smith also describes the film's half-starved shaven-headed workhouse boys as 'an image that echoes the concentration camps of the Second World War' (Smith, *Dickens and the Dream of Cinema*, p. 130); an irony, given later accusations of anti-Semitism and historical insensitivity levelled at the film.
69 Cineguild press release, 15 September 1947. Microfiche for *Oliver Twist*, BFI Library.
70 Cineguild press release, 1 October 1947. Microfiche for *Oliver Twist*.
71 *Oliver Twist* shooting script dated 12 May 1947, p. 41. DL/3/1, BFI Spec Coll.
72 *Life*, 7 March 1949.
73 Al McKee, 'Art or outrage? *Oliver Twist* and the flap over Fagin', *Film Comment*, January 2000, p. 44.
74 *Guardian*, 22 February 1949. The same incident was also reported in more anti-Semitic terms, claiming that it involved 'Fewer than 100 Polish Jews, many of whom are known to the Berlin police as black market operators' in *Daily Telegraph*, 22 February 1949. For a full discussion of the response to the film, see Brownlow, *David Lean*, pp. 245–9, and Al McKee, 'Art or outrage?', pp. 40–5.
75 *News Chronicle*, 21 February 1949.
76 *Oliver Twist* pressbook, BFI Library.
77 Samuel, *Theatres of Memory*, p. 421.
78 Tomalin, *Charles Dickens*, p. 374.

79 *Oliver Twist* shooting script dated 12 May 1947, p. 112. DL/3/1, BFI Spec Coll.
80 Silver and Ursini, *David Lean and His Films*, p. 70.
81 Al McKee, 'Art or outrage?', p. 41.
82 See McFarlane, *An Autobiography of British Cinema*, p. 594.
83 Tomalin, *Charles Dickens*, p. 98.
84 Brownlow, *David Lean*, p. 242.
85 John Ruskin, *Sesame and Lilies* (London: George Allen, 1865), p. 73.
86 Quoted in Andrew Pulver, 'Adaptation of the week: *Oliver Twist*', *Guardian* (Review), 10 April 2004, p. 19.
87 Pratley, *The Cinema of David Lean*, p. 80.
88 *Madeleine* pressbook, BFI Library.
89 As well as being the subject of numerous popular accounts, academia's interest in this case is also evident from the large number of publications on it, most recently Eleanor Gordon and Gwyneth Nair's *Murder and Morality in Victorian Britain: The Story of Madeleine Smith* (Manchester: Manchester University Press, 2009).
90 Mary S. Hartman, 'Murder for Respectability: The Case of Madeleine Smith', *Victorian Studies*, Vol. 16, No. 4 (June 1973), p. 382.
91 Quoted in Briggs, *Victorian People*, p. 16.
92 Ibid., p. 59.
93 Quoted in Nick Rance, '"Victorian Values" and "Fast Young Ladies": from Madeleine Smith to Ruth Rendell', in Gary Day (ed.), *Varieties of Victorianism: The Uses of a Past* (Basingstoke: Macmillan, 1998), p. 222.
94 Ibid., p. 223.
95 The phrase provides the title of Steven Marcus's book *The Other Victorians: A Study of Sexuality and Pornography in Mid-Nineteenth-Century England* (London: Weidenfeld & Nicolson, 1966).
96 Brownlow, *David Lean*, p. 266.
97 Ibid., p. 289.
98 Ibid., pp. 269 and 275.
99 *News Chronicle*, 18 February 1950.
100 *Sunday Chronicle*, 19 February 1950.
101 *The Times*, 18 February 1950.
102 *Madeleine* pressbook, BFI Library.
103 Anderegg, *David Lean*, p. 69.
104 On the extra-narrative importance and sexual symbolism of hairstyles in 1940s melodrama, see Sue Harper, 'Historical Pleasures: Gainsborough Costume Melodramas', in Christine Gledhill (ed.), *Home Is Where the Heart Is: Studies in Melodrama and the Woman's Film* (London: BFI, 1987), pp. 182–4.
105 Lean was in psychoanalysis from 1948 to 1950 and drew on his consultations in his filmmaking, particularly in the use of sexual symbolism. See Brownlow, *David Lean*, pp. 238–9.
106 Silver and Ursini, *David Lean and His Films*, p. 91.
107 See Brownlow, *David Lean*, p. 270.
108 *Sunday Chronicle*, 19 February 1950.
109 John Orr, 'David Lean: The Troubled Romantic and the End of Empire', *Romantics and Modernists in British Cinema* (Edinburgh: Edinburgh University Press, 2010), p. 65.
110 Ibid., p. 76.
111 *Observer*, 19 February 1950.
112 Sweet, *Inventing the Victorians*, p. 75.
113 *Madeleine* pressbook, BFI Library.
114 *Reynolds News*, 19 February 1950.

115 *Daily Herald*, 17 February 1950.
116 *New Statesman*, 25 February 1950.
117 Hartman, 'Murder for Respectability', p. 399.
118 *Madeleine* pressbook, BFI Library.
119 Pratley, *The Cinema of David Lean*, p. 95.
120 E. R. Wood, 'Introduction', *Hobson's Choice* (London: Heinemann, 1964), p. vii.
121 Granada TV Network, *Granada's Manchester Plays* (Manchester: Manchester University Press, 1962), p. vi.
122 Quoted in Andrew Higson, 'Space, Place, Spectacle: Landscape and Townscape in the "Kitchen Sink" Film', in Higson (ed.), *Dissolving Views: Key Writings on British Cinema* (London: Cassell, 1996), p. 133.
123 *Daily Mail*, 26 February 1954.
124 Brownlow, *David Lean*, p. 297.
125 Ibid., p. 398.
126 Reported in *Manchester Guardian*, 9 September 1953. The *Bolton Evening News* complained of 'how they stole our only day of Summer, to make a darker background for a mummer', 16 September 1953.
127 *Sunday Times*, 28 February 1954.
128 Shepperton Studios press release dated 5 August 1953, replicated on BFI microfiche on *Hobson's Choice*.
129 A convincing intertextual link could be made between this moment and Charles Laughton's section of the portmanteau film *If I Had a Million* (1932), which concludes with Laughton's character leaving his job and blowing a raspberry at his boss as his parting gesture.
130 Brownlow, *David Lean*, p. 307.
131 Ibid., p. 299.
132 Ibid., p. 300.
133 *Picture Post*, 27 February 1954, p. 35.
134 *Star*, 26 February 1954.
135 *Daily Telegraph*, 27 February 1954.
136 Briggs, *Victorian People*, p. 27.
137 Wood, 'Introduction', *Hobson's Choice*, p. vii.
138 Brownlow, *David Lean*, p. 298.
139 Silver and Ursini, *David Lean and His Films*, p. 112.
140 Brownlow, *David Lean*, p. 307.
141 *Evening News*, 26 February 1954.

Women in love: *Brief Encounter* (1945), *The Passionate Friends* (1949) and *Summer Madness* (1955) 4

The American title for Lean's romance *The Passionate Friends* – *One Woman's Story* – could have been applied to several of the films the director made during the course of his career. As noted earlier, six of Lean's sixteen films were decisively women's stories with 'preeminent female protagonists'[1] and fit very comfortably into the generic category of woman's film as defined by Maria LaPlace ('distinguished by its female protagonist, female point of view and its narrative which most often revolves around the traditional realms of women's experience'[2]) or Jeanine Basinger (a film that can 'articulate female concerns, angers, and desires, [and] give substance to a woman's dreams and a woman's problems'[3]). And yet Lean has seldom been considered a woman's director in the manner of a George Cukor, instead accruing a 'reputation of having heroes rather than heroines',[4] reflected in Judy Davis's fears that he didn't actually know how to direct women. This skewed perspective on Lean's work has something to do with the acclaim and critical pre-eminence accorded to the epic war films *The Bridge on the River Kwai* and *Lawrence of Arabia*, and his designation as 'the poet of the far horizon', a more masculine domain than the domestic settings more commonly associated with women's pictures.

Lean himself was keen to avoid being stereotyped as a 'man's director' and in interviews made plain his allegiance to female-led stories as much as male-led stories, and heroines as much as heroes: 'I like women. A couple of films with men and you get typecast'; 'I like making films about women, I like telling love stories, I think they are fascinating.'[5] Latterly celebrated for his work with Alec Guinness and discovery of Omar Sharif and Peter O'Toole, back in the 1950s Lean had been hailed as a woman's director, 'always a Svengali with actresses'.[6] Significantly, the actors for whom he had the greatest admiration were both women, Celia Johnson and Katharine Hepburn, the latter also described by Lean as 'my best friend'.[7] He singled them out as exceptionally gifted and professional in a number of interviews[8] and wrote to Robert Bolt, 'I think I've done my best work with women – not my ex Ann Todd – but with Celia and Katie'.[9] Of all his films, Lean picked as his personal favourite not the film generally acknowledged as his masterpiece, *Lawrence of Arabia*, but his story of late-blossoming romance starring Hepburn, *Summer Madness*: 'I like [it] more than any other film I've done, I think.'[10]

The masculinisation of Lean's reputation despite the available evidence to the contrary connects with the broader tendency identified by Justine Ashby to see the woman's picture as an emotionally excessive interloper in British cinema, 'an unwelcome cuckoo-in-the-nest'.[11] Because of this blind spot, British films that might otherwise be considered woman's films are either ignored or 'swept under the umbrella of other film movements or genres ... in order to fit them, however reductively, into a dominant scheme of national cinema'.[12] Applying this to David Lean's *Brief Encounter*, for instance, one can recognise how its dominant designation as 'quality' realist cinema in the 1940s might have disguised the fact that it is simultaneously 'a masterpiece of "melodramatic emotionality" and "dramatic intensity"',[13] featuring a woman's romantic dilemma at the centre of its dramatic universe.

In re-examining three of Lean's films and bracketing them together as women's pictures, this chapter aims to foreground the absolute centrality of women and women-centred narratives to much of Lean's filmmaking. *Brief Encounter* was the first of Lean's films to provide a sustained focus on the inner life of a heroine, detailing an ordinary middle-class woman's experience of unexpectedly falling in love. *The Passionate Friends* provided a more psychologically opaque and socially upscale variation on the theme of illicit romance with a compelling central performance from Ann Todd. The trilogy is completed by *Summer Madness*, Lean's first Hollywood co-production and first film to be shot entirely on location overseas as well as the director's favourite among his own films. 'Women in love' is the shared subject matter of all three films but, unlike Lean's later 'story of love' *Ryan's Daughter*, these three particular films also focus on slightly older heroines, not ingénues but mature women who have each, in different ways, missed out on a grand romance and are making up for lost time. In addition, all three films place 'a woman's consciousness and a woman's will, at the centre of the text'.[14] But at the same time, as Richard Dyer points out with specific reference to *Brief Encounter*, while women tell the story on screen, 'behind the camera, men authored the film'.[15] This creates an irresolvable tension common to all women's films, according to Mary Ann Doane, between the text's 'attempts to trace the contours of female subjectivity and desire' and its entrenchment in 'traditional forms of conventions of Hollywood narrative – forms which cannot sustain such an exploration'.[16] When read symptomatically, such internally divided films can illuminate 'certain contradictions within patriarchal ideology'.[17] Even at the time, the schematic nature of the woman's picture's appeal was patently and insultingly transparent to some critics and Lean's forays into the form came in for flak: '*Summer Madness* is one of those films men love to make for women' complained one reviewer, featuring 'some *divine* man, of mature charm, Like Mr Rossano Brazzi. Throw in a foreign locale, some breath-taking clothes (never mind who the heroine is, she always looks as if she were dressed by Dior), a little heartbreak, and a moral problem (moral problems always mean sex) and you'll have the ladies pounding at the box office.'[18] Such disdain for the culture of women, even among women, is an attendant danger in making women's pictures and, I would argue, the possible reason for the lower critical standing of Lean's female-focussed films in comparison with his male-focussed films. Even *Brief Encounter*, the exception to that rule of neglect, had to be rescued from damning associations with women's mass culture in order to be reified. Being promoted for BBC television transmission in the 1960s, the film's seriousness was defended thus: 'Although the situation – an unsatisfactory love affair between two married people – is the basis of most women's magazine stories, *Brief Encounter* has an emotional maturity virtually unknown in British films.'[19]

There are certainly contradictions galore in the attempts of all three films to tell 'one woman's story', each one riven with the ideological paradoxes of femininity. But there are also indications of the presence of a female discourse in each film, what Richard Dyer calls a 'feminine angle'. He identifies certain elements of *Brief Encounter* such as 'Celia Johnson's performance and Laura's reading habits' as providing 'a space for the articulation of a woman's view at variance with male perceptions'.[20] Likewise, in the star performances of Ann Todd and Katharine Hepburn in *The Passionate Friends* and *Summer Madness* and in the privileging of fashion in those two films, both on screen and in their marketing and promotion, one might discern a similar 'feminine angle' in evidence. But there seems to be a further, much deeper tributary of feminine discourse running through these films, one that is linked to authorial subjectivity. David Lean is not necessarily an obvious director to be co-opted into feminism, given his inveterate womanising (according to his secretary Pamela Mann he left 'broken hearts strewn across the world'[21]) and preference for 'passive' women over 'cerebral' ones.[22] But a revisionist approach to Lean's films might make productive use of Tania Modleski's work on Alfred Hitchcock in which she argues that despite Hitchcock's appearance as the patriarchal director *par excellence*, he actually internalises a female discourse in his work that runs parallel to and disrupts the more obvious male discourse. In the case of *Rebecca* (1940) Modleski suggests that 'by being forced to maintain a close identification with du Maurier's "feminine" text to the point where he felt the picture could not be considered his own ("it's not a Hitchcock picture"), Hitchcock found one of his "proper" subjects – the potential terror and loss of self involved in identification, especially identification with a woman.'[23] Here the feminine discourse not only invigorates but actually galvanises the artistic identity of the director. Previous critics had posited the notion of a cinematic 'discourse of the woman' which could 'render the dominant discourse of the male fragmented and incoherent',[24] but it had always been linked to a woman director. Modleski cuts the 'woman's discourse' free of its biological moorings and argues that films directed by men also have the potential to contain it.[25]

This conceptual framework has obvious pertinence for thinking through the gender politics of David Lean's films. One of their recurring and central dramatic concerns, the conflict between restraint and abandon, duty and desire, is arguably developed primarily through Lean's films about women. Just as *Rebecca* made an irrevocable mark on Hitchcock's subsequent career, Lean's later film *Lawrence of Arabia* would probably be very different had it not been preceded by films such as *Brief Encounter* and *Summer Madness*. Moreover, Modleski's comments about the terror of identification with a woman seem particularly pertinent in relation to Lean. He spoke of all his characters being 'an extension of one's self'[26] and I think there is compelling evidence for his strong identification with a number of his female protagonists. Lean's descriptions of leaving Croydon's 'very, very grey' suburbia, catching the train and losing himself at cinemas like the Tivoli on the Strand – 'a journey into another world' – or of waiting around in the refreshment room of Victoria Station to catch the last train home, strongly recall aspects of both Queenie in *This Happy Breed* and Laura in *Brief Encounter*.[27] Those heroines' desires for excitement and escape, and even their action of catching trains, correspond closely with Lean's own autobiographical comments and seem to reverberate with his own personal memories. *Lawrence of Arabia* is often characterised as the film in which Lean had the deepest personal investment, becoming an obsessive 'desert-loving Englishman' just like the film's hero. But it was *Summer Madness* of which Lean said: 'I've put more of myself in that film than any other I've ever made.'[28]

It may be that the adoption of a female persona enabled a degree of licence, the freedom to confess while in disguise. Thinking about the reasons behind the younger Lean's desire for escape (particularly the emotional pressure exerted by his mother after his father had deserted the family), it may be that using female characters to animate and work through personal feelings offered a way of managing personal trauma and uncomfortable vulnerability. To quote Kaja Silverman, 'at the heart of women's otherness there remains something strangely familiar, something which impinges dangerously upon male subjectivity. From the very outset the little boy is haunted by this similitude – by the fear of becoming his sexual other.'[29] Lean's frequent collaborator Robert Bolt certainly seems to have felt troubled by those kind of feelings, commenting in an interview that it was disagreeable to recognise elements of feminine vulnerability within one's character when writing from a woman's perspective: 'What one does is draw on the feminine in oneself. The difficulty about this is not that there is insufficient feminine in oneself but that one is reluctant to admit how much there is in oneself.'[30] Bolt admitted that in writing certain situations, when trying to adopt the mantle of female subjectivity, the result was that 'your subconscious starts to panic. It doesn't want to know.'[31] Those troubling feelings of loneliness, of vulnerability, of wanting to yield but fearing the consequences, are powerfully worked through in Lean's female-centred romances. But they offer much more than masculine crisis iterated through female ciphers. This trio of films also constitutes one of the high points of Lean's career, presenting highly sympathetic insights into the dilemmas faced by women in love.

Brief Encounter (1945)

One of the best-known and best-loved of British films, *Brief Encounter* also has a totemic status that goes far beyond film. It has been endlessly parodied by everyone from Elaine May and Mike Nichols to Victoria Wood, pastiched in everything from *The Seven Year Itch* (1955) to *Dad's Army*, and clips from it are embedded in films ranging from *A Touch of Class* (1973) to *Brick Lane* (2007). It was (in)famously remade in 1974 with Sophia Loren and Richard Burton in the starring roles, but even today the original *Brief Encounter* continues to be the object of worshipful homage, both indirect – as with the romantic renunciation scenes in *Atonement* (2007) – or direct, as with Kneehigh's 2008 stage production based on the film. *Brief Encounter* is also *the* example, beyond any other book, play, film, poem, anecdote or event, chosen by Jeremy Paxman as the starting point for his study of national character, *The English: The Portrait of a People*. In the unconsummated love affair of Laura Jesson (Celia Johnson) and Alec Harvey (Trevor Howard), Paxman discerns the representation of core English values; 'the importance of a sense of duty', and the idea that 'the emotions are there to be controlled'.[32] The film's claims to national specificity are only bolstered by the incomprehension it has often met in other countries. In postwar France, audiences concluded 'Laura a eu tort!', that the heroine was mistaken in returning to her husband rather than running away with her lover.[33] In 1946, a British newspaper reported that in Germany the film was met with 'boos, catcalls, and a 30 per cent drop in theatre attendance wherever it was shown' (a hidden agenda of national superiority is suggested by the British Military Government spokesman's explanation: 'Some Germans profess total inability to understand the moral scruples on which the plot hinges').[34] Some years later, the Neapolitan students taught by Richard Dyer were also confounded by the film: 'All that suffering, and for what?'[35] As Dyer suggests, the very national specificity of the film – its British-ness, or perhaps more especially English-ness – can be both 'its glory but also a stick to beat it with'.[36]

From the moment of its initial release, *Brief Encounter* was drafted into a kind of national service, not only for being morally exemplary but also cinematically exemplary. It featured heavily in 1940s film criticism's construction of 'quality' cinema which signalled British cinema's new confidence and prestige.[37] André Bazin praised it for 'combining a highly refined aestheticism with the advances of a certain realism' – although he had significantly revised his opinion by 1956 when he saw his earlier admiration of the film merely as the expression of 'critical illusions about English cinema which I was not the only one to entertain'.[38] The film won the Grand Prize at Cannes in 1946, was Oscar nominated in 1947 and in 1952 featured in the first *Sight and Sound* top ten of greatest films ever made, tying with Renoir's *La Règle du jeu* (1939). It has not, however, appeared in any of the subsequent ten-yearly polls; an indication of the rapid depreciation in its critical esteem after the high-water mark of the postwar years. By the mid-1960s, its ethos of restraint – its motto, Raymond Durgnat observed, could be 'Make tea not love'[39] – provoked impatience and irritation in some viewers. Durgnat recalls that at one screening he attended 'Even the name of the town enraged a well-spoken young lady who finally cried out, "Where the hell is Milford Junction anyway?"'[40] However it is important to remember that *Brief Encounter* had also met with antipathy in some quarters back in the 1940s. When it was first test-screened in a cinema near the docks of Rochester in Kent with a working-class clientele, it was heckled and laughed at throughout because of the (much parodied) middle-class speech of its protagonists, not to mention its unimpeachably 'correct' morality.[41] Although the film had a certain degree of success at the time, especially in 'the better class halls'[42], it was greatly superseded in popularity by other contemporaneous British films *The Wicked Lady* (1945), *The Seventh Veil* (1945) and *Piccadilly Incident* (1946), which offered versions of the British 'woman's picture' less in thrall to notions of realism and, at least in the case of *The Wicked Lady*, more attuned to blood-and-thunder melodrama and bodice-ripping fantasy.

Brief Encounter may be a national icon, but from the moment of its initial release onwards there have been any number of iconoclasts who have called into question its ability to speak for them and their national identity. Perhaps the critic Gavin Lambert was correct when he called the film a 'definitive document of middle-class repression',[43] the last word on a particular kind of Britishness, specific to a time and a place and most crucially a *class*. Even within the film, we see the operation of a slightly different moral code via the parallel relationship between Myrtle Bagot (Joyce Carey), the station tearoom manageress, and Albert Godby (Stanley Holloway), the guard, who belong to a different social class from Alec and Laura, and are on the whole less inhibited about acting on their feelings for each other. Laura can eavesdrop on Myrtle's discussions with waitress Beryl (Margaret Barton) about leaving her husband and setting up in business with a friend but she cannot envisage doing the same thing herself. These moments are played as comedy, as is Albert's playful slap on Myrtle's behind – which takes place off-screen and is presented through Laura's good-humoured reaction to it – but it also suggests a liberated attitude to sexual relationships inaccessible within Laura's middle-class habitus.

However, it is not just class that is at stake in *Brief Encounter*'s depiction of forbidden love. Andy Medhurst has offered a very persuasive reading of the film in terms of the 'queer authorship' of its writer, Noël Coward. The thwarted relationship at the centre of *Brief Encounter* is heterosexual, but the film's depiction of 'the pain and grief caused by having one's desires destroyed by the pressures of social convention'[44] clearly makes sense as a coded reference to the tribulations of – then still illegal – homosexuality. Several decades on, Richard Kwietniowski's short film *Flames of Passion* (1989) paid homage to *Brief Encounter*'s queer subtext by offering a gay re-imagining of the original film, taking its own title from the torrid blockbuster film that Alec and Laura leave halfway through.

In terms of authorial agency, the film was marketed, reviewed and generally understood as 'Noël Coward's *Brief Encounter*' rather than David Lean's when it was first released. However, it was a sign of Lean's growing confidence as a director in his own right and not just Coward's technician-for-hire that he encouraged the eminent author to rethink the chronological structure of its source, the one-act playlet *Still Life* from his compendium *Tonight at 8.30* (1935). Lean insisted that the original dramatic structure lacked sufficient intrigue and surprise, suggesting that the film version could play with audience expectation by beginning with an enigmatic scene showing the couple's final parting, 'and then you go back and explain that this is the last time they see each other. They were never going to see each other again. And you play the first scene in the picture – it made no sense to you at all and you didn't hear half the dialogue – again, and that's the end of the film.'[45] This narrative strategy comes to full fruition at the end of the film when we return to the beginning with a different and wiser perspective.

Even when we see those events for the first time, we may not realise their full implications but a strong sense of *something* significant taking place is nonetheless conveyed. From its outset, the pounding piano chords of Rachmaninov accompanying the image of an express train thundering past immediately prepare the viewer for an intense experience, even if it is followed by the more homely image of Stanley Holloway checking his pocket watch to reassure himself of the train's punctuality. We may not be able to hear the dialogue of the couple seated at the corner table of the station tearoom, but the incidental dialogue that dominates the soundtrack is anything but incidental. It's full of talk of class infringement (trying to get in a first-class carriage with a third-class ticket) met by punitive authority (the often invoked but never seen stationmaster 'Mr Saunders'). It's while hearing about the malefactor being 'ticked off' and the police being called to sort him out that we first see Alec and Laura, thus subtly preparing us for a story peppered with similar fears about flouting proprieties and violating rules. Myrtle's casual admonishment to Albert that 'time and tide wait for no man' has a more penetrating relevance for the couple about to be torn apart by unforgivingly punctual train departures.[46] When Dolly Messiter (Everly Gregg) bursts in on the couple's final moment of intimate communion over the teacups, it is as obvious 'as though there were a flaming meteor'[47] overhead, in the words of C. A. Lejeune, that a moment of some importance has been interrupted. Our first proper view of Laura's face captures her in a moment of acute social embarrassment: 'Really, you're quite a dark horse. I shall telephone Fred in the morning and make mischief', Dolly teases Laura about her husband, and Celia Johnson's watery smile, although unnoticed by Dolly, suggests an inadvertently accurate guess on Dolly's part. And there's also Alec's firm hand on Laura's shoulder as he leaves, a parting gesture which combines public formality with private resonance, made more special by being captured in close-up. After Alec's departure, Dolly's words, like Albert and Myrtle's before, seem to have a resonance beyond their immediate meaning, especially her mentions of a woman nearly being knocked down and something being 'battered to bits' – rather like Laura.

Laura seems vague and distracted, especially after returning from her brief sojourn outside the tearoom; it won't be until the end of the film that we discover where she went and why. However, on board the train home to Ketchworth, we begin to find out a little more, via one of *Brief Encounter*'s most distinctive features: Laura's confessional and intimate voice-over narration. First instigated in response to Dolly's unstoppable flow of chitchat, it functions to block out Dolly's voice and takes the form of a prayer for a sympathetic listener, 'I wish I could trust you. I wish you were a wise kind friend instead of just a gossiping acquaintance I've known for years and never particularly cared for.' The questing lone brass motif of Rachmaninov's concerto begins and will recur throughout the film's soundtrack as an expression of Laura's desire to confess, to articulate her feelings. Laura's appraisal of Dolly is harsh, as it is of several of the other women who feature in her flashbacks such as 'that awful Mrs Leftwich' she sees in Boots 'wearing one of the silliest hats I've ever seen', the lady musicians and 'that idiot of a waitress' at the Kardomah, a contemptuous cinema usherette, Mary Norton's 'rich over-made-up cousin', or even 'refined' Mrs Bagot. It's intriguing that she identifies so strongly with Donald Duck's 'blind rages', as though there's an anger in her that can find no outlet. Although Dolly is actually very kind to Laura, buying her brandy when she faints (to 'buck you up') and seeing her back to Ketchworth safely, that character's main narrative function is to be a baseline of middle-class, middle-England femininity in all its supposed superficiality and conservatism. Her consumerism ('I've been shopping 'til I'm dropping!'), remarks on servant trouble (her maid Phyllis has left her), her gossipy tone and casual snobbery ('provincial, you know, and very nouveau riche') offer an absolute contrast to Laura's soliloquy, which transcends petit-bourgeois English life and works on a grander scale of deep sorrow and human mortality:

> This can't last – this misery can't last – I must remember that and try to control myself. Nothing lasts really – neither happiness or despair – not even life lasts very long – there will come a time in the future when I shan't mind about this anymore – when I can say quite peacefully and cheerfully 'How silly I was' – No, no – I don't want that time to come ever – I want to remember every minute – always – always – to the end of my days.[48]

This moment's sublime combination of Coward's words, Rachmaninov's music (the delicate but insistent chords played by pianist Eileen Joyce),

Lean's direction (the slow track in on Laura's face, the manipulation of lighting to isolate her in her thoughts), *and* Celia Johnson's vocal and physical performance (the soft, intimate timbre of her speech, so different from her sharper public voice, and her closed eyes during 'always – always', halfway between exhaustion and ecstasy) sets the tone for what is to come.

The quotidian world of a 1930s English housewife, centred on a weekly shopping trip to Milford, with its station tearoom, Boots lending library, cinema and Kardomah café, will be fastidiously recreated by the film (hence its reputation for realism) but so will the emotional depths beneath the apparently banal surface. Laura says at one point 'I'm an ordinary woman – I didn't think such violent things could happen to ordinary people'. But it is precisely that interaction in the film between ordinary suburban mundanity – going to the chemists to buy a toothbrush, having fried sole and soup for lunch at a café – and violent unexpected emotion – falling in love, wanting to die if one cannot be with one's lover – that makes *Brief Encounter* so resonant. And those contradictory extremes have to be contained within Laura (and to a lesser extent Alec) who is, most of the time, unable to express her deepest feelings because she must behave correctly in public. But through her voiceover narration, we are granted privileged access to her inner emotions, which are often in conflict with her outward appearance; in an emblematic phrase from later in the film she says, 'I tried not to show it, but I was quite hysterical inside'. As Richard Dyer argues, 'To see *Brief Encounter* as only cups of tea, banal conversation and guilt is not really to see or hear it at all ... Far from lacking emotion, the film is throbbing with it.'[49] Indeed, the film thrives on the dramatic tension created by simultaneously hiding innermost emotional states while also eloquently 'outpouring' them, whether in meaningful looks and confessional speech, or through expressionistic *mise en scène* or pounding surging orchestral music which articulates the passion felt when words fail.

Brief Encounter's impeccably careful construction is evident in our introduction to Fred (Cyril Raymond), Laura's husband. He is first represented by his bowler hat (stockbroker conformity?) dominating the foreground of the *mise en scène* of the hallway as Laura enters, and then by his disembodied voice calling her. Laura has to attend to her children's disagreement over birthday treats and when she joins her husband downstairs, their discussion also centres on the children. It's only a mention of going to the cinema and the distant sound of a train whistle that forces Laura back into tortured recollection of Alec, and she has to disguise her tears as embarrassment at her fainting spell at the station. Laura helps Fred with the *Times* crossword, providing the missing seven-letter word 'romance'. She knows it's correct because as a 'poetry addict' she knows from memory the line from Keats that provides the clue ('When I behold upon the night's starred face, huge cloudy symbols of a high romance')[50] while by contrast Fred knows it is correct because 'it fits in with delirium and Baluchistan'; fever and foreignness. A concise portrait of a marriage is offered. Ostensibly settled, normal and happy – as Laura rather over-emphatically insists 'we are a happily married couple, and I must never forget that. This is my home, you are my husband and my children are upstairs in bed. I am a happily married woman' – the crossword collaboration nonetheless suggests a profound difference in temperament between husband and wife.

The selection of Rachmaninov on the wireless ushers in the first flashback, as Laura sits with her sewing on her lap and via a very slow lap dissolve is transported back to the refreshment room of Milford Junction station. During this long transition into flashback, Laura is seated with her back to us viewing her memory almost like a film. Remembering Freud and Breuer's note that 'hypnoid states' may 'grow out of the day-dreams which are so common even in healthy people and to which needlework and similar preoccupations render women especially prone',[51] it is tempting to read the romance with Alec as pure fantasy, predicated on a chance meeting with a handsome doctor (a perpetual hero of romantic fiction and female fantasy; Dolly admits her own 'passion for doctors') which is then spun into an elaborate narrative of wish-fulfilment by a woman very attuned to romance narratives, as a keen cinemagoer, reader of romantic fiction and not just a lover of poetry but an 'addict'. Is this whole story nothing more than the compulsive feeding of her addiction?

However, if it is a fantasy, it begins in realist mode, detailing one of Laura's ordinary 'Milford days' just a few weeks ago. The small pleasures of everyday life are suggested by her enjoyment of the clean herbal smell of the chemists and her collection of a new library book by her favourite writer, Kate O'Brien. Even the incident at the station which engineers the first meeting between Alec and Laura is ordinary and un-dramatic – a speck of grit in the eye – although it is caused by a kind of romanticism on Laura's part; the thrill of watching the express train thunder through the station (something that Celia Johnson and David Lean also used to enjoy doing during filming in Carnforth).[52] The pain in Laura's eye and Alec's ability to relieve that pain engenders a brief moment of physical proximity but within the acceptable circumstances of medical attention. Grit removed, doctor and patient say their goodbyes and go about their normal business once more. The next Thursday, they meet again on the way to hospital and grocer's respectively, exchange ironic comments about the 'exciting lives we lead', and part again. A guilt-ridden Laura later wonders if her idle thoughts about the doctor catching his train home were a portent of things to come. But it's only on the following Thursday that circumstances conspire to push them together for longer. Moreover, this occurs when Laura is in a 'reckless and gay' mood, fresh from buying an extravagant birthday present purchase, and enjoying the music from a barrel organ on the street corner and the feel of warm sunshine on her face.

It's fascinating to observe how much the subsequent forging of the bond between Alec and Laura depends upon their shared lampooning of others, often in terms of social inferiority; their shared laughter over the lady musicians at the Kardomah and cinema, over the trashy hyperbole of cinema trailers aimed at the undiscriminating picturegoer, over the conversations between Myrtle and Beryl to which Laura encourages Alec to be an amused eavesdropper. A certain smugness and class-determined fellow-feeling brings them together as much as any nascent flames of passion. The point at which friendship transforms into love occurs during Alec and Laura's conversation about his 'special pigeon' as a medic, his enthusiasm for preventative medicine. Noël Coward's words in *Shadow Play*, another of the *Tonight at 8.30* playlets, apply equally well to what happens in this scene: 'small talk – a lot of small talk with quite different thoughts going on behind it'.[53] Medical explanation is placed in counterpoint to a deeper unspoken communication of longing looks and Laura's sudden unbidden outburst: 'You suddenly look much younger. Almost like a little boy.' It's a touching moment but, once again, it's interesting how the middle-class couple bond over the bodies of the working classes, the debilitating lung diseases of miners and steelworkers just deployed as a conversational vehicle for the couple's growing romantic connection.

Over their next few meetings, Laura oscillates between denial and deprecation of her connection with Alec and a recognition that it may be something momentous, as when she intuits an 'awful feeling of danger' punctuated by the sharp grating sound of train brakes and an enclosing cloud of hissing steam. Laura resolves to undertake preventative medicine of her own by not meeting Alec again but when their next meeting actually fails to happen (because Alec has to attend to an emergency at the hospital), Laura is quick to agree to a rescheduled meeting the following Thursday.

Flames of Passion, the jungle film which had been trailed as the 'stupendous, colossal, gigantic, epoch-making' forthcoming attraction at their first cinema visit, is now the main picture. But its bombastic stylings put off Alec and Laura, with the filmmakers using this meta-cinematic moment to offer their own critique of the ramped-up extremities of Hollywood romance, perhaps in favour of their own more 'realist' approach. Leaving the cinema, the couple head for the botanical gardens and hire a boat to row on its ornamental lake. At this point *Brief Encounter* presents its most direct meditations on national identity, as Laura reflects that 'we should all behave quite differently if we lived in a warm, sunny climate all the time. We shouldn't be so withdrawn and shy and difficult' and later, when Alec falls in the water and has to dry his clothes in the boatman's shed, that 'the British have always been nice to mad people. That boatman thinks we're quite dotty.'[54] Unseasonably warm quasi-foreign weather and a moment of madness lead to a mutual confession of love in the boatshed, just as 'Baluchistan' and 'delirium' led to 'romance' in Fred's crossword. Laura is more resistant to admitting it and acting upon it than Alec, who leads the way, but when he initiates a kiss in the railway underpass she yields to it. But that glorious passionate embrace is interrupted, first by the arrival of other people in the underpass, and then by Fred, breaking into Laura's flashback with a request to turn down the deafeningly loud music. It is, as Richard Dyer suggests, 'a husbandly call to order'[55] just as Laura's romantic self-expression is reaching its zenith.

When Laura's flashback recommences, the barely begun affair seems to be increasingly coloured by guilt and shame. The soundtrack of the second part of the film is even more marked than the first by recurrent aural interruptions: whistles, bells, announcements, and other kinds of alerts and warnings. The affair may in fact have realised its fullest expression not in any physical contact between the lovers but in the fantasies concocted by Laura as she catches her train home the evening after her first kiss with Alec. Lean astutely uses the image of the train window as a screen onto which Laura projects her dreams, gazing both at her own reflection and at the scenery rushing past beyond the glass. She admits that her fantasies are those of 'a romantic schoolgirl' but sets them running all the same, with glamorous scenes in a ballroom, at the Paris Opera, in a gondola in Venice, in an open-top car, on an ocean liner, and even a tropical desert island (not that far removed from the jungle kitsch of *Flames of Passion*). These, Laura says, are 'all the places I've always longed to go', but in the end, rueful realism wins out. The palm trees of her imagination turn back into 'those pollarded willows by the canal just before the level crossing' and Laura gives up her ticket at Ketchworth and walks home 'without wings, without any wings at all', Coward's words made more poignant by Celia Johnson's peerless vocal delivery of them. The closest Laura will come to achieving those dreams is when she drinks champagne with Alec, although the setting is a provincial hotel rather than a French chateau. The open-top car of her daydreams motors through a foreign landscape; although Alec borrows a similar car, it's for a trip to the more homely environs of the English countryside.

When Laura examines her reflection again that evening, romantic reverie has been replaced by self-disgust at her capability first to deceive her husband, then to co-opt her friend Mary Norton into 'the most appalling domestic lie' to cover her tracks. Whereas earlier, the narrative dealt with Laura's self-deception about the depth of her feelings, now it shifts into her deception of others. She discovers she has a remarkable – and perhaps unsuspected – facility for lying, but finds this discovery 'humiliating' and 'degrading'. The enforced mendacity of her situation oppresses Laura, and so does the sexual dimension of an affair. Initially resistant to taking things further, Laura resolves to catch her train home despite Alec's suggestion that they go back to his friend Stephen's empty flat. But she then suddenly relents at the last moment and hurries to meet Alec; Lean often cited the little skip Celia Johnson puts into Laura's step at this moment as evidence of the actress's intuitive brilliance.[56] Back at the flat the couple's meeting is initially awkward, with talk – rich in metaphorical significance – about the damp wood in the grate failing to ignite; although Trevor Howard failed to see the point of the scene's conversational preamble.[57] However, when the flames of passion do finally begin to flicker they are swiftly doused by the arrival of Stephen Lynn. Like 'Mr Saunders' the stationmaster, Stephen had previously been a character frequently mentioned but never seen; only for him to make a sudden and unexpected appearance. His exchange with Alec as Laura scuttles away ashamedly down the tradesman's staircase is a model of English confrontation through insinuation and indirectly expressed anger. Both the casting choice for Stephen (the creepy dead-eyed Valentine Dyall) and the carefully dressed *mise en scène* of the flat, decorated with, amongst other things, a cranial x-ray (an anatomical rather than spiritual view of the human psyche?), conspire to make it, in Lean's words, 'a hostile place, uncosy, unwelcoming ... guilt is all over the place'.[58] *Brief Encounter* is often spoken of in terms of its refusal of sexual passion – Durgnat's 'make tea not love' – but it's important to remember that the non-consummation of Alec and Laura's affair has more to do with unfortunate interruption than moral restraint. As Kevin Maher summarised the film, reviewing it in 2007: 'They did the decent thing but only just.'[59]

Laura runs away and then wanders the streets after her hurried eviction from the flat, finally sitting down on a park bench for a smoke. She

8 Sweet sorrow: Laura (Celia Johnson) and Alec (Trevor Howard) say goodbye in *Brief Encounter* (1945)

notices a policeman looking at her 'rather suspiciously', with the inference that he suspects her of soliciting. It seems that once the respectable middle-class woman has been tainted by illicit sex, her status is rapidly reduced to that of 'common' prostitute. Later that evening, back in the station refreshment room, working-class waitress Beryl reluctantly responds to Laura's request for paper and pen and a nip of brandy, refusing to be deferential to her lady customer, and even leans back on the table swinging her keys in a mocking manner when trying to evict Laura and Alec, looking them up and down with an appraising eye. The coarse world of bum-slapping and cheeky soldiers who make ribald sexual remarks is no longer something that Laura can laugh at, firmly removed from the fray; adopting an attitude of superiority no longer works when you've just been caught almost *in flagrante delicto* yourself. However, the safe return of Alec and Laura to middle-class respectability is assured by their decision to renounce their affair because, as Alec ventriloquises for Laura, 'the feeling of guilt, of doing wrong is too strong, too great a price to pay'.

They resolve to meet one final time, and the sequence that depicts their parting after that sad decision is, I think, one of the loveliest moments in British cinema (Plate 8). Little wisps of steam float across the frame, echoing the loose tendril of hair that moves across Laura's forehead.

Their clasped hands are broken apart by the movement of the departing train, a literal illustration of the fact that the terms of their affair are determined by train timetable. The camera tracks alongside Laura in the window momentarily, fixed on her emotional state, before being left standing as the train pulls away with Laura in it. On the soundtrack, we hear a particularly gentle moment of the Rachmaninov concerto, with soft and delicate solo piano, intermingled with the rhythmic sounds of the departing train and Alec's voice asking 'Thursday?' Laura doesn't answer him, retreating into the carriage's interior as the screen fades to black. Romantic renunciation has seldom looked – or sounded – so bewitchingly beautiful.

This moment in the narrative also marks the point at which *Brief Encounter*'s chronological Mobius strip returns to its beginnings: the present Thursday, which we have already seen in 'real time' rather than via flashback. As Lean planned, when we see the final parting of the couple, cut short by another intruder, Dolly Messiter, we have the benefit of hindsight, and that changes everything. This time we are placed with Alec and Laura, rather than just viewing them as only one aspect of the tearoom's *mise en scène*. Furthermore, what we see is also supplemented by Laura's intimate expository voiceover narration and, to focus our attention further, Lean and cinematographer Robert Krasker manipulate the lighting to plunge Laura's surroundings into shadow during her most extreme moments of introspection. The piercing shriek of the express train's whistle (a sound described perfectly by Eric Lomax as 'that high note of inhuman relief'),[60] and Dolly's perfectly innocent remark 'of course, that doesn't stop, does it?' are matched by a sudden dramatically canted close-up on Laura. When Laura runs from the room, we go with her rather than staying with Myrtle and Dolly as we had before. The express train had called her before – her romantic fondness for watching it thunder past might be a sublimated desire for oblivion – but this time she nearly answers its call, nearly behaves in the manner of an Anna Karenina and throws herself under it. Roger Manvell eloquently described the 'terrifying shot when the express screams by with its windows flashing a staccato rhythm of white lights across Laura's agonised face'[61] before the camera angle untwists, her wildly blown hair settles back again, and the moment of danger passes. As with the non-consummation of the affair, the non-consummation of the suicide occurs not because of a stiffening of moral fibre but something less courageous, according to Laura's narration: 'I wasn't brave enough – I should like to say that it was the thought of you and the children that prevented me – but it wasn't.' Husband and family have become totally marginalised in Laura's pursuit of 'high romance'.

Laura re-enters the refreshment room, and a straight cut – not a slow lingering dissolve – takes us back to her home and the present moment. As Silver and Ursini note, it looks 'as if the abrupt change of scene had jarred her, rudely, awake'.[62] A close-up on Laura's desolate expression is followed by a reaction shot of Fred, the editing suggesting that he may have actually heard her unspoken confession, as though its sheer emotive force has necessarily broken free of its restraints and reached him: 'Whatever your dream was, it wasn't a very happy one, was it?' Cyril Raymond's Fred transcends the character's initial tendencies towards Basil Radford-style caricature to become a more rounded figure; warm and empathetic, he is a genuine rival to Alec rather than a stuffy cipher. But Fred's apparent understanding of Laura's innermost thoughts also makes him a benignly omniscient patriarch. He explains Laura's experience for her, as Alec has repeatedly done before in the film. One of the ironies of a film ostensibly given over to a female authorial voice[63] is that Fred literally has the last word(s): 'You've been a long way away. Thank you for coming back to me.' But Laura has the last sound, her stifled sob finally breaking out after so many weeks of repression before being muffled against her husband's shoulder. Her eloquent, often poetic, voiceover narration has ended but the closing chords of her carefully chosen personal soundtrack of Rachmaninov accompany 'The End'. Contemporary publicity material for *Brief Encounter* presented the final reunion of husband and wife in approvingly traditional terms: 'It is Laura's later acceptance of Fred, and his quiet understanding, that underlies the real strength of her ties to her home – and family life.'[64] However, some decades later, Raymond Durgnat read the same moment less positively, seeing it less as a happy ending and more as 'a nadir of abjectness',[65] the final extinguishing of those flames of passion. It seems to me that the power of the scene comes from that finely nuanced combination of comfort and despair, the warm embrace that might equally be read as suffocation.

One final point. Although it may not be immediately apparent to today's viewer, the cinemagoer of 1945/46 would have recognised instantly that *Brief Encounter* was not a contemporary drama but set a few years earlier, in the pre-war period. The original play *Still Life* was staged in 1936, while the published screenplay for *Brief Encounter* places events in the winter of 1938–39. The film carefully depicts its period milieu with pointed details like Laura and Fred being able to leave their curtains open with lights blazing (no blackout), trains running on time, and no coupons required to buy items like chocolate. The sugar is in the spoon, not on the ration. Indeed, much was made in its publicity material of the film's deployment of dummy chocolate bars, mock icing, and moulded plaster fruit: 'many commodities, now completely forgotten and "off the market" were an everyday sight and L P Williams has made clever improvisation in the minute details of set dressing.'[66] But there is more to *Brief Encounter*'s temporal shift than simple nostalgia for the un-rationed luxuries of the recent past. As Antonia Lant has argued, 'a contemporary audience member could view the film with a sense of historical superiority that appealed to his or her sense of place, knowing that the constructed epoch on the screen had a definite and catastrophic endpoint.'[67] Neither Alec nor Laura seems to realise that their affair is taking place in the larger historical context of the final days before unprecedented global conflict. As the film's publicity material confirms, 'little thought was then given to the approach of war'.[68] With hindsight, the couple's renunciation of each other in favour of stability and continuity is imbued with dramatic irony. 'Wild horses wouldn't drag me away from England and home and all the things one's used to. One has one's roots after all, hasn't one?', Dolly states, a sentiment with which Laura agrees, wide-eyed but rather half-heartedly. But the world is about to change immeasurably, and roots are about to be ripped up, no matter what one couple chooses to do.

Brief Encounter gains a great deal of its resonance from the specificities of its chronology and its timing, set in an England on the cusp of the Second World War and then being made just as that war was finally drawing to a close. It is very much a film of its moment, whose appeal for modern audiences partly derives from its ability to be a time capsule of vanished manners and attitudes; in critic William Cook's words, it has become a 'metaphor for an idea of England that has almost completely disappeared'.[69] But *Brief Encounter* is also more than that. The terror and shame sparked by adultery might have receded in the intervening years but, as Richard Dyer so rightly points out, 'many of the emotions it mobilises are not in fact things of the past: betrayal and deception, divided loyalties, the pull between safety and excitement, cosiness and abandon'.[70] Few films animate the eternal conflict between restraint and abandon as vividly or as movingly as *Brief Encounter*. What film critic Joan Lester said of it in 1945 still rings equally true today: 'This film lives.'[71]

The Passionate Friends (1949)

The Passionate Friends was initially conceived and scripted by Ronald Neame and Eric Ambler, adapting a novel by H. G. Wells. However, it would become subject to a kind of unofficial coup at Cineguild when David Lean and Stanley Haynes persuaded Neame to relinquish the project and let them take over, subjecting Neame to professional humiliation which provoked near-suicidal despair.[72] Thereafter, Neame and Anthony Havelock-Allan would begin to withdraw from Cineguild, setting in train the company's ultimate demise. Cineguild would, in any case, soon be subject to the chill wind of John Davis's desire for absolute cost-efficiency at the Rank Organisation; quite a contrast with J. Arthur Rank's warm lenience. Thus *The Passionate Friends* marked the beginning of the end of a professional alliance which had enabled David Lean to become one of the most respected of directors in 1940s British cinema. The casting of Ann Todd in the film – ironically, secured by Neame and Ambler's original script – would also mark a new beginning for Lean himself, since Todd was soon to become the director's third wife, and the star of this and his next two films, *Madeleine* and *The Sound Barrier*. The couple's first meeting on the set of *The Passionate Friends* was recalled in the most dramatic and indeed mythic terms by Todd: 'Then on "action", strapped to the camera crane, he swooped down out of the darkness like Jupiter on Leda into a close-up of me. It was sudden, dramatic and possessive – and my introduction to David Lean.'[73]

If *The Passionate Friends* was a harbinger of the future in some ways, in others it looked backwards, recalling Lean's earlier film, *Brief Encounter*. Both films focus on a woman torn between her husband and her lover, and driven almost to the point of suicide before reconciling herself to marital fidelity. Both films make use of flashback structures that play with chronology and both employ female voiceover narration. However, *Brief Encounter*'s decidedly ordinary milieu of 'railways and respectability, rain and Rachmaninov'[74] had been exchanged in *The Passionate Friends* for something glossier and more upmarket. Laura Jesson's middle-class tweediness was replaced by a heroine with an 'expensive wardrobe and aristocratic manner',[75] while Milford Junction's cramped refreshment room had given way to an expansive hotel terrace on the sunny shores of Lake Annecy.

The 1913 novel by H. G. Wells covered events of the late nineteenth and early twentieth centuries, but Lean's adaptation moved it forward into the 1930s and 1940s. Its newly contemporary setting is evident in the film's opening scenes, with its heroine Mary Justin (Ann Todd) revelling in the ready availability of rationed or scarce commodities such as butter, white bread, cream and fresh fruit as soon as her aircraft takes off and leaves British restrictions behind. The sudden abundance delights Mary and matches her excited anticipation of what is to come: 'a holiday! A holiday in Switzerland.' *The Passionate Friends* deliberately deploys a tourist gaze, aiming to provide vicarious enjoyment for audiences undergoing British austerity. Its very first establishing shots provide panoramic postcard-style views of Mary's destination, Alpine lakes and snow-capped mountains, before going on to show the shoreline 'Hotel Splendide' re-opening for business. The focus then shifts back to the tourist on her way there, pictured glamorously attired in her stylish veiled hat and comfortably seated in the plane while through the window the landscape whips past her and eventually falls away as she becomes airborne. The composition of the shot recalls Laura's romantic daydreams in *Brief Encounter*, which used the train window as a screen on which to project her exotic romantic fantasies of foreign travel. But here, prosaic train has been substituted for exciting plane and Mary's foreign travel is real rather than imagined.

Upon arrival, Mary finds that her room (with a view) is as beautiful as she had hoped, but the guest about to take up the adjoining room is, unbeknownst to her, her former lover Stephen Stratton (Trevor Howard). Unaware that Stephen is only a few feet away, she is nonetheless thinking about him and their chance encounter on 'a new year's eve nine years ago'. Thus begins the first of the film's many and often highly complex flashback sequences. Reviewers of *The Passionate Friends* at the time of its release often singled out this feature of the film as problematic. Comparing it unfavourably with Lean's previous romance, the *Evening Standard*'s Milton Shulman called *The Passionate Friends* a 'brief encounter with inflammation of the flashback' which 'would appear to have been shot with a time machine rather than a camera'.[76] Its flashbacks within flashbacks were unnecessarily confusing for the *News of the World*'s reviewer, who describes 'trying to extricate Wells' eternal triangle from David Lean's maze'.[77] The *Sunday Dispatch*'s critic simply fumed 'enough Mr Lean! Get on with your story!'[78] However, the temporal intricacies of *The Passionate Friends*, going far beyond the more straightforward chronological manipulation in *Brief Encounter*, have the effect of turning the film into a meditation on the processes of memory. As Anderegg suggests, the film's style 'sets up reverberations among past and present events that break down accepted categories like cause and effect, before and after, now and then'.[79] Recollections beget more recollections until the film isn't merely a matter of a woman reminiscing over the great lost love of her life (although it is that too) but a reflection on how she has *turned* him into the great love of her life through the process of reminiscence and her creation of potent and often highly romanticised memory-images of that romance.

Eric Ambler recalled how David Lean and Stanley Haynes were both in psychoanalysis, 'going to sessions every day' during the time they were preparing *The Passionate Friends*. Lean's analysis, under Dr Willi Hoffer, had begun during the production of *Oliver Twist* and would continue unabated for the next three years.[80] Lean's second wife Kay Walsh later reflected that while Lean 'didn't like analysis ... it's very painful facing up to who you really are', he had entered into it because of a deeply felt internal conflict: 'I think he really did want to hang on to something normal, healthy and substantial – clock-winding and sharpening the knife for the Sunday joint. He was very aware that with this fire burning inside him something very destructive could happen. He was always on the verge of it.'[81] Ambler noted how, during the re-scripting of *The Passionate Friends*, the director 'tried to work his analyst's observations into the film';[82] one way, perhaps, of making a 'stolen' project his own. The influence of psychoanalysis permeates Lean's filmmaking during those three years: *Madeleine* in particular was redolent with self-conscious Freudian symbolism particularly fixed on Emile's cane. In the specific case of *The Passionate Friends*, knowledge of Lean's psychoanalysis lends a new resonance to the film's evocations of memory, and its emphasis on an obsessive return to the past which determines and dominates the present.

The first set of flashbacks-embedded-within-flashbacks in the film begins with Mary's memory of the New Year's Eve Chelsea Arts Ball welcoming in the year 1939, and a slowly falling cluster of balloons (filled with a special mixture of compressed air and hydrogen to make them fall unnaturally slowly).[83] Former lovers Mary and Stephen are reunited in the noisy scrum on the dancefloor, shouting their greetings to each other and embracing affectionately. The melee in which they are engulfed is observed from a balcony above by Mary's husband Howard (Claude Rains), underlit and in opera cloak, closely resembling the sinister figure of Bela Lugosi's Count Dracula. When Mary returns to Howard in their private balcony, their more decorous celebrations of the new year are intercut with the raucous Auld Lang Syne below. The kiss from her husband, a restrained peck on the cheek, contrasts sharply with the warm spontaneity of Stephen's embrace. While Howard enjoys his position as surveyor of the crowds (commenting that the revellers look like they're suspended from the ceiling by wires – his puppets?), Mary's yearning looks suggest that she would rather be a participant.

In the cab home, Mary's face is almost totally obscured by dark shadows, and as in her lakeside hotel room, darkness begets memories of Stephen; now memories within memories. A slow dissolve ushers in a highly romanticised image of Mary and Stephen's faces reflected in a pool of water. 'Will you always love me Mary?', Stephen asks. 'Always', Mary replies, as the swelling orchestral score accompanies their kiss, only for sound and image to be curtailed by the sharp sound of the car's brakes, jolting Mary out of her memory and back into the present moment. However, she soon slips back into reminiscence mode, and even further into romantic territory. The camera tilts down from a hazy soft-focus canopy of leaves to find Mary and Stephen lying beneath the trees, looking up. Stephen recites from Keats's *Endymion* – 'but at the tip-top, there hangs by unseen film, an orbed drop of light' – and Mary completes the line as she clasps Stephen's hand, 'and that is love'; like her romantic predecessor Laura Jesson, Mary knows her Keats. But again, the beauty of the memory (within a memory) is broken up by prosaic reality; the taxi door opening as they arrive home. The editing here is quite superbly sharp, underlining the dislocation felt by the heroine.

Later, ensconced in her neat twin bed next to Howard's, the bedside clock rapidly ticking away the seconds, trees outside casting wavering shadows across her face, Mary's thoughts turn again to the past and to Stephen, this time conjuring up a memory of their separation, the end of the affair. Alone in a moonlit room, the couple dance to a gramophone record. Although Mary insists she will never love anyone as much as she loves Stephen, she still turns down his marriage proposal. 'If two people love each other, they want to be together, they want to belong to each other', Stephen urges, but Mary corrects him: 'Stephen, I want to belong to myself.' She pleads with him: 'Why can't there be love without this clutching, this gripping?' Mary's desire for independence makes sense in the context of Wells's original novel, with its lengthy meditations on free love (partly inspired by Wells's affair with Rebecca West) and stinging critique of the lot of women, their enforced destiny as 'pretty silken furry feathery jewelled *silences*'.[84] But at the time of the film's release, such feminist sentiments seem to have been met with impatience or incredulity. 'This film has no core of feeling' complained the *News Chronicle*, while the *Daily Mail* made a guess 'that the average woman, if there is such a person, will sharply decide that there is little wrong with this silly girl that the back of a hairbrush would not swiftly put right'.[85] The *Daily Herald*'s reviewer briskly summed up the heroine as 'one of those girls who want to have their cake and eat it too'.[86] If Laura's dilemma in *Brief Encounter* had been fairly clear-cut, Mary's seems far more opaque. Publicity material for *The Passionate Friends* tried to clarify it as 'the story of a woman's conflict between love and emotional security', in which the heroine cannot 'reconcile herself to a future in which possessive love takes the place of personal freedom and security', and so 'she turns her back on romance',[87] but this is far more abstract and far less compelling a dilemma than the lonely passion of Laura Jesson. Instead, as John Orr observes, the film offers something more akin to an art film like Resnais' *Last Year in Marienbad* (1961), another film which makes 'love enigmatic and time problematic'.[88]

This sense of opacity and obscurity is only exacerbated by the casting of Ann Todd in the role, astutely described as 'wistful, fastidious, passive', a 'moon actress', by Raymond Durgnat.[89] Todd's stardom had been built on notions of enigma, a template set by her breakthrough role as Francesca in *The Seventh Veil* (1945) whose desires are unfathomable even to herself until revealed under hypnosis (and then they turn out to be rather perversely masochistic). She had been hailed in France as 'la petite Garbo', and her silky blonde glamour was something quite different for British films, as a 1945 article in *Picture Post* noted, describing her as 'the nearest thing to a star, in the Hollywood sense, that we have yet confected' in comparison to Britain's other 'well-known screen actresses – the Margaret Lockwoods, the Phyllis Calverts – [who] remained leading ladies, gracious, charming, competent no doubt, but leading ladies, not stars'.[90] But Todd's aura of mystery and transcendence from earthly concerns sometimes seems to work against the creation of sympathy for her character in *The Passionate Friends*.

Stephen's response to Mary's desire to belong to herself is to tell her baldly 'your life will be a failure'. The same words are repeated as Mary wakes from her recollection, standing in judgement on her current choice of life as a trophy wife in a marriage of convenience. A montage sequence shows both ex-lovers, going about their usual lives, unable to stop thinking of each other, leading irresistibly towards an ostensibly innocent lunch invitation for old times' sake. But Mary and Stephen's lunch stretches out into evening, and they slip back into an easy familiarity, reanimating their previous conversational intimacy. The mood shifts when Mary plays a phrase on Stephen's piano and the framing of the shot makes Mary, and the viewer, suddenly aware of the erotic potential of Stephen's bodily proximity. Just as Lean would present one of the most revelatory emotional moments in *The Bridge on the River Kwai* almost counter-intuitively through a shot of the character's back rather than his face, here too the couple's slow inching towards romantic reunion is presented via a shot of their backs as they both gaze out from Stephen's balcony at the darkening skies. When Mary turns to face Stephen, and the couple kiss, the camera suddenly elevates as if to convey their mutual sense of elation and it tracks towards them to frame their kiss tightly, suggesting the exclusion of everything else in their world at this moment.

All this occurs while Mary's husband Howard, a banker, is away on business in Berlin. As John Orr suggests, 'the war itself is an absent-presence'[91] throughout the film and, given that the year is 1939, there is a strong suggestion of appeasement for the purposes of financial expedience in his actions, even if he does regard the Germans as 'a dangerous mob'. Howard's absence enables Mary and Stephen to pursue their relationship reasonably freely, and certainly much less furtively than Laura and Alec's cramped courtship conducted according to the dictates of branch line timetable. A higher level of affluence *and* a different model of morality are in evidence here. Where Alec and Laura reach their decision to part permanently over teacups in a suburban station buffet, Stephen and Mary decide that she will leave her husband over brandy balloons at a classy-looking supper club.

Upon his return, Howard begins to suspect his wife of adultery, with his disillusionment and the confirmation of his worst suspicions presented in a series of compelling sequences. It begins when Howard is dictating a letter to his secretary but his thoughts keep returning to his wife's forgotten theatre tickets (she is meant to be seeing a musical comedy 'First Love'). The letter's contents seem strangely relevant to his current state of mind, culminating in the phrase 'earlier protestations had been quite insincere' being immediately followed by a telling shot of his wife's photograph. Finally he picks up the theatre tickets on the table with a snap, acting as a sound bridge to the theatre where Howard hopes to have his fears allayed. When he sees the two unoccupied theatre seats – shocking confirmation of his wife's dishonesty – stage lights strobe across his face and a tinny cymbal strikes incessantly. His pain and humiliation is heightened by its mocking juxtaposition with the musical's lightweight theme tune ('my first love's the best love of all') and audience applause.

Back home, the scene of confrontation that follows between Howard and the lovers is very carefully choreographed, in terms of composition of figures within the frame (often symbolically triangulated; Plate 9), camera movement, and editing (it was a textbook example of the craft for Karel Reisz and Gavin Millar[92]). The sequence's meticulous craftsmanship mimics Howard's own careful engineering of the situation in which the lovers' perfidy will be exposed; as Lean put it, he is 'having them on toast' and it's 'rather a sadistic scene'.[93] Howard invites Stephen in for a drink leaving the evidence of their deceit (a theatre programme) on the table for his wife to see. Just as with Stephen Lynn and Alec Harvey in the flat in *Brief Encounter*, anger is expressed indirectly, through insinuation and sarcasm. Howard takes Stephen's coat for him then contemptuously tosses it aside. His offer of 'ice?' in their drinks is pure intimidation masquerading as polite hospitality. As in the dictation scene earlier, ostensibly neutral observations are loaded with meaning, from that word 'ice' to Mary's comment that the irises sent by the florist are 'spiky and unfriendly' (analogous to her or possibly Howard?). Howard's comments on the German and Italian governments' 'taste for intrigue', 'pathetic faith in themselves' and 'romantic hysteria' obviously relate as much to his faithless wife and her lover as to their immediate referents. The truth out, Stephen is ejected from the house, leaving husband and wife together to work out their problems.

Mary's planned escape from her loveless marriage does not materialise and she decides to stay with Howard. Her motivations seem rather enigmatic (assuming she is not purely mercenary) and, as Michael Anderegg observes, in Mary we have 'a character who, although at the centre of her own narrative, remains essentially mysterious'.[94] When Stephen comes to rescue her, she tells him that while she wants his love she also wants 'the affection and security Howard could give me'. 'Do you always want to belong to yourself?' asks Stephen (again), prompting Mary to flee upstairs. She throws herself on her opulent, neatly made single bed, and sobs, the camera tracking back to isolate her further. This moment of emotional dejection ends the flashback and the film returns to the Hotel Splendide with the tortured backstory of Mary and Stephen's relationship firmly established.

It seems inevitable that the ex-lovers staying in adjoining rooms will meet. When it happens on the sunny breakfast terrace the next morning, once again (a recurring phrase when discussing this film) their pretence at plain friendliness disguises a deeper connection. There follows an

9 The love triangle of *The Passionate Friends* (1949): Mary (Ann Todd), Howard (Claude Rains) and Stephen (Trevor Howard)

idyllic day out, making the most of what might be their last chance to make amends for the past. It begins with a rapturous speedboat ride on the lake, leaving white-water in its wake, followed by an ascent above the clouds and into the mountains via cable car. 'White is the colour of Lean's muse', Raymond Durgnat once observed,[95] and *The Passionate Friends* offers a particularly pronounced example of the director's predilection for *film blanc*, lovingly capturing the pale, fair-haired beauty of Ann Todd, often wearing white, and making use of recurrent motifs of bright sunlight, spray, cloud and snow. One particularly striking moment has the couple passing through a band of cloud. As they stand side by side in the cable car, semi-obscured by the surrounding mist, Mary tells Stephen he looks like a ghost, which is true in a way – a spectre from her former life and what might have been if she had made a different choice years ago. Among these 'cloudy symbols of a high romance', they discuss their respective marriages and the fact that they have found happiness, before the moment passes. They have broken through the clouds to their final destination: a mountaintop picnic.

Where the film had previously been dominated by flashbacks, now there are flash-forwards or visions of an alternative reality, Mary's daydreams. While Stephen prepares the picnic, Mary drifts into a reverie. First she imagines hearing herself and Stephen saying marriage vows, and then she envisages a different version of their cable car trip in which Stephen tells her 'I could never marry anyone but you' and they kiss passionately. However, she cheerfully dismisses her thoughts as 'dreaming nonsense', a lost cause. The irony is that at the moment of Mary's personal settlement with the choice she made nine years before, Howard arrives back at the hotel sooner than expected. Lean directs a gripping suspense sequence, once again centred on Howard's dictation of a letter to his secretary, but with the banker half-distracted from the task and picking up his binoculars to view distant sights. The secretary knows that Mary and Stephen are (innocently) spending the day together and are about to return, and fears that Howard will spot them in the distance. After several heart-stopping false alarms, it is the secretary's anxious gaze that gives the game away, prompting him to look at what she's looking at: his wife disembarking from a boat with Stephen and their farewell kiss. Reeling from the shock of another perceived betrayal, he is haunted by warped images of passionate kisses between Mary and Stephen, his shifty-looking secretary, a smarmy, knowing concierge, all conspiring to cuckold him. His humiliation is capped when Mary rushes past him, unseen, to wave goodbye to Stephen's departing boat from her room, clearly besotted in a way she has never been by him. Howard watches her, as though watching a play or a film, as she desperately waves her scarf, and then turns away, half-obscured by the voile curtain, dejected and with tears in her eyes. Too late she sees him and immediately he leaves, slamming the door behind him. A matching sound bridges the transition to the next image: a typewriter carriage return slamming across a divorce petition for Justin vs. Justin.

A race then ensues between Mary and Howard's lawyers to be the first to contact Stephen with the damaging news. Both parties use every form of modern telecommunication – communiqués overheard among a babel of voices carried by the telegraph wires – but the lawyers get there first, presenting Stephen with the legal papers when he is met at Victoria station by his wife. Mary can only observe from the shadows as Stephen and his wife argue, their conversation drowned out by loud train noises. In a trancelike state, Mary wanders into what she calls 'some sort of restaurant' but which is clearly a fairly ordinary café, and her non-comprehension of this fact, and annoyance at 'a man who kept asking me for money' (behind the counter, to pay for her cup of tea) demonstrate a certain ethereal inability to operate in the real world. Maybe she did make the right choice all those years ago; she is dependent on the cushioning provided by Howard's wealth, the 'security' it provides from prosaic reality.

Desperate for an answer and rebuffed in her attempts to plead with the lawyers, Mary, like Laura before her, is drawn towards railway tracks, and suicide, as the only means of escape. She attempts one last time to persuade Howard to call off the divorce to prevent Stephen's ruin but Howard responds with a vituperative demolition of Mary's 'love and kindness and loyalty' towards her husband: 'it was the love you give a dog, and the kindness you give a beggar, and the loyalty of a bad servant.' Claude Rains's performance of wounded pride and unsuspected vulnerability is particularly superb here, with echoes of his usurped lover Alex Sebastian in *Notorious* (1946). As in many Lean films, this moment of emotional revelation is presented with the speaker turned away from the camera. But this has an additional purpose here; he doesn't realise that the latter part of his confession, that he had unexpectedly fallen in love with Mary, goes unheard. Mary has already fled the house for the street, dwarfed in a high angle shot by the sign for a London Underground station, the destination that is calling her. As she enters, the station's numbered signs present a horizontal countdown, 5–4–3–2–1, and an arrow to a 'way out'. The noise of an incoming train rumbles below and disarrays Mary's hair, a sign that her glacial poise has deserted her. She glides past the ticket inspector, ignoring his request for her ticket, and continues her descent on the escalator, not looking back. The film had begun with holiday excitement and ascent into the clouds on a plane; it ends with a death-driven downward movement beneath the earth. Mary drifts through thick crowds of disembarking passengers like a sleepwalker. Once she reaches the platform, there is little noise apart from the whistle of a workman. The signs and lights announce the arrival of a train, and are intercut with a close-up of Mary, isolated further by bands of dark shadow above and below her white face. A shot of the curving skeletal rail, accompanied by the nearing sound of the train, is followed by an even tighter close-up of her face, her eyes and billowing hair picked out in striplight. She closes her eyes and begins to fall forward, semi-ecstatically, into her suicide but is pulled back from the brink at the last moment. The immediate cut reveals that her rescuer is Howard, holding Mary tightly while her fine-boned face jolts and shudders, indicating her extreme inner agonies. This is the point where the cool impassive Todd seems to come fully to life, most expressive when being pushed – sadistically – to her limit, as with *The Seventh Veil*. Something akin to the Hitchcockian approach to icy blondes seem to be at work here – and in fact Todd came to this film fresh from working with Hitchcock on *The Paradine Case* (1947). Moreover, given the psychoanalytically inflected context of the film's production, and the burgeoning relationship between director and star, it seems reasonable to see in *The Passionate Friends* a more personal investigative quest, to get behind the cool surface not only of Mary Justin but also of Ann Todd.

In an echo of 'well-meaning, interfering' Dolly Messiter, an elderly lady bystander asks 'is anything the matter, can I help?', but Howard gently escorts his wife to a nearby bench, where the two of them sit down together (underneath a briefly glimpsed advertisement for Guinness ironically urging 'Keep Smiling'). Mary begins to sob and Howard comforts her, displaying the greatest degree of physical closeness in the film. 'Shall we go home now?' Howard asks and Mary, like Pip before her and Lawrence after her, repeats the word 'home' with interrogative disbelief. The lone sound of the whistler on the platform is then displaced by the orchestral score which now surges to accompany the couple's upward movement, holding onto each other closely. Mary had remarked earlier in the film about 'the pleasure of walking arm in arm with a man' and Howard rather than Stephen now fulfils that role.

In Wells's novel, Mary Justin commits suicide, upholding the author's belief that society always destroys the liberated woman. In this adaptation, Mary lives but one might read her fate in a variety of ways. For John Orr, the film's ending is decisive and boldly reactionary: 'the triumph of the patriarch'.[96] However, I read its conclusion in more ambivalent terms, like the ending of its sister picture, *Brief Encounter*. Fervent love is forsaken in favour of homely security and the losses as well as the gains entailed in that choice remain all too apparent. But despite its definite resemblance to *Brief Encounter* in some respects, *The Passionate Friends* retains a distinctive identity of its own, as the comments of its more positive reviewers at the time indicated. For *The Times*, it moved 'up and down like the erratic temperature of a feverish patient' lacking 'the easy unforced line of *Brief Encounter*',[97] while the *Express* found it 'a butterfly of a film – and not an easy one to put a net over. It keeps fluttering around, showing the gossamer brilliance of its wings, but somehow it never gets close enough to be pinned down.'[98] Although *The Passionate Friends* was being gently criticised for its lack of steadiness and certainty, by choosing to compare the film to a gorgeous shimmering butterfly or an unsettling fever dream, the critics also managed to suggest something of its particular and peculiar powers.

Summer Madness (1955)

Summer Madness – known as *Summertime* in the US – marked the transitional point between the two stages of David Lean's career: the 'small' British films up to that point and the international epics in the years to come. If its promotional taglines were to be believed, the film promised an experience defined by expanse: 'Big romance ... big spectacle ... big suspense ... In Eastman colour'. Shot entirely on location in Venice, it outranked the foreign interludes of Lean's earlier *The Passionate Friends* and *The Sound Barrier* and also marked Lean's return to colour photography after the bold early experiments of *This Happy Breed* and *Blithe Spirit*. By 1955, the technology was no longer exceptional in Hollywood, with 61 per cent of major studio productions made in colour.[99] Even so, its renewed use connoted something significant in Lean's career: his decisive move towards lovingly rendered large-scale foreign spectacle. After Lean had experienced this style of runaway production, returning to a British studio would be, he said, 'like going down a mine'[100] and so he scarcely did so for the remainder of his career.

Summer Madness was based on Arthur Laurents's 1952 play *The Time of the Cuckoo* about a middle-aged unmarried American woman on vacation who finds herself seduced by Venice and by one particular Venetian, a married shopkeeper. For the film version of the play, adapted by Lean and H. E. Bates, small, stout Shirley Booth who had played the female lead on stage gave way to tall, wiry Katharine Hepburn, a different kind of spinster altogether. Being able to cast a major American star like Hepburn indicated Lean's growing stature as a filmmaker, but what

Richard Dyer referred to as the 'powerfully inescapably present, always-already-signifying nature'[101] of the star's persona impinges much more, playing a major role in determining the meaning of the text. In the case of Katharine Hepburn, a famed Hollywood maverick, this meant that her character in *Summer Madness* inevitably carried with her traces of the star's reputation for unconventionality, independence and integrity. Hepburn's perceived difference from Hollywood's feminine norms was emphasised in one review of the film, which described the star as 'the Garbo of the great outdoors ... freckled by the sun, shiny with the rain and roughened by the wind. Her lean Olympic legs are made for striding uphill, not curving fatly on the pin-up settee. She has fuzzy hair, carpenter's hands and a nose which defies make-up.'[102] In her earlier career, her image and very particular beauty had often been figured in terms of the amazon or 'virgin goddess' to cite *The Philadelphia Story* (1939). Continually typed as headstrong, Hepburn's films reiterated the need for her to be humanised by a rougher complementary male, exemplified by her frequent teaming with Spencer Tracy. As Hepburn aged, the virgin goddess slowly metamorphosed into the old maid. This type could be a doughty, admirable figure, echoing Hepburn's off-screen status as a survivor. She might have lost her youthful bloom but the ageing process only seemed to distil and sharpen her remarkable angular looks, dominated by cheekbones deemed 'the greatest calcium deposit since the white cliffs of Dover'.[103] But the cultural connotations around the old maid, especially in the 1950s, were not generally positive. Hepburn was continually cast in those roles in the later decades of her career. Andrew Britton identifies her 1950s films, among them *The African Queen* (1951) and *The Rainmaker* (1956), as a 'spinster cycle';[104] *The Iron Petticoat* (1956) stands as a representative title with its suggestion of forbidding, impenetrable femininity. Britton persuasively reads these films as a way to 'punish the independent woman by redefining her as a frustrated spinster and getting her to acknowledge what she has always really wanted',[105] namely a man. Her show of autonomy must be revealed as a defence mechanism and a barrier to true fulfilment, and relentlessly broken down. To a certain extent, this describes very well the narrative of *Summer Madness*. And yet I think to read it simply in terms of the ritual humiliation of a spinster is to miss some of its deepest resonances. Lean described *Summer Madness* as his personal favourite among his own films and his most personal film: 'I've put more of myself into that film than any other I've ever made.'[106] In *Summer Madness*, as in several other 'women's films' made by Lean, the female protagonist is less a cultural scapegoat and more a powerful vehicle for authorial identification and self-expression.

Jane Hudson is presented to us first as a director, a definite sign of Lean's personal investment in the character. Lean, who once said cameras were 'like a friend'[107] to him, was a notably avid amateur filmmaker and photographer, shooting countless reels of cine-footage when travelling across the globe, and applying the same meticulous craftsmanship to his home movies as he did to his professional work. Jane is similarly fastidious in her filmmaking. She directs the very first shot that we see, accompanied by her off-screen instructions to her 'actor', fellow train passenger (Andre Morell), getting him to hold up the cover of her guidebook to Venice ('in a little closer, up a little higher') so she can use it as her movie's establishing shot. As her train steams over the lagoon into Venice, she enthuses 'oh boy, gotta get a shot of this!', thinking in terms of cinematic spectacle – a born director. It is her desire to get a perfectly framed shot that will later cause her to fall backwards into the canal in the film's most famous moment. Our first sight of Jane in the film is with cine-camera clamped to her eye, and so strongly are we encouraged to identify with Jane's 'kino-eye' that some of the film's most visually sumptuous views of Venice are presented as though coming diegetically through her camera, accompanied by its whirring sound and her 'voiceover'.

As well as being somewhat bossy, Jane adopts a masculine physical stance, straddling seats to get the best shot. The film's presentation of Jane in these initial moments plays on recognisable aspects of the Hepburn persona – her disregard for conventional femininity – but it also belongs to a long-standing tradition of British caricaturing of Americans. It's no accident that Jane is played off against Morell's reserved *Horse and Hound*-reading English gentleman making gentle fun of her brash manner and guileless (and slightly materialistic) enthusiasm for her European holiday: 'Like it? I've got to. I've come such a long way. I've saved up such a long time for this trip.'

But this slightly superior lampooning of an ingenuous heroine isn't sustained for very long. Soon the film pitches us right into Jane's experiences through her eyes, using shots indicating her point of view. As she arrives at Venice's central station, the sheer noise and the density of bodies are presented as near to overwhelming but then the sound dims and the camera pulls back for a wider shot as Jane emerges into the heart of Venice; a brief moment of quiet revelation among the clamour. Boarding the floating bus she is quickly recognised as a fellow American tourist by another couple, the McIlhennys (MacDonald Parke and Jane Rose), and henceforth they, rather than Jane, become the butt of the film's anti-American jokes about American tourists in Europe. They are all Midwesterners – Jane from Akron, Ohio, the McIlhennys from Kankakee, Illinois – and all tourists, but just as with Dolly in *Brief Encounter*, Lloyd and Edith McIlhenny become the standard version of their type against which the more exceptional heroine can be defined. The McIlhennys have a relentless and packed itinerary taking in all of Europe within the space of a couple of months, with only a few hours each day devoted to 'I. A., Independent Activity'. Lloyd McIlhenny's philistinism is confirmed by his comment that Venice is 'just Luna Park on water', while by comparison Jane is breathlessly impressed by the superb views from the canal: 'Isn't that wonderful?' From now on, Jane's recourse to her camera no longer suggests a crass commodification of Europe's splendours. Rather, it indicates her fervent desire to imbibe fully all that the city has to offer, to commit it to celluloid memory, from its ancient palatial façades and magnificent domed churches to a chance encounter with waterborne firefighters responding to an alarm. Their boat is red, the first significant flash of that colour in Venice, the colour that will recur throughout the film as an invitation to excitement but also danger; it is the colour of the glass goblet she is drawn to, the colour of the single shoe she later abandons, Cinderella-style.

Jane is seduced by the sights and also, crucially, the sounds of Venice with *Summer Madness* eschewing 'Ruskin's silent stones' in favour of a much noisier city.[108] As Jane is led by her porter through a tight alleyway between high-sided houses, the camera tilts up to frame the narrow strip of blue sky above while the soundtrack is a rich and beguiling mixture of ambient noise: conversation, laughter, a singing lesson, piano, a dog barking, footsteps. When Jane reaches her destination, the Pensione Fiorini, its view of the canal with gondolas sailing past is so ravishing, her involuntary sigh takes over her whole body. It is the first of many moments of rapturous contemplation. Her reaction is similar when she is presented with her room with an astonishing view over the city's rooftops stretching out across the lagoon to Murano. Lean clearly heeded Alexander Korda's advice not to neglect the city's landmarks: 'They're not a cliché for nothing. For God's sake don't be shy of showing these famous places.'[109] At moments like these, the film amply fulfils the hopes the Venetian authorities had of it that it would help to attract tourists to their city; in fact, it more than doubled visitor numbers according to Stephen Silverman.[110] Publicity material for *Summer Madness* also made pains to emphasise the tourism angle, with promotional tie-ins to manufacturers of suitcases and other travel accessories and Italian guidebooks and maps, all encouraging foreign holidays.[111] The pressbook boasted of 'The world's most fabulous city as you've never seen it' and Lean aimed to create aesthetic 'eyefuls', his own phrase for such moments of spectacle.[112] Many critics, Dilys

Powell among them, responded to the film in kind: 'The eye is endlessly ravished.'[113] Reviewers waxed rhapsodic over its stunning evocation of Venice: 'the beauty, the colour, the evanescent shadow patterns, the opulence of the famous architecture cheek-by-jowl with the city's dark by-ways ... in an effort to capture the transience of the moment, the million fleeting fragments of which make up the glory, past present and future that is Venice, Mr Lean has filmed some of the loveliest scenes of the city ever, surely, to appear in the cinema.'[114] However, the film does not shy away from showing the less salubrious side of the city. One of Jane's beautiful daydreams is shattered by the sudden emptying of a slop bucket from a great height into the limpid blue-green water. *Summer Madness* shows us the incomparable beauty of the Doge's Palace and the Bridge of Sighs but banal and dirty human life goes on; there's still a slop bucket to empty, or a television aerial on a tenement roof, or a homeless child selling dirty postcards and begging cigarettes. The film gets a lot of dramatic mileage out of this juxtaposition, alternately evoking Venice's extraordinary loveliness *and* its capacity to be a setting for venality, echoing Jane's own movement between the two extremes of enchantment and repulsion.

Settling into her hotel with an Italian-American cocktail of Cinzano and bourbon, Jane chats with its owner Signora Fiorini (Isa Miranda) disclosing desires that go far beyond the usual tourist agenda of 'seeing things and getting some culture' or 'buying perfume cheap'. Instead she hopes to remedy a much deeper lack, expressed through the proxy of 'a girl I met on the boat': 'But way back, way way back in the back of her mind was something she was looking for ... a wonderful mystical magical miracle ... I guess to find what she'd been missing all her life.' For Jane, Europe is much more than an authenticated Luna Park. As so often in fictional relationships between the new and old worlds, Europe promises to round out the spiritual and sensual education of an American pilgrim. Jane's desire for a magical miracle is teamed with a sense of melancholy as she waits and hopes. After all its other inhabitants have departed for other engagements, Jane walks the sun-dappled terrace, lone footsteps echoing, looking out at the picturesque passing gondoliers. A violin plays – diegetic sound coming from nearby – but it works like a non-diegetic score to underline Jane's loneliness. The camera pulls back a little as if to further emphasise her isolation within the frame. Her only company is the statuary far above and a cat she tries to call over but who refuses to come. A dissolve suggesting the slow passage of time brings in a shot of Jane still on the terrace, picking at olives, seated but full of restless energy. The camera tracks in as she leaves her seat and resumes walking. She throws a stone into the canal and is embarrassed when it accidentally calls a gondola. The film's lushly romantic main theme plays over the scene, but diegetically via the sound of one of the square's orchestras being carried by the breeze then taken up by a male tenor. As the music reaches its crescendo, Jane looks across at a couple crossing the nearby bridge but it's the overheard sound of another woman's laughter that brings her close to tears, framed in unsparing close-up. For Lean, this scene contained the kernel of a film whose central theme was 'loneliness': 'a more common emotion than love, but we speak less about it. We are ashamed of it. We think perhaps that it shows a deficiency in ourselves.'[115] Hepburn's delicate wordless performance of someone putting up a brave front against her loneliness but feeling overwhelmed by it nonetheless, along with the careful manipulation of *mise en scène*, soundtrack, editing and camera movement, make this sequence one of the most affecting in the film.

Seeking respite from her isolation, Jane follows the sound of the singing and goes out onto the streets. The loud tolling of bells then draws her into the Piazza San Marco. She rushes through bustling side streets until she finally reaches her journey's end, and the camera tilts upwards to take in the full height of the campanile, rendered even more beautiful via the warm golden tones of Jack Hildyard's 'magic hour' photography. In the most striking example of the film's focus on Venice's most 'obvious places', high-angle shots of the famous square and its pigeons are alternated with cutaway close-ups of bells and gilded statuary. The sequence also makes a feature of Hepburn's reaction shots, showing Jane being overwhelmed by what she hears and sees, confirming the sheer impact of the spectacle before her. However, it's notable that the final verdict on the beauty of Venice comes not from Jane but from another American lady tourist who is heard telling her tour guide 'don't change a thing, not one thing' (only New World naivety could countenance that a place as ancient as Venice *could* change). Although the anonymous woman seems like an unusual choice to ventriloquise Jane's feelings after we've become used to the film sending up American tourists, the patent sincerity in her expression of awe and wonder, however imperfectly expressed, means that it is granted due credence and authority.

As evening begins to draw on, Jane is shown seated alone at a table outside one of the square's busy cafés. As Dilys Powell was to note, the film conveys exceptionally well the sometimes 'painful excitement' of being alone in a wonderful city.[116] Jane surveys the passers-by and reaches for her camera to film one pair of girls walking past in their finery (Plate 10). However her panning shot then takes in a matching pair of young men who appraise the girls and then follow them. Sexual desire and pursuit seem to be everywhere, much to Jane's disapproval or perhaps envy. When the camera returns to Jane at her table, the man behind her who had previously been obscured by his newspaper is now visible. The reframing of the shot emphasises his presence, as does the recognisability of Rossano Brazzi, already familiar from another Italian spectacular *Three Coins in the Fountain* (1954). The sound of Jane's camera whirring as she films draws his attention, and in a shot/reverse-shot pattern typical of classical cinema, shots of him looking at Jane are alternated with shots of Jane being looked at, particularly her slim ankle and foot in white slingback heel.[117] The camera tracks in on her back, as if to mimic the increasing intensity of the man's appraisal. Jane realises she's being watched, then confirms it with a quick look behind, and she puts on her sunglasses, a protective shield which allows her to look without being looked at. Being the object of a male gaze, just like the young women she'd captured on film a moment before, makes Jane uncomfortable. She quickly flees, to the bemusement of Brazzi's character, retreating to a lonely canalside step where she contemplates the semi-submerged lion statues, worn away by tide and time, un-admired and forgotten.

Shopping the next day, Jane finds herself inexorably drawn to a single red glass goblet in the window of an antique shop. The shop owner of course turns out to be Brazzi's character, Renato De Rossi. There is an awkward moment of mutual recognition when Jane removes her protective sunglasses. Their first conversation centres on the purchase of the goblet and illuminates their underlying cultural differences, as he encourages her to bargain but she insists on paying the full named price. He continues to look at her admiringly while her evident attraction to him is expressed through her verbal stutters and physical stumbles, even tripping up on the bridge as she walks away from his shop; a touch that was Hepburn's own invention.[118]

Back at the pensione, the comedy of social awkwardness continues as Jane tries to invite herself along to Harry's Bar with a younger couple, the Yaegers, only to find herself rebuffed. However, she puts on her brave face and decides to go out to the same café as the night before, hoping that she might meet again the man she hopefully referred to as 'mio amico' in her letter home. Seated alone at her table, she sees the Yaegers walk past and hastily pretends she has company at her table by spreading out her drinks and tipping up the seat next to her. However, as the camera tracks back from Jane, the wider shot reveals Renato De Rossi in the background searching for a table. They see each other, exchange greetings but too late Jane realises that her attempt at averting embarrassment – her faked occupancy of two seats – has sent Renato on

10 Jane (Katharine Hepburn) and her camera in *Summer Madness* (1955)

his way. As he moves on, the camera once again tracks away from her leaving her alone with trembling lip and teary eyes. If *Summer Madness* conveys nothing else, it shows repeatedly the terrible pain of trying to maintain a façade of contented independence while inwardly crying out for human contact.

Jane seeks solace the next day in relentless sight-seeing and filming while all the Venetian natives are asleep in the midday sun – except her little urchin companion Mauro (Gaetano Autiero). It's while she's trying to get an ideal image of De Rossi's shop, some remnant of their brief encounter, that Jane falls into the canal attempting to frame the perfect shot.[119] Although Jane tries to wisecrack her way out of it ('you should've seen me in the Olympics'), her embarrassment at becoming a highly visible spectacle for a crowd of Italian passers-by is all too plain, and she begs Mauro to take her home before De Rossi sees her. It's interesting that the moment most often excerpted from this film (for instance, in the 1990 American Film Institute tribute to Lean) is this impeccably timed comedy pratfall. Comic moments recur throughout *Summer Madness* and one paper's review of the film was even headed 'Mr Lean's new comedy',[120] suggesting a different generic reading from its designation elsewhere as woman's film. But both genres hinge on a sense of extremity and the discomfort of their protagonists. The melodramatic and comic elements of *Summer Madness* are different ways of mediating the same underlying emotion: humiliation, or at least Jane's fear of it. The fear of being a laughing stock – an old bore trying to gatecrash other people's parties, an old maid taken in by a smooth gigolo – is what prevents Jane from being able to act on her desires. Andrew Britton felt that the film assembled an 'inexhaustible arsenal of degradations' each one 'triggered to go off whenever the heroine experiences romantic longing'.[121] But Hepburn's own collusion in this (*her* addition of the stumble outside De Rossi's shop) complicates the idea of such moments being externally imposed misogynist ridicule. Jane's fall in the water is perhaps not so much a ritual humiliation as a kind of baptism. As with the dousing of her spinster character in the rapids in *The African Queen*, it's a pivotal moment; another soaking to the skin that effects another deeper transformation.

Still drying off, hair loose, towel round her shoulders, Jane is visited by Renato De Rossi, and their initial stilted pleasantries soon shade into much deeper conversation. Reminiscent of Noël Coward's 'small talk with quite different thoughts going on behind it',[122] De Rossi remarks 'we talk about glasses, we talk about Venice but we are not speaking about them, are we?' The subtext is his attempt at courtship, but Jane is resistant, insisting on intractable national difference as a barrier to coming together: 'I am not an Italian, I am an American.' Several critics noted that Brazzi's dialogue, here and elsewhere, was within the well-worn tradition of the Latin lover, and was in danger of lapsing into cliché at times, with gnomic but beautifully delivered lines like 'The most beautiful things in life are those we do not understand.'[123] But his comment to Jane that 'you make many jokes but inside I think you cry' is highly astute and signals a change from the previous set-up – a two shot tracking in closer on the couple – to an over-the-shoulder shot of Jane's reaction as De Rossi's comment hits home and she begins to cry. Jane's carefully guarded defences have been broken down by De Rossi's candour and simplicity ('we saw each other, we liked each other') and she is on the brink of accepting his invitation for coffee in the piazza, when the McIlhennys burst in and interrupt (more echoes of Dolly Messiter). They have been glass shopping and Edith McIlhenny proudly flourishes – dead centre shot – a bright red goblet, blown that day in Murano, identical to the one De Rossi had sold Jane as an antique. Mrs McIlhenny then lifts the lid from a wooden crate containing another five the same. What Jane had hoped was unique, authentic and antiquated turns out to be modern, still hand-made but mass-produced, an easily purchased souvenir. But if the goblets are beautiful, does it matter? These dilemmas turning on authenticity and truth have a larger application to Jane's situation, and the matter of whether or not De Rossi is to be trusted. Her internal conflict between desire and fear is finally angrily and violently expressed as Jane knocks over a chair, raging to De Rossi, 'What do you expect me to feel? What do you want me to do?' It's an emotionally explosive moment in a film which has hitherto dealt with someone trying to hold back emotion, to fight tears. Jane goes to the balcony and, in a typical Lean touch, the ensuing moment of emotional surrender is staged with the protagonists' backs to the camera.

De Rossi encourages Jane to take a deep breath and take a chance on him: 'Relax and the world is beautiful.' The film fully vindicates his sentiments in its lushly romantic presentation of the evening concert. The camera ranges over the architectural opulence of a floodlit St Mark's Square as the orchestra play the overture to Rossini's *The Thieving Magpie*. Jane and Renato are seated together at their table and while Jane takes in the romantic sights and sounds and sighs contentedly, Renato enjoys Jane's enjoyment. When a flower seller comes to their table, Jane picks out a white gardenia, a flower which has Proustian resonances of lost youth: as a younger woman she was denied one as a corsage because it was too expensive for her date to buy. But now De Rossi tells her 'you have your gardenia. Everything happens sooner or later.' The sequence presents an accumulation of sensual details such as Jane's cool green glass of crème de menthe frappé, the warm evening breeze making the tablecloth flutter slightly, and the suggestion of the scent of gardenia. As C. A. Lejeune commented, 'the air itself seems to sing of summer and Italy'.[124]

It is indicative of Jane's relaxation that the next morning, after a passionate parting embrace with Renato, she's forgotten her camera. Rather than insisting on being in control of the gaze, now she's happy to be its object as she readies herself for her evening with De Rossi. We see her under the hairdryer, having her fingernails and toenails painted vivid red. Just as she was drawn to the red goblet in the window earlier, she is now drawn to a scarlet and gold high-heeled shoe and a strapless black dress with red trim and white chiffon scarf. Makeover complete, she descends the pensione staircase in the complete outfit, and is complimented as 'a real Italian' by the maid Giovanna.[125] But Jane's successful makeover is not crowned by the arrival of a handsome prince and desire fulfilled. Instead, once again, her burgeoning relationship is thrown into disarray, this time by the revelation that De Rossi not only has children but is also still married. Distraught, Jane goes to prop up a nearby bar. When she returns to the pensione she is confronted with more Italian immorality – an affair between Eddie Yaeger and Signora Fiorini – confirming her worse suspicions of native moral corruption, compounded by the couple's use of the young boy Mauro as their helper like a sullied modern Cupid. Jane observes unseen from the shadows but then angrily confronts Mauro for his 'immoral earnings' and snatches his money away. De Rossi arrives, sends the child away, and accuses Jane of puritanism and immaturity. 'You Americans get so disturbed about sex', he tells her, 'Stop behaving like a schoolgirl', rather like the rebuke Brazzi's character will offer to another narrow-minded American girl abroad in *South Pacific* (1958). Then, in one of the most memorable lines of dialogue in *Summer Madness*, De Rossi likens Jane's rejection of him to that of a hungry child offered ravioli but who stubbornly holds out for beef steak. He counsels her: 'My dear girl, you are hungry, eat the ravioli.' In courtship Italian-style, sexual and gastronomic consummations are inextricably linked. Jane might have been hoping for something more akin to the refined cuisine she enjoyed in France but Renato urges her to accept something less delicate but more satisfying.

Jane still tries to hold out against Renato's pleas – 'I come from such a different world and I'm not going to be here long' – and walks away from him, trying to lose herself in the labyrinthine walkways of the city. Only when she walks into a dead end trying to evade his pursuit does she finally relent, admitting 'this is ridiculous'. There is no spoken agreement to go together but the cut to the next shot shows both of them seated at a café table, laughing at a pedlar's display of mechanical toys: two little marching kittens with red ribbons around their necks (like Jane), a bucking donkey, two manic monkey musicians, and a juggling clown. Their funny jerky movements send Jane into paroxysms of laughter that seems to go beyond mere enjoyment towards something more hysterical. Is it that she recognises herself in the clockwork toys? She is no more in control of her actions than an automaton, compelled by drives and desires as comically as the dog frantically kicking a ball or the cat condemned to continually chase a fish across their tabletop.

The next shot also focusses on involuntary movement, framing the couple's feet as they halt outside a supper club advertising dancing. Their feet begin to dance and they are irresistibly drawn inside: intellect has been bypassed by rhythmic instinct. On the dance floor, Jane copies an Italian woman's clasp of her partner's neck while dancing, trying out new gestures even though they feel strange to her. The night passes and a dissolve brings in their final dance of the night, to a lone violin playing a slow waltz. Jane now revels in her lover's cultural difference; the fact that Renato will gently croon the song to her 'because you're Italian'. The barriers of language and nationality have been broken down. Jane says she knows what the song is 'really about' even though she doesn't speak Italian, reaching a stage of empathetic understanding, of instinctive knowledge, that previously she had resisted.

After the couple meander back to Renato's apartment (Jane barefoot), fireworks begin, their loud explosive sounds followed quickly by images of their colourful starbursts. Jane and Renato's blissful kiss on the balcony is intercut with a barrage of sky-rocketing fireworks and dancing red sparks; it is as hackneyed an image of romantic fulfilment or, more bluntly, of orgasm as the cinema has produced, but is no less beautiful or spectacular for that. Whereas Hitchcock seemed to be semi-mocking similar imagery when he deployed it the same year in *To Catch a Thief* (1955) – while still unashamedly using it to complement the visual pleasure of Grace Kelly in seductive mode – Lean seems to be using the imagery straight, while still recognising its hyper – no, more like hysterical – romanticism. Jane discards one of her red shoes on the balcony and the camera frames it in close-up while in the background of the shot the movement of the curtain indicates the lovers' retreat inside. The increasingly tumultuous score accompanies further pyrotechnic display. Korda's advice to not be afraid of clichés, to go to the obvious places, seems to have been heeded at a deeper level beyond mere geography in *Summer Madness*. The film constantly teeters on a knife-edge of absurdity in its hyper-romanticism, its embrace of all the clichés of exotic romance. The highly sensual *mise en scène* of Venice, with its suggestions of scent and warmth, and the constant sonic envelope of lovely lyrical music, collaborate in creating a setting which seems too good to be true, just like the handsome, ardent lover who croons lyrical songs in Jane's ear. Our response to it mirrors Jane's response within the film: do we maintain a sceptical distance and reject it, or do we accept it in all its glorious hokeyness and sigh over the undeniable visual and aural pleasures it offers?

Lean worried continually over this dialectic of expressiveness/understatement throughout his filmmaking career. For instance, Robert Bolt's *Lawrence* script had a sequence in which the hero grasps a stone so tightly that it draws blood from his hand, but Lean pulled it fearing that it was over-the-top.[126] However, he would later upbraid Bolt and himself for lacking the courage of their dramatic convictions: 'We must stop this throwing away of pearls! We are both guilty and if we can only see the reasons we can do so. ... It's something to do with this English politeness I'm always talking about. We both "want to say it" ... but don't *quite* want to say it. Too obvious. Too vulgar. We almost take a pride in those scenes which are caught on to only our brightest friends, and bugger the hoi-polloi. I'm scared stiff of being thought a ham.'[127] Lean's worst fears would be realised several years later when the hyper-romanticism of *Ryan's Daughter* came in for stinging criticism. In a more critically respected film like *Brief Encounter*, such full-blooded romantic imagery is always tempered, ironised and undercut (consider the appearance of the pram advert just after the *Flames of Passion* trailer) whereas in *Summer Madness* it is given full and sincere expression. And although it attracted nothing like the level of critical opprobrium directed at *Ryan's Daughter*, the film still came in for some criticism for being 'almost a glossary of romance', according to critic Milton Shulman: 'Lean digs down into the deepest of molasses barrels for his sugary effects', he observed, adding that 'no woman's magazine could go to press without them'.[128] The critic need only invoke feminised popular culture in order to damn the film by association. Even those who praised the film often did so by re-masculinising it, claiming '*Summer Madness* is a woman's picture made with a man's intelligence.'[129]

There is no let-up in the hyper-romantic tone in the scenes detailing the morning after. Panoramic shots of Venice at dawn eventually reveal a distant lone couple wandering through an empty St Mark's Square. As the deep orange sun rises, Jane finally gets her gondola ride, back to the pensione, waving goodbye to her lover. This is the real thing, the film suggests, not the jostled gondola jam that the McIlhennys find themselves stuck in, being hollered at to turn to page 37 of their guidebooks. Arriving back at the pensione, she glides her lost red slipper up the staircase to her room in a haze of sexual fulfilment. She even conducts a conversation with Giovanna entirely in Italian; American virgin no longer, she has 'gone native'.

Jane and Renato meet again the next day to journey by speedboat across the lagoon to Burano, described by Renato as 'the island where the rainbow fell'. A quick montage showcases the tonal harmony of its blues and dark oranges, interspersed with patches of green and yellow, accompanied by harp on the score as if to intensify its magical ambience (or suggest that it is too beautiful to be real?). The film returns to the couple at sunset. The camera pans across orange-tinted clouds reflected in the glassily perfect waters disturbed only by a lone gondolier. Jane and Renato lie together on the nearby shore and in a single take the film captures their idle lovers' conversation while in the background a perfect orange-red sun, reflected in the water, sinks below the horizon (testimony to Jack Hildyard's skills, and a rehearsal for a similar sundown scene in *Kwai*). Cut back to an ominous clock tower automaton striking a bell the following morning: *tempus fugit*.

Renato waits for Jane at their usual café table and gets the orchestra to play their song (and the film's main theme) as she approaches. Even though Jane recognises this as carefully confected romantic gesture, she still derives pleasure from it, knowing it's a cliché but enjoying it all the same. As they sit together, Jane takes in the sights of Venice – the pigeons fluttering across St Mark's Square, the tall campanile piercing the blue sky – and seems to extend her body up to try and reach them just as the music in turn reaches its crescendo. Renato senses 'you are far away' but Jane corrects him: 'I am very close', an ambiguous phrase; close to him, close to staying rather than going home, close to some kind of ultimate ecstatic fulfilment? The retrospective turn of her thoughts, recalling the first evening she came to the square, the first time she saw Renato and he was wearing a yellow tie, seems to indicate the end of something. Jane Hudson shares with Lean's other romantic heroines Laura Jesson and Mary Justin a compulsion to commit to memory. As Jane vows: 'I don't want to forget any of it, not a single moment.' A large flock of pigeons take off as Jane and Renato leave the square. Where *Brief Encounter* had steam, and *The Passionate Friends* had clouds, *Summer Madness* uses birds to the same effect; to create a sense of fluctuating fluttering movement across the screen, in counterpoint to the more fixed elements of the *mise en scène*. They are an image of feminine aspiration and desire; both Laura Jesson and Rosy Ryan imagine having wings.

Jane announces to Renato that she plans to leave Venice in just two hours, news that he greets with disbelief, asking her 'why throw it away?' The question is a pertinent one, and Andrew Britton's reflections on this moment in the film are very interesting. Britton argues that the spinster is caught in a double-bind: just as she is perceived as necessarily being 'in a perpetual seething torment of ungratified heterosexual desire',[30] and has to be forced to recognise that fact, she cannot be granted romantic fulfilment beyond a brief ecstasy. Instead 'through some subtle flaw of her own (the flaw involved, presumably, in having become a middle-aged spinster), a life with men is impossible anyway.'[31] But it is possible to read Jane's curtailing of the affair in another way, as a recognition of the unsustainability of 'high romance' beyond a brief moment. Jane likens it to knowing when to leave a party at the right time, recognising that the enjoyment must wane as time passes. It has to end in order to stay perfect. In a way, the romantic high pitch of the film's style also points to this; the glory of the sky-rockets, the Rossini, the abandoned red slipper, is altogether too hysterically overwrought, too 'perfect' to be sustainable. Although Lean preferred the American title for the film, the more neutral and gentle *Summertime*, the inclusion of 'madness' in the British title is entirely appropriate to the film's tone, indicating its typically Leanian conflation of romance and delirium.

This touch of madness also marks Hepburn's performance which, as Britton suggests, is 'pitched consistently on the edge of hysteria ... One is struck by the violence of the performance – a violence which appears as a conflict between desire and resistance.'[32] Britton reads Hepburn's hysterical performance as a feminist 'counter-text', which 'makes the film's project untenable' by exposing 'everything that the film cannot afford to admit. It makes present the oppressiveness of a cultural situation that entails a norm (a woman should have a man) by which the woman, socially and emotionally, has everything to lose.'[33] Hepburn's performance is truly remarkable and does register how much is at stake for Jane through its vehemence and its pathos. But to suggest that Hepburn's performance is the sole locus of these discourses of hysteria is to simplify the film's project. I think *Summer Madness* is very much attuned to the sense of terror felt by Jane Hudson at the prospect of surrender felt by Jane Hudson, a reverberating thematic concern throughout so much of Lean's work, and arguably within Lean himself. Certainly the critic David Denby makes a persuasive case for seeing *Summer Madness* as a highly personal film for its director: 'Lean, I think, genuinely identifies with Jane's love of beauty and her fear of it, her longing for sensuality and her terror of being engulfed by it. Her fervency and stiffened resistance are emblematic of his whole career.'[34]

As *Summer Madness* nears its end, it only remains for Jane to say her goodbyes at the station. She has told Renato not to see her off but still seems disappointed when he fails to appear. Instead, the little boy Mauro arrives to say goodbye to Jane, demonstrating his fondness for the eccentric American lady by giving her a stolen fountain pen as a parting gift. Incidentally, the utterly superficial treatment of the Italian street child remains one of the film's failings, showing little concern for his fate, reassuringly insisting instead on his picaresque cuteness and contentment with his lot, his suitability as a funny foil to solipsistic American self-discovery. Once Mauro leaves, Jane boards the train and a series of close-ups reveal her mounting sense of panic, a weakening of her previous resolve, as the whistle blows, the light turns from red to green and the train's wheels are set in motion, taking her away from Venice and Renato. But suddenly we see Renato moving frantically through the crowds, along the platform, trying to reach Jane. He has a little white parcel with gold ribbon, knocked out of his hand but then retrieved. He runs to catch the train and within the train's interior Jane runs back towards him, a wonderful physical dramatisation of mutual yearning (showing again the formative influence of one of Lean's favourite films *The Big Parade*, in which Renee Adoree desperately tries to catch up with John Gilbert's departing truck). But despite his running and her outstretched hand, he can't quite catch her to give her the parcel. At the end of the platform, realising it's hopeless, he opens the box and holds up a white camellia, a kind of parting salutation, similar but less ominous than the one Godbole offers to Mrs Moore as her train leaves in *A Passage to India*. Jane nods and silently mouths 'I see it, I see it' to Renato and blows him expansive kisses. The gesture, the holding up of the camellia, so that it becomes a perfect white flower of memory, is far more powerful than receiving the actual material object, which would wilt and wither within a few hours.

The writer H. E. Bates' original concept for Renato (closer to the darker tone of Laurents' play) was to have him be precisely the gigolo Jane suspects, and to end the film with him looking down the platform for his next pick-up as soon as Jane's train leaves. But Lean thought this 'too cynical, too harsh',[135] and instead Renato's interest in Jane, and his protestations of love, are positioned as totally sincere. Also, in the completed film, the final emphasis rests not with the man left behind on the platform but the woman who is leaving him behind. The camera stays on Jane's train as it pulls out from the station and curves away down the track. Her slowly waving arm fills the foreground while Renato becomes an ever-more-distant dot. There follows a close-up of Hepburn's teary but triumphant and confident goodbye to the city. I think this moment problematises Andrew Britton's assessment that Jane 'has nothing to go back to: her life without him has been, by this time, thoroughly devalued ... The act of renunciation is pure loss.'[136] One might equally read the moment as a new beginning, a late blooming, not the end of the story but a fresh, re-invigorated start for Jane who 'is determined to get on with her life'.[137] 'Her romance, though illicit, has brought her to full stature' was the verdict of *Kine Weekly*.[138] The final shot of her train steaming back across the lagoon is not a dying fall of an image but a visually dynamic shot and the accompanying music is powerful and percussive rather than plangent or melancholy. The ending embraces another familiar romantic cliché: that it is better to have loved and lost than never to have loved at all.

The motif of the train inevitably sends one back to *Brief Encounter*, to which all of Lean's subsequent female-centred dramas were inevitably compared, with *Summer Madness* hailed as a 'Brief (Venetian) Encounter' and 'Latin-styled *Brief Encounter*' in various reviews.[139] But there have been definite changes in the way Lean presents a fleeting romance between 1945 and 1955. The ultra-English milieu of the station refreshment room or suburban cinema shot in black and white has been replaced by the sunny spectacular spaces of Venice, presented in glorious Eastmancolor. Where Laura only dreams about a gondola ride, Jane makes that dream come true through her own savings. Both Jane and Laura's affairs are held back by the woman's guilt and doubt but whereas Laura's love remains stymied, Jane's illicit affair is triumphantly consummated. She enjoys her romance but also ends it on her own terms. Unlike her Leanian predecessors, Laura Jesson and Mary Justin, Jane Hudson has no husband she has to lie to, and she is never driven to suicidal extremes like those earlier Lean heroines. She never contemplates flinging herself under a train. Her equivalent plunge over the edge actually happens but it's comedic rather than tragic; the harmless fall into the canal. The 'boat train' that Laura likes to watch rushing through the station, destined for exotic foreign locations, and that she almost throws herself under is also, in a way, the same train on which Jane is a passenger at the end of *Summer Madness*. The stirring wide shot of that train on the Venetian lagoon horizon – not rushing through the narrow confines of Milford Junction – marks the liberation not only of Jane Hudson but also of David Lean, now that the new international direction of his career had begun.

Notes

1 Silver and Ursini, *David Lean and His Films*, p. 3.
2 Maria LaPlace, 'Producing and Consuming the Woman's Film: Discursive Struggle in *Now, Voyager*', in Christine Gledhill (ed.), *Home is Where the Heart Is: Studies in Melodrama and the Woman's Film* (London: BFI, 1987), p. 139.
3 Jeanine Basinger, *A Woman's View: How Hollywood Spoke to Women, 1930–1960* (New York: Knopf, 1993), p. 36.
4 Silver and Ursini, *David Lean and His Films*, p. 3.
5 Lean interviewed by Cathy Furniss in 1971 anthologised in Organ (ed.), *David Lean: Interviews*, p. 52. Lean quoted in Pratley, *The Cinema of David Lean*, p. 85.
6 Harold Conway, *Daily Sketch*, 30 September 1955.
7 Lean interviewed by Michel Spector in 1989 in Organ (ed.), *David Lean: Interviews*, p. 113.
8 Furniss interview in Organ (ed.), *David Lean: Interviews*, p. 52.
9 Undated letter circa summer 1963 from David Lean to Robert Bolt. UoR Spec Coll.
10 Quoted in Pratley, *The Cinema of David Lean*, p. 120.
11 Justine Ashby, 'It's Been Emotional: Reassessing the Contemporary British Woman's Film', in Melanie Bell and Melanie Williams (eds.), *British Women's Cinema* (London: Routledge, 2010), p. 154.
12 Ibid., p. 155.
13 Melanie Bell and Melanie Williams, 'The Hour of the Cuckoo: Reclaiming the British Woman's Film', in Melanie Bell and Melanie Williams (eds.), *British Women's Cinema* (London: Routledge, 2010), pp. 5–6.
14 Anderegg, *David Lean*, p. 90.
15 Richard Dyer, *Brief Encounter* (London: BFI, 1993), p. 16.
16 Mary Ann Doane, *The Desire to Desire: The Woman's Film of the 1940s* (Bloomington: Indiana University Press, 1987), p. 13.
17 Ibid.
18 Eleanor Wintour, 'Do women really want this?', *Tribune*, 7 October 1955.
19 Promotional material for the BBC transmission of the film on 9 October 1965. Microfiche on *Brief Encounter*, BFI Library.
20 Dyer, *Brief Encounter*, p. 16.

WOMEN IN LOVE 129

21 Brownlow, *David Lean*, p. 364.
22 Lean recalled by Norman Spencer quoted in ibid., p. 326.
23 Tania Modleski, *The Women Who Knew too Much: Hitchcock and Feminist Theory* (London: Methuen, 1988), p. 55.
24 Claire Johnston, 'Dorothy Arzner: Critical Strategies' (first published 1975), in Constance Penley (ed.), *Feminism and Film Theory* (London: Routledge, 1988), p. 39.
25 Kaja Silverman provides an important brake on too much free play of gender identity by pointing out that the male director's adoption of female voice 'must be read in relation to the biological gender of the biographical author, since it is clearly not the same thing, socially or politically, for a woman to speak with a female voice as it is for a man to do so, and vice versa.' Kaja Silverman, *The Acoustic Mirror: The Female Voice in Psychoanalysis and Film* (Bloomington and Indianapolis: Indiana University Press, 1988), p. 217.
26 Lean interviewed by Joseph Gelmis in 1970 in Organ (ed.), *David Lean: Interviews*, p. 47.
27 Silverman, *David Lean*, p. 9, p. 22.
28 Lean quoted in Brownlow, *David Lean*, p. 312.
29 Kaja Silverman, 'Lost Objects and Mistaken Subjects: Film Theory's Structuring Lack', *Wide Angle*, Vol. 7, nos. 1–2 (1985), p. 23.
30 Bolt quoted in Adrian Turner, *Robert Bolt: Scenes from Two Lives* (London: Vintage, 1999), p. 302.
31 Quoted in Turner, *Robert Bolt*, p. 302.
32 Jeremy Paxman, *The English: A Portrait of a People* (London: Penguin, 1999), p. 5.
33 Cited by Isabel Quigly in NFT programme notes. BFI microfiche on *Brief Encounter*.
34 Unspecified newspaper clipping dated 6 November 1946, BFI microfiche on *Brief Encounter*.
35 Dyer, *Brief Encounter*, p. 10.
36 Ibid., p. 41.
37 See John Ellis, 'The Quality Film Adventure: British Critics and the Cinema, 1942–1948', in Andrew Higson (ed.), *Dissolving Views: Key Writings on British Cinema* (London: Cassell, 1996), pp. 66–93.
38 Andre Bazin, *What Is Cinema? Volume 2*, translated by Hugh Gray (Berkeley: University of California Press, 2005), p. 49.
39 Raymond Durgnat, *A Mirror for England: British Movies from Austerity to Affluence* (London: Faber, 1971), p. 181.
40 Ibid., p. 180.
41 Brownlow, *David Lean*, p. 203.
42 Lean uses this phrase in his piece on the film while also noting that the film was 'not a big box-office success'. David Lean, 'Brief Encounter', *Penguin Film Review*, Vol. 4, 1947, p. 29. Richard Dyer notes that its popularity is a slightly contentious matter since it does appear in *Kine Weekly*'s yearly round-up and was retrospectively declared a money-spinner by *To-Day's Cinema* in 1948. See Dyer, *Brief Encounter*, pp. 56–7.
43 Gavin Lambert in conversation with Stephen Frears and Alexander Mackendrick, during Frears's documentary *Typically British: A Personal History of British Cinema*, Channel Four/BFI, 1994.
44 Andy Medhurst, 'That Special Thrill: *Brief Encounter*, Homosexuality and Authorship', *Screen*, Vol. 32, No. 2, Summer 1991, p. 204.
45 Brownlow, *David Lean*, p. 194.
46 As Richard Dyer suggests, Coward and Lean's attendance to these micro-details make this an extraordinarily carefully crafted classical narrative in which 'every

detail contributes to the overall thematics of the work.' Dyer, *Brief Encounter*, p. 44. For some readers this is pleasurable while others may find it, as Dyer acknowledges, 'honed and created to a point of rigidity' (p. 48).
47 *Observer*, 25 November 1945.
48 Roger Manvell, screenplay of 'Brief Encounter', *Masterworks of the British Cinema* (London: Faber, 1990), p. 127.
49 Dyer, *Brief Encounter*, pp. 66–7.
50 Keats' poem 'When I Have Fears' is a well-selected reference point, echoing the sentiments of Laura's previous monologue with its intimations of mortality ('When I have fears that I may cease to be' and 'I stand alone, and think till love and fame to nothingness do sink') and the brevity and power of love (the 'fair creature of an hour' inspiring 'the fairy power of unreflecting love'). The section quoted, with its mention of 'huge cloudy symbols of a high romance' inevitably suggests the steam and smoke of the railway station.
51 Sigmund Freud and Josef Breuer, *Studies on Hysteria* [1893–95] (London: Pelican, 1974), p. 64.
52 Silverman, *David Lean*, p. 60.
53 Noel Coward, 'Shadow Play', *To-Night at 8.30* (London; Methuen, 2009 [1936]), p. 141.
54 Despite its Cowardian flourishes, Ronald Neame actually wrote the dialogue for the boatshed scene. Neame, *Straight from the Horse's Mouth*, p. 96.
55 Dyer, *Brief Encounter*, p. 28.
56 Brownlow, *David Lean*, p. 201.
57 Ibid., p. 199. 'Why doesn't he fuck her?' was Howard's rather basic line of questioning.
58 Ibid., p. 200. The scene also famously gave Billy Wilder the inspiration for his film about borrowed flats and affairs, *The Apartment* (1960).
59 *Times* (T2 section), 2 August 2007, p. 15.
60 Eric Lomax, *The Railway Man* (London: Vintage, 1996), p. 2.
61 Quoted in introduction to Manvell, 'Brief Encounter', *Masterworks of the British Cinema*, p. 116.
62 Silver and Ursini, *David Lean and His Films*, p. 40.
63 Dyer offers a penetrating analysis of the film's simultaneous loquaciousness and silence of its heroine, *Brief Encounter*, pp. 15–31.
64 Undated publicity material, BFI microfiche on *Brief Encounter*.
65 Durgnat, *A Mirror for England*, p. 181.
66 Undated publicity material, BFI microfiche on *Brief Encounter*.
67 Antonia Lant, *Blackout: Reinventing Women for Wartime British Cinema* (Princeton: Princeton University Press, 1991), p. 170.
68 Undated publicity material, BFI microfiche on *Brief Encounter*.
69 William Cook, *New Statesman*, 26 March 2001, p. 44.
70 Dyer, *Brief Encounter*, p. 10.
71 Joan Lester, *Reynolds News*, 25 November 1945.
72 See Neame, *Straight from the Horse's Mouth*, p. 120.
73 Ann Todd, *The Eighth Veil* (London: William Kimber, 1980), p. 69.
74 *Sunday Express*, 25 November 1945.
75 Silver and Ursini, *David Lean and His Films*, p. 122.
76 *Evening Standard*, 27 January 1949.
77 This reviewer saw the origins of its complicated structure – 'so highbrow and clever' that it would soar 'high above the heads of ordinary cinemagoers' – stemming from the malign influence of European cinema and stated: 'Suggestion: that no British producer, director or writer shall be permitted to see any continental film for a year.' *News of the World*, 30 January 1949.

78 *Sunday Dispatch*, 30 January 1949.
79 Anderegg, *David Lean*, p. 64.
80 Brownlow, *David Lean*, pp. 238–9.
81 Ibid.
82 Quoted in Neame, *Straight from the Horse's Mouth*, p. 119.
83 Cineguild press release, undated. BFI microfiche on *The Passionate Friends*.
84 H. G. Wells, *The Passionate Friends* (New York: Harper, 1913), p. 300.
85 *News Chronicle* and *Daily Mail*, both 28 January 1949.
86 *Daily Herald*, 28 January 1949.
87 *The Passionate Friends* pressbook, BFI Library.
88 Orr, 'David Lean: The Troubled Romantic and the End of Empire', p. 70.
89 Durgnat, *A Mirror for England*, p. 189.
90 'A new star made in Britain', *Picture Post*, 24 November 1945, pp. 26–7.
91 Orr, 'David Lean: The Troubled Romantic and the End of Empire', p. 66.
92 Karel Reisz and Gavin Millar, *The Technique of Film Editing* (London: Focal Press, 1953).
93 Brownlow, *David Lean*, p. 258.
94 Anderegg, *David Lean*, p. 67.
95 Durgnat, *A Mirror for England*, p. 188.
96 Orr, 'David Lean: The Troubled Romantic and the End of Empire', p. 70.
97 *The Times*, 28 January 1949.
98 *Daily Express*, 28 January 1949.
99 Statistic cited in Sheldon Hall and Steve Neale, *Epics, Spectacles and Blockbusters* (Detroit: Wayne State University Press, 2010), p. 140.
100 Brownlow, *David Lean*, p. 330.
101 Richard Dyer, *Stars*, 2nd edition (London: Routledge, 1998), p. 129.
102 *Evening Standard*, 29 September 1955.
103 Quoted in James Spada, *Hepburn: Her Life in Pictures* (London: Columbus Books, 1986), p. 135.
104 Andrew Britton, *Katharine Hepburn: Star as Feminist* (London: Studio Vista, 1995), p. 214.
105 Ibid., p. 209.
106 Quoted in Philips, *Beyond the Epic*, p. 216.
107 Quoted in 1990 interview with Kevin Brownlow, in Organ (ed.), *David Lean: Interviews*, p. 115.
108 Campbell Dixon, *Daily Telegraph*, 1 October 1955.
109 Brownlow, *David Lean*, p. 316.
110 Silverman, *David Lean*, p. 110.
111 Pressbook for *Summer Madness*, BFI Library.
112 Brownlow, *David Lean*, p. 316.
113 *Sunday Times*, 2 October 1955.
114 *New Statesman*, 8 October 1955.
115 Quoted in Brownlow, *David Lean*, p. 312.
116 *Sunday Times*, 2 October 1955.
117 Of course, extra-diegetically, the beautiful close-up provided of handsome and immaculately dressed Brazzi frames him as potential object of a female gaze, especially as it figures in a film aimed specifically at women cinemagoers.
118 Brownlow, *David Lean*, p. 319.
119 Apocryphally blamed for an incurable eye infection suffered by Hepburn thereafter – although several other people working on the film dispute this – Hepburn's much cited anecdote only provides extra-textual support for the idea of her plunge into the canal being life-changing and irrevocable.
120 *Financial Times*, 3 October 1955.

121 Britton, *Katharine Hepburn*, p. 219.
122 Coward, 'Shadow Play', p. 141.
123 See for instance review in *Evening News*, 29 September 1955, which picks on his later 'I am a man, you are a woman' line.
124 *Observer*, 2 October 1955.
125 Publicity for *Summer Madness* made a lot of capital out of this aspect of the film, with one retail tie-in advising 'How to make a big splash in your "Summertime" sales', while *Cosmopolitan* magazine ran a feature on 'fashions inspired by *Summertime*'. DL/5/1, BFI Spec Coll.
126 Turner, *The Making of David Lean's 'Lawrence of Arabia'*, p. 131.
127 Letter from David Lean to Robert Bolt dated 15 June 1964. UoR Spec Coll.
128 Milton Shulman, *Sunday Express*, 2 October 1955.
129 *Evening Standard*, 29 September 1955, p. 18.
130 Britton, *Katharine Hepburn*, p. 209.
131 Ibid., p. 220.
132 Ibid., p. 230.
133 Ibid., p. 231.
134 David Denby, 'A Romance in Venice', *Premiere*, March 1990, p. 30.
135 Brownlow, *David Lean*, p. 316.
136 Britton, *Katharine Hepburn*, p. 220.
137 Philips, *Beyond the Epic*, p. 215.
138 *Kine Weekly*, 15 September 1955, p. 19.
139 *Evening News*, 29 September 1955 and *Picturegoer*, 1 October 1955, p. 16.

Men of vision: *The Sound Barrier* (1952), *The Bridge on the River Kwai* (1957) and *Lawrence of Arabia* (1962) | 5

I was ten when I saw the film *Lawrence of Arabia*. I vividly remember the image of the lonely inhospitable desert, the soaring emotional music and the man alone. ... He reminds me of all those other boyhood heroes who had to be free of the ties that bound them down – women, children, emotional relationships – before they could get on with doing what a man's got to do ... The male hero is in flight from women.[1]

In his evocative recollection of the personal impact *Lawrence of Arabia* made upon him as a child, Jonathan Rutherford makes clear the avowed masculinity of the film's dramatic world, focussed on a man 'in flight from women'. *Lawrence of Arabia*, along with Lean's preceding film, *The Bridge on the River Kwai*, and to a slightly lesser extent *The Sound Barrier*, all present male-dominated realms, and all three films fix their attention on male visionaries determined to bring their visions to full fruition. The aircraft pioneer Ridgefield in *The Sound Barrier* is determined to make supersonic flight a reality. Colonel Nicholson in *Kwai* is obsessed with building a bridge to last six hundred years and, according to his creator Pierre Boulle, is a man possessed of 'the sort of faith which moves mountains, builds pyramids, cathedrals or even bridges'.[2] British Army officer T. E. Lawrence transmogrifies himself into a semi-mythical figure 'El Aurens' who victoriously galvanises revolt in the Arabian desert. The visions of all three men hinge on notions of conquest: of the skies, the jungle and the desert. Harking back to Ruth Benedict's deployment of the opposing categories of Apollonian and Dionysian, each of their projects attempts to impose Apollonian order and structure on worlds that threaten to be Dionysian in their irrationality or inscrutability. Apollo the sun god has an additional pertinence in relation to *Lawrence of Arabia* which often shows its hero framed against the sun and depicted as a kind of solar deity.

That this dichotomy is deeply gendered has been noted by several scholars, among them Camille Paglia, who uses Apollonian and

Dionysian (or her preferred variation, 'chthonic' meaning earthy or subterranean) to distinguish between the masculine drive for progress and civilisation and a dark disorderly realm associated with the feminine. But rather than rehabilitate chthonic chaos, Paglia celebrates the Apollonian: 'Everything great in western civilization comes from struggle against our origins.'[3] Ridgefield's jets fly over Ancient Greece and Egypt in *The Sound Barrier*, the birthplaces of Western linearity for Paglia, while Lawrence is drawn to the Arabian desert not only to fulfil his military destiny but because 'it's clean', an aridity in total contrast with chthonic swampy fertility ('the male hero is in flight from women'). In the steamy jungle between Burma and Siam, Nicholson proposes to construct a structure of Apollonian beauty and linearity over the river Kwai (and Boulle describes it in ultra-Apollonian terms: 'he saw it only as something abstract and complete in itself: a living symbol of the fierce struggles and countless experiments by which a nation gradually raises itself in the course of centuries to a state of civilisation.'[4]) The male hero in *The Sound Barrier* is not just metaphorically but literally in flight, piercing the heavens in aircraft that resemble perfect silver darts. For T. E. Lawrence – later an aircraftman himself – 'speed, and the conquest of the air, was the greatest achievement of civilisation,'[5] although speed would also be a contributory factor in his premature death. Apollonian progress might easily be diverted to the ends of Dionysian abandon.

What is interesting about Lean's three films centred on 'men of vision' is the extent to which they show the limitations and strains of trying to fulfill Apollonian destiny. Viewing *Kwai* and *Lawrence* together in a 1963 twin release, the critic Felix Barker noted how the 'final frustration of great endeavour is the tragic irony of both films. Nicholson blows up the bridge he has so lovingly created; Lawrence sees his revolt become a shambles. In his own way, each soldier is a single-minded fanatic.'[6] The fanaticism of Ridgefield's assault on the sound barrier is different in that he achieves his goal, but even he succumbs to a moment of doubt over its human cost. *The Sound Barrier* also differs from the other two films in including a significant female voice offering a more sceptical perspective. But overwhelmingly in all three films, gender determines genre, and their emphasis on 'physical movement, violence and suspense, with often perfunctory motivation and romance'[7] would see them categorised as action/adventure and, as Yvonne Tasker observes, 'it remains commonplace to critically designate action as a male or masculine genre'[8] in opposition to 'melodrama's "female" or "feminine" status'.[9] However, in spite of each of these three films' moments of dynamic action, melodrama actually seems like a far more appropriate description. The feats and achievements of the male heroes are presented with sincerity and visual intensity but the darker, tortured, obsessive, *excessive* aspects of their Apollonian personalities are also on full display.

The Sound Barrier (1952)

After the claustrophobia of *Madeleine*'s courtroom scenes, Lean's next project would open out into the wide open spaces up above the clouds, an ethereal realm glimpsed only briefly in *The Passionate Friends* but explored in detail in this aviation saga. *The Sound Barrier* marked the beginning of a new strain of epic-scale adventure to Lean's cinema that would eventually see him dubbed 'the poet of the far horizon'. The director had briefly considered stories relating to Scott's polar expeditions and Mallory and Irvine's attempted conquest of Everest, but later decided that 'the mystery has gone out of them. They are dated.'[10] Instead, Lean's film would explore the latest expression of that same ethos of discovery, one that married the traditional trope of courageous voyages into inhospitable places with a new scientific spin, entirely appropriate for what would soon be the 'new Elizabethan age': a film about the designers and pilots committed to pushing air travel into new supersonic dimensions, breaking the sound barrier. Alexander Korda had overseen several aviation-themed films back in the 1930s – *Conquest of the Air* (1936), *Q Planes* (1939) and *The Lion Has Wings* (1939) – and his belief in the project was matched by Lean's enthusiasm. The director had been fascinated with flight since his boyhood in Croydon, site of Britain's first aerodrome (where he had seen Charles Lindbergh land in 1927[11]), and he enjoyed his extensive preliminary research for the project, interviewing pilots and visiting aircraft manufacturers.[12] The playwright Terrence Rattigan, a former pilot who had drawn on his RAF experiences in writing his play *Flare Path* (1942) and the screenplay for *The Way to the Stars* (1945), was then brought in to convert anecdotes and statistics into a gripping narrative.

The Sound Barrier's aerophilia reflected the zeitgeist of postwar Britain. Ever since the huge Bristol Brabazon had flown over the Festival of Britain site in 1951, advances in British civil aviation had been a significant source of national pride, although the Brabazon's embarrassing demise – sold by the Ministry of Supply for scrap a little over a year later[13] – might have provided a hint of the disappointments to come. But in the early 1950s, not only had Frank Whittle been acclaimed as an exemplary 'new Elizabethan'[14] for his invention of the jet engine, but Britain had also created the first jet airliner, the de Havilland Comet, which entered service in May 1952 to 'jubilant headlines', offering 'the world's first scheduled jet service – to South Africa. Eleven months later it had brought Tokyo within 36 hours of London.'[15] Korda made full use of this aeronautic triumph in promoting *The Sound Barrier*, which in turn provided a unique showcase for Britain's star planes; the sleek silver Comet makes an impressive cameo appearance and all the planes featured are granted their own credit screen in the manner of guest stars. In a superb publicity coup, Korda even sponsored the Comet's maiden flight to Paris in October 1952, with himself, David Lean, producer Norman Spencer and Ann Todd on board, an event which received international press coverage.[16] Lean and Todd, the new golden couple of British cinema, would go on to do further publicity work for de Havilland, flying over to New York for the film's US premiere as well as jetting to Africa as unofficial ambassadors for the company. Ann Todd later recalled being 'entertained like royalty everywhere. At one reception in Cape Town a couple of ladies even curtseyed to me!'[17]

The buoyant mood would not last. The apparently happy marriage of the golden couple was on the brink of collapse, with Lean resenting their promotional status as husband-and-wife team ('Do we have to have all this Bert and Anna lark?' he complained to a stills photographer bent on depicting them in the style of Herbert Wilcox and Anna Neagle[18]), and the triumph of the British Comet would swiftly turn to tragedy. The plane had been 'rushed through by de Havilland from drawing board to commercial operation in record-breaking time',[19] with the company overlooking important safety details in their haste. When the first Comet crashed in May 1953, tropical storms were blamed and there were dark mutterings of sabotage. But when a second and then a third crash occurred in January and April 1954, the real problem was soon diagnosed: metal fatigue causing the planes to break up. The Comet was grounded for good, its certificate of airworthiness withdrawn, and, as Harry Hopkins points out, this was 'not merely an industrial setback. It was a national catastrophe. It was like defeat in battle.'[20] Britain irrevocably lost its lead over other countries in the field of jet aviation. De Havilland would soon be usurped by America's Boeing and by 1956 B.O.A.C. had put in an order for fifteen of Boeing's 707 jet passenger planes.[21] However, this downward trajectory in British aviation was yet to occur when *The Sound Barrier* was conceived and made, and the film belongs to that earlier optimistic moment when Britannia looked set to rule the skies, proving to be one of the top British box-office successes of its year.[22] It was promoted with stunts that built upon that contemporary fascination with jet aircraft, with one cinema installing in its foyer a 'real wind tunnel model of supersonic aircraft', and another offering free flying trips.[23] The Broadway cinema, Southampton, proudly put on display the 'painting "Comet over the Channel" loaned from the de Havilland board room'.[24]

From its pre-credit sequence showing RAF fighter pilot Philip Peel (John Justin) first running up against the sound barrier above the White Cliffs of Dover – a scene Dilys Powell said she wanted to applaud for being 'suffocatingly exciting'[25] – to its mirror sequence near the end when he finally breaks through the invisible wall, *The Sound Barrier* glories in aerial spectacle and suspense. The music matches this mood; composer Malcolm Arnold said he 'made a rhapsody of it'[26] when a plane broke through the cloudscape. Yet again, a Lean film hinged on 'huge cloudy symbols of a high romance'. Pre-empting *Lawrence of Arabia*, Lean wanted to show the human presence as tiny in comparison with the immensity and sublimity of his environment: 'I want to get the feel of the immensity of space. I'd like to see a wonderful cloudscape with just a little dot.'[27] Through its stunning photography, unanimously praised by the critics, and razor-sharp editing, *The Sound Barrier* sought to express, in producer Norman Spencer's words, 'the wonderment and fascination of a new element ... *the intoxication of six hundred miles an hour at forty thousand feet.*'[28]

The test pilots Philip (John Justin) and Tony (Nigel Patrick) are central to evoking this airborne ecstasy but its darker aspects also find expression through the character of J. D. Ridgefield (Ralph Richardson), the aircraft tycoon obsessed with breaking the sound barrier. Richardson's performance is marked by two distinctive features: his adoption of a bluff, no-nonsense Yorkshire accent, and his terrifying appraising stare which sometimes seems to look past its ostensible object, fixed instead on some inward distant horizon – the look of a fanatic, looking forward to Colonel Nicholson and T. E. Lawrence, and also referring to the director himself (Ralph Richardson even copied Lean's bushy eyebrows for the character[29]). Ridgefield does not attempt to cover up the driving force behind his vision – 'I could talk about the national security, beating the potential enemy bomber, flying to New York in two hours. But that's not the real point. The real point is it's just got to be done' – and expresses it in sexualised language: 'We can *force* through this barrier.' He is an all-powerful patriarch, depicted in full flying gear in the imposing portrait that hangs on the chimney breast, who holds sway over his son Chris (Denholm Elliott) and his daughter Sue (Ann Todd). It is while attempting to live up to his father's imprimatur that Chris dies in a plane crash, forcing himself to fly solo too quickly despite feeling he was never really 'born to fly'. Sue's attempt to escape the family home is thwarted when the people selling her dream cottage are warned off by her father. The masculinity of the Ridgefield family dynasty is made clear. Sue feels that her father despises her for being a daughter rather than a son who can work in the family business, and there is a more subtle hint of female marginalisation in the only allusion to the late Mrs Ridgefield in the film; at dinner, Sue mentions that her mother liked modern music. 'If she did, she didn't let on about it to me', her father bluffly insists, and Sue's response is a soft, unnoticed 'no', suggesting how far her mother's personality may have been repressed by her husband.

Ridgefield's chief engineer, Will (Joseph Tomelty), half-jokingly calls his boss a 'vile seducer', a description that is upheld in the scenes showing Sue's husband Tony being lured into the role of test pilot. First, Ridgefield takes him into the lab to show him their prototype jet engine (Sue and Chris are excluded, looking in through a window) and then does a little conjuring trick, nonchalantly tossing in a white silk handkerchief which instantly vanishes, all the while surveying Tony's face to check his new protégé has been properly spellbound. Second, and more disturbing, is the scene that ensues shortly after Chris's funeral. Back at the house for a drink, Ridgefield slowly unwraps a box and pulls from the tissue paper an impeccably sleek model aircraft, holding it aloft and gazing lovingly upon it. With no apparent remorse or regret at his son's death, and no pause for a period of mourning, he has gone back to the

11 Ridgefield (Ralph Richardson) seduces Tony (Nigel Patrick) with a model of the new Prometheus in *The Sound Barrier* (1952)

pursuit of his vision. His hope is to mesmerise Tony with the prototype for the new (and significantly named) Prometheus, and Arnold's music with its low semi-atonal woodwind suggests a snake charmer exerting hypnotic control, while the silver dart of the plane appears incongruous and unreal, representative of a new element, a new world, within the otherwise solidly domestic *mise en scène* (Plate 11).

The demonic and inhumane dimensions of Ridgefield's vision become even more apparent in the scenes that follow Tony's subsequent death on a test flight. Again, a death in the family is apparently not mourned but just scrutinised for useful evidence. Ridgefield is pictured alone in his office with the tape recorder playing back Tony's final words from the cockpit. Unknown to him, Sue has entered the room and, horrified and disbelieving, flees just as her husband's dying scream is broadcast through the dark echoing aircraft hangar. Although *The Sound Barrier* is full of remarkable visuals, its soundtrack is hugely important too, as one critic noted: 'The terrifying whoosh of a jet plane meets your ear the second after you have seen the plane go by. While Ann Todd's voice is like a whisper on a pillow. Everything here is to do with sound.'[30] The success of supersonic flight is proven by a sound, the sonic boom, that soon became a defining noise of modernity in the early 1950s, as Harry Hopkins suggests: 'fusillades of supersonic bangs saluted science's new omnipotence and drove gardeners mad by shattering their greenhouse panes.'[31] This distinctive sound was also used as a marketing ploy, with one cinema in Bognor Regis using the 'shattering thunderclap' people heard during the first supersonic flight over the town to entice people to the film, 'hence cards printed with "The Big Bang – you have heard it, so be sure to see it."'[32] The moment in the film when the sound barrier is broken also makes highly effective use of sound. The physically distant pilot Philip is made aurally present via the speaker in Ridgefield's office. Ridgefield has pleaded with his alienated daughter not to leave him and so the pair listen together, in suspended animation as they wait to hear the result. As the plane accelerates, the close-up on Ridgefield's face twists on its axis, reminiscent of the emotional duress of Laura's suicidal impulse in *Brief Encounter*. Finally, the tension is broken with the loud sonic boom, which causes the white curtains at the open window to flutter.

Terence Rattigan originally conceived Sue as another son, changing the character's sex when Korda made a throwaway suggestion about it and Rattigan seized upon the idea: 'My God, the whole thing works. Why didn't I think of that? I don't want a father and son. I want a father and daughter...'[33] Because of this change, the two polarised ideological positions in the film are heavily gendered. The father represents the visionary pioneer, and the notion of progress at any cost, while his daughter questions the impulse to break through frontier after frontier regardless of the human attrition rate. Their increasingly bitter arguments, separation and eventual reconciliation form what one critic called the 'counter melody'[34] of the film. Although the father's arguments finally win out, Sue's position is given weight and credence by Rattigan's writing, as she asks: 'is the ability to travel at two thousand miles an hour going to be a blessing to the human race?' She offers a sharp economically grounded critique of who will really benefit from this advance; Ridgefield's shareholders, and the very wealthy few who are able to afford supersonic travel (anticipating criticisms of Concorde). I feel that Michael Anderegg is mistaken in his suggestion that Sue 'presents no coherent argument ... she merely whines continually about not being able to understand. Her opposition is reduced to the "Feminine Principle", the woman who cannot fathom what it is that men can do.'[35] Sue does represent a feminine principle, as Anderegg suggests, but it is one that is granted some credence and authority rather than merely being whining; losing her brother and her husband to her father's vision, she refuses to lose her son as well and instead, as one reviewer noted, 'is fiercely determined to protect him from the ideology which can lead to sudden death'.[36]

Sue's position was echoed in several female reviewers' responses to the philosophical dilemma posed by the film. The *Daily Graphic*'s Elspeth Grant aligned herself with a female critique of the need for speed:

> I cannot see what useful purpose will be served if we are ultimately able to put a girdle about the earth in 40 minutes. Shall we have peace through that? Shall we be one whit happier? I do not think so. I am for the slow boat to anywhere – which shows how unprogressive I am. Mine is, of course, a strictly feminine point of view – but I think there must be millions of women like me, for the Amy Johnsons and Amelia Earharts are surely few. In his script for the film, Mr Terence Rattigan makes out a case for the masculine viewpoint. To a man, it seems, the world is a challenge. Armed with imagination and courage, he sets out to conquer it – to wrest from it its secrets.[37]

The *Daily Mail*'s Iris Ashley asked women how they would feel in Ann Todd's position and 'got the same answer from most. "Human life is more valuable than progress – and, anyway, what's all the hurry?" But how can we separate life and progress? If we were deprived of the benefits of science half of us would not survive long.'[38] In considering who shouldered the heaviest burden in the exploration of the stratosphere, Ashley spoke up for the unsung heroism of those who, in the words of the film's pressbook, 'earthbound, can only sit and wait':[39]

> I am inclined to think there are times when it is far easier for a man to go out and be a hero than it is for his wife to stand quietly by and let him get on with it ... It is in no way belittling to suggest that there can be excitement, even exaltation, in the bravery of the pioneer of science, the explorer, and the test pilot. What is there to sustain his wife? ... Personally, I'd sooner be a coward down here than a brave man up there, but if I had to choose I'd rather be a hero than a hero's wife any day.[40]

Perhaps because of this feminine scepticism about technological progress, several reviewers worried whether the film could appeal equally to both male and female cinemagoers. Their desires were seen as unambiguously gendered, with men relishing the twin spectacles of action and advanced technology, while women would be interested in the human story exemplified by Ann Todd's dilemma (making her addition to the film all the more strategically significant). *Kine Weekly* expressed relief that despite having 'the most superbly photographed flying sequences ever screened', the film 'never allows technicalities to overshadow essential feminine appeal'.[41] Along similar lines but more outspoken is Reg Whitley's piece, 'Faster than sound but is it too slow, girls?':

> The trouble with flying films, my cinema friends tell me, is that while the boys will always go for a good one it has to be something really super-colossal to interest the girls. They usually prefer a spot of romance and a good laugh – or cry – to anything dealing with mechanics, even when they're supersonic... [The film has] unsurpassed aerial thrills that will make strong men grip their seats with excitement. But what about the girls? How will they react – especially to the necessarily technical talk?[42]

The incongruity of femininity and flight was illustrated by the accompanying image of Ann Todd unrecognisable in full flying gear, captioned 'Guess who?' with the solution underneath. The film was greatly admired by reviewer Margaret Shipley for its action sequences (which 'will have everybody gripping their seat-arms with communicated horror') but she took issue with the depiction of women in the film: 'When a test pilot marries, neither the individual not the sum of human progress is greatly assisted by a wife who clings like a stricken vine, perpetually bleating "What about ME?".'[43] Interestingly, Shipley's criticism echoed David Lean's disputes with Ann Todd about how to play the part of Sue, and in particular the scene in which she pleads with Tony not to go on the dangerous test flight. Todd insisted that it should be a fight: 'I felt that women, when they have something important to say, are inclined to get rather fierce. It's an animal thing. At some terrible hour of the morning I played it the way I thought it ought to be played. And then I cried at the end and became very feminine.'[44] Lean's reaction was silence and a row ensued between the couple, with Lean insisting that if Todd played it her way 'no man would stay in the audience. They'd just walk out.'[45] In the end it was Lean's vision of polite entreaty and stoic acceptance rather than Todd's atavistic fury that made the final cut. However, Todd's vision of the emotional underpinnings of the scene would become the dominant image used on posters for the film: a desperate woman clinging onto a man by the lapels of his flying suit.[46]

Ann Todd plays slightly against her usual type here, cast not as ethereal ice maiden but pregnant earth mother. She is grounded in *The Sound Barrier* in contrast with her romantic alpine ascent in *The Passionate Friends* or her aura of enigma in *Madeleine*. Here, her white gloves are held to her mouth in horror as she watches her brother perish in a fireball spewing black smoke. She cries out involuntarily as she looks down into the deep crater containing the mangled wreckage of her husband's plane, grasping her side with the onset of labour pains. We share her point of view here via a horrible crane shot looming over the smouldering pit. But Sue is not totally earthbound. Earlier in the film, we had seen her up in the clouds alongside her husband, enjoying a daytrip to Egypt, and revelling (like the viewer) in the spectacular aerial views on display over France, Belgium, Holland, the Mediterranean, Greece and North Africa.[47] However, while she looks down at the earth, and worries that everything below looks 'very small and insignificant', her husband urges her to look up: 'There's our future: space. You can't make that insignificant.' Thus the jet plane figures as the latest expression of a continuum of technological achievement that goes back to the civilisations of ancient Greece and Egypt (striking images of the Parthenon and the Sphinx are juxtaposed with the sound of the jet roaring overhead). There is no room for the sentimental nostalgia for older forms of technology in contemporaneous British films like *The Titfield Thunderbolt* (1953) or *Genevieve* (1953); here we see nineteenth-century engineering marvels surpassed when the plane zooms over and beyond a speeding train on the ground below.

Sue frequently escapes from Ridgefield's patriarchal household to the resolutely feminine space of Jess (Dinah Sheridan) and Philip's cottage, a 'roses-round-the-door' bucolic idyll with a *mise en scène* dominated by the trappings of domesticity and motherhood: a giant teddy bear, children's toys, baby shoes, a mixing bowl, chintzy soft furnishings and a baby's high chair. Sue presents an image of ultra-femininity as she goes out to the cinema to distract herself from Tony's activities, heavily pregnant in sprigged floral cotton blouse and carrying her wicker shopping basket.[48] The suburban skyline above her head, with the clouds suddenly bisected by a plane's vapour trail, then dissolves to a new shot: the Andromeda galaxy seen through Ridgefield's telescope, bringing in a discussion between father and son-in-law about the death and rebirth of distant stars. Male and female spheres are truly polarised; the women doing the suburban round of shopping and cinemagoing (not unlike Laura Jesson's weekly trip to Milford) while the men ponder and attempt to conquer the mysteries of the universe.

This binary opposition of masculine and feminine finds its apotheosis in the scene that follows Philip's first successful supersonic flight. Before he has a chance to tell his wife Jess about his epoch-making achievement, she has launched into a hurried conversation about new coats for the children: 'We've got to make up our minds now. Do you think the colour's too much? ... Look, darling, pay attention. This is very important.' Of course, there is obvious dramatic irony in her insistence that such domestic trivia is 'very important' when her husband has just descended from conquering the stratosphere. Nonetheless, when Philip's laughter morphs into sobs, it is perhaps because of his sudden sharpened awareness of the importance of his wife and family, and exactly what he might have lost through his aerial expeditions. As Silver and Ursini suggest, Philip possesses an 'admirable ability to balance between the two worlds'[49] more than any of the other men in the film, but the character's hysteria at this moment speaks of an impossible rupture: can the worlds of supersonic flight and children's coats ever comfortably coexist?

The final reconciliation of father and daughter struck several critics as 'a false soft note'[50] and 'merely a sentimental evasion'.[51] Despite her earlier insistence that her father's ambition for dominion over the skies might be 'an evil vision', and the loss of her brother and husband, Sue is moved by her father's admission of self-doubt which finally humanises him in her eyes. The last sequence of the film shows her coming back home with her young son, John. They call on Ridgefield in his observatory, and there is a slightly chilling moment when the toddler is placed on an image of the moon's surface, 'presaging, possibly, his astronautical future'[52] which Sue had tried specifically to prevent before. The newly reconstituted family exit the room together, a touching crossgenerational image, but the camera remains with Ridgefield's telescope. The final shot has a model for the new Prometheus, screen left, and the telescope, screen right, both angled upwards towards space; the next step for Ridgefield's vision. The music is far from triumphant but repeats instead the semi-atonal 'enchantment' piccolo motif previously connected with both Chris's and Tony's deaths. As Gene Phillips suggests, 'this unearthly music spirals upward'[53] and seems distinctly sinister when paired with the relentless gesturing skywards of inanimate objects in anticipation of men following the same path. This closing image puts me in mind of the title of Wernher Von Braun's autobiography: 'I aim at the stars.' The Nazi rocket scientist who created the devastating V2 bomb using slave labour but ended up the lynchpin of NASA's space programme proves an object lesson in the amorality of technological vision and the barbarities committed in its service (it was Mort Sahl who made the sardonic suggestion that Von Braun's book should have the subtitle 'but sometimes I hit London').[54]

However, the notion of aiming at the stars might be a good motto for David Lean at this time; a highly ambitious director engaged in film-making on a grander scale than many of his British contemporaries, and not nostalgically cosying up to the past but pointing to the future instead. Lean wanted to make more films of this adventurous ilk but ironically ended up with the period comedy *Hobson's Choice* as his next film, a complete departure from *The Sound Barrier* although it shares with its predecessor the theme of a dissident daughter defying her overbearing father, and it does feature a character hankering after the moon (albeit reflected in a puddle). Lean's passion for the skies, the stratosphere and what lies beyond had not really abated though. After making *Lawrence of Arabia*, Lean wrote to Bolt about his idea for a film encompassing the remarkable achievements of humanity, from our primordial origins as the 'jelly in the sunlit pool' to the supreme human achievements of jet-powered aviation and satellites gracefully orbiting the earth, which would empower the downtrodden common man with its transcendent 'anti suburban mentality'.[55] However, one might say that in *The Sound Barrier*, most specifically in the eerie sublimity of its closing sequences, Lean had already achieved many of those aims.

The Bridge on the River Kwai (1957)

David Lean's working relationship with Sam Spiegel, simultaneously highly productive and highly antagonistic, began with their large-scale war film *The Bridge on the River Kwai*. Lean's carefully planned previous project, an adaptation of Richard Mason's interracial romance *The Wind Cannot Read*, had fallen through (Lean and Mason's script would eventually be directed by Ralph Thomas for Rank), enabling him to take up Spiegel's offer. It is interesting to reflect that *Kwai*, the film that is often seen as marking the watershed in Lean's career, his first in the epic mode that would become his hallmark henceforth, and such a military, masculine spectacle, could so easily have been supplanted by an epic widescreen love story instead. In some senses, that former project would have followed on more cogently from Lean's previous cross-cultural love story, *Summer Madness*. Certainly *Kwai* marked Lean's decisive entry into the world of big-budget spectacular filmmaking, 'bloody millionaire stuff' in the words of his prop man Eddie Fowlie. The emblematic image of this high-end production is its bridge; meticulously constructed at great expense and effort, to be dramatically destroyed in the film's explosive climax (a departure from Pierre Boulle's original novel, where it remained intact).[56] However, despite being characterised as an 'absolutely perfect example of an action film' by admiring filmmaker John Milius, *The Bridge on the River Kwai* actually has fewer spectacular set-pieces than one might expect from this description, relying instead on its 'wonderful characters' to propel the narrative.[57] Indeed, Lean felt that the 'size' of *Kwai* was dependent not on magnificent expansive locations or booming ballistics but on the central performances, especially whoever played Colonel Nicholson. In a lengthy letter to Sam Spiegel, he explained his viewpoint on the character and his central importance to the film:

> The Colonel is the great central pillar of our story. He is a magnificent tragic-comic figure well out of the usual run of film characters. He is unusual because although he is a heroic figure, his actions are well-nigh foolhardy, as above all his main objective is to build a bridge for the enemy in the best possible way. As a director I have to make this extraordinary hero understandable to an audience. If they don't understand and admire him in spite of his misguided actions, his stature will diminish – and being the cornerstone of the film – the size of the film will diminish with him ... Colonel Nicholson is a misguided hero as seen from the inside. A fool and a maniac as seen from the outside ... I want to put a microscope on Colonel Nicholson. At the moment you are trying to show the workings of a complicated Swiss watch, and you don't even remove the casing ... If this is going to be a big picture, it will be a picture of character and not of plot.[58]

Nicholson is juxtaposed with a host of other male figures: the cheerfully cynical American Shears (William Holden), the sardonic medical officer Clipton (James Donald), the Don-turned-commando Warren (Jack Hawkins) and Nicholson's opposite number on the enemy side, the Japanese camp commandant Colonel Saito (Sessue Hayakawa). Although with hindsight it is impossible to imagine anyone other than Alec Guinness playing Nicholson, at the time Lean worried that the actor wouldn't be able to imbue the role with sufficient stature, and his preference was for Ronald Colman or Ralph Richardson. It was Sam Spiegel who finally persuaded a reluctant Guinness to take on the role;

one of many important contributions made to the film by its producer. He would also manage, where many others had failed, to persuade A. W. Lawrence to permit a film to be made of his brother's life, thus enabling Lean to create the film usually considered his masterpiece. Lean would subsequently denigrate Spiegel as a meddler and a crook, and even sympathetic accounts of the producer depict him as 'a charming buccaneer who could have slit your throat and convinced you that it was necessary'.[59] But as Kevin Brownlow reminds us, *Kwai* could not have been achieved without Spiegel's backing: 'a film of this scale, however brilliant the director, depends on enormous financial support.'[60] Not only that, but Spiegel was 'often brilliant' in his interventions at the scripting stage, with an 'ability to put his finger on what was wrong',[61] according to Norman Spencer. Lean's playing of 'the pukka gentleman to the producer's "Big cigar, baby, let's buy them out" approach'[62] was partly mutual self-caricature, but the idea of the two men as complementary, albeit quarrelsome opposites has considerable substance to it. Indeed, when Lean wrote to Spiegel about the conflict between Nicholson and Saito as 'a tremendous clash of wills',[63] he could have been describing his own working relationship with the producer.

Lean experienced a similar clash of wills with the first writer assigned to the project. Carl Foreman's initial script met with disappointment, with Lean feeling that it failed to convey the ironies inherent in Boulle's novel, turning it into 'an adventure story pure and simple'.[64] Writers Calder Willingham and Michael Wilson worked on subsequent drafts, although the former's revisions were rejected wholesale by Lean. The long-standing injustice of inaccurate credit for the film, due to the pressures of the Hollywood blacklist, was finally corrected for the film's 1992 video release, with Foreman and Wilson named as its writers (although Lean would remain unaccredited for his considerable script work). One notable example of the authorial struggles in the film's creation comes with the film's opening sequences, and the entry of Nicholson and his men into the camp. Spiegel was far from keen on Lean's idea of using the overly English tune 'Colonel Bogey' to accompany their arrival, while Foreman insisted that Lean's ambition to make an entire sequence out of this moment betrayed his origins as 'an art-house director' with 'no experience of the international market': 'You can't take up three minutes with British troops walking into a camp whistling a tune nobody's ever heard of – you can't expect people to sit in their seats.'[65] In the end, of course, the scene did hold, and remains one of the film's most memorable moments – and even made an international hit of the old marching song. After the opening shots of a train thundering past the trackside graves of perished labourers and a brisk funeral cynically conducted by

Shears ('To the greater glory of...?'), the whistling of the new arrivals signals the audacity of hope even in the most uncompromising of environments. As the men under Nicholson's command march, Lean picks out details of their physical dilapidation; the dirty bloody bandages, the ragged uniforms, the boot that flaps apart with its owner's rhythmical movement. Cutaways to Nicholson surveying his men coincide with the swelling of the music from diegetic whistling to Malcolm Arnold's full orchestral version; music which Lean hoped would have 'a grandeur, a real swagger'.[66] Although the ostensible reading of the moment is in terms of defiance and indomitability – Eddie Fowlie speaks of 'pride in the human animal' upon watching the sequence[67] – one might also discern a hint of incipient mania, in Nicholson's expression at least. The pulsing of his cheek muscles suggests strong emotion being kept under control (to overflow later), while the heightening of the music inaugurated by Nicholson's point of view is not that far away from the 'tunes of glory' that Guinness's character hears in Ronald Neame's 1960 military drama of the same name, used to signify his increasing mental instability.

Despite their dramatic richness, the scenes of marching men overlaid with swaggering martial music have also acted as a flashpoint for those critical of Lean's film, particularly in terms of its inaccuracies in representing the experiences of those who had worked on the Burma–Siam railway during the Second World War. Typical is one review of Ian Denys Peek's war memoir *One-Fourteenth of an Elephant*, which begins by mentioning *Kwai* and 'that uplifting tune' but concludes that facing up to the grim reality of Peek's account 'makes it impossible for me to watch that film again'.[68] Another death railway veteran, Ian Watt, in a 1959 BBC radio programme on the film, found the film's first shots 'very exciting; there they were, the vultures, the narrow cuttings, the bedraggled prisoners', and admitted that the 'Colonel Bogey' marching scenes were 'passable, perhaps probable; but I also remembered how early the prisoners in Siam had lost the boots and the energy that one needs for marking time properly – to say nothing of their tolerance of regimental nonsense'.[69] Others with the same experience of one of the war's cruellest episodes were repulsed by the film's iconic status in representing that part of the conflict. Memoirist Eric Lomax accused it of conveying 'a false picture ... who ever saw such well-fed POWs?'[70] while artist Ronald Searle criticised it as 'romantic nonsense' during his 2005 *Desert Island Discs* appearance.[71] The controversy surrounding the film has raged ever since its initial cinema release, as members of the National Federation of Far Eastern Prisoners of War passed a resolution at their 1958 conference 'deploring the fact that the story of the film was not described as fiction' and 'falsely represented prisoners' conduct',[72] and angry letters were written to the newspapers, like this one from a Maisie Sheed: 'Remembering soldiers I knew from that theatre of war who returned shattered wrecks, knowing of the many others who died through sabotaging and impeding Japanese war efforts, I felt it intolerable that such a picture should be shown without explanation.'[73] Lean's response to these criticisms is not recorded but one would imagine that they stung, especially given Lean's own self-doubt about the tone of his work while he was filming, confessed in a letter to Spiegel: 'It's just like a group of jolly boy scouts having pranks with the scoutmaster ... sorry to go on like this but it has given me an awful hit below the belt. I didn't realise the thing could be so misinterpreted.'[74]

The first section of *Kwai* centres on the aforementioned battle of wills between Nicholson and Saito. The unequal power relations between captor and captives are suggested visually by the shot of Saito's shiny immaculate high boots as he bestrides the platform through which we glimpse the troops with their (as we have just seen) much shoddier footwear. Saito's attempt at benevolent dictatorship ('be happy in your work') is challenged by Nicholson's insistence on adherence to the letter of the Geneva Convention, a protest which earns him a slapped face and several days locked in the baking heat of a tiny corrugated iron prison nicknamed 'the oven'.[75] Physical punishment doesn't break him and nor does the temptation of English corned beef and Scotch whisky offered by Saito. Guinness's physical performance in these scenes makes us acutely aware of a man undergoing terrible bodily suffering but forcing himself to maintain his upright demeanour for the sake of his men; Guinness later said Nicholson's 'curious, slightly lurching, bent walk' was an imitation of the gait of his son while recovering from polio.[76] In the end Saito's only option is a humiliating climb-down, and hence Nicholson enjoys victory, raised on the shoulders of his cheering men, while Saito is overcome by choking sobs back in the privacy of his quarters, clenching his fists to his head at his shame. Allegedly it was Lean's harsh treatment of Sessue Hayakawa for necessitating retakes that partly instigated the actor's intensely poignant performance in the scene.

Despite their obvious cultural differences, and Saito's insistence that he hates the British and does not want to 'hear of rules. This is war. This is not a game of cricket', the two colonels nonetheless occupy common ground in obeying their respective military codes, as the opening line of Boulle's novel insists: 'The insuperable gap between East and West that exists in some eyes is perhaps nothing more than an optical illusion.'[77] Mirroring face-to-face profile shots become a presentational trope of scenes featuring the two men together. During the course of one of their exchanges we find out that Saito is a frustrated artist who studied for three years at the London Polytechnic before being compelled to switch to engineering (this is in ironic counterpoint to Nicholson's later admission that, despite appearing to be the acme of Englishness, he has actually spent fewer than ten months in the mother country in the past 28 years – less than Saito). Neither man's identity, national or otherwise, is as monolithic as it initially appears, and with Saito this cultural complexity is also indicated by the odd details in the *mise en scène* of his quarters which mixes traditional Japanese tatami mats and wall hangings with the tacky Americana of a girlie pin-up calendar for 'Joey's Garage, Elk City, Ohio'.

The destinies of the two men are intertwined, and, in Boulle's words, Nicholson's 'confidence asserted itself in direct proportion to Saito's increasing embarrassment'.[78] As Nicholson enjoys his triumph at the celebratory concert party (the first and only time we see him laugh in the film), Saito prepares for ritual suicide. The preceding scene where the two men meet on the bridge, beautifully shot in the warm glow of 'magic hour', and movingly performed by both actors, manages to encapsulate simultaneously the men's kinship and the gulf between them (Plate 12). Saito declares the sunset beautiful, but Nicholson mistakenly (and symptomatically) thinks he's referring to the newly completed bridge. However, Nicholson's consideration of his life, expertly timed by Guinness to coincide with the setting of the sun, applies just as well to Saito:

> But there are times when suddenly you realise you're nearer the end than the beginning. And you wonder, you ask yourself, what the sum total of your life represents. What difference your being there at any time made to anything. Hardly made any difference at all, really, particularly in comparison with other men's careers. I don't know whether that kind of thinking's very healthy; but I must admit I've had some thoughts on those lines from time to time.

The camera focuses on Nicholson's back, partly to suggest Saito's point of view but also to make this a fittingly restrained and underplayed moment of English emotional revelation, as Neil Sinyard suggests: 'Nicholson's awkward, covert way of expressing his deepest feelings in *Kwai* is complemented by Lean's eloquently oblique, indirect framing.'[79] Guinness had wanted to play it in close-up, and the closer profile shot later on during his speech marked a kind of compromise. But the maintenance of distance is crucial to the sequence's power. This is a man inadvertently, accidentally, revealing his deepest feelings through what seems to be an idle conversation, in little details like the way he stretches out the words 'from time to time', or telling unconscious gestures like his stroking the wood on the bridge lovingly – a sudden outbreak of

12 Nearer the end than the beginning: Nicholson (Alec Guinness) and Saito (Sessue Hayakawa) at sundown in *The Bridge on the River Kwai* (1957)

sensualism in an otherwise buttoned-up man (borrowed from Lean's own gesture of stroking the camera that had filmed *Roses of Picardy* (1927) when he first entered British Gaumont studios[80]) – and unexpectedly releasing his baton upon the words 'But tonight' to let it fall into the river below, a sign that he is 'losing his grip' in the thrill of the moment.

As Boulle suggests, East and West have much in common. The honourable self-sacrifice of Saito's 'bushido' military code mirrors the ethos of riding faithfully 'into the valley of death' that Shears associates with Nicholson. Shears also draws Warren into this comparison with his angry outburst during their jungle mission:

> You make me sick with your heroics! There's a stench of death about you. You carry it in your pack like the plague. Explosives and L-pills – they go well together, don't they? And with you it's just one thing or the other: destroy a bridge or destroy yourself. This is just a game, this war! You and Colonel Nicholson, you're two of a kind, crazy with courage. For what? How to die like a gentleman, how to die by the rules – when the only important thing is how to live like a human being.

Thus William Holden's Shears, the established American star of the film, is characterised as the true lover-of-life in contrast to the military men of other nations half in love with easeful death. Shears is 'a civilian at heart' by his own appraisal, despite his eventual death in action. But it is a significant development that the figure who questions obsessive vision and human sacrifice in its service in *Kwai* is a man, in contrast with *The Sound Barrier*'s female interrogative voice.

Although Ann Todd described her role in *The Sound Barrier* as 'only a woman in a man's film',[81] that description actually seems much more fitting for Ann Sears and the four Thai actresses in the male-dominated *Kwai*. In fact, Sears's role was only introduced because of Columbia's fears that the film 'was too "male-orientated" to do business',[82] with

MEN OF VISION 151

Lean later deeming Sears and Holden's brief love scenes 'bloody awful'.[83] They may well be perfunctory but in their evocation of beachy sensuality and unapologetic sexuality (with Sears's brazenly cheerful 'good morning' as she leaves Holden's bungalow after their night together) they provide a contrast with the majority of the film's action, and underline Shears's difference from his more uptight comrades.[84]

According to Norman Spencer, Lean was altogether keener on the Burmese girl bearers who assist Warren, Shears and Joyce (Geoffrey Horne) in their mission to blow up the bridge, and 'went to town' on filming them.[85] Perhaps Lean was making up for his lost opportunity to eulogise submissive oriental femininity in *The Wind Cannot Read*, characterising Asian women (in the most sexist and Orientalist terms) as sweet, charming, gentle, kind, not at all tough, scrupulously clean, and 'brought up to look after men'.[86] The film's publicity material follows along similar lines, sighing over 'beautiful almond-eyed' girls whose names apparently translate into English as 'All Beautiful, Beautiful Eyes, Young Lady and Flower'.[87] Although the slightly anomalous presence of women in the otherwise all-male film was criticised as unlikely by some – Derek Hill described the bearers as 'apparent finalists in a Miss Siam contest'[88] – no less an authority than André Bazin spoke up in their favour. The film's romantic relationships were 'a bit conventional' and 'sentimental', Bazin argued, but they could be justified in terms of 'the psychological and dramatic usefulness of an erotic aura, which serves as a prelude to the heroes' death', and 'not only was the screenwriter not wrong to sketch in these love affairs, but he also would have been mistaken not to do so'.[89] Although they are marginal and often silent, the Burmese women in *Kwai* still have a significant, albeit stereotypical, function as gentle feminine counterpoint to a masculine ethos of destruction. They suggest a lost paradise, made explicit in the Gaughin-esque sequence where they bathe with the men in beautiful pools and waterfalls, wrapped in bright-coloured sarongs: Lean's homage to Flaherty and Van Dyke's *White Shadows of the South Seas* (1928).[90] The shocking intrusion of a Japanese soldier (presented in the same fashion as Magwitch's first appearance) turns the idyll into a bloodbath, with Hildyard's colour photography making a striking tableau of the spreading red in the clear blue water, and the frightened women marooned on the rocks, with the flying foxes startled by the gunfire suddenly darkening the skies.

The parallel plots of the building of the bridge and the commando mission to destroy it finally converge in the film's climactic sequences. Isabel Quigly conveys very well in her review the film's mounting sense of moral and ethical equivalence:

It shows war up from various points of view ... and each point of view is criticised by another, its opposite and complement. One ends up stimulated, wondering and confused. Heroism one cannot fail to admire, but where does it begin and end? What is courage and what mere flag-waving, what cowardice and what prudence?[91]

Ambiguity is the keynote of the drama, as Lean himself emphasised in a letter to Sam Spiegel: 'It is a story of shades and tones, of half rights and half wrongs – of human dilemma.'[92] In order to explore this, irony is one of the primary tools deployed by the film, introduced in the questions posed by medical officer Clipton, who dares to suggest to Nicholson quite early on in proceedings that 'what we're doing could be construed as – forgive me sir – collaboration with the enemy. Perhaps even as treasonable activity', only to be met with Nicholson's dismissive response that he has 'a lot to learn about the Army'. There is a lovely moment of misunderstanding when the men on the mission spy through their binoculars what they think is a commanding officer shamefully reduced to enforced labour on his knees when what they are witnessing is actually Nicholson's proudest moment: the erection of a plaque commemorating his men's work on the magnificent bridge. However, as Quigly suggests, there is no simple condemnation of Nicholson. Instead there is an undeniable validity to his view that it is better to maintain morale and to construct something of lasting significance than to let his men deteriorate into squalid dissipation. Although Clipton is clearly the voice of reason juxtaposed with Nicholson's blinkered monomania, some of the Colonel's responses to Clipton's inquisitions are harder to answer, such as when he evokes medical ethics as a comparison to his own decision to do the best possible job on the bridge: 'if you had to operate on Saito, would you do your best or would you let him die?' There is something deeply counter-intuitive and morale-sapping about building a bridge badly, as former POW Ian Watt testified: 'our lives had been one long and meaningless compromise between our notion of duty and our instinct of workmanship; one minute we'd be doing a bit of casual sabotage with a faulty bolt or a well-placed ants' nest, and the next we'd be trying to make a neat job of a mortise and tenon joint or straining to get some heavy timber into perfect alignment.'[93] Although Anderegg constructs a plausible reading of the film as an allegory of the Suez crisis,[94] far more persuasive is Brownlow's suggestion that what the Frenchman Pierre Boulle was doing in his novel, and what bleeds into its subsequent adaptation, was examining some of the paradoxes of collaboration, using the captured British to elucidate his own country's recent history.

Nicholson's insistence that he is doing it for his men's morale belies his vanity and his own Ozymandian tendencies to construct a lasting monument that might endure for 'six hundred years, that would be quite something.' For all his efforts to retain composure and self-possession during his terrible punishment in the oven, something changes irrevocably for Nicholson during that ordeal; in the crucible of the heat, his future compulsion has been forged.[95] It is shortly after his triumphant release from incarceration and victory over Saito that Nicholson first announces his intention to cooperate in building the bridge in order to 'rebuild the battalion' and to 'teach these barbarians a lesson in Western methods and efficiency that will put them to shame. We'll show them what the British soldier is capable of doing.' Interestingly, this speech takes place on a floating platform crossing the river, indicating Nicholson's parallel movement across a moral boundary, from resistance to collaboration. That great admirer of Lean, Steven Spielberg, used a very similar setting for the scene in *Jaws* (1975) in which the Mayor of Amity cynically decides to hush up the shark's first attack; another physical journey across water used to indicate the crossing of an ethical point of no return. However, there is nothing cynical about Nicholson's resolution, and the improved morale of his men in constructing a beautiful bridge is vindication enough for his decision, until the moment of his face-to-face confrontation with Shears. Yet another piece of mirroring between characters takes place, this time in the dialogue, with Nicholson's incredulous 'You?' met by Shears's accusatory 'You!' From this point onwards, Nicholson's rationalisation of his actions and his determination to protect the bridge cannot hold, and his movement is suspended, as he removes his hat and scratches his head as if emerging from a daydream, finally asking himself 'What have I done?' His salvation only comes through an action that can be interpreted as partly premeditated or wholly accidental: falling onto the plunger that in turn detonates the explosives packed under bridge. Isabel Quigly found this an 'over-strained coincidence' but there is a pleasing serendipity in Nicholson's final act bringing about the destruction of what he had hoped would be his lasting monument.

Lindsay Anderson found *Kwai*'s ending glib, briskly dismissing it thus: 'it takes more than the word "madness" repeated three times at the end of a film to justify comparisons with *All Quiet on the Western Front*',[96] referring to Clipton's final summation of the carnage. Charles Barr has also provided a cogent critique of James Donald's unexplained disappearance from the final scenes, only reappearing to utter the concluding words, which inaugurate the camera's airborne withdrawal and the swelling score: 'how crudely the film here manipulates him, and wastes him ... He simply doesn't need to *say* "madness" once, let alone three times: he can speak much more forcefully through eyes, eyebrows, the set of the mouth.'[97] Perhaps so, but in some respects it seems that 'madness' is the only word that *Kwai* could end on, a word harped on and played with throughout its script, from Saito's 'He's mad, your Colonel. Quite mad' echoed by Warden's later 'He's gone mad' through to Nicholson's counter-accusation of Saito, 'Actually, I think he's mad', and finally Clipton's 'Are they both mad or am I going mad? Or is it the sun?' In Boulle's novel, Clipton loses his cynicism and goes along with Nicholson's scheme, whereas in the film he never loses his ironic distance, although he does begin to doubt his sanity.[98] In representations of English identity, intense heat and incipient insanity are often intrinsically linked: a notion given its supreme comic expression by Noel Coward's song 'Mad Dogs and Englishmen' and outstanding tragicomic expression in *The Bridge on the River Kwai*. However, Lean's next film would explore in even greater depth the obsessive English male forged under the hot foreign sun, whose magnificent actions tread a fine line between sanity and madness.

Lawrence of Arabia (1962)

The contemporary reputation of *Lawrence of Arabia* is as an undisputed classic of epic film-making, lionised by the likes of Steven Spielberg as the inspiration for his own directorial career and greeted with acclaim upon its 1989 restoration and re-release. Back in 1962, when the film first came out, Lean's peers were also more than fulsome in their praise of the film, with both George Cukor and Billy Wilder telling the director that they couldn't get the film out of their minds, King Vidor, a favourite director of Lean's from the silent days, expressing his admiration, and Fred Zinnemann declaring Lean to be 'a bloody poet'.[99] *Lawrence of Arabia*'s initial critical reception was also generally positive in tone, praising its magnificent spectacle ('this is just about the *best-looking* film in the whole of my experience')[100] as well as its more cerebral qualities as 'an epic with intellect behind it'.[101] However, an influential group of British critics clustered around the emergent magazine *Movie* firmly rejected the film, as Philip French later recalled: '[they] huffily announced that they were off to see a truly serious film in the NFT's first Howard Hawks season.'[102] For these nascent auteurists, the other new releases reviewed in the same week as *Lawrence* would have been of much greater interest: Hawks's latest, the African adventure film *Hatari!*, and Godard's cinephiliac character study *Vivre sa vie*. Even in more recent years, dissenting voices have still been raised about *Lawrence*'s canonical status, and the prestige of the kind of epic cinema it

MEN OF VISION 155

epitomises. In Stephen Frears's 1995 authored documentary on British cinema, *Typically British*, *Lawrence*'s raid on Aqaba sequence is overlaid on the soundtrack with the theme music for the soap opera *Coronation Street* (1960–), indicative of a contemporaneous mode of British drama with entirely different – and perhaps to some eyes preferable – priorities: small-scale, small screen, domestic, quotidian.

This implicit comparison of *Lawrence*'s large-scale spectacle with small-scale soap opera, often seen as a quintessentially feminine form, raises some important questions of gender. Lean's cinema appeared to be taking a distinctly masculinised turn, with *Lawrence* following and extending the logic of *Kwai* in focussing on male military life. Whereas women had still been a marginal presence in the previous film, here they are virtually invisible. Despite running for over three hours, *Lawrence of Arabia* has no female speaking part and women's physical appearances in the film are also remarkably restricted. They exist only as the swathed masses bidding farewell to the Arab menfolk departing to war, their stasis contrasting dramatically with the dynamic galloping movement of the men leaving for Aqaba, or later as the anonymous victims of that war; a briefly glimpsed young girl and woman in the cutaway to Wadi Rumm after Auda's invitation to dine with him, or the glimpse of a jewelled hand of a woman riding camelback in purdah – actually belonging to the film's second assistant director David Tringham.[103] The lack of women in the film caused some anxiety to those marketing it, fearing its lack of appeal for female viewers. This is evident in the pressbook's slightly over-compensatory encouragement to exhibitors:

> 'Lawrence' could hardly be called a woman's picture – but by listing all the famous names in the star-studded cast on leaflets, milk bottle collars, etc. you could have a good angle for aiming specifically at the ladies. Well-worded leaflets, for example, distributed on a door-to-door basis, would probably bring in many women to the theatre – and don't forget they would be bringing their husbands along too.[104]

Women's fashion tie-ins were another popular strategy to increase female interest, with Columbia promoting a range of women's fashions inspired by *Lawrence of Arabia* with names such as 'desert dazzle' and 'chic sheik'.[105]

However, in its total evacuation of women characters on screen, *Lawrence of Arabia* could claim absolute fidelity to its main source text, T. E. Lawrence's *Seven Pillars of Wisdom* in which the author remarks that 'from end to end of it there was nothing female in the Arab movement, but the camels'.[106] Indeed, Jonathan Rutherford suggests that it was precisely this lack of women wherein lay the attractions of Bedouin existence for Lawrence. The desert offered an all-male utopia representing 'social exclusion from bourgeois familial culture and its sexualities: a "spiritual ice-house" of personal renunciation and "cleanness".'[107] For Rutherford, this latter quality offered by the desert environment, that of 'cleanness' (a word Lawrence frequently employs in *Seven Pillars*), was inextricably linked to 'its absolute lack of fecundity and its absence of women. Its sparseness and dryness were the antithesis of the imaginary maternal body with its enveloping softness and its fluids.'[108] There is certainly a strain of gynophobia in some of Lawrence's writing that is notable, ranging from his evocation of the repulsive decrepitude of Queen Alexandria in *The Mint* (written 1928, published 1955) to the disgust he expresses at a crowded troopship's latrine being blocked by a sanitary towel, the situation exemplifying for him a 'horror of almost final squalidity'.[109] Here, repudiation of the body and its potential for decay and degradation is vectored directly into repudiation of the female. However, there was also a more specific female presence from which Lawrence was anxious to extricate himself: his mother. He writes in a letter of 1927 about the encroachment upon his identity caused by his mother 'always hammering and rapping to come in'.[110] Escaping this powerful maternal influence seems to have played no small part in Lawrence's attraction towards the woman-free world of Arabian expedition.

And yet, as Lawrence goes on to elaborate after his comment on the camels, the absence of women from the Arab revolt did not mean an absence of femininity, more that its mantle was adopted by men rather than women, giving them a kind of 'double endowment' of gendered qualities: 'Like women, they [the Arabs] understood and judged quickly, effortlessly, unreasonably. It almost seemed as though the Oriental exclusion of women from politics had conferred her particular gifts upon the men.'[111] This gender discourse continues into the film in which no women may be prominent but nonetheless, as Steven Caton notes, 'the category "woman" is always present'.[112] This is most obviously true of the characterisation of T. E. Lawrence himself, strikingly described by Anderegg as 'a surrogate woman, a figurative white goddess'.[113] While Lawrence embodied manly imperial valour, he also possessed a number of qualities, often negative ones, typed as feminine. Indeed, for his 1950s biographer Jean Beraud-Villars, Lawrence could be like a 'hysterical woman, perfidious, lying, unstable, with a taste for travesty and treason, and a love of causing quarrels'.[114] But Caton also argues for a more positive identification of Lawrence with the feminine, even suggesting, quite contentiously, that 'O'Toole's androgynous performance, combined with his sensitive and introspective characterisation, allowed identification with him *as* a woman.'[115] Caton cites as proof the testimony of several female fans including critic Janet Maslin ('As a

MEN OF VISION 157

young adolescent, I became so desperately obsessed with [it] that I saw it over and over again, spent years studying the life of its hero, regarding him as a kind of role model') and another anonymous woman, who calls the film 'my secret obsession'.[116] Peter O'Toole's appearance and performance in the film suggested sexual ambiguity or androgyny, combining chiselled good looks and tall stature (unlike the real T. E. Lawrence) with dark make-up to accentuate his deep blue eyes, the fluid drapery of Arab costume (of which more later), a soft mellifluous voice and a repertoire of gesture tending at times towards the effeminate. For critic David Robinson, O'Toole's Lawrence resembled 'a medieval Madonna' in the Arab conference scenes[117] and, more famously, Noël Coward was to remark that the actor was so pretty that the film would have been more appropriately titled 'Florence of Arabia'.[118]

Although the marketeers of the film noted its divergence from anything resembling a 'woman's picture', in fact the film hinges on one of the key motifs of that genre, the make-over, with a physical transformation through clothes allegorising a deeper personal metamorphosis. Thinking of women's films like *Now, Voyager* (1942), Jane Gaines suggests how 'dress tells the woman's story',[119] but that statement seems equally true of the male-centred narrative of *Lawrence*. Just as *Now, Voyager*'s downtrodden spinster Charlotte creates a new confident self by assuming a new appearance (and thus disengages from the malign influence of an overbearing mother), so Lawrence discards the ill-fitting British army uniform (deliberately sized incorrectly for O'Toole by costume designer Phyllis Dalton) in favour of beautifully becoming white Arab robes trimmed with gold, reminiscent of Western bridal clothes. Lean's script notes on the significance of Lawrence's adoption of Arab dress point to the romance but also the potential delusionary quality to his change of clothes:

> We should pull out all the romantic stops in order to dramatize it in action for the first time. In the opening of the sequence, Lawrence should be Lowell Thomas's Twentieth Century Arabian Knight and the desert should be Ethel M. Dell's Garden of Allah. The dreamer is beginning to act out his dream with open eyes.[120]

Lawrence first adopts Arab headdress, in combination with his khaki uniform, on the eve of his triumph in Aqaba, signalling a growing ease in the Arab world. After his rescue of Gasim from the desert, and his important assertion that 'nothing is written', a more intimate scene sees him discuss his illegitimacy with Sherif Ali (Omar Sharif). Ali then applies Lawrence's logic to his friend, counselling him that without a father 'you are free to choose your own name then, to write yourself'. Lawrence has a new name 'El Aurens' given to him by his Arab comrades, but what seals his transformation is Ali's decision to burn his old clothes and present him with new ones. In one of the film's most memorable scenes we see him 'try on' this new self, enjoying the fit and fluidity of his new clothes and drawing his dagger, not in an act of martial aggression but to admire his reflection in the blade (Plate 13).[121] However, this is where the logic of the scene parts company with parallel moments of sartorial transformation in women's pictures. Whereas female self-interest in an attractive appearance is condoned, in a man it is condemned as narcissism. Lawrence's increasingly extravagant enjoyment of his attire, running back and forth to make the flowing garments billow behind him, is suddenly and embarrassingly interrupted when it is revealed that Auda has been watching him all along. One critic suggested that the 'effeminacy' of O'Toole's vain, posturing Lawrence was thrown into even greater relief through juxtaposition with Auda, played by 'completely masculine Anthony Quinn'.[122] Despite his adoption of beautiful becoming clothes, there are still limitations on Lawrence's metamorphosis. Auda's young son easily identifies the crestfallen Lawrence as English despite his Arab guise, and the verbal sparring that ensues between Ali and Auda hinges on paternity and bastardy, questions impossible to evade even in the world into which Lawrence has tried to escape and create a new 'legitimate' self. Clothes only partly make the man, and the insubstantiality of appearance is suggested through costume as Lawrence's story develops, with his robes made to look ever 'thinner, even more wraith-like' (Phyllis Dalton and wardrobe master John Wilson-Apperson used deliberately weathered organza to achieve the effect)[123] as his sense of self-assurance increasingly deteriorates.[124] Lawrence once described his life as 'the intact course of a snowflake',[125] and the film's costumes do an excellent

13 T. E. Lawrence (Peter O'Toole) surveys his new white robes in *Lawrence of Arabia* (1962)

job of suggesting something of that metaphor in fusing pristine whiteness with extreme vulnerability, especially in the context of what Dryden (Claude Rains) calls the 'burning fiery furnace' of the desert.

Lawrence's adoption of flowing white robes does not speak merely of 'gender trouble'. It also indicates his cultural border-crossing as an Englishman 'going native' in Arabia. The familiar trajectory of rise and fall in telling Lawrence's story is also evident in his relationship with the Arabs. He is gradually integrated into the Arab milieu, enjoying warm comradeship with Ali and astounding military success then followed by humiliation, disillusionment and ultimately exile. At two strategic moments in the film, Lawrence is mistaken for an Arab. The first comes in triumph, when the Arabs have captured Aqaba, and Lawrence and Farraj have returned to Cairo to report the victory, but are barred from the British officer's bar for being 'wogs'. In the conversation with Brighton (Anthony Quayle) that ensues, Lawrence's confused allegiances are made plain through Bolt's superb scripting of Lawrence's explanation of who has taken Aqaba: 'We have – Our side in the war has – the wogs have. We have.' (Later in the scene he changes to 'I did it'.) Peter O'Toole brilliantly brings to life Lawrence as a divided man, a British officer disgusted by the racism of his compatriots, and attempting to maintain military sangfroid in face of mounting hysteria – ice rattling in the glass of lemonade that has to be steadied by a second hand – hardly believing the achievements he has come to report. The second moment of 'passing' happens near the end of the film in the horrific environs of the Turkish hospital, unrelieved by British assistance, full of the dead and dying. A British medical officer pushes Lawrence aside with a brusque 'Get out of my way, you filthy little wog', angrily slapping him when Lawrence's incredulity turns to peals of laughter. The same man will later want to shake the great T. E. Lawrence's hand when he sees him in British battledress – 'Haven't we met before? Lawrence sardonically enquires – and we realise that he is the same man from the film's opening scenes who was enraged by the suggestion that Lawrence was a 'shameless exhibitionist'.

Placed between these two scenes of ethnic misrecognition is another where Lawrence's Arab disguise fails, his capture in Deraa. His robes are stripped away, revealing the lily-white skin underneath, which is then fingered lasciviously by the Turkish Bey (José Ferrer) as prelude to sexual assault. Later, Lawrence will mimic the Bey's gesture in explaining to Ali what he now regards as the irreducible reality of race, pinching the flesh on his chest: 'I'm not the Arab revolt, Ali. I'm not even an Arab. Look. That's me ... That's what makes us want what we want.' His hopes of refuge in another culture, questionable at the best of time, have proven impossible. In *Seven Pillars of Wisdom*, Lawrence reflects on the dangers of the process of cultural translation he had undergone and what he regarded as the harmful effects of his living within a foreign culture:

> In my case, the effort for these years to live in the dress of Arabs, and to imitate their mental foundation, quitted me of my English self, and let me look at the west and its conventions with new eyes: they destroyed it all for me. At the same time I could not sincerely take on the Arab skin: it was an affectation only ... I had dropped one form and not taken on the other.[126]

There is no sense of optimistic hybridity in this account, more the trauma of becoming stranded between two cultures. Drawing on the postcolonial theory of Homi Bhabha, one might characterise those moments of pathos when we see Lawrence desperately try to embody hegemonic white masculinity, by jogging up to fellow soldiers and enthusing about sport ('jolly good about the squash court') in terms of an imperfect act of mimicry of the colonial male, which is immediately detected as bogus: 'lays it on a bit thick, doesn't he?'[127] Nonetheless, there is an obvious danger in refracting all elements of East–West cultural exchange solely through the lens of the single personage. In a criticism that also works of Lean's film, Edward Said suggests that, in an act of solipsistic Orientalism, 'Lawrence reduces the entire narrative of the revolt (its momentary successes and its bitter failure) to *his* vision of himself as an unresolved, "standing civil war".'[128]

However, *Lawrence of Arabia* is very much alive to the idea that its protagonist is a flawed figure. His provocative initial comments about Arab barbarism are heavily ironised or directly challenged, and his leanings towards demagoguery are revealed to be delusionary. Feisel (Alec Guinness) reminds him that his love for the arid Arabian landscape, as one more of the 'desert-loving Englishmen', is perverse when Arabs themselves long for 'water and green trees'. True that there are questionable moments of Orientalism within the film's diegesis: Alec Guinness and Anthony Quinn's 'brownface' performances appear more fraudulent now than in 1962, while the scenes of Auda smashing up the telegraph machine and being disappointed by paper money rather than gold, or the chaotic tribalism of the Arab conference, seem to adhere to the worst kind of stereotyping of the backward native in need of colonial instruction.

But conversely the film is never a straightforward celebration of imperial derring-do, and this partly comes from the imprint of the two leftist writers who worked on the project, blacklisted Michael Wilson followed later by Robert Bolt, who admitted that he was strongly inclined to 'disapprove of figures like T. E. Lawrence as being the colourful ornaments and stalking horses of imperialism'.[129] Thus Lawrence's military and personal triumphs are always qualified by doubt and guilt. His defiant rescue of Gasim from the sun's anvil is paired with the scene in which he must execute the same man which, as Kevin Jackson notes, inflicts 'a stinging blow to Lawrence's faith in himself as a Nietszchean superman'.[130] His victory in Aqaba and the journey to announce it are is coloured by his culpability in Daud's death in quicksand during the course of it. This double-edged approach seems fitting for a life of a man described by one biography as the 'new heroic type for the modern age – a hero who is concerned about the loss of human life resulting from his commands and who feels ambiguous about his very desire to rule others'.[131] The historical context of the making of this film about earlier British colonial adventures in the Middle East, specifically its appearance in the wake of the Suez crisis of the mid-1950s, is also an important factor in how questions of colonialism are dealt with; the Suez canal is not only used as the site where Lawrence's identity is questioned (the motorcyclist who calls across it 'Who are you?') but is also directly named as 'an essential British interest' by Feisal. For James Chapman and Nick Cull, *Lawrence of Arabia* constitutes a watershed in the cinema of Empire between the traditional 'projection of imperialism as a force for political and social stability' and the critique developing in the 1960s 'of the imperial project in films such as *Zulu, Khartoum*, and *The Charge of the Light Brigade*',[132] while Steven C. Caton goes even further in designating it 'anti-Imperialist' while still deeply 'Orientalist'.[133] For him, *Lawrence of Arabia* offers one of 'those moments in colonial discourse that allow for possibilities of self-criticism on the part of the colonizer and thus would further place in abeyance the colonial project or even subvert it'.[134] It recognises that Imperialism is 'an inherently unstable project',[135] here incarnated by an inherently instable hero.

The first half of the film is more optimistic in tone but its final moments prior to the intermission hint at the darker and more ambivalent tone to follow. Dryden looks dubious as Lawrence insists 'Arabia's for the Arabs now'. While Lawrence receives appreciative cheers from an audience of British officers for his military feats, both Dryden and Allenby (Jack Hawkins) confess their disquiet about what the future will hold for the 'poor devil riding the whirlwind'. Bolt's scripting of this moment is certainly much less obviously victorious than Michael Wilson's original script which closed the first half with 'LAWRENCE alone on the mountain top, a prophet with a vision'[136] cheered rapturously by the Arab troops down below. But both Wilson and Bolt shared the concept of *Lawrence* as an interrogative biography, with Wilson's idea of moving immediately from Lawrence's death into newsreel accounts of his life demonstrating the direct influence of *Citizen Kane*. The memorial sequence in the completed film still contains the legacy of that Wellesian approach, juxtaposing varying opinions of Lawrence's character and achievements, and even raising questions about Lawrence having a rightful place in St Paul's, before using the reminiscence of Brighton (Anthony Quayle) to launch the flashback to Cairo and the beginning of Lawrence's brilliant military career in Arabia. What *Kane* and *Lawrence* share is a refusal to draw final conclusions about the meaning of a man's life, instead sustaining multiple and contradictory readings of their protagonists' personality and motivations. One of the great works of literature Lawrence admired and wanted to emulate in his own writing was Walt Whitman's *Leaves of Grass*, with its famous lines 'Do I contradict myself? Very well then I contradict myself. (I am large, I contain multitudes)',[137] and, as his biographers suggest, in many ways 'Lawrence *is* his contradictions'.[138] Maintaining this sense of paradox and enigma whilst also undertaking a lengthy and detailed character study is a difficult balance but one the film achieves precisely by giving us a multitude of Lawrences all coexisting within the same man. As its canny producer Sam Spiegel pointed out at the time of its release: 'We did not try to resolve the legend of Lawrence of Arabia. We tried to perpetuate it.'[139]

As a film detailing the life of a fictional newspaper baron, *Citizen Kane* is very mindful of the growing power of the mass media during the late nineteenth and early twentieth centuries, and this is just as true of *Lawrence of Arabia*. The most important character in this respect is the reporter Jackson Bentley (Arthur Kennedy), based on Lowell Thomas, the American journalist who had made Lawrence a global celebrity through flamboyant reportage and showmanship. Thomas's illustrated presentations on Lawrence certainly didn't shy away from Orientalist kitsch, being preceded by a Dance of the Seven Veils and Lowell's wife singing a Muslim call to prayer.[140] After the upward trajectory of the film's first half, the second half begins with Bentley, the reporter and myth-maker, and his encounter with Feisal. It signals the film's shift from the portrayal of Lawrence as a brilliant strategist and courageous warrior to a portrayal of the mechanisms by which his fame is promulgated; the self-conscious creation of Lawrence as hero, and the uses to which this heroic persona might be put. In the grim context of the First World War's mass mechanised slaughter, T. E. Lawrence offered 'a powerful and regenerative myth for a disenchanted age',[141] an image of war heroism becoming increasingly scarce.

And as Feisal points out, in the American context, his propaganda value is indisputable: 'You are looking for a hero who will draw your people towards war ... Lawrence is your man.' Immediately after this line of dialogue, the film cuts to a shot of Lawrence pushing down the plunger to detonate explosives and derail a train, and then quickly to a shot of the photographer capturing the moment for public consumption. What we are seeing, the film seems at pains to remind us, is a mediated event, and indeed it looks too aesthetically perfect to be true; Lawrence looking far too clean, elegant and well-groomed – not a mark on his white robes, not a hair out of place – for the reality of the situation, and in distinct contrast with his generally more dishevelled appearance in the first part of the film. The derailing of the train with explosives looks like a perfectly stage-managed event.

As the sequence develops it plays on the dual meaning of 'shooting', with Lawrence shot alternately by a camera and by a gun. Only Auda seems to recognise the danger of the former as much as the latter, destroying Bentley's photographic equipment when it is used to capture his image, believing it has stolen his soul – a fear partly upheld by the change in Lawrence's behaviour that we witness as he is turned into a media personality. The real T. E. Lawrence spoke of his simultaneous 'craving to be famous; and a horror of being known to like being known',[42] and here we see the film deal with the effects of fame upon Lawrence, strongly suggesting that becoming 'known' has only helped to nurture the megalomaniac side of his personality. Has he begun to believe his own publicity? He speaks of his immortality, impossible to kill except with a golden bullet, and indeed a gun fired at close range only wounds him. Finally he jumps up onto the overturned train and parades along its carriages (like a model on a catwalk?), the camera tracking alongside to follow his feet, before he stops to pose as the midday sun silhouettes his figure. This is a self-consciously created image of Lawrence as sun god, a perfect photo opportunity, and Bentley responds to it with characteristically down-to-earth glee: 'Yes sir, that's my baby!' In this moment, the film supports biographer Richard Aldington's view that T. E. Lawrence actively colluded in his own mythologisation by Lowell Thomas. We see Lawrence allow Bentley to arrange his robes more becomingly for a photo and he happily provides good pithy copy for the reporter, telling his amanuensis he simply likes the desert 'because it's clean'.

However, replicating the film's repeated motif of pride coming before a fall, Lawrence's hubris and burgeoning Christ complex (believing he can walk on water and enact miracles) are soon punished by his most absolute humiliation: his capture and assault by the Turks in Deraa. This also marks the moment in the film in which Lawrence's homosexuality is most directly addressed. Lean conceived of the relationship between

Lawrence and Ali as a great love story, comparing it to the unconsummated affair of his earlier film *Brief Encounter*,[143] and Philip French was to note how much of the film centred on 'romantic encounters of a dune kind between the sad blue eyes of Peter O'Toole and the liquid brown eyes of Omar Sharif'.[144] But that relationship outwardly remains at the level of the fraternal, unlike the encounter with the Bey in Deraa, which is more vividly sexualised. Lawrence describes it in *The Seven Pillars of Wisdom* as 'that night the citadel of my integrity had been irrevocably lost'[145] and strongly intimates, although never finally confirms, that he was raped by his captors as well as being whipped and beaten. In the film the Bey's desire for Lawrence is expressed fairly unambiguously through dialogue: 'If I were posted to the dark side of the moon I could not be more isolated. You don't have the slightest idea what I'm talking about, do you? ... That would be too lucky.' 'A man can't always be in uniform.' It's also intimated through performance and framing, with a strategic close-up of the Bey's moist mouth and the use of what Paul Dehn calls his 'expectant little cough'[146] to punctuate the scene, which Lean directly instructed Ferrer to imbue with an orgasmic quality'.[147] Lawrence is forced face down onto a bench, his legs pulled apart and arms held out in front of him by one of the Turkish soldiers, who stares directly into his eyes and leeringly smiles as the beating commences. The Bey observes from a discreet distance, suggesting a connoisseur's enjoyment of the spectacle. The focus now shifts to outside the prison, and Ali's concern for his friend. There is 'a slight, ominous pause in the sound of the beating'[148] which indicates that some other kind of violation might be taking place before Lawrence finally reappears, cast outside onto the street without ceremony, not walking on water now but thrown into a filthy wet gutter.

High in the mountains, in a ruined castle (another citadel which has lost its integrity), Ali nurses Lawrence back to health and tries to reconcile him to his corporeality ('Sleep. Eat. You have a body like other men.'). But the events in Deraa leave their irreconcilable imprint upon Lawrence thereafter. The enforced defilement of his body in Deraa is presented as the wellspring of his subsequent act of unmitigated vengeance on retreating Turkish troops on the road to Damascus. Enraged by the sacking of an Arab village and already on the brink of hysteria, Lawrence gives the order 'No prisoners!' and what follows is an utter bloodbath. Lawrence's incipient sadism, hinted at by his shameful admission of enjoying having to shoot Gasim, is given full vent. The only hiatus in the slaughter comes when Lawrence pauses to survey his reflection in his dagger, just as he had earlier in the narrative. But the weapon is no longer shiny and silver, just as he is no longer pristine and white; instead both are smeared with red gore. Whereas before Lawrence had been in flight from corporeal reality, here he wallows in the visceral. As Bentley remarks, it is literally a 'rotten bloody picture', and a far cry from Lawrence's earlier photogenic escapades.

The actions of the Turks have created a damaged traumatised man hardly able to maintain his sanity, but the British military establishment are even more culpable in their insistence on sending him out on their 'big push' in full knowledge of his unstable state. Ali draws a direct equivalence between the two attacks on Lawrence's integrity. In response to Bentley's question 'What did that Turkish general do to him in Deraa?', Ali counteracts 'What did the English general do to him in Jerusalem?'. Allenby, the English general in question, chooses to ignore Lawrence's obvious distress, expressed through his stated wishes to have his 'ration of common humanity' as well as his cringing semi-foetal body language. Most eloquent of all in expressing the residual trauma of Deraa is the re-opening of the wounds on his back, with blood slowly seeping through his shirt. The sequence that follows became referred to by Lean and Bolt as 'the "seduction" scene'.[49] Allenby achieves his objective of keeping Lawrence in the field through flattery and, in the cruellest manipulation of all, showing Lawrence a picture of his own son and inviting him to visit the Allenby family after the war. As Steven Caton argues, 'The thrust meets its mark. To be clasped in the paternal embrace, to be assured some sort of domestic inclusion is all that Lawrence, the illegitimate son, wants, and in exchange for which he is willing to pay any price.'[50] It is telling that, in relation to this sequence, Bolt's original script uses the same language of citadels being breeched that Lawrence used to invoke his assault in Deraa in *Seven Pillars of Wisdom*,[51] only underlining further the moral equivalence of the assaults upon Lawrence from generals of both sides.

The original scene between Allenby and Lawrence would eventually be significantly trimmed by Lean, fearing it was too dialogue-heavy, and it seems that a fear about the film becoming off-puttingly discursive and cerebral haunted Columbia's marketing department, who stated in the British campaign manual:

> *Lawrence* has been presented in some of the more highbrow newspapers as a film for deep-thinkers, probing into the enigma that was T E Lawrence. Of course, this is very true, but we suggest that in aiming publicity materials at the masses the emphasis should be placed on the all-action, all-colour and all-starring aspects of the picture ... present the film as a colourful slice of action-full movie-making.[52]

However, if they were worried that talk would overwhelm spectacle in *Lawrence of Arabia*, they must have failed to comprehend the film's extraordinary visual power exemplified by moments such as the 'match' cut, which transports us straight from Dryden's office to sunrise over the dunes of Jebel el Tubeiq (incidentally the first shot of the production to be filmed). Lean rhymes the swirling sand clouds of the desert with the stardust of the Milky Way in the night sky, he evokes the shimmering undulating quality of sand dunes and the near-abstraction of the desert landscape (for critic Tom Wiseman, these shots had 'the pictorial simplicity – and impressiveness – of Picasso landscapes'[53]), communicating something of Lawrence's obsession with this world as well as Lean's own fascination with it, both of them 'desert loving Englishmen', and trying to transmit this to the viewer.[54] The spell was certainly cast over Dilys Powell who spoke rapturously of 'The sun rising on the rim of blood-orange sand; dust-storms like the smoke trails of a djin; the shapes of infinity, the clouds of heat – I think it is the first time for the cinema to communicate ecstasy.'[55]

The film's most celebrated sequence, the long introduction of Sherif Ali as he rides towards the well, is testimony to the collaborative brilliance of Lean, director of photography Freddie Young and designer John Box. The gradual transformation of Ali from abstract black shape on the horizon, a floating shimmering mirage, to a real flesh-and-blood man is a remarkable cinematic achievement. It also alludes to the origins of cinema itself. A mirage and a movie both offer flickering images in which we see something we think is physically present but which isn't really there: both depend on optical illusions to bring them to life. It seems right that one of Lean's most memorable *coups de cinéma* was inspired by the desert. Lean was fascinated by the character of Lawrence but seems to have been even more entranced by the landscapes of Arabia, as suggested by a letter he wrote to Michael Wilson while filming: 'It somehow threw me back on myself and made me very conscious of being alive. There you are. Just you and it. You can't sit down and be entertained. Everyone is somehow much more on their own out there, and perhaps they just have to come face to face with themselves.'[56] According to continuity supervisor Barbara Cole, Lean would sometimes spend the best part of an hour gazing through the viewfinder 'in a sort of trance', not realising that the crew were waiting for filming to start.[57] Although Lean bitterly resented Sam Spiegel's enforced relocation of the production from Jordan to Spain, the producer had become convinced, perhaps correctly, that 'if he didn't pull the rug from under his [Lean's] feet, he would be there till now shooting pretty pictures'.[58]

If the film's visuals are stunning, then no less notable is its ingenious use of sound, from the intoxicating romanticism of Maurice Jarre's score to other more subtle manipulations of soundtrack. Critic Alexander Walker identified as particular aural highlights the use of the sound of a ship's horn, the metal ladles knocking together on a traveller's baggage and the 'stereophonic tomfoolery of an echoing gorge'[59] as particular highlights. This latter moment has Lawrence sing 'The Man who Broke the Bank at Monte Carlo', sharing the 'independent air' of the song's protagonist while experimenting with the echo his voice creates in the rocky chasm. But suddenly the void answers back with 'Hey you!': it comes from Brighton, who has been sent to find him. As Steven Caton notes, the word 'you' reverberates, providing 'an aural image of hollowness that sums up the problem of a self that will claim multiple identities and loyalties'.[60] Another voice from afar questions Lawrence's identity later in the film. 'Who are you?' shouts the motorcyclist repeatedly from the opposite bank of the Suez canal (dubbed by Lean himself), and Lawrence is unable to answer this question on even the most literal level of self-identification.

The exemplary use of cinematic sound and vision come together in the film's final sequences, after a disillusioned and exhausted Lawrence's leave to transfer has finally been granted by Allenby and he has been made a Colonel as a parting honour. It seems that Lawrence's future life is telescoped into his drive to the ship that will take him home; it presents his destiny in microcosm. The car's dusty windscreen obscures his face as he slumps in his seat, unlike that of his driver, which can be clearly seen above it. The great man, statuesque on a turned-over train, now seems shrunken. Their car passes a column of Arabs on camels and we hear the distinctive noise of the animals as they pass by, an aural link to Lawrence's days in the desert. Lawrence stands up briefly, thinking he has seen someone he recognises (Ali?) but soon sinks back into his seat, disappointed, unrecognised. His anonymity may be felt as a slight here but anonymity is what T. E. Lawrence would seek back in England, adopting a lowly 'everyman' status and a variety of names – Private Ross, Private Shaw – to disguise his infamy. 'Well sir, going home' says the driver, to a muffled response from Lawrence and the man repeats 'Home, sir!', inadvertently reminding Lawrence of what he lacks rather than the expectancy of home comforts (will Allenby honour his invitation to his family home?). At this point the roar of a motorcycle is heard as it speeds past the car towards the horizon, and it is passed in the opposite direction by a truckload of British troops, overheard singing a music hall song of poignant departure, 'Goodbye Dolly, I must leave you, though it breaks my heart to go'. Lawrence's two future directions are thus both suggested: his attempt to lose himself in the ranks through the company of the common man and total immersion in the routines of military life, as he would describe in his RAF memoir *The Mint*, or his mania for velocity especially on his beloved Brough motorcycle. 'In speed we hurl ourselves beyond the body'[161] he wrote in a 1929 poem, and we know from the beginning of the film (and from the fact that it is to the shot of the motorcycle disappearing into vanishing point that the film returns, not the truck full of Tommies) that this will be the path Lawrence ultimately chooses, finally transcending his body by annihilating it. The final shot of the film teases us with simultaneous proximity and distance; it is a close-up of Lawrence but his face remains an indistinct blur, impossible to see, impossible to read. Jarre's main 'Lawrence' theme is reprised but only in the most fragile, tentative way and as a solo as well, underlining the character's isolation. The warrior of genius and the global celebrity who we have spent the last few hours engaged in investigating ends the film as he began it: an enigma.

Notes

1. Jonathan Rutherford, 'Who's that Man?', in Rowena Chapman and Jonathan Rutherford (eds.), *Male Order: Unwrapping Masculinity* (London: Lawrence & Wishart, 1988), p. 47.
2. Pierre Boulle, *The Bridge on the River Kwai*, translated by Xan Fielding (London: Fontana, 1957), p. 121.
3. Camille Paglia, *Sexual Personae* (London: Penguin, 1992), p. 40.
4. Boulle, *The Bridge on the River Kwai*, p. 91.
5. Letter from T. E. Lawrence to Robert Graves quoted in Stanley Weintraub and Rodelle Weintraub, *Lawrence of Arabia: The Literary Impulse* (Baton Rouge: Louisiana State University Press, 1975), p. 121.
6. Felix Barker, *Evening News*, 3 January 1963.
7. Brian Taves, *The Romance of Adventure: The Genre of Historical Adventure Movies* (Jackson: University Press of Mississippi, 1993), p. 4.
8. Yvonne Tasker (ed.), *Action and Adventure Cinema* (London: Routledge, 2004), p. 9.
9. Ibid., p. 5.
10. *The Sound Barrier* draft pressbook copy, BFI microfiche.
11. Silverman, *David Lean*, p. 18.
12. Brownlow, *David Lean*, p. 281.
13. Harry Hopkins, *The New Look: A Social History of the Forties and Fifties* (London: Secker and Warburg, 1963), p. 385.
14. Depicted in doublet and hose in a *Daily Express* tableau of 'modern Elizabethans'. Hopkins, *The New Look*, p. 288. Whittle was a guest at the film's premiere, filmed for television, as was wartime flying ace Douglas Bader. Brownlow, *David Lean*, p. 292.
15. Hopkins, *The New Look*, p. 389.
16. Brownlow, *David Lean*, pp. 292–3.
17. Todd, *The Eighth Veil*, p. 72.
18. Brownlow, *David Lean*, p. 289.
19. David Kynaston, *Family Britain, 1951–57* (London: Bloomsbury, 2009), p. 123.
20. Hopkins, *The New Look*, p. 391.

21 Kynaston, *Family Britain*, p. 378. For further discussion of *The Sound Barrier* in the aviation context of its moment of production and exhibition, see Adrian Smith, 'The Dawn of the Jet Age in Austerity Britain: David Lean's *The Sound Barrier* (1952)', *Historical Journal of Film, Radio and Television*, Vol. 30, No. 4, 2010, pp. 487–514.
22 *Kine Weekly*, 18 December 1952, p. 9.
23 *Kine Weekly*, 30 October 1952, p. 33.
24 *Kine Weekly*, 23 October 1952, p. 39.
25 Dilys Powell, *Sunday Times*, 27 July 1952.
26 Brownlow, *David Lean*, p. 292.
27 Ibid., p. 286.
28 Ibid., p. 284.
29 Silverman, *David Lean*, p. 93.
30 Paul Holt, *Daily Herald*, 25 July 1952. Indeed, the film would go on to win the Academy Award for sound.
31 Hopkins, *The New Look*, p. 386.
32 *Kine Weekly*, 25 September 1952, p. 27. Another cinema used a 'loudspeaker on top of the canopy [which] relayed to general public roar of a plane's engine when going into a dive'. *Kine Weekly*, 9 October 1952, p. 36.
33 Quoted in Brownlow, *David Lean*, p. 283.
34 Fred Madjalany, *Daily Mail*, 25 July 1952.
35 Anderegg, *David Lean*, p. 78.
36 Iris Ashley, 'I'd rather be a hero than be his wife', *Daily Mail*, 11 December 1951.
37 Elspeth Grant, 'Jet film has me in its grip', *Daily Graphic*, 25 July 1952.
38 Ashley, 'I'd rather be a hero than be his wife'.
39 UK campaign sheet for *The Sound Barrier*.
40 Ashley, 'I'd rather be a hero than be his wife'.
41 *Kine Weekly*, 24 July 1952, p. 18.
42 *Daily Mirror*, 25 July 1952. See also the question posed by the *News of the World*, 27 August 1952: 'But how are you women cinemagoers going to react to this sombre tragic story?'
43 Margaret Shipley, 'Not wives like these, please!', *Sunday Chronicle*, 27 July 1952.
44 Brownlow, *David Lean*, p. 290.
45 'Old boy, never put your wife in pictures', Lean complained to Anthony Squire, who concurred that 'she argued the toss for every single shot.' Ibid., p. 289.
46 The US poster campaign also used 'How much can a woman take!' as one of its main taglines. *The Sound Barrier* pressbook, BFI library.
47 The striking aerial photography of Paris and the Alps was undertaken in a plane piloted by John Derry, the test pilot who was later killed, along with 26 spectators, when his plane broke up at the Farnborough Air Show in September 1952. See Kynaston, *Family Britain*, p. 122. David Lean and Ann Todd were there and witnessed Derry's wife's stunned reaction to the accident: she 'just sat there as if nothing had happened'. Brownlow, *David Lean*, p. 295.
48 Interestingly, there was some use made of discourses of fashion in promotional material to appeal to women. A London Film Studios press release dated 1 October 1951 (available on BFI microfiche for the film) noted that although Ann Todd's role 'is down-to-earth and so is her wardrobe ... with typical elegance, she has concentrated on unusual accessories which can make the plainest outfit fashion-right.'
49 Silver and Ursini, *David Lean and His Films*, p. 105.
50 Dilys Powell, *Sunday Times*, 27 July 1952.
51 *Monthly Film Bulletin*, September 1952, p. 124.
52 Silver and Ursini, *David Lean and His Films*, p. 108.
53 Phillips, *Beyond the Epic* p. 183.

54 It also echoes the RAF motto 'Per ardua ad astra' (Through adversity to the stars), alluded to in the title of the Rattigan-scripted *The Way to the Stars* (1945).
55 Brownlow, *David Lean*, pp. 490–1.
56 Although the cost of the bridge was often cited in publicity as a quarter of a million dollars, it was closer to $52,000. Production designer Don Ashton says that Spiegel quoted the higher figure 'to make the picture sound more important'. Natasha Fraser-Cavassoni, *Sam Spiegel* (London: Time Warner, 2004), p. 200.
57 Milius speaking on 'An Appreciation', *The Bridge on the River Kwai* DVD, 2000 special 2–disc edition (Columbia Tristar Home Video).
58 Letter with extensive script notes to Sam Spiegel dated 31 January 1956. DL/6/5, BFI Spec Coll.
59 Fraser-Cavassoni, *Sam Spiegel*, p. 153.
60 Ibid., p. 194. It is telling that only Sam Spiegel managed to get approval for a film based on the life of T. E. Lawrence where many others – Herbert Wilcox, Rex Ingram, Alexander Korda, Anthony Asquith – had failed.
61 Ibid., pp. 196–7.
62 Ibid., p. 193.
63 Brownlow, *David Lean*, p. 349.
64 Letter from Lean to Spiegel, quoted Brownlow, *David Lean*, p. 351.
65 Ibid., p. 356.
66 Ibid., p. 381.
67 Interview in 'The Making of *Bridge on the River Kwai*', *The Bridge on the River Kwai* DVD, 2000 special 2–disc edition (Columbia Tristar Home Video).
68 Jonathan Mirsky, 'Working on the Railroad', *Guardian* (Review), 27 November 2004, p. 6.
69 Ian Watt, 'Talking of Films', BBC broadcast, recorded Monday 23 March 1959, transcript on BFI microfiche for *Kwai*.
70 Lomax, *The Railway Man*, p. 232.
71 Anthony Barnes, *Independent on Sunday*, 10 July 2005, p. 22.
72 *Evening News*, 9 May 1958. Also reported in *Star*, 19 May 1958. The leader of the group, A. E. Percival, repeated this in a letter to the *Daily Telegraph*, printed 2 June 1958: 'The members of our federation deeply resent the use of conditions such as these as a basis for a story of fiction which brings dishonour to Servicemen.'
73 *Daily Telegraph*, 10 June 1958. John Smyth, in command of 17th division in Burma at time of the Japanese invasion, also wrote that he could 'appreciate the slight feeling of revulsion which is felt by some of those who were compelled to build a bridge for the Japanese in almost exactly the same location as that in the film on the infamous railway of death', concluding with ambivalent praise for the film as 'wonderful entertainment and true art: and it poses deep human problems. But it is, of course, fiction – glorious fiction.' *Manchester Guardian*, October 1957 (no specific date listed, BFI microfiche on *Kwai*). Another area of continuing controversy is the suggestion that the fictional Colonel Nicholson bore a strong resemblance to the real Colonel Toosey, strongly refuted by Peter N. Davies, *The Man Behind the Bridge: Colonel Toosey and the River Kwai* (London: Athlone, 1991).
74 Fraser-Cavassoni, *Sam Spiegel*, p. 210.
75 Guinness hid a blood capsule in his mouth, which he bit when he was slapped, much to the shock and distress of Hayakawa, who thought he had really hurt his co-star. Phillips, *Beyond the Epic*, p. 219.
76 Ibid., p. 247.
77 Boulle, *The Bridge on the River Kwai*, p. 7. Simone Signoret's letter to Lean drew a comparison with Renoir's humanist anti-war film *La Grande Illusion* (1937), which drew similar equivalences between French and German generals. Letter dated 11 January 1958. DL/6/8, BFI Spec Coll.

78 Boulle, *The Bridge on the River Kwai*, p. 63.
79 Neil Sinyard, 'Sir Alec Guinness: The Self-Effacing Star', in Bruce Babington (ed.), *British Stars and Stardom* (Manchester: Manchester University Press, 2001), p. 148.
80 Silverman, *David Lean*, p. 25.
81 London Film Studios press release, 5 September 1951 (available on BFI microfiche for *The Sound Barrier*).
82 Fraser-Cavassoni, *Sam Spiegel*, p. xiii.
83 Brownlow, *David Lean*, p. 363.
84 Lean maintained the importance of Shears's easy and uncomplicated sexuality in the face of attempts to make the character more tortured: 'Don't let's have any Don Juans who spend their time jumping into bed with everyone in order to prove their virility – which they doubt. Freud page 1. We'll only get complication and guilt. We need simplicity and normality.' Letter to Spiegel dated 10 August 1956. DL/6/5, BFI Spec Coll.
85 Interview in 'The Making of Bridge on the River Kwai', *The Bridge on the River Kwai* DVD.
86 Brownlow, *David Lean*, p. 334. It was because of this that Lean avoided Foreman's original idea of a strapping Amazonian woman making a play for the men, since it violated his notion of Asian femininity. See Brownlow, *David Lean*, p. 349. An interesting addendum: Sam Spiegel's wife, Betty, scurrilously suggests that the four Thai actresses were 'all friendly – shall we say – they liked to have fun' and sexually propositioned Holden, Hawkins, Guinness and Lean in turn. Fraser-Cavassoni, *Sam Spiegel*, p. 208.
87 Columbia press release, 22 February 1957, BFI microfiche on *Kwai*.
88 *Tribune*, 11 October 1957.
89 André Bazin, *Bazin at Work: Major Essays and Reviews from the Forties and Fifties*, translated by Alain Piette and Bert Cardullo (London: Routledge, 1997), p. 227.
90 Turner, *The Making of David Lean's Lawrence of Arabia*, p. 177.
91 Isabel Quigly, *Spectator*, 11 October 1957, p. 482.
92 Letter with extensive script notes to Sam Spiegel, 31 January 1956. DL/6/5, BFI Spec Coll.
93 Ian Watt, 'Talking of Films', p. 3. However, others, such as Eric Lomax, speak of their indentured labour for the Japanese purely in terms of wanting 'to delay them, to hinder their efforts, to do shoddy work'. Lomax, *The Railway Man*, p. 97.
94 Anderegg, *David Lean*, pp. 100–1.
95 For a parallel in real life, see Lomax's words on the psychological effects of extended exposure to 'a blazing hot sun': 'you have nothing to do but think; yet thought is a process that should be directed by the will, and under extreme stress thoughts spin away on their own, racing faster and faster like a machine out of control'. Lomax, *The Railway Man*, p. 116.
96 Lindsay Anderson, *New Statesman*, 12 October 1957, p. 460. Lean was so stung by this dismissal that he still recalled it thirty years later. Brownlow, *David Lean*, p. 385.
97 Charles Barr, 'Madness, Madness!: The Brief Stardom of James Donald', in Bruce Babington (ed.), *British Stars and Stardom* (Manchester: Manchester University Press, 2001), pp. 164–5.
98 Boulle, *The Bridge on the River Kwai*, p. 92.
99 In letter to Robert Bolt dated 3 December 1962. UoR Spec Coll.
100 Alan Dent, *Sunday Telegraph*, 16 December 1962.
101 Alexander Walker, *Evening Standard*, 13 December 1962.
102 Philip French, *Observer*, 28 May 1989, p. 44.
103 Turner, *The Making of David Lean's Lawrence of Arabia*, p. 113.

172 DAVID LEAN

104 British 1962 pressbook for *Lawrence of Arabia*, BFI Library. Columbia's Leo Jaffe is also quoted as voicing his concerns about it being 'another male film' like *Kwai* in Fraser-Cavassoni, *Sam Spiegel*, p. 236.
105 See fashion spread inspired by the film in the *Saturday Evening Post*, 9 March 1963, pp. 30–1: 'Lawrence inspires the Arab look – the chic sheik look ... a fluid line borrowed from the robes worn by Lawrence.' The US exhibitor's manual also included tie-up opportunities with beachwear designers, milliners and other designers with exhortations to 'work with local stores and women's page editors' to maximise publicity for the film. *Lawrence of Arabia* exhibitor's manual, available at http://cinefiles.bampfa.berkeley.edu/cinefiles.
106 T. E. Lawrence, *Seven Pillars of Wisdom* (London: Jonathan Cape, 1935), p. 214.
107 Jonathan Rutherford, *Forever England: Reflections on Masculinity and Empire* (London: Lawrence & Wishart, 1997), p. 84.
108 Ibid., pp. 87–8. Although one might argue that the desert sinkhole that swallows Daud in the film offers a strong image of the terrifying potential of the desert to engulf and overwhelm. Equally, it may be one of a number of images in the film that evoke anality, from the dark hole/trench that Lawrence mentions in his first lines of dialogue to the well that is his first meeting place with Ali, from inside which the camera looks out at one point.
109 Quoted in John Mack, *A Prince of Our Disorder* (New York: Little, Brown and Company, 1976), p. 361.
110 Quoted in Rutherford, *Forever England*, p. 83.
111 Lawrence, *Seven Pillars of Wisdom*, p. 214.
112 Steven C. Caton, *Lawrence of Arabia: A Film's Anthropology* (Berkeley: University of California Press, 1999), p. 206.
113 Anderegg, *David Lean*, p. 110.
114 Quoted in Stephen E. Tabachnick and Christopher Matheson, *Images of Lawrence* (London: Jonathan Cape, 1988), p. 66.
115 Caton, *Lawrence of Arabia*, p. 22.
116 Ibid., pp. 3–4.
117 David Robinson, *Financial Times*, 11 December 1962.
118 Brownlow, *David Lean*, p. 480. Steven Caton also notes that satirical US magazine *MAD* had Lawrence sing 'I Feel Pretty' in their spoof comic strip of the film. Caton, *Lawrence of Arabia*, p. 212.
119 Jane Gaines, 'Costume and Narrative: How Dress Tells the Woman's Story', in Jane Gaines and Charlotte Herzog (ed.), *Fabrications: Costume and the Female Body* (New York and London: Routledge, 1990), p. 180.
120 Undated script notes for *Lawrence*. DL/7/5, BFI Spec Coll.
121 This touch seems to have been O'Toole's improvisation. See Jackson, *Lawrence of Arabia*, p. 69.
122 Nate Wheeler, 'A Freudian Oasis', *Scene*, 27 December 1962.
123 Turner, *The Making of David Lean's Lawrence of Arabia*, p. 140.
124 Howard Kent's memoir of *Lawrence*'s making offers an admiring if slightly patronising account of Dalton's remarkable achievements: 'Phyllis looked much too young and pretty to be capable of handling a job of such magnitude, but her looks were strictly deceptive.' Howard Kent, *Single Bed for Three: A Lawrence of Arabia Notebook* (London: Hutchinson, 1963), p. 126. He praises her for managing to work within an ever-changing shooting schedule, 'spending days on detailed research, translating that research on to the drawing-board and then going off to buy the material and equipment for the costumes she had designed' (p. 127) and still being indefatigable: 'When eight o'clock strikes, Phyllis Dalton is still trotting round as full of energy as ever. It is only when she sees the traders beginning to pull down their shutters that she realises the day's shopping must

come to an end. By that time she has ordered clothes and materials running into many hundreds of pounds, and done it as coolly as a girl going out to buy three yards for a skirt and a new blouse for Spring' (p. 132).
125 Quoted in Jackson, *Lawrence of Arabia*, p. 2.
126 Lawrence, *Seven Pillars of Wisdom*, pp. 31–2.
127 Homi K. Bhabha, 'Of Mimicry and Man: The Ambivalence of Colonial Discourse', *The Location of Culture* (New York and London: Routledge, 1994), pp. 121–31.
128 Edward Said, *Orientalism* (Harmondsworth: Penguin, 1991), p. 242.
129 Quoted in Caton, *Lawrence of Arabia*, p. 177. For detailed accounts of the contribution of Wilson and Bolt to the film and subsequent controversy surrounding the allocation of screen credit, mirroring similar disputes around *Kwai*, see Caton, *Lawrence of Arabia*, pp. 100–41 and Turner, *The Making of David Lean's Lawrence of Arabia*, pp. 53–99.
130 Jackson, *Lawrence of Arabia*, p. 19.
131 Tabachnick and Matheson, *Images of Lawrence*, p. 76.
132 James Chapman and Nicholas J. Cull, *Projecting Empire: Imperialism and Popular Cinema* (London: I. B. Tauris, 2009), pp. 87–8.
133 Caton, *Lawrence of Arabia*, chapter 5, 'An Anti-Imperialist, Orientalist Epic', pp. 172–99.
134 Ibid., p. 10.
135 Ibid., p. 12.
136 Turner, *The Making of David Lean's Lawrence of Arabia*, p. 76.
137 Tabachnick and Matheson, *Images of Lawrence*, p. 157.
138 Ibid., p. 160.
139 Quoted in Fraser-Cavassoni, *Sam Spiegel*, p. 273.
140 Turner, *The Making of David Lean's Lawrence of Arabia*, p. 25.
141 Rutherford, *Forever England*, p. 72.
142 Lawrence, *Seven Pillars of Wisdom*, p. 563.
143 Turner, *The Making of David Lean's Lawrence of Arabia*, p. 73.
144 French also recalled that while the *Movie* critics left the press screening in search of Hawksian virility, the rock impresario Kit Lambert, who also happened to be present, hailed the film as 'British cinema's first queer epic'. Philip French, *Observer*, 28 May 1989, p. 44.
145 Lawrence, *Seven Pillars of Wisdom*, p. 447.
146 Paul Dehn, *Daily Herald*, 11 December 1962.
147 Phillip Bergson, 'The Remaking of an Epic', *What's On*, 17 May 1989, p. 65.
148 Turner, *The Making of David Lean's Lawrence of Arabia*, p. 121.
149 Ibid., p. 133.
150 Caton, *Lawrence of Arabia*, pp. 233–4.
151 Quoted in Turner, *The Making of David Lean's Lawrence of Arabia*, p. 136.
152 British pressbook for *Lawrence of Arabia*, BFI Library.
153 Tom Wiseman, *Sunday Express*, 16 December 1962.
154 In this respect, Ella Shohat's accusations that the film represents a gendered colonial gaze wherein its 'unveiling of the mysteries of an unknown space becomes a *rite de passage* allegorizing the western achievement of virile heroic stature' do ring true. Shohat, 'Gender and Culture of Empire: Toward a Feminist Ethnography of Cinema', *Quarterly Review of Film and Video*, Vol. 13, Nos. 1–3 (1991), p. 52.
155 Dilys Powell, *Sunday Times*, 16 December 1962.
156 Turner, *The Making of David Lean's Lawrence of Arabia*, p. 157.
157 Ibid., p. 128.
158 Roy Stevens quoted in Fraser-Cavassoni, *Sam Spiegel*, p. 256.

159 Alexander Walker, *Evening Standard*, 13 December 1962.
160 Caton, *Lawrence of Arabia*, p. 125.
161 Quoted in Weintraub and Weintraub, *Lawrence of Arabia*, p. 117.

Feminising the epic: *Doctor Zhivago* (1965), *Ryan's Daughter* (1970) and *A Passage to India* (1984)

6

At the acme of its popularity and power, the epic film's entanglement with questions of masculinity was unquestionable. There had been female-centred film epics before, most famously *Gone with the Wind* (1939) but during its postwar Hollywood heyday, the genre's heroes were almost without exception men and its concerns predominantly masculine in tenor. Films such as *Ben-Hur* (1959), *Spartacus* (1960), *El Cid* (1961) and indeed Lean's own *Lawrence of Arabia* provided lengthy mediations on male identity and heroism. They focussed extensively on close male relationships often heavily marked by elements of homoeroticism, which was also evident in the frequent recourse to male bodily display in texts themselves and the promotional materials used to market them. Vivian Sobchack notes the epic's recurrent use of 'patriarchal "voice of God" narration'[1] to frame narrative events and our understanding of them, further masculinising the form's address. But for Sobchack, the gendering of the genre runs much deeper than its selection of male-oriented stories and storytelling devices. Instead, epic's insistence on 'surge and splendour' (the title of her article) makes it 'cinema tumescent: institutionally full of itself, swollen with its own generative power to mobilise the vast amounts of labour and money necessary to diddle its technology to an extended and expanded orgasm of images, sounds and profits'.[2] Following Sobchack's imagery, epic cinema functions not only as a display of masculine potency – in Ted Hovet's phrase, a demonstration of 'representational prowess'[3] – but also as a kind of male masturbatory solipsism. But epic's 'extended and expanded orgasm' could not last indefinitely, and, as Sobchack notes, after the genre's peak in the late 1950s and early 1960s came an inevitable decline.

It is interesting that the epic film often read as indicative of the genre's unsustainability was actually 'the only epic in the grand tradition with a woman as the lead':[4] Fox's multi-million-dollar production *Cleopatra* (1963), three years in the making. Although its box-office takings were impressive, it struggled to recoup anything near the level of return on their investment that Fox had hoped for, despite starring the globally famous real-life lovers Elizabeth Taylor and Richard Burton.[5] *Cleopatra*'s disappointing performance heralded the beginning of the end for films of that ilk, the colossal historical epic, and presaged the later even more seismic crisis in Hollywood towards the end of the decade. The enormous success in the mid-1960s of *The Sound of Music* (1965), a female-led blockbuster albeit in musical mode, disguised a deeper decline and momentarily encouraged studios to see a profitable future in more and bigger musicals. However, the expensive results – the likes of *Camelot* (1967), *Doctor Dolittle* (1967), *Star!* (1968) and *Hello, Dolly!* (1969) – were outperformed by a new wave of much cheaper, defiantly un-family-oriented films such as *Bonnie and Clyde* (1967), *The Graduate* (1967) and *Easy Rider* (1969).[6] These were the films favoured by the powerful youth market, which was much less enchanted by older versions of film spectacle; MGM surreptitiously switched its marketing of *2001: A Space Odyssey* (1968) from more traditional Hollywood epic terms to selling it as 'The Ultimate Trip' for younger audiences 'in acknowledgement of its hallucinogenic properties and countercultural resonance'.[7]

This particular institutional and cultural context is indispensable for understanding the development of David Lean's work in epic mode in the 1960s. The commercial and critical success of *Kwai* and *Lawrence* with their Oscars and impressive box-office receipts would be surpassed, at least in one of those dimensions, by Lean's next film *Doctor Zhivago*, a film that made its director more money than all of his other films put together. Second only to *The Sound of Music* in being the top performing film not only of 1965 but of the entire decade, *Doctor Zhivago* cost $11.9 million and had eventual world rentals in region of $100 million, approximately two-thirds of which came from the US but, as Hall and Neale note, the film also 'set many all-time records in territories such as Italy and Spain'.[8] Certainly a huge popular success, *Zhivago* was by no means a critical success. Its reviews were distinctly chillier and more disparaging than those which had greeted *Kwai* and *Lawrence* before it, and despite its ten Oscar nominations, it eventually won in only five categories, none of them major awards (by contrast, *Kwai* and *Lawrence* had both won Best Picture and Best Director). By the time it came to Lean's next epic production, *Ryan's Daughter* (1970), the Oscar nominations had slunk down to four, the wins to two, and the critical knives were being sharpened. Garnering praise for pioneering intelligent epic cinema in the late 1950s and early 1960s, by the close of the decade Lean was being derided as an old-fashioned exponent of an outmoded model of filmmaking. This culminated in his harrowing appearance before the National Society of Film Critics at a disastrous reception at the Algonquin Hotel in New York, where Lean was mercilessly grilled for several hours on his latest release *Ryan's Daughter*. As the meeting's chair Richard Schickel recalled: 'Pauline Kael launched a brutal critique, and this opened the floodgates. And it was an angry torrent. I pretty much lost control.'[9] According to Nicolas Roeg, the showdown left the director 'in a state of catatonic shock'[10] which played a large part in his withdrawal from filmmaking for over a decade: 'I thought "what's the point?"'[11] His eventual return to the screen would come with *A Passage to India* (1984), although in the intervening 'wilderness' years he would come close to setting up a number of projects, including a Gandhi biopic (bubbling under since the late 1950s) and the saga of the mutiny on the *Bounty* told through two films, *The Lawbreakers* and *The Long Arm*, to be produced by Dino De Laurentiis. A version of Karen Blixen's *Out of Africa* was mooted to David Puttnam in the early 1980s. But the next film Lean would actually make, which would also be his last film, was *A Passage to India*, another feminised epic set in an outpost of empire. It completed a trio of films in which expansive and spectacular modes of filmmaking are used to frame stories which prioritise the feminine.

Doctor Zhivago, *Ryan's Daughter* and *A Passage to India* are assuredly epic in their monumental scale and expansive themes and yet they eschew the usual masculine epic hero. In divergent ways, each film feminises the epic. *Kwai* and *Lawrence* had queried the codes of behaviour governing their military central protagonists but the two men (Nicholson and Lawrence) nonetheless remained the locus of the drama. After a near eradication of women from those films, *Doctor Zhivago* returned Lean to a more inclusive approach to gender in which a female character, Lara, occupied a position of equal dramatic importance to her male counterpart. Zhivago is the titular hero but, as many reviewers were to complain, he was not an active, destiny-forging hero but an observer and recipient of history. However, if the critical reaction to *Zhivago* was lukewarm then, as we have seen, it was positively venomous for Lean's subsequent production. *Ryan's Daughter* was conceived and made on an epic scale but dealt with the 'small' topic of an Irish girl's journey from adolescence to adulthood: her marriage, her affair and the subsequent punishment for that transgression. It is the film where that growing tension between epic and feminine in Lean's later career is most pronounced, having been judged a deficient epic on the grounds of a perceived incompatibility between feminine subject matter and epic grandeur. It is worth quoting Virginia Woolf at this juncture on this deeply gendered critical bias on what does or doesn't constitute serious subject matter: 'This is an important book, the critic presumes, because it deals with war. This is an insignificant book because it deals with the feelings of women in a drawing room. A scene in a battlefield is more important than a scene in a shop – everywhere and much more subtly the difference of value persists.'[12] Both *Doctor Zhivago* and *Ryan's Daughter* touch on war, revolution, national struggle but were condemned for being more preoccupied with smaller stories – love stories, in other words – deemed unworthy of epic treatment. Lean would defend his position on *Ryan's Daughter*: 'What I am doing is telling an intimate story of people with the rumbling of the guns of the first world war and the Irish rebellion just over the horizon. It is human emotions – not circuses – that give a story its size.'[13] But this was to little avail, at least in terms of the film's critical reception (although the trade press could be more sympathetic to the merging of intimate romance and epic adventure, as *Kine Weekly*'s review of *Doctor Zhivago* suggests, with its awareness of a dual address: 'The film has two angles of appeal: it is a simple, heroic love story, or an ironic social commentary on the cruelty and illogicality of revolutions. Either way it should fill the Empire. Big prestige offering'[14]).

Despite a long interregnum between Lean's penultimate and ultimate productions, it is interesting that his last film, *A Passage to India*, once again combined epic style with an interest in female subjectivity, remaking the dull prudish Adela Quested of E. M. Forster's novel into an engaging questing heroine who is, in the words of critic Derek Malcolm, 'neither a fool nor entirely an innocent but a real woman in the throes of a panicking self-discovery'.[15] When Lean had anonymously attended screenings of *A Passage to India*, he feared that when the audience went quiet at the end 'you just don't know what they're thinking'.[16] He needn't have worried: the film was a success with audiences and critics alike. In his remaining seven years of life, his advancing age and concomitant illness, combined with the vagaries of the film business, would prevent Lean from being able to make further films so that *A Passage to India* would become both his glorious resurgence and his final testament. The critic David Denby judged it 'large scale and spectacular [but] also debonair, intimate, light on its feet',[17] suggesting that with *A Passage to India* Lean finally managed to achieve a successful synthesis of the epic and what the director referred to as the 'little gem'. But its orientation towards the woman in romantic crisis placed it firmly in a well-established lineage of Lean's female-focussed film. As Silver and Ursini point out, Adela Quested is the 'last in a line of heroines searching for fulfillment stretching back forty years to Laura Jesson'.[18] While Lean's telling of women's stories in epic mode differed significantly from his female-focussed films of the 1940s and 1950s, not least in budget and style, there were nonetheless remarkable continuities between those early films and the epic femininities of his late career.

Doctor Zhivago (1965)

In its opening chapters, Boris Pasternak's *Doctor Zhivago* contains a remark that suggests how well suited the novel was for adaptation by David Lean: 'The succession of huge views aroused in the travellers a feeling of spaciousness and made them think and dream of the future.'[19] Huge views that inspire dreams; this might have been written with Lean in mind, especially as expounded in his previous film, *Lawrence of Arabia*. However, Lean was keen to make a distinction between that earlier epic and what he envisaged for this film, writing to MGM's Robert O'Brien: 'Zhivago is not Lawrence. I mention this because I don't want you to think that I visualise the greater part of this film played against enormous backdrops. This is an intimate study of people and most of the scenes will be played in intimate surroundings.'[20] As with all of Lean's epic films, there is a tension between the immense and the intimate, and an awareness of the need to keep them in perfect balance. A certain embarrassment about epic is also in evidence, corresponding with Sobchack's view of the epic as challenging 'for those who have been culturally trained to value asceticism, caution and logic' because 'there is something uncomfortably embarrassing about the historical epic's visual and aural excessiveness, about the commercial hype that surrounds its production, about its self-promotional aesthetic aura ... its spectatorial invitation to indulge in wantonly expensive, hyperbolic, even hysterical acts of cinema.'[21] Despite receiving notable acclaim for his work in epic, David Lean expressed qualms about being bracketed as a maker of that type of film: '"When Robert Bolt and I did Lawrence we thought of it as an intimate story, but obviously one had to have a lot of camels and horses. It becomes an epic." Lean made a face. "I hate that word. It sounds like *Ben Hur* or *The Ten Commandments*."'[22] In taking on *Zhivago*, Lean seemed keen not only to distance himself from epic labelling but also from the unrelieved masculinity of his last film, stating in a 1965 interview 'I've done two films now with no women in them, and I like love stories very much and I found this a superb love story'.[23] *Doctor Zhivago* takes its title from its male hero but Lean conceived of its heroine, Julie Christie's Lara, having equal if not greater dramatic stature to Omar Sharif's Yuri Zhivago. In discussion with his collaborator on the film, Robert Bolt, Lean made clear how pivotal she was to the story: 'even if we didn't have a good film about Dr Zhivago we'd have a good one about Lara.'[24]

Pasternak's novel was a literary sensation of the late 1950s, a candid attack on the Soviet Union from within which had been smuggled to the West for publication. Pasternak was awarded the Nobel Prize for Literature in 1957, to the great annoyance of the Soviet authorities, but the author's fears of being forced into exile prevented him from receiving the award in person. Given the novel's infamy, it is unsurprising that it should be a prime candidate for film adaptation, and producer Carlo Ponti bought the rights. David Lean had his misgivings when first approached to direct, but when he read the novel on a long sea voyage he found it so gripping and profoundly moving that he was hardly able to finish it for the tears in his eyes, and agreed to take it on. However, as critic Raymond Durgnat noted, Pasternak's novel was 'an adaptor's nightmare' hinging on 'long separations and passing decades' while invoking both 'a huge, complex historical process' and 'a poetic sense of nature'. It also insisted upon the importance of personal happiness, which may have been heretical to Stalinism but was unfortunately also 'a Western romantic cliché'.[25]

A lot happened in Pasternak's novel. As Robert Bolt later remarked, if you included all the novel's incidents, 'the resulting film would run for at least sixty hours'.[26] Because of this, Bolt worried about how to compress the novel while also maintaining its poetic expanse. As he wrote on the endpapers of his copy of *Doctor Zhivago*:

> Contrary to most books and almost all films the style (details, observations, insights) is the essence, the story is the accidental. It is a poem. This is a long book and a complex story. It will in any case have to be grossly simplified to get it into (say) 2½ hours. But if we merely simplify to that end, to get it into 2½ hours, we shall have merely an ordinary 'fast moving' story, an ordinary film. We must <u>further</u> simplify so that the story we are left with can be told in 2½ hours *at leisure*. Only then can we be true in our film to the essence of the book.[27]

Adapting *Zhivago* repeatedly pushed Robert Bolt, who was simultaneously experiencing the break-up of his marriage, to tears of frustration, howls of 'rage and helplessness'[28] and several periods of writer's block. As he confessed in a letter: 'I've never done anything so difficult, that *bugger* Pasternak! It's like straightening cobwebs.'[29] It took a lot of intensive work from both Lean and Bolt to straighten those cobwebs: Adrian Turner notes that one of Lean's memos on just one section of the film ran to thirty-six pages of single-spaced typescript, and this was while Bolt and Lean were staying in adjoining rooms in Madrid and had already worked on the script all that day.[30]

FEMINISING THE EPIC   181

One particularly pressing matter, dominating Bolt's endpaper notes, centres on the novel's hero, Yuri Zhivago, and his relationship to the dramatic action. Bolt writes that Pasternak's *Doctor Zhivago* presents

> An adventure of the mind and heart, not of the body: Dr Z is almost always physically passive. If he were also mentally and spiritually passive there would be no story, but in fact he is the most active mind and spirit possible: a poet. *This* is our story and 'action' (meaning physical action) must be subservient to this ... But contrariwise NB how important to Dr Z's inner life is the background of the revolution and how violently Pasternak contrasts it – its harshness, its hard, sharp outlines, its ruthless *action* – to the gentle contemplating inner life of Dr Z ... this contrast between the violent events and his *experience* of them and what his inner life makes of them, is the whole point and we must preserve it. He must not, cannot, be the 'hero' of the action. He *must* be the 'hero' of the film. Therefore it is not a film *of* action ... it is a *quiet*, thoughtful book, though quietly thinking about violent things. Ergo a quiet thoughtful film.[31]

To some, a quiet, thoughtful roadshow blockbuster might seem like an impossible objective if not a contradiction in terms. However, Bolt's insistence that Zhivago must not be made over into a more obvious kind of hero would find its echo in Lean's notes on the character, suggesting a screenwriter and director in total agreement. Lean admitted that 'in film terms, Doctor Zhivago himself is a non-hero – doesn't flash a sword or lead men into battle',[32] and as Lean would write to the actor eventually cast in the role, Omar Sharif, Zhivago 'blossoms out like a flower bud into somebody very special. It's not easy to make a hero of a really good man. He doesn't take sides – doesn't condemn. He's a watcher and observer of life and has no easy answers in the way most of us have.'[33] Prior to the selection of Sharif, Paul Newman had been suggested by MGM but was decisively rejected by Lean because he could 'only see him as a very practical young man' with 'nothing of the dreamer about him'.[34] But while Zhivago was someone for whom 'all the big crises of his life are taken out of his hands by fate', Lean was insistent that the character must not be a 'dreaming bore'.[35]

Despite the intention to make Zhivago a deliberately passive figure, a hero who doesn't *act* so much as *react* to things perpetrated upon him, reviewers of the completed production still took issue with the passivity of its central protagonist. Alexander Walker suggested that the film's failings were partly due to a profound mismatch between the material and the director: 'Lean likes fanatics: men who are driven by an obsession ... men who make events happen even if they perish by them. But the essence of Dr Zhivago is that everything happens to him, he remains passive and introspective.'[36] Likewise, in the American publication *Saturday Review*,

Arthur Knight commented that 'Poor Zhivago, although he dominates the film, is the sort of fellow that things happen to. Not part of the revolution, he is repeatedly engulfed by it.'[37] Critical animus was frequently directed against Omar Sharif's performance and his failure to live up to the active status of an epic lead, with comments on his 'unchanging spaniel eyes and an idiot smile',[38] that he is 'rarely more than soft brown eyes with a smile which sometimes approaches a simper',[39] that he 'smoulders damply'[40] and that he offered a 'soft and colorless core for a film that requires a strong centrifugal force to bind together its disparate elements'.[41] Passivity is seen as being antithetical to heroism; a hero must act, not be acted upon. Lawrence's will-to-power, albeit damaged and hysterical, is preferable to Zhivago's acceptance of destiny and reflection upon it through his poetry. The film attempts to make a case for Zhivago's as a kind of alternative heroism, a passive resistance, in his insistence on the private life, in contradistinction to its attempted obliteration by a destiny-forging but destructive individual such as Strelnikov. Sharif's soft yielding Zhivago is actually a more faithful rendition of the man in Pasternak's novel who sums up his life thus: 'History hasn't consulted me, I have to put up with whatever happens.'[42]

Bolt's endpaper notes on adaptation say a lot about Zhivago but very little about Lara; a telling absence. She is only briefly touched upon in a reflection on casting: 'My God the difficulties! Zhivago and the two women (particularly Lara) have got to have moral dignity – without posturing or pomposity. Where on earth do we find this?'[43] However, in his subsequent letters, Bolt went into much more detail on Lara, particularly after Lean had expressed concerns that Bolt was building up the sympathetic dimensions of Tonya (a character Lean failed to see much interest in) at the expense of Lara, who was being made to seem 'chippy'.[44] Lean surmised that Bolt's marital breakdown was being mapped onto the film and that when Bolt's script extolled Tonya's virtues 'maybe Robert is really saying, "Jo [Bolt's wife] is a wonderful character".'[45] For Lean, Lara was much more important and he envisaged her as absolutely central to the audience's emotional involvement in the film:

> This is our heroine! [I] add the exclamation mark because this is no heroine by screen standards of twenty years ago. Even the word heroine is old-fashioned because heroines are part of a myth about perfect human beings. Laras and lesser Laras will be sitting in our audience, fathers and mothers of Laras, husbands of Laras. They all know that such women exist *and* that they are fine human beings in spite of their frailty. She is in all of us. That is what makes her a great and touching character ... I believe that audiences will be riveted by this girl's story, but they will only be riveted if we don't cheat, soften and sentimentalise her.[46]

FEMINISING THE EPIC   183

Elsewhere Lean insisted to Bolt that Lara should match Zhivago in dramatic power and be 'a noble partner' for the hero: 'This is a very big and unusual woman. We haven't a Garbo to play her so for heaven's sake draw her in bold heroic strokes.'[47] In response, Bolt apologised for his skewed characterisation, and endeavoured to reflect more accurately his underlying feeling for Lara: 'In fact she's the most powerful person in the film; damn nearly an earth mother.'[48]

As well as being one of the film's most important characters, Lara also seems to have figured as a sexual fantasy of the eternal feminine for Lean: 'I think Lara was always adult. Those sort of women are. They're deep pools not mountain rapids ... Only the few know the depth of their passion because it's well down below the surface *only to be guessed at* by all except their lovers. They are *quiet*, not jumpy.'[49] In his correspondence with Robert Bolt, a discussion of her character occasioned a long comparative discussion of male and female sexuality, with Lean musing that 'women, real women, are fathomless. A man will rise only to his limitations, but a woman will go up the scale alongside the man until *he* can go no further. The imaginative lover must surely take her further up the scale than Mr Jones.'[50]

When it came to casting the film, Lean said in an interview that he 'decided to take the plunge on youth and make some stars of my own'.[51] Lean's discovery from *Lawrence*, Omar Sharif, was cast as the eponymous hero. However, several other principal actors were drawn from the British New Wave, not only Julie Christie – cast on the strength of her sexy introductory saunter in *Billy Liar* (1963) – but also Tom Courtenay from that same film and *The Loneliness of the Long-Distance Runner* (1962) as the young revolutionary Pasha, and Rita Tushingham from *A Taste of Honey* (1961) as Lara and Zhivago's daughter. Lean was very keen to have a young dynamic central cast, rejecting producer Carlo Ponti's implicit suggestion that his wife Sophia Loren might play Lara, on the grounds she could never convince as a teenage virgin. Instead Lean felt that the audience's understanding of the main characters depended on 'see[ing] them flower into adult human beings. If we present them in full bloom their behaviour will seem inexcusable ... Our story is *so* topical and well-timed; don't let's turn it into a routine story about middle-aged promiscuity.'[52] The supporting casting was highly eclectic, with English acting traditions represented by Ralph Richardson and Alec Guinness while Rod Steiger was inculcated in method acting. But ironically it was Geraldine Chaplin, a virtual newcomer to films but possessed of an impeccable cinema pedigree as the daughter of Charlie Chaplin, who received the greatest amount of press attention during production, 'an avalanche' according to one journalist.[53] However, once the film had been released, and Julie Christie had been awarded her Best Actress Oscar for *Darling* (1965), the focus would swerve onto the young British star, who came to epitomise the liberated 1960s woman. Her very contemporaneity would prove a stumbling block to plausibility when she took on period roles. Although Robert Bolt thought Christie was 'perfection' and 'lovely' as Lara in *Doctor Zhivago*, he admitted privately to Lean that sometimes her characterisation seemed nearer to the Kings Road, Chelsea than Moscow's Nevsky Prospekt.[54]

Although her performance as Lara was criticised by some reviewers along similar lines to Sharif's Zhivago – Alexander Walker, for example, said Christie had 'the glow of a lustre jug. I still wonder if there is anything inside'[55] – many other critics were effusive in their praise for the actress. According to Arthur Knight, Christie flourished in 'the one truly dynamic role in the entire film',[56] while David Robinson stated that she became 'the dominant figure ... her graceful Lara is perhaps the nearest thing to the original in the film'.[57] Kenneth Tynan concurred: 'But it is Julie Christie who dominates the film – smouldering, vulnerable ... Her erotic scenes have an urgent warmth that few British actresses could rival.'[58] Raymond Durgnat even discerned 'all Pasternak's sadness, all Pasternak's world, in her clear and inscrutable green eyes, in the tragic set of her finely sensual mouth, in her haunting air of being smoothly firm and subtly docile ... her partners are virtually a backcloth for her sole performance which is by far the maturest in the film.'[59] Dilys Powell added: 'Almost alone this vivid young actress makes you believe.'[60]

Robert Bolt's original notes in his copy of Pasternak's novel concluded by emphasising the fragility of the source text: 'We are going to have to be *delicate*. Therefore it is at some point going to seem to us that we are being merely *faint* ... The love story should be – must be – heartbreaking ... But we must take great care of this, great care; he [Pasternak] knows what he's about and if we try to be more overt than he is we may bring it all crashing to the ground. The whole thing is airborne, not *built*.'[61] The irony inherent in Bolt's observation is that in order to appear airborne, the film must be *built*, hence his terrible struggles with the adaptation. In a further irony, Bolt's images of delicacy and subtlety could not contrast more vividly with the promotional ballyhoo surrounding the production 'stressing *labor* and *quantity*',[62] in common with Sobchack's observations on the epic mode. Zhivago's publicity campaign, masterminded by Robert J. McGrath, former FBI agent turned senior executive at MGM, placed great emphasis on the production's huge scale. One MGM press release recounts how the Madrid set and facilities covered 10 acres, that 780 men worked on that set over 5 ½ months of construction, that it had

90,000 fittings, and that in decorating it 57,692 pounds of paint were mixed, and 820 paintbrushes were used, of which 370 were completely worn out by the assignment.[63] Seven thousand daffodil bulbs had to be imported from Holland for the film's springtime sequence, and, as journalist Helen Lawrenson waspishly observed, every reporter who came on set 'was told the story, usually by all three press agents in turn'.[64]

As befits a roadshow presentation, *Doctor Zhivago* commences with an orchestral overture, accompanied by vivid oil paintings of the sun behind silver birches, indicating the centrality of the natural world in the film to come. The first human figure we are introduced to, through a slow pan up his body, is Major Yevgraf Zhivago, played by Alec Guinness. He oversees the exit of a flood of workers, mostly headscarved young women, from a dark tunnel overhung by a large red star. We later discover that these young workers are responsible for the monumental task of moving earth by hand to facilitate the construction of a massive hydroelectric plant. 'What are they like, these girls?', Yevgraf asks the engineer, the question which sets off the framing narrative for the film, Yevgraf's search for his niece, who he suspects may be among the workers at the site. This device was arrived at as a way of accommodating the story of Lara and Zhivago's daughter, a vital element of the original novel but presented as a coda, one of several extra endings that Bolt would describe as 'very vigorously wagging tails to the main story'.[65] While they might be acceptable in an episodic novel, such narrative add-ons were much harder to make work in a film. The solution arrived at was to promote Pasternak's elusive figure of Yevgraf Zhivago, the hero's half-brother, to the role of narrator, placing him 'half in and half out of the story',[66] and to use his quest to bookend the film. Yevgraf acts as narrator/commentator, compelling events forward, contextualising them, shaping them into a coherent narrative, and thus abdicating Yuri Zhivago from non-poetic expository duties. In order to invest Yevgraf with sufficient gravitas and interest, Lean was determined from the outset to have Alec Guinness play the role and sold it to him with reference to an earlier 'small' film: 'I love so-called commentary in films. If it's well done I think it gives a special sort of intimacy. I wonder if you remember Brief Encounter? It was told almost 50–50 commentary and dialogue, and the curious thing is that no-one remembers it as such.'[67]

In this opening sequence, Yevgraf not only initiates the flashback into the past, and into his brother's story, but he is also vital in setting the tone for the film. His summary of the Revolution and the establishment of the Soviet Union simultaneously evokes remarkable progress – 'We've come very far very fast' –but also its dark terrifying undertow: 'do you know what it cost? There were children in those days who lived off human flesh. Did you know that?' This startling line is the sole remnant of Bolt's original plan to foreground the 'bezotchaya' from Pasternak's novel, the abandoned feral children of the revolution who were forced to survive by any means necessary.[68] But in the process of script revision they were excised in order to prioritise the central love story of Yuri Zhivago and Lara over the broader historical canvas of suffering. Despite his sensitive attention to the plight of suffering children in *Great Expectations* and *Oliver Twist*, it seems that Lean was simply not interested in the children caught up in revolution. We can see it in Lean's terse instruction to Bolt to play down Lara's daughter Katya's discovery of new playthings when she, her mother and Zhivago enter the ice house at Varykino: 'Bugger Katya and her toys.'[69] It was romance rather than family that Lean saw as paramount, and he expressed definite unease at Bolt's idea that Zhivago should listen to his unborn baby's heartbeat through Tonya's 'extended stomach': 'it's the sort of intimacy that makes me feel I shouldn't be there.'[70]

However, the pathos of childhood vulnerability is not completely removed from the picture. Tonya Komarovsky (Rita Tushingham), the young woman who may be Yevgraf's niece, plainly and poignantly reproduces a child's perspective when forced to recall her earliest memory: asked for her mother's name, she can only remember 'mummy', and when pressed on what she looked like replies, 'Big. I was little. She looked big.' The theme of the bereft child carries over into the film's first flashback, and our entry into the story of Yuri Zhivago. He is first introduced as a young boy at his mother's funeral, one of a number of distant black figures walking across the steppes against the backdrop of massive snow-capped mountains (exactly the kind of 'enormous backdrop' that Lean said he would generally avoid) before the film cuts to a closer shot of the little boy. Dressed in black, he carries a sprig of lily-of-the-valley as he follows his mother's coffin, shot from a low angle to suggest the child's point-of-view. The camera lurches forward vertiginously when they reach the grave (rather like the shot over the crash crater in *The Sound Barrier*) and then the film returns to a close up of the child's pitiful face as he contemplates his mother's final resting place. Yuri's gaze is drawn up towards the swaying trees shedding their leaves but is then brought back down to earth by the rhythmic noise of nails being hammered into her coffin. It is sealed, and he will never see his mother's face again. Jarre's score provides 'four thunderous claps of music (kettledrums, tubular bells, zither) as the earth hits the coffin'[71] to underline the moment's shock and finality. But there follows a shot that seems to come from Yuri's imagination: the mother 'asleep' inside the sealed coffin. In its weird yet lucid beauty, the image offers, according to one critic, 'the first indication we have that Yuri is also a poet'.[72] Finally, the little boy places his flowers on the grave and reluctantly walks away. Back at his home, in the care of family friends the Gromekos, Yuri is supplied with his mother's legacy, her beautiful red balalaika. Left alone to sleep, Yuri's eyes keep returning back to it, visually striking in comparison with the generally gloomy and foreboding *mise en scène*. The soundtrack's sudden reverberation with balalaika music suggests the little boy's recollections of his mother playing, briefly reanimating the instrument and resurrecting her memory. But the music has to fight against the sound of a storm outside, a howling blizzard that blows the flowers from the mother's grave. A branch taps on the icy window incessantly, recalling similar moments in Lean's Dickens adaptations. The scene ends with the boy looking out at the snow, the first instance of a recurrent motif in the film of Zhivago positioned at a window or doorway, a perpetual observer.

The icy white blizzard dissolves to an inexplicably bright abstract image in orange and jade green. It turns out to be a cluster of cells that Yuri is observing through his microscope, part of his medical training now he is a young man. The medical student expresses his desire to forego 'pure research' in favour of general practice because he wants to see 'life' and gain inspiration for his poetry. The impression of a young man, scholarly but eager to go out into the wider world, is established just as the film prepares to introduce Lara, a young woman Yuri doesn't yet know but with whom his life will be intermingled. The tinkle of a discarded microscope slide bridges to the screech of a departing tram, the one that Yuri has just missed. He runs to catch it and inside sits Lara, swathed in black hat and scarf, only her eyes visible. Yuri sits behind her and their imminent connection is suggested by the quick cutaway to the tram's overhead power line throwing off a spark, an image repeated when Lara then moves past him to dismount the tram and their anonymous bodies touch for the first time.[73]

Walking down the street – John Box's remarkable exterior set recreating Moscow in Madrid[74] – Lara then meets Pasha (Tom Courtenay) on the street, handing out revolutionary propaganda to workers despite Lara's entreaties to be more careful. Unafraid despite Tsarist intimidation, Pasha is animated by powerful political convictions. Although Lara is engaged to Pasha, she pretends he is her brother (a similar sibling trope applies to Yuri and Tonya Gromeko) but the entrance of Komarovsky (Rod Steiger) into the action interrupts this adolescent ambience. Komavosky is a figure of unambiguous adulthood, the mature lawyer lover of Lara's mother who makes the daughter feel distinctly uncomfortable in his presence. Surrounded by the unclothed mannequins in her mother's dressmaking workshop, Lara is asked by Komarovsky how old she is now (seventeen). As Lean described the scene in his notes, 'Komorovsky starts his seduction and twirls a piece of light material around her face. Understand me when I say that the key to this scene is the girl's *genuine* aura of youthful innocence.'[75]

When her mother is taken ill, Lara is drafted in to take her place at dinner with Komarovsky that night, and thus in spite of her immaturity she is ushered into a world of plush adult opulence, a restaurant carefully colour coded in deep red and gold, adorned throughout with sparkling crystalware. The colour red connects the restaurant with a very different scene unfolding in parallel; it is the colour of the banners carried at the protest march in which Pasha is participating. While Komarovsky is spinning Lara round in a waltz, plying her with red wine, Pasha's march passes on the street below. Just as Lara and Komarovsky begin their journey home, they pass a mounted solider giving his cavalry troops the order to 'Prepare'. Their planned target is the march but another parallel attack is taking place in the sleigh, as Komarovsky grips Lara's face and forces himself upon her, accompanied by the high-pitched jangle of sleigh bells. The film then cuts back to the cavalry waiting at the end of the street for their quarry to approach. The protestors' homely, slightly out-of-tune brass band, and the sound of their marching feet in snow announces their arrival, unaware of what awaits them. At this point, Yuri is woven back into the story as he emerges onto the balcony of his home to look at the march, which is about to take a horrifying turn. The soldiers raise their sabres, which glint threateningly in the dark and we hear the sound of galloping hooves in the snow as they mount their attack on the marchers, who try frantically to flee. Although the sequence borrows certain motifs from Eisenstein's depiction of a similar attack on unarmed civilians by Cossack troops in *Battleship Potemkin* (1925), such as trampled individuals and fearful children isolated within the melee, Lean deliberately avoids a replication of that film's montage technique. Instead he chooses to focus on Yuri's reaction to what is unfolding on the street below, using the character's facial expression and an emotive soundtrack of slashing and screaming to imply the horror. On his balcony, Zhivago is removed from the fray, forced to watch transfixed while the massacre takes place. The direction Lean suggested to Sharif for this moment is intriguing: while the camera tracks in on his reaction shot to the carnage, he was told to 'think of being in bed with a woman and making love to her' and to suggest the moment 'just before orgasm'.[76] Is this to suggest a sexualised response to the spectacle or a canny piece of counter-intuitive advice to invoke a sense of something overwhelming and unstoppable without overdoing

FEMINISING THE EPIC 189

the pathos? In any case, the sabre charge is sexualised by its intercutting with the loss of Lara's virginity, faithful to Robert Bolt's idea of 'the unity of two parallel actions – the meeting and massacre, and the restaurant and rape'.[77] The film cuts from a large bloodstain on the snow after the massacre directly to a close-up of Lara's face, suggesting the latter as a reaction to the former, implying cause and effect.[78] A threefold loss of innocence has taken place: Lara's loss of sexual innocence, and Pasha and Yuri's loss of political innocence as victim and witness of the tsarist attack. The young doctor is forced back inside by government troops when he goes out to tend the wounded. Back in the workshop, Lara surveys her reflection in the mirror, tears in her eyes, surrounded by semi-clothed headless mannequins draped in various bits of feathered frilly finery, taking us back to Komarovsky's first act of 'seduction'.

Immediately after this shot of a devastated Lara, the final member of the young quartet of central characters is introduced: Tonya Gromeko (Geraldine Chaplin). There is a striking contrast between the deflowered Lara of the previous shot and unsullied perfect pink powder puff Tonya waving happily from a train. She trails heaps of expensive luggage, with hatboxes that look like wedding cakes against the dark brown and black relief of the station setting. Tonya is the only one of the quartet yet to lose her innocence, and her effusive use of 'mummy' and 'daddy' to greet her parents suggests someone still thinking as a child. However, in other respects, she is emerging into adulthood like her peers. Costume designer Phyllis Dalton took particular care in getting right Tonya's show-stopping outfit of 'shell pink, pearl grey and a marabou muff', trying to balance the character's 'newfound sophistication, her break-away from family supervision' (she is returning home from Paris) while maintaining 'the youthful bloom and wonder of her first grown-up outfit'.[79]

Privileged young Tonya is juxtaposed with others the same age who are far less fortunate. When we next see Pasha, he is disfigured by a gaping vertical (vaginal?) sabre wound on his cheek, and Lara contemplates her reflection in the mirror once again after her forced sexual initiation by Komarovsky the night before. She goes to church seeking comfort but is warned by the priest that the 'flesh is not weak, it is strong. Only the sacrament of marriage will contain it.' After confession, leaving the church, a sleigh rounds the corner and the high-pitched jangle of its bells, recalling the sound that accompanied her violation, seems to suggest the call of insistent irrepressible sexuality. Lara consents to meet Komarovsky at closed dining-rooms used by men of the upper echelons of Tsarist society to entertain their mistresses, and as with the restaurant, the milieu is dominated by rich velvet reds.

The chamber's antique mirrors, candelabras and heavy drapes imbue it with a gothic feel. When Komarovsky enters the room, the opening door reveals the visual shock of Lara wearing a very low-cut tight red dress with black gloves and black choker at throat, all chosen by him, a far cry from the girlish dove grey high-necked dress she had worn for their last meeting. Her voluptuous body is framed in a mirror, headless (like the workshop mannequins), and she is urged to turn around for Komarovsky's perusal. He forces her to drink, holding the glass to her mouth and tilting it up to the point of overspill. Then, in an intensely eroticised moment, he catches the drizzle of wine under her chin while the rest glazes her mouth moistly. Lara's reaction to all of this is marked by her twinned repulsion and attraction – described by Bolt as 'half abhorred, half relished depravity'[80] – towards the older man who in Oedipal fashion is her own mother's lover.

When Lara's mother subsequently attempts suicide, Yuri and his professor happen to be the doctors who attend the scene, called by Komarovsky. After pumping her stomach, the professor throws back the covers to expose the woman's sweating naked body and remarks with misogynistic relish, 'That's not how poets see them, is it? That's how GPs see them. That's how they are.' But Yuri, the poet, provides a gentle corrective to his teacher's disgust: 'Do you know, from here she looks beautiful.' Even in the most sordid circumstances, Yuri is able to find beauty. This is clear in his moment of quiet observation alone in the dressmaking workshop after the panic has subsided. The score's main theme is subtly picked out as he moves around the room observing his surroundings. As a train rumbles nearby and makes the ceiling rattle, he trails his hand over the table and over Lara's open schoolbooks, taking it all in, preparing for its conversion into poetry. He sees himself reflected in a glass partition separating the rooms but then sees something through the glass: a girl's hand overhanging the arm of a chair as she sleeps, the only point of light in the dark room. 'An almost black screen and a lighted hand ... Not realistic. Magic', wrote Lean of this moment devised by Freddie Young.[81] A candle suddenly illuminates the room, held by Komarovsky, who has come to tell Lara her mother will survive. Yuri watches from other side of the glass as Lara kisses Komarovsky in relief while on the soundtrack the noise of another overhead train dominates, replicating Pasternak's description of the two lovers 'acting a dumb-scene'[82] before Yuri's eyes. However, the observer then becomes the observed once Komarovsky notices Yuri looking and looks directly back at him (and us as well) in a confrontational manner, rather like the moment when Thorwald looks back at Jeffries in *Rear Window* (1954). *Doctor Zhivago* has firmly established its hero as an observer, perpetually at one remove from the action but always ready to alchemise it into poetry. But this look back from Komarovsky gives the first hint that passive observation will be a hard stance to maintain as time passes.

When Lara states her desire to marry Pasha, Komarovsky responds with misogynistic name-calling. For him, there are 'two kinds of men' in the world, the 'high-minded' and 'pure', and 'another kind. Not high-minded not pure but alive.' In similar fashion, he categorises women: 'And you as we well know are not the first kind.' She slaps him, and in a marked refusal of chivalry, he hits her back (Steiger did not tell Christie he was going to do it and so her shock is genuine; likewise in the sleigh scene, she was not expecting the French kiss Steiger sprang on her to make her look of shock at his advances more pronounced[83]). He continues 'You, my dear, are a slut.' However, just as his bifurcation of men is problematised by the existence of Zhivago, who is both high-minded *and* alive, a doctor *and* a poet, so Lara is a woman who is sexual and yet not a sybarite reduced to sex. The film makes plain her disgust and resistance at being cast in that role by her seducer.

Nonetheless, the film repeats a common but disturbing trope of pre-feminist depictions of female sexuality, in that her libidinous desire is awoken by assault. After his 'slut' accusation, Komarovsky again forces himself on Lara on a couch in the mother's workshop. Her initial protestations and attempt at fighting him off merge into an embrace of her attacker. But afterwards she lies abandoned on the couch and he spits out his parting words – 'And don't delude yourself that was rape; that would flatter us both' – we remain with her, in close up and bathed in sweat, still in disarray after the assault.[84] Her confrontational look back to the camera suggests her anger – at him and at herself – and (rightful) desire for revenge. A sudden cut to Pasha's abandoned gun segues into the next sequence where once again the destinies of all four young protagonists are entangled, with Tonya and Yuri witnessing Lara's attempt on Komarovsky's life at a grand Christmas party. She even – presciently – interrupts the announcement of their engagement with her gunshot. But Komarovsky is only mildly wounded and Lara is led away by Pasha. Back home, he reads the confessional letter she left for him, in another 'dumb-show' scene, framed through a little porthole in the frosty window pane made by a single candle's flame. For *Time* magazine's reviewer, this was a highly eloquent symbolic moment: 'the circle becomes a poetic, crystalline metaphor for his swollen anguish and the inevitable burning away of youth's illusions'[85] – although, slightly less poetically, the circle was actually melted by the endlessly inventive Eddie Fowlie operating a hairdryer.

The return of Yevgraf's narration announces the outbreak of the First World War, and an accompanying montage presents the corresponding fates of principal characters. Both Yuri and Tonya, and Lara and Pasha, are now married and each couple has a child. Births and marriages, the usual subject matter of domestic drama, are conveyed via ellipsis and instead the focus shifts back onto the public and political, as Pasha and Yevgraf volunteer in the hope of stirring up revolutionary ferment among the troops, and Yuri is conscripted as a medic. Civil war and revolution presage chaos but also (conveniently, in narrative terms) occasion the coming together of Zhivago, drafted to a frontline hospital, and Lara, looking for her husband on the front and then working as a field nurse. Although their mutual attraction is clear, restraint conquers abandon and their friendship remains platonic. When the field hospital finally closes, Yuri is left behind to watch the departing wagon train with Lara on board. Once again, he walks around an empty room that contains traces of her, this time her vase of sunflowers rather than schoolbooks, and again, through the use of the central musical theme, it is suggested that Yuri is storing up a memory of this place for conversion into later poetry.

'Adapt yourself', the advice given to Zhivago by one of his patients Comrade Kuril (Bernard Kay), proves highly prescient upon his return home and reunion with Tonya. The family home has now been taken over by grim-faced bureaucrats demanding his discharge papers and taking offence at his bungled attempt at hospitality: 'it is not for you to welcome us'. The film encourages us to place our sympathies entirely with the beleaguered former gentry, holed up in one small room and enjoying the last cigar in Moscow, rather than the workers or revolutionaries. Yuri is a model of bourgeois endorsement of a fairer society ('There was room for 30 people in this house. This situation is more just') and Tonya is shown to be a cheerful and resourceful young woman making the best of their straitened circumstances. By comparison, the 'comrades' are at best pettifogging and at worse duplicitous, even looting the family's belongings. Indeed, one major criticism made of *Doctor Zhivago* was the lack of any optimism in its depiction of the initial revolutionary moment. As Kenneth Tynan remarked, 'You will look in vain for any sign of the vast upsurge of jubilant idealism that overthrew the Romanovs. The Bolsheviks are presented as mean and envious bullies, eager to impose a despotism worse than the one they have supplanted ... The traditional cold-war view of the October Revolution has seldom been more blatantly expounded.'[86] Responding to criticisms that his script was slanted against the Bolsheviks, Bolt grumpily insisted 'I know damn well it's not'.[87] Given Bolt's former communist affiliations and continuing leftist sympathies, the film was by no means a simple denunciation of the revolution and its aftermath. Rather more, like its source novel, the film offered a markedly downbeat vision, commensurate with increasing recognition of subsequent Stalinist tyranny. Lean's approach to the politics of the piece was blithe avoidance, as he told an interviewer: 'This is not a political film. I'm an ignoramus about politics.'[88] Lean's intention was to dramatise the revolution less as ideological experience and more as 'a great, big human earthquake'.[89] When Yevgraf meets his half-brother Yuri for the first time, the voiceover narration lets us know the great danger his brother is in: 'He approved of us (the party) but for reasons that were subtle, like his verse ... he was walking about with a noose round his neck and didn't know.' The only hope for this 'personal, petit bourgeois and self-indulgent' poet and his family is to flee Moscow, and Yevgraf aids their passage east. As the family waits to leave, the massed sleeping bodies huddled in the railway station are juxtaposed with declamatory revolutionary posters of Lenin with extended hand, as though offering to help, and Trotsky with raised fist. Compared to the people desperately seeking an exit, their gestures necessarily appear empty.

The extended sequence on the train to Varykino as Zhivago and his family flee an increasingly dangerous Moscow is not only one of the most striking sections of the film, it also provides a strong counter-argument to the critical tendency to characterise the film as little more than sumptuous spectacle. Bolt saw an opportunity to present a microcosm of Russian society in transit – 'the train, ramshackle, makeshift, crammed with heterogeneous helpless folk and led by revolutionaries with red banners'[90] – and Lean urged him to 'pull out your biggest cinematic stops to date. We are running up to the interval; we've done with Moscow and are heading East into a new centre of gravity for our story. I'm sure we should bend everything to giving them a cinematic display – and a train's not a bad prop!'[91] The train sequence also boasts the remarkable presence of Klaus Kinski, all burning blue eyes and pulsing veins on his forehead, as Kostoyed, an anarchist intellectual who is being extradited as forced labour. He barracks anyone he hears spouting revolutionary cant and directly contradicts their falsehoods about 'voluntary labour'. Even as he is in chains and in all likelihood being deported to his death, he insists upon his independence of thought: 'I am a free man, lickspittle and there's nothing you can do about it. I am the only free man on this train. The rest of you are cattle!' He laughs out loud at Zhivago's faltering attempts to derive some aesthetic pleasure from the sight of the moon glimpsed through a tiny wooden hatch in the carriage (which is soon kicked shut in any case by a fellow traveler feeling the cold). The dominant truth of their environment is not natural beauty but immersion in the most squalid aspects of dense human habitation: pitching out excrement-sodden straw from the carriage door and dousing the floor with disinfectant. Although Kostoyed seems a very different kind of man from gentle, passive Zhivago, he is entranced by a humanist spectacle of the kind that might captivate the poet: the elderly couple who cuddle up against each other by red stove-light in the dead of night, a minor miracle of human affection. The camera tracks into a tight close-up of Kinski's almost awed reaction to the sight, denuded of any cynicism. But it is not clear whether his response is admiration at the stubborn continuance of connubial warmth or just disbelief.

When the carriage door is next opened, it offers the sight of sacked and burnt villages, dead livestock, starving freezing people. One desperate woman tries to get on the passing train with her baby, and is helped on by Zhivago, only for Tonya to discover that the infant is already dead and was just being used as a prop to aid her rescue: 'It wasn't my child and his little soul is in heaven now, that's certain.'[92] The atrocities she is fleeing are the work of the merciless and mysterious Commander Strelnikov, already subject to a certain amount of mythologising: 'No one knows where he comes from and they never know where he is.' However, just before the film breaks for its intermission – and the necessity of an intermission is the mother of superb narrative invention here – it reveals the identity of Strelnikov. Steaming past on his own customised bright red locomotive, a close-up accompanied by train whistle and the sound of a flapping flag suddenly shows us that he is Pasha. Of all the personal transformations forged by war and revolution, his shift from young idealist to ruthless ideologue seems the most dramatic.

The return to the action after the intermission begins with a shot from the front of the train, 'phantom ride'-style, as it emerges from a dark tunnel. Part of its aim was dazzling spectacle; as Lean noted, it would look 'as if the shot from the train until now had been on small film and we'd now banged on the Panavision lenses'.[93] But the metaphorical connotations of seeing the light at the end of the tunnel are obvious. The train's passengers are now nearing their final destination and although they can still hear artillery fire, it's distant and counterbalanced by an equally powerful natural sound, a waterfall. Yuri dismounts the train and looks around, absorbing the beauty and warmth of an orange sun shining through the branches of tall pines. However, just at this contemplative moment, he is seized by Red Guards and taken off for questioning by Strelnikov on suspicion of being a White Guard spy. Clearly, the attainment of a rural idyll will not be that easy.

FEMINISING THE EPIC 195

The confrontation between Zhivago and Strelnikov affords the film its most direct explication of opposing worldviews. Strelnikov criticises Zhivago for his 'absurdly personal' poetry and states unequivocally: 'Feelings, insights, affections, it's suddenly trivial now. You don't agree, you're wrong. The personal life is dead in Russia. History has killed it.' Strelnikov's self-imposed transcendence of personal bonds extends to shelling Yuryatin, the town in which Lara and his daughter Katya are living, news that Zhivago receives with horror. Although Strelnikov insists that 'private life is dead for a man with any manhood', Yuri questions a concept of masculinity commensurate with murder and destruction. 'What will you do with your wife and child in Varykino?' Strelnikov asks Zhivago. 'Just live', he responds. Although Strelnikov is the more formidable figure, it is absolutely clear that the film's sympathies lie with Zhivago's modest ambitions. His apolitical ethos may have been lambasted – perhaps unsurprisingly – by the communist *Morning Star*'s Nina Hibbin as 'I'm all right Ivan ... a plea for the right of a poet to consider himself something special and apart, responsible to no one but himself'.[94] But those in the film who denounce Zhivago's desire to disengage and 'just live', like Strelnikov, and later Razin (Noel Wilman) who censures Zhivago for being a 'dubious poet hugging his private life', are presented as deeply flawed characters.

Once Zhivago is free to go, the family returns to their beautiful onion-domed dacha at Varykino. Their old servant Petya (Jack MacGowran) is as deferential as before. But the main house is locked, commandeered by the local 'people's committee', so the family must make a home for themselves in the little cottage on the estate instead. The idyll of a simple life, unimpeded by revolutionary turmoil, is briefly attained. Yuri tills their little patch of land, and Tonya works away at her ironing with their son Sasha's help. But the thump of the iron, previously associated with Lara's hospital duties, sends Yuri's mind to her probable location, the nearby Yuryatin. Distracted, he sits down to write when his wife suddenly voices his secret thoughts: 'Yuri, why don't you go to Yuryatin?' He refuses on the grounds that the roads there are blocked by snow – just as his writing is blocked – but winter is just about to thaw into spring in one of the film's most visually stunning sequences, as Zhivago's poetic inspiration returns along with his reconnection with Lara.

The feathery frost crystals on the window pane are illuminated by spreading sunlight and a dissolve introduces the sudden eruption of bright yellow into a *mise en scène* kept deliberately muted up to this point.[95] The daffodils that fill the screen are 'a kind of visual Lorelei calling to him'.[96] In early script discussions, Robert Bolt argued that the daffodil scene could bring to life the vivid thought processes of creative inspiration, contrasting the apparently inactive man standing among the flowers with the intense activity going on within: 'His POV: the daffodils again, the birch leaves, the white birch branches, we hurl the camera through them, we race, we are drunk, we soar, we return, we skim the daffodils and settle at the man's broken-booted feet, ascend slowly to his face. He is as before; but we have been the poet's *mind* for a minute.'[97] The final version of the scene is not quite as visually dynamic as this but it does suggest that pantheistic sympathy between poet and environment as well as the intensity of his contemplation, tracking right in to the stamen within a single daffodil. Visually, it is very much a 1960s sequence, even prophesying 'flower power' several years before the Summer of Love. From the absolute centre of one flower, the film dissolves to a close-up of Lara, her blue eyes and blonde hair lit up by a beam of sunlight, corresponding to the colours of nature seen just a moment before. The music is also vital. Bolt's original notes called for a score that 'must be sparing, modest, mostly solo, duet, trio, an octet (say) for climaxes. *Not* an orchestra. It's an intimate story against an epic background. The music must strengthen the story, must not side with the background.'[98] But in the end, Maurice Jarre was chosen to compose the score, building on his spellbinding work on *Lawrence of Arabia*, and what he supplied was certainly not sparing or modest. Instead its melodic core refrain, 'Lara's theme', became a huge hit, played on a million music boxes and in a million lifts. Raymond Durgnat suggested that for a Russian epic, the music was strangely Italian, 'irresistibly evocative of Venice, gondolas and pizza pie'.[99] But in providing a score dominated by a love theme rather than music for revolutionary action, Jarre adhered to Lean and Bolt's original aim of emphasising the more intimate personal story over the events which form their backdrop.

Pasternak's novel was 'full of "co-incidences"'[100] and Bolt worried that Zhivago and Lara's second fateful reunion in Yuryatin might stretch credibility. However, Lean took a slightly different view of supposedly implausible events, perhaps drawing on Dickens' facility with coincidence: 'I think it would be a dreadful mistake to drop the idea of "Destiny" out of this picture. It adds an extra colour to so many of the scenes ... something to do with legends.'[101] The resumption of their love affair, now passionately consummated rather than platonic, is not only absolutely necessary but also faithfully Pasternakian. But it also casts Yuri in the least sympathetic light in the entire narrative, as he shuttles between his heavily pregnant wife at home in Varykino and his lover in Yuryatin, only later deciding that he must break from Lara. His resolution to end his affair is never tested though, as war and revolution once again intrude into private existence and Zhivago is kidnapped by Red partisans on the road home to his wife. With Zhivago's enforced conscription into the Red Guard, the film returns once more to the masculine realm of warfare and scenes combining horror and stunning spectacle; the sabre charge across the frozen river, recalling the battle on the ice in Eisenstein's *Alexander Nevsky* (1938), and the machine-gunning of young volunteers in a golden cornfield speckled with poppies. Coming upon their dead bodies, one of the partisans says 'It doesn't matter' in perhaps the film's most shocking moment of anti-humanist expression. Uncomprehending, Yuri tries ineffectually to reinstate the principle of love – 'did you ever love a woman?' – but is met with a stonewall of nihilism. Strelnikov's proclamation that the personal life is dead in Russia seems to have come to pass. Women and children are the primary victims of that edict. The partisans encounter a group of them fleeing something, tramping across snowy wastes, the blankness of the *mise en scène* heightening the moment's universal symbolism. A deranged woman among them, wild-eyed and blue-lipped, cries 'soldiers, soldiers' at the passing partisans. Red or white, they ask her, but she makes no distinction, just reiterates 'soldiers' and moves on further into the white abyss. Zhivago's reaction shot, with only his tired eyes visible, is an augury of the 'thousand yard stare' of those forced to witness similar atrocities.

Zhivago's recurring recourse to nature, even in the most grim of situations, now seems to fail him. The 'Lara/inspiration' musical theme plays as he looks up at the moon again but this time it is obscured by mists, its light dim. The partisans have refused to release him but to continue with them would mean an irrevocable move into nihilism and death. So, like Lawrence rescuing Gasim from the sun's anvil, Zhivago repudiates the wisdom of the group and instead rides in the opposite direction, back towards home. His connection with the Russian landscape is now a matter of pain rather than pleasure, as he is the only human figure in the extreme bleakness of an unending snowscape which threatens to claim him; the icicles in his moustache suggest as much, he is *becoming* the icy landscape. After his impossible epic journey across immense landscapes, and the extreme challenge to his physical and spiritual self, he finally reaches Yuryatin, and Lara's home. She is not there but Zhivago is overwhelmed to find everything as it was before; the tiny miracle of a floral china plate and bowl set for lunch on the table. In such carefully maintained domesticity, the ragged ravaged Zhivago is an incongruous presence and he recoils from his reflection in the mirror, cadaverous aside from his red-ringed eyes. Rather like Pip in *Great Expectations*, Zhivago reaches the point of unsustainable anguish and collapses, hallucinating Tonya's face as the shot irises in on him. As its blur encroaches, he cries out. When he comes to, it is Lara's face that he first sees, just as Pip woke to see Joe Gargery tending to him.

For all the moments of large-scale spectacle in *Doctor Zhivago*, its true dramatic climax is not physical but cerebral and takes place in a closeted interior. It comes when Yuri, Lara and Katya retreat from the encroaching world and hide out in the Gromeko dacha, which has been transformed into a place of enchantment, a magical ice palace. One of the inspirations for John Box's design was a photograph of Captain Scott's hut in Antarctica, where a small hole in the wall had allowed the snow and ice to enter and colonise its interior. Here, a combination of candle wax, pressurised icy water and glittering mica was used to achieve the same effect.[102] The setting has to be unforgettable as the ultimate refuge for the lovers, the place where Yuri's poetic self *and* his romance with Lara can be perfectly fulfilled. This battered but somehow even more beautiful remnant of pre-revolutionary elegance is the last place where poetry and love can flourish, even while the wolves surround them, even while, as Lara states, it is 'a horrible time to be alive'. A subjective camera mimics the new occupants' point-of-view as they move through the shut-up rooms. The camera halts as it reaches the most important spot: a desk. Zhivago wipes off a thick top layer of snow to reveal that it is still intact underneath, as are the paper and ink in the drawer. The stage is set for the creation of what we already know, with the benefit of Yevgraf's framing narration, will be his finest artistic achievement (Plate 14).

For Lean, the composition of the 'Lara' poems had to be 'a real scene' in which we 'know and see the moment when this man's talent, so long dammed up, was released on its greatest and final work'.[103] It begins

14 Zhivago (Omar Sharif) and Lara (Julie Christie) seek refuge from revolution in *Doctor Zhivago* (1965)

FEMINISING THE EPIC 199

with a sense of Yuri being lured by the desk. He takes his candle over, sits down, and at the top of a pristine sheet of paper writes Lara's name. A faltering version of Jarre's Lara theme on the soundtrack is temporarily silenced by the sound of a wolf howling in the distance. Like other dangerous external forces, they pose a threat but they can be held off for now, and Yuri shoos them away easily. He is drawn back inside by the sight of the candle on the desk seen though the frosty window. As Lara and Katya sleep nearby, he writes through the night. However, the equally important counterpart to Zhivago's creation of the poems is Lara's discovery of them when she wakes. Lean advised Bolt: 'Robert, this is the sort of thing the cinema can do so well. There's a wonderful 30 seconds of screen time here. A girl coming to a desk and finding a poem written to and about her with music supplying the poetry as she reads it to herself – mounting and mounting until tears run down her cheeks – putting it back on the desk with great care and siting back for a moment or two in wonderment at him and the something in her which sparked his genius. When he comes and stands beside her I think she could hardly speak.'[104] The sequence lives up to Lean's expectations, and Julie Christie's performance of delighted astonishment (her small gesture of holding up her hand so she can read to the end without interruption) is exquisitely done. A tender dispute over the poem's provenance follows. 'This isn't me, Yuri', she insists. 'Yes, it is', he counters. 'No, it's you', she replies but he simply points to her name at the top of the page and she reads it aloud: 'Lara'. Woman is unquestionably entrenched in the role of muse here (as Lean's notes put it: 'Yuri is a looker at life. Lara is life'[105]) but in that role she is granted a kind of joint authorship and creative status. The lovemaking that follows, the film implies, is when their daughter is conceived, and so artistic creation and the creation of new life are strongly aligned. In *Doctor Zhivago*, women's allotted role is very traditionally conceived as inspiring love and poetry – never writing it themselves – and bearing children. However, in its elevation of the domestic and personal, far above the public and military, the film argues for the importance of qualities usually considered feminine and (therefore) insignificant.

Komarovsky reappears with the news that Strelnikov has shot himself while awaiting trial. His insistence on being called Pasha Antipov when captured along with the fact that he was trying to get back to his family all suggest his repudiation of his former nihilism. Like Zhivago, now he wants to 'just live'. As a result of Pasha's death, his surviving family are placed in grave danger and Komarovsky, now a high-ranking Soviet Commissar, offers to escort Lara and Katya to safety further east. The ice palace idyll is over and the lovers' goodbye, although they don't admit it to each other, is final. Desperate to get a last look at Lara's departing sleigh, Zhivago runs upstairs, clawing at the window to open it and, when that fails, smashing it to get a final glimpse of her before she disappears over the horizon forever; a reversal of Sharif's slow arrival over the horizon in *Lawrence*. On the train, Lara's revelation to Komarovsky that she is pregnant with Yuri's child yanks the action out of its flashback and back into the framing narrative. 'You were born in Mongolia, you were born that year' Yevgraf presses upon the girl he believes to be his niece, trying forcibly to connect past and present.

After the dramatic climax of Yuri's poems and Lara's pregnancy comes the film's denouement and Yevgraf's explanation of what happened to the protagonists beyond this point. Zhivago, we discover, dies of a heart attack on the way to start a new job at the hospital. Events come full circle as his first and last encounters with Lara both happen while he rides on a Moscow tram. Once again observing through a window, at one remove from the action, Zhivago notices a woman who looks like Lara walking down the street. When the tram swings very near to her, his hopes are confirmed – it is Lara. He hammers frantically on the window, then tries to open it but can't. All the while, she walks on implacably, showing no signs of recognition or of even having noticed him. He disembarks the tram to try to catch her, tries to call out her name but can't make a sound. Grasping his collar, he collapses to the ground, dead. His prone body is juxtaposed with a golden statue nearby, thrusting its fist in the air, the model of heroic Soviet masculinity. But in death, Zhivago becomes a hero and his grave is visited by countless mourners laying flowers (as Yevgraf says, 'Nobody loves poetry like a Russian'). The daffodils inform us that Lara has been there too.

Yevgraf tries to help Lara find her lost child Tonya but without success. And then without ceremony Lara promptly disappears from the narrative. Lean and Bolt's aim was to replicate the power and shock of Pasternak's brief summary of the character's mysterious but commonplace demise: 'One day Lara went out and did not come back. She must have been arrested in the street, as so often happened in those days, and she died or vanished somewhere, forgotten as a nameless number on a list which was afterwards mislaid, in one of the innumerable mixed or women's concentration camps in the north.'[106] As Lean wrote to Bolt, 'It's one of the most awful lines in the book and it's haunted me since first reading.'[107] Yevgraf's voiceover mobilises much of Pasternak's original text but the clinching detail is the visual juxtaposition of the tiny figure walking alone down the grey street dwarfed by an enormous poster of Stalin overhead, a striking metaphor for the fate of all those forcibly 'disappeared' by totalitarian regimes.[108]

Lean was concerned that beyond the deaths of the two lovers, the film might suffer from an anti-climax and urged Bolt to provide something as emotionally powerful as one of the key scenes in *Lawrence of Arabia*:

> I think you've got a problem quite as big as the problem you solved with the train-top walk and I think it needs the same sort of audacious approach ... You will suspect me of being a ham – and I suspect myself, but I also suspect you of that English politeness we've often spoken about. After all the high drama can we drop so suddenly into a minor key? I think you can do it with the actual dialogue between Yevgraf and the girl, but haven't you got to launch them into it with a certain dash?[109]

In the end, Bolt rose to the challenge with aplomb. The film returns to the fate of the child upon which it opened. After being pressed and pushed, the girl finally gives Yevgraf her heart-breaking account of how she came to be lost: 'We were running in a street. My father...' 'Not your father, Komarovsky', Yevgraf corrects her before she continues her story, using the simple language and the disconnected images of the traumatised child: 'The street was on fire. There were explosions and the houses were falling down. He let go of my hand. He let go of my hand. And I was lost.' But what had seemed to be irrevocable loss, complete abandonment, so much so that she 'wanted to die' as a child, has now been altered. She has the possibility of a family in the shape of her uncle. Yevgraf, previously agnostic towards anything 'personal, petit bourgeois and self-indulgent', now finds that he wants a family connection. The girl is wary, only willing to believe she is the daughter of a great poet 'if it's true'. Yevgraf smiles at this indication that she is her father's daughter, commenting 'That's inherited'. But the film's final insistence on the heredity principle is its most memorable. Yevgraf notices the balalaika she slings over her shoulder as she walks away and the girl's boyfriend tells Yevgraf she's 'an artist', even though no one taught her how to play. Despite the revolution's attempts to remake men and women, it seems that inherited qualities stubbornly continue to make their presence felt. 'Ah then, it's a gift', Yevgraf says of this unexpected resurgence of her grandmother's musicality. As Neil Sinyard argues, Guinness 'is enormously moving in the light lift and lilt he gives to the phrase',[110] amply fulfilling Lean's hopes for the delivery of those final valedictory words: 'I can imagine – with a bit of encouragement – what he will give in emotional punch to them. Put it in Alec's lap. He will be very moved and I think he'll release the full flood of emotion in the audience.'[111]

The closing images of *Doctor Zhivago* have proven to be among its most contentious. The young lovers walk away over a colossal dam as water thunders out of it. Where the water meets the river below, the spray that is thrown up creates a rainbow. As the end credits roll, the film returns to those torrents pouring out of the dam, the gushing water echoing the movement of the cast's names. For the critic Patrick Gibbs, 'the final scene with its background of a Soviet-made dam and introduction of a nice Communist youth to look after Zhivago and Lara's daughter suggests that the end has, indeed, justified the means'.[112] Raymond Durgnat called the ending 'crashingly banal' but he had actually misremembered the rainbow going over the heads of the young couple walking hand in hand across the dam, a rather more obvious benediction of Soviet progress than what actually appears in the film.[113] In the film's planning stages, Lean was very anxious to avoid these kinds of interpretations of the film's conclusion, writing to Robert Bolt: 'Do let's be careful not to make it look like a jolly boost for the new USSR now that dear old Khrushchev is in power and all those other chaps we saw posters of in the film are out of the way and the Revolution is over – and was worth it after all because see those lovely new buildings [referring to the construction site setting] and the way people really mix now.'[114] Perhaps the rainbow is not a blessing but a sign of nature's unstoppable continuity, no matter what kind of man-made construction is placed in its path; it can as easily materialise over a man-made waterfall as a natural one. Nature can't help throwing forth wonders, even if it seems that nobody is looking or caring. The hydroelectric dam is an impressive human achievement (partly built by bare hands, as the film informs us at the beginning) but it is locked in a continual struggle against the water, managing for the time being to control and divert this natural force in particular directions but it is the water, not the dam, that will win out in the end. The 'achievements' of the revolution are epic but they are dwarfed by ahistorical eternity; a ceaseless flow whether of water or of human life.

As detailed earlier, *Doctor Zhivago* did not enjoy unanimous critical acclaim. So it was with a certain amount of trepidation that Robert Bolt finally approached the result of his and Lean's cobweb-straightening when he went to see the film at the beginning of 1966 with his agent Peggy Ramsay. But he and his companion were knocked out, as he wrote to Lean:

> It is a *tremendously* good film, and anyone who doesn't like it condemns himself. It's moving, powerful, beautiful, serious and continuously held my rapt attention; Peggy and I sat like a pair of housemaids and ended with sodden handkerchiefs. I can't tell you how proud I am to be your lieutenant in the enterprise. It's in a different street from *Lawrence* and that's saying a lot. Peggy was almost reeling. She kept saying, in a whisper that shook the chandeliers, 'But it's over*whelming*! One is *overwhelmed*!'[115]

Doctor Zhivago would be Lean's biggest commercial success but although Bolt thought it surpassed *Lawrence of Arabia*, it has never garnered the same level of critical esteem as that earlier film instead enjoying a lesser status as high-1960s chocolate-box-pretty romantic slush. This is entirely unfair for a film which is far richer than its kitschy reputation suggests. Luchino Visconti's alleged comments after having seen the film – 'Let's see it round again. But don't tell anyone!'[116] – suggest that part of the problem was that the film became a guilty pleasure, one that couldn't be openly admitted among the cognoscenti. But *Doctor Zhivago* had some fans in high places nonetheless who were prepared to admit it. Responding to Bosley Crowther's cruel review which said the film 'reduced the vast upheaval of the Russian Revolution to the banalities of a doomed romance',[117] Alexandra Tolstoy wrote a personal letter to Lean to say 'many of my friends and I do not agree with the criticism of New York Times ... I consider that the film was excellent and I, as Leo Tolstoy's daughter with whom the Pasternaks were very friendly, as a Russian – thank you for the brilliant job you have achieved.'[118]

Ryan's Daughter (1970)

The project that would eventually evolve into *Ryan's Daughter* was marked from its conception by a sense of ambivalence about size and scale. Immediately after *Doctor Zhivago*, Robert Bolt forcefully (and somewhat hypocritically) rejected the large canvas filmmaking of his previous two films with David Lean, stating in a letter to John Huston about a different possible project, 'I loathe epics. I think our film should aim at two hours flat. I also loathe runaway budgets – they lead to flabbiness and uncertainty of story. Do you agree? There's something sharply distasteful about those mindlessly expanded millions.'[119] In a letter to Lean about their next collaboration, Bolt expressed similar sentiments albeit in far more diplomatic terms, envisaging 'something simpler in its mechanics, with more emphasis on atmosphere (like Brief Encounter if you like), less sheer strained ingenuity of story-telling. A simple but grand theme that could be told in lesser length.'[120] A month later, perhaps aware of Lean's irritation at having his recent work continually compared back to that particular film, Bolt slightly revised his stance: 'I don't mean another Brief Encounter in the sense of anything as "small" as that ... It ought to be a simple story with an important or exciting theme ... We want something we can expand instead of compress.'[121] Bolt had been working on ideas for suitable vehicles for his new wife and muse, Sarah Miles. An early idea of adapting Jane Austen's *Emma* gave way to his more sustained attempt to adapt Gustave Flaubert's *Madame Bovary*, which Bolt then pitched to Lean.[122] Lean agreed in principle but argued for a very loose adaptation of the basic situation of Flaubert's novel: a romantically disillusioned young wife of an older man has an affair with a younger suitor with disastrous consequences.[123] Although Lean and Bolt had considered other potential locations for their Bovary-esque story – Kevin Brownlow mentions Sicily, the Shetlands, Sardinia and India as possibilities[124] – they finally settled on the West Coast of Ireland as their setting.

Ironically, given the final expanse – and expense – of the film, it seems that for Lean too the original intention behind *Ryan's Daughter* was a partial retreat from the epic and a return to the smaller scale of filmmaking that defined his early career. In correspondence and conversation, Lean repeatedly described the Bovary project as a 'little gem', filmable in ten weeks,[125] something 'much more intimate and private than the last two films'.[126] However, he later modified his position: 'I don't want an epic, and I don't want a "little gem". I want something that has size and that size must be emotional.'[127] It seems that with *Ryan's Daughter*, Lean's aim was to synthesise two sides of his career, his early British miniaturism and the giant canvases of the later epics, with a story that held the personal and political in perfect balance. However, judging from the critical response to the film, this endeavour should be judged an unmitigated failure. The film's reception was truly punitive with critics, in Adrian Turner's words, 'not so much roasting the film as incinerating it'.[128] Leading the attack were the members of the National Society of Film Critics (formed in deliberate reaction against the exclusive, more conservative New York Film Critics Circle) wishing to act as midwives to a new kind of cinema and feeling constrained by the film establishment's gerontocracy. Pauline Kael, who had led the Algonquin assault on Lean, concluded her brilliantly acerbic review of *Ryan's Daughter* with a clear statement of the pervasive 'them-and-us' mind-set of the moment: 'the publicity machine has turned it into an artistic event, and the American public is a sucker for the corrupt tastefulness of well-bred English epics. One begins to feel like a member of a small cabal, powerless to fight this well-oiled reverence.'[129] With hindsight, one can see how Kael underestimated the power she and her fellow critics had. They may have felt, like British critic Gavin Millar, that Lean was 'a solid enough target to sustain a tiny barb'[130] but as we have seen they were entirely wrong in that estimation.

But although many critics mobilised against *Ryan's Daughter*, the film also had its defenders. A booking form for the British roadshow presentation of the film at the Empire Leicester Square collated the comments of a number of US critics who were highly supportive. The terms of their defence were particularly significant. Headed up with the title 'American critics welcome the return of a great tradition ... the motion picture!', their comments continued along similarly traditionalist lines: 'David Lean is an artist, a giant at a time when the pygmies are taking over. He has come up with the kind of film – no – *Ryan's Daughter* is a movie, which is what they were called when we first began to love them – that you haven't seen in years, and things being as they are, that you may never see again.' (Bernard Drew); 'a narrative film that the foolish may find "old-fashioned" simply because it is near-classic in its structure and universal in its humanity' (Judith Crist); 'David Lean's direction is a reminder of the days when movies were works of art. Every young filmmaker in the world should be required to see *Ryan's Daughter* before shooting another foot of film' (Rex Reed); 'To those complaining they don't make movies the way they used to – it's a winner' (Bruce Bahrenberg).[131] These were the conservative middlebrows, resistant to the products of the new Hollywood, longing instead for old-fashioned narrative cinema of the kind proffered by Lean, and highly defensive about what they saw as its demise. This position is exemplified by British critic David Lewin's argument that *Ryan's Daughter* should be a success because the public 'want romance now, not a hippie revolution; they want hope and not despair'.[132]

Examining the divergent reviews of the film, it becomes clear that David Lean and *Ryan's Daughter* were unfortunate enough to be caught in the crossfire of a battle for the soul of contemporary cinema, and the fractious critical reception of the film pointed to cultural disagreement on a much larger scale. Rightly or wrongly, *Ryan's Daughter* was seen as representative of a whole school of filmmaking that its advocates wanted to support and its antagonists wanted to destroy. The film seemed representative of all that was indefensible about large-scale movie-making of the time – the sprawl of its production schedule, the extravagance of its expense account, even the length of its running time – summed up by Alexander Walker's damning comment that 'instead of looking like the money it took to make, the film feels like the time it took to shoot'.[133] Another review put it even more succinctly: 'It's an all-star six million quid bore'.[134] Never mind that much of the expansion in its budget was due to delays caused by poor weather, something entirely out of Lean's control, and a controversial relocation to South Africa was undertaken in order to complete production and circumvent the technically challenging Irish climate, whose 'pea-soup mist' followed by 'blazing sunlight' presented the most 'horrendous matching problems'.[135] Lean was a 'tall poppy' asking to be cut down to size by both critics *and* envious industry insiders. The film's assistant editor Tony Lawson remembered an encounter with another director who was furious about Lean's multi-million-dollar budget: 'He said he could make three films for that budget. He was incensed that he [Lean] had essentially stolen it from other film-makers.'[136] But due to the disappointing performance of many high-budget productions in the late 1960s, and – conversely – the enormous success of several micro-budget films, the kind of economic largesse extended to Lean by MGM would not be repeated. Although it would eventually turn a profit (nowhere near as much as *Zhivago* but still the fourth most profitable film of its year[137]), it would be the destiny of *Ryan's Daughter* to mark 'the end of an age', to be 'The Last Epic'.[138]

In some respects the film was proud to position itself as old-fashioned, as indicated by its British promotional strategy, with Lean himself boasting 'we've made an old classical type of film with no improvised quality' and claiming that the modern notion that 'you have to be under thirty without experience but with flashy cutting to tell your story' was 'silly'.[139] But this commitment to an older cinematic idiom led the film to be described as 'a throwback, a film out of time',[140] with one critic calling it 'an epic love story from the 1940s or early 1950s'.[141] Even so, this was not an entirely old-fashioned piece of film-making. The romance was explicitly sexual in contrast to the restraint exercised by films of thirty years before, not least Lean's own. Even though one critic congratulated the director 'for having the nerve to make a blazing love story when everyone else in the business is stripping down to raw sex',[142] *Ryan's Daughter* still included scenes of a sexual nature and fleeting moments of female nudity which were enough to jeopardise its family film status and have it threatened with an R (over-17) certificate in the US.[143]

Moreover, in spite of its period trappings, this was a film with youth at its centre, as suggested by its earlier working title, 'Coming of Age'. More specifically it dealt with the problems of a young person chafing against society's established mores while seeking free self-expression and a more utopian existence, a topic with great contemporary relevance not to mention considerable commercial appeal. Through clever casting which maximised its emphasis on 'the strength of teenage sexual passions',[144] Lean and Bolt had managed to give the historical literary adaptation *Doctor Zhivago* great youth appeal, 'acclaimed by teenage America' as the top film of its year according to a survey conducted by *Seventeen* magazine[145] and may have hoped to replicate its success with young cinemagoers with *Ryan's Daughter*. Bolt stated that with *Ryan's Daughter* they 'wanted to do something about youth which was modern in spirit'[146] even if it was 'not consciously and overtly or deliberately about the generation gap'.[147] Bolt's inspiration for the film came from 'trying to sort out with myself what the balance is between the marvellous, natural, instinctive upsurge of energy and impatience and aspiration and idealism in youth; the balance between that on the one hand, and the knowledge of reality and probability which comes to you only with the passage of the years. At what point do you make a compromise, *do* you make a compromise, or do you have to make *no* compromise at all?'[148]

One might argue that the film is weighted too heavily on the side of maturity, and develops into an unintentional riposte to youth (including the young filmmakers taking over the cinema), reminding them firmly that youth is not unique to them, that it is a passing phase and that in the end individuals must accommodate themselves to the world, not demand that the world change to fit their needs. After all, this is a film that takes an aspirant young protagonist and cuts her firmly down to size, making her suffer a horrible sexualised punishment at the hands of her community before reuniting her with a much older sexless husband whose worth she now sees; a sour allegory of the containment and chastisement of errant youth post-1968, and a piece of wishful thinking for those on the wrong side of the generation gap. Christopher Hudson certainly saw it this way, arguing that the moral of the tale is the heroine being 'shown that aspiration is dangerous, and that love is a dogged responsibility like any other'.[149]

But this doesn't seem quite right as an assessment of the film's mood: it is much more morally ambiguous than that. Indeed, if the main sympathies of the film lie anywhere it is with the young female protagonist and seeker-after-truth, Rosy Ryan (Sarah Miles). The film offers a passionately conceived account of the state of adolescence, that sense of being on the brink, as described by Lean: 'When we are young, we expect there's going to be some wonderful something or the other in life ahead. We don't quite know what it is. This is what Rosy is after.'[150] Lean and Bolt, according to one piece on *Ryan's Daughter*, 'were drawn to this story because of the idealism, the romanticism of the girl. The character lured them just because of her quality of something more. Not an ordinary girl willing to accept whatever her lot turns out to be, but a girl who yearns for something more, who has a desire to strive to be bigger, who has an acute sense of the importance of her own life, who seeks a larger happiness. An idealist.'[151] The decision to focus on a young woman was partly rooted in Robert Bolt's desire to write something for his wife. But it was also driven by Bolt's recognition that the theme of individual versus society would be more fully realised if he and Lean focussed on a young woman, deciding that 'a girl would be more interesting as a central figure than a boy, because there are more social pressures on a girl.'[52] The film's title hints at the fact that we see the character through her various and changing relationships to men: daughter to the fond foolish old publican Thomas Ryan (Leo McKern) – it is notable that Rosy's mother is dead and not even mentioned until the film's closing scenes; wife to the gentle village schoolteacher Charles Shaughnessy (Robert Mitchum); lover to the shell-shocked Major Randolph Doryan (Christopher Jones); admired from afar by the village idiot Michael (John Mills); worried about by the village priest Father Hugh Collins (Trevor Howard). Even the romantic novelette we see her reading, 'The King's Mistress', has a woman as the possession of a man, just as Rosy herself is 'Ryan's daughter' in the film's title. But that does not mean that Rosy is defined solely in terms of her relationships to men and their views of her. Silver and Ursini suggest that '*Ryan's Daughter* belongs more to the title character than any other'.[53] Indeed, the film places at its centre the experiences of the young woman, with the male characters as satellites to her development and growth. As Margaret Hinxman points out, it is 'a story of love' (the tagline used to advertise the film) 'not only between the Irish heroine and the men in her life but between the girl and her idealised expectancy of love'.[54] *Ryan's Daughter* is dominated by Rosy Ryan's dreams and expectations and experiences, and in an age when filmmaking was becoming increasingly dominated by male buddy relationships, according to Molly Haskell,[55] that is both laudable and rare. The sense that a film like *Ryan's Daughter* might have been answering the prayers of certain cinemagoers is suggested by a reader's letter to *Photoplay* magazine in February 1971 (when *Ryan's Daughter* was still at the beginning of its year-long run at the Empire, Leicester Square): 'Producers of motion pictures nowadays ignore a large – and once profitable – section of the public altogether, namely us, the women. Pictures rather scoffed at as "women's pictures" made money and were extremely successful ... Does the film industry as a whole despise the average woman moviegoer? We, who like gentle, wholesome stories, fine heroes and superb actresses?'[56] *Ryan's Daughter* could well be the kind of woman's picture this female letter-writer appears to crave, albeit in the guise of epic spectacular cinema.

A great deal of the negative commentary on *Ryan's Daughter* suggested that a small story had been falsely inflated and expanded, that what should have been a little gem had been pimped into a gigantic flashy rhinestone in order to meet the demands of epic roadshow cinema.[57] For Pauline Kael it was '"Ecstasy" blown up to the proportions of "The Decline and Fall of the Roman Empire"'.[58] *Time*'s critic unequivocally stated: 'small lives are not the stuff of spectacle.'[59] Other critics decried its 'blatant ambition is to give cosmic importance to a trivial story of a young wife's coming of age' and complained that 'three hours is a bit long for a trifling little love story [which] stubbornly resists being pressed in the epic mould'.[160] But the critics' sense of what constitutes a big or small story, what merits epic treatment and what doesn't, is cast in deeply gendered terms. Underlying much of the dismissal of the film is a marked contempt for female-oriented or female-associated popular culture and the film's perceived connection to it: for Tom Milne, it 'looks and sounds as though it had been conceived as a circulation-booster for a struggling women's mag'[161] (and there is an undertow of misogyny in his descriptions of the heroine 'prancing ecstatically into the woods with her passion' or 'parading along the cliff top before provocatively dropping her parasol'[162]); for Alexander Walker, it was 'a tale whose basic triteness places it in the class of palliatives designed in earlier and more innocent decades to lighten the lot of tired housemaids'.[163] Even for a more supportive reviewer like Felix Barker, *Ryan's Daughter* was like 'a paper-covered novelette', 'a film which is – in that damnable phrase – "a woman's picture"'.[164] Barker's review ends with an interesting moment in which he invokes a different perspective from his own: 'The public will probably echo the feelings of a young girl whom I overheard say: "I loved it" adding a little defensively, "You see, it's rather my sort of film."'[165] If Barker can be trusted, this overheard comment suggests an audience response to *Ryan's Daughter* – moreover, a specifically female one – that strongly diverges from the critics' chorus of disapproval.

Surprisingly, few critical objections were raised at the time to *Ryan's Daughter*'s highly problematic representation of the Irish, although this has figured more prominently in subsequent critiques of the film. Although Lean emphasised the universality of the story ('It happens to be in Ireland, but I think it could happen anywhere'),[166] it is revealing of the filmmakers' subconscious attitudes that a story about 'the wild and darker parts of our natures ... the primitive emotions'[167] should be set in that particular country which has so often served as primal 'other' for the dominant colonial power. The choice of Ireland as location would not only let the film capitalise on the photogenic possibilities of the Irish landscape, specifically its Atlantic coast, but also make use of the country's political situation. The film was set during the First World War, just after the Easter Rising, events that could widen the scope of the 'little gem' and provide, Lean said, 'an outside conflict, something over the hill to come in and affect the characters. The 1916 Irish situation suited us rather well.'[168] To have events of huge formative importance to the Irish nation reduced bathetically to something that 'suited us rather well' indicates a slightly superficial approach to Irish politics on the part of the film's makers, and, as Ruth Barton has argued, *Ryan's*

Daughter 'is not interested in trying to understand the causes and consequences of the trajectory of Irish historical events but reproduces them as signifiers of incomprehensible otherness'.[169] The presence of the IRA in the village affords the film its biggest set-piece, when the villagers all join together to land smuggled German arms from the sea during a violent storm, but their motivation for doing so is left rather opaque. The majority of Irish characters in the film seem to be, in Alexander Walker's phrase, 'on hire from Rent-a-Peasant',[170] figuring merely as the backdrop against which the refined characters can be defined; thus sensitive Rosy is juxtaposed with the cruel taunting Maureen (Evin Crowley). The villagers rise up as one when required, whether for the purposes of taunting Michael, supplying lurid local colour at a wedding, or wreaking vengeance on an informer and, as Fidelma Farley argues, their behaviour is 'explained in terms of their "primitive" nature, shaped by the raw, natural, elemental forces which surround them'.[171] Perhaps more disturbingly, E. Butler Cullingford notes that Michael's distorted simian features recall the derogatory images of the Irish that appeared in *Punch* and similar publications throughout the nineteenth century, suggesting that the film is drawing on a deeply embedded racist heritage.[172] However, this pejorative depiction is slightly complicated by the film's apparent popularity in Ireland, running for nearly a year in one of Dublin's major first-run cinemas.[173] Cullingford and Farley also suggest that *Ryan's Daughter* presents a partial critique of colonial occupation. As with *Lawrence of Arabia*, the Imperial hero is a wounded damaged man, represented here by the limping shell-shocked Major Doryan VC, whose 'physical and psychic vulnerability is repeatedly underlined by the film, and serves to emphasise the instability of the Empire he represents'.[174]

The Irish landscape provides the film's primary spectacle in its opening sequence. A vista of rolling black clouds gradually becomes illuminated with orange and red as dawn breaks. The first person to appear cuts a tiny figure in comparison with the scale of the sea cliffs. A cut to a medium shot reveals this to be the film's heroine, Rose, who has dropped her frilly parasol over the edge of the precipice. She leans over to watch it parachute down to the sea. It is rescued and returned to her by Father Hugh and Michael out fishing in their little boat, although Rose shows scant gratitude, clearly repulsed by Michael's grotesque appearance. In the film's early sequences, Rose is established as a solitary and rather aimless girl, wandering the cliffs and the beaches with little to occupy her except the daydreams engendered by her choice of reading matter. Rose's mercurial moods are evoked by the shots showing the continual movement of the clouds and the constantly changing dappled shadows they cast on the hilltops; nothing is fixed and everything is mutable, just as it is in her developing personality. She is in a liminal state, no longer a schoolgirl but not yet a wife and mother with 'floors to scrub', and as the priest has warned her earlier, 'doing nothing's a dangerous occupation'. It soon becomes clear that her romantic fantasies have fixed themselves onto her former schoolteacher Charles Shaughnessy, recently arrived back in the village from a conference in Dublin, inadvertently bringing to Rose's isolated existence a whiff of metropolitan glamour with his talk of concerts by the Royal Philharmonic and scholars from the Sorbonne. Charles gives Rose a window on the wider world, telling tales of heroic figures encompassing the range of 'Byron, Beethoven and Captain Blood', although he is the first to admit that he is 'not one of them fellas' himself. However, his gentle self-deprecation is lost on Rose, who insists he should be 'standing on a heap of pride' rather than putting himself down. Her intentions towards him are revealed in the shot just before his arrival on the beach when, in a sudden gesture of resolve, she casts her book into the sea, which claims it with a roar (a striking juxtaposition of human culture and atavistic nature, in the shape of a flimsy paperback tossed into thunderous foaming waves). Rose will no longer need to read about love in novels because she is about to make her romantic dreams reality.

While he goes for a drink in her father's pub, she remains on the beach, walking in her bare feet in the imprints of his boots, an image used to convey Rose's sexual desire, according to Lean: 'what we wanted to say was that she's also very physically attracted to him and so we got the idea of a big close-up of his footprints in the sand and after a moment her naked foot comes in and treads in them. At the end, a wave comes up and engulfs her and she's sort of like a tightrope walker, sort of swept away by these erotic thoughts of hers.'[75] A note of disquiet is sounded by a pause in the sequence, where the emphasis shifts from Rose's bare feet to her face just as she looks up from what she's doing, furtive and unsure of herself. The wind blows her about as she tries to remain fixed in Charles' tracks, and the longer shot reveals the tide coming in to knock her off balance. She looks a rather absurd figure with her girlishness laden down with the almost parodic trappings of mature femininity, her second-hand parasol, pendant, net gloves and flower-decked hat. Certainly, such fashionable niceties look rather incongruous and almost hubristic in such an elemental landscape. Rose is trying to assert her identity in the face of an impassive nature that cares not one whit for her existence, and will whip that parasol out of her hand without a moment's notice. She's not in tune with nature but trying to resist it, or only acknowledge its picturesque qualities.[76] The music takes on an oddly tremulous and discordant, almost nauseous, dimension, as if presaging the danger to come if Rose tries to follow through on her teenage crush. It is one of the few occasions when Maurice Jarre's music for the film is entirely successful; elsewhere it comes across as overly strident. The sequence suggests something the force of Rose's infatuation 'engulfing' and overpowering her, an idea supported by Robert Bolt's direction in early draft of screenplay: 'her own sensations have amazed her'.[77]

Back at the schoolhouse, Rose waits for Charles's arrival and readies herself for her declaration of love. She listens attentively to the door opening and Charles's footsteps in the adjoining room. The camera pans across the bare whitewashed wall between them as Rose envisages exactly what Charles is doing next door. He puts on a slightly scratched gramophone record of Beethoven's Fifth, perhaps a sign that he's thinking of Rose, since they were discussing Beethoven on the beach. Its decisive chords also provide the perfect score for Rose's nervous anticipation while waiting to confess all. When she tells Charles she loves him, it happens in the schoolroom, where the teacher and pupil origins of their relationship are painfully clear, in spite of Rose's insistence that she's not a child any more. Although Charles tries to explain that she has 'mistaken a penny mirror for the sun', Rose refuses to back down. The turning point comes with a touch of his hand upon her shoulder, accompanied by a rippling harp glissando on the soundtrack and a slow tracking movement towards the couple. In *Brief Encounter*, the same gesture was used as the final point of contact between two lovers, but here it signals the beginning of a relationship. Charles's protests continue ('you were meant for the wide world, not this place ... it wouldn't do') but when Rose poses her final question, 'So you don't want me then?', his resistance fails him. 'Don't want you?' he asks in disbelief, before answering her question with a slightly stilted but heartfelt kiss. The playing between the two principals in this scene is beautifully judged, particularly Robert Mitchum's ability to convey in a single half-gasped 'oh' as he embraces the young girl a whole lifetime of repression and the sudden impulse to yield to temptation. Appropriately, the very next scene shows the arrival in the village of the IRA leader Tim O'Leary (Barry Foster), who shoots a policeman who recognises him and then disposes of a body by tipping it into a mineshaft; the long wait for the sound of the impact and the cloud of dust thrown up from the depths seems emblematic of the similar disturbance deep in Charles's ossified psyche.

When we next encounter Rose, she is talking to the priest in preparation for her forthcoming marriage to Charles. Rose is still a girl hungering for excitement but the dialogue emphasises how far her wishes for change and self-transformation have been funnelled into sexual aspiration. She hopes that her first experience of 'the satisfaction of the flesh' will make her into a different person. Rather than sex just being 'a function of the body' as the priest has it, Rose believes it will provide airborne transcendence. 'What are you expecting? Wings, is it?' the priest asks as Rose looks towards the seagulls hovering overhead, another of Lean's heroines with lofty aspirations. Charles and Rose's wedding is a sedate affair but the celebrations afterwards take a ribald turn. The use of cross-cutting recalls the ceilidh scene in *Madeleine* but, whereas the repressed couple and the libidinous villagers were geographically quite separate in the earlier film, here they are in close proximity. The teenage boys and girls of the village kiss and carouse but nearby the head table of the wedding breakfast presents a very different and very static tableau. Charles's stilted arrhythmic clapping gives a hint of the carnal disappointment that awaits Rose. In fact, the bridegroom seems very reluctant to consummate the marriage, despite the winks and pointed looks at pocket-watches from the wedding guests. Finally persuaded to go upstairs, Rose and Charles have to make their way past the red-faced, panting dancers who break off from their reel to watch the couple depart for bed. The ritual of the village men kissing the bride soon descends into near-riot, presaging Rose's mobbing by vengeful villagers later on in the film.

Upstairs, Rose hastily underdresses, puts on her nightgown and gets under the bedcovers to wait for her husband, her sense of anticipation made clear by her trembling hands as she turns down the covers. A number of shots show the room from her perspective in the bed; first the warm orange light cast through the little bedroom window from the continuing revels downstairs and then, more tellingly, the bedroom ceiling, dully whitewashed, cracked and mottled with damp. It is as though Rose is taking in these homely ordinary views for the final time before the great change attendant upon sexual initiation. When Charles enters the room, there is no abatement in the scene's tension. He undresses shyly behind the screen and reacts awkwardly when Rose's wedding dress falls on the floor (collapsing in a heap, as her marital ambitions are soon to). Charles kisses his new wife and tells her she's 'a wonderful girl', but she protests 'no, I'm not', trying to indicate a carnal readiness that passes her husband by completely. Lying in bed together, they kiss again but are suddenly surprised by the sound of a handful of grain hitting the window pane, thrown by the revellers below to offer encouragement. A panning shot then follows Charles's hand as he reaches down under the bedclothes to pull up Rose's nightgown and shortly afterwards the sudden expression of pain on her face indicates that penetration has occurred. The cut to the dancers downstairs and the up-and-down movement of the fiddler's bow presents the consummation through sly metaphor before the film quickly returns to the bedroom. The sex comes to a perfunctory close and Charles rolls off Rose's body. The next shot of the window, framed exactly the same as it was through Rose's pre-coital perspective, demonstrates that everything has remained the same; no dramatic change has taken place. Even more telling are the respective reaction shots of the newlyweds as they lie back to back, Charles spent and sad, and Rose trying to put on a brave face but completely disillusioned, her great expectations of sex totally thwarted. Sarah Miles's acting, showcased in extreme close-up, is particularly fine here, as she shows Rose's terrible disappointment fighting with her equally powerful desire not to let her husband know.

The ensuring portrait of their marriage consolidates the sense of a profound mismatch. Dropping her honeymoon luggage, Rose stands facing her husband open-palmed and welcoming an embrace from Charles but he scurries off to play one of his Beethoven records instead. Charles's music had once soundtracked erotic anticipation but now it connotes oppressive domestic routine. Rose prettifies and domesticates their home with bright new paint and furnishings but can't disguise their underlying incompatibility. She likes growing living flowers while Charles likes to press them inside heavy books. In one vignette of awkwardness, Rose encourages Charles not to cover up with a shirt after working bare-chested in the garden, but his self-consciousness at sitting half-naked at the tea table is evident and the couple end up bickering. While Charles leads the schoolchildren in their recitation of multiplication tables, Rose tries to escape from an existence by rote. Unhappily married and frustrated with her lot, she returns to walking the beach alone. Confronted by the village priest, who quizzes her on the cause of her unhappiness, Rose is unable to explain. What she wants remains inchoate, lacking a frame of reference and a means of recognition: 'How can I know? I don't even know what more there is.' She has her health, a good husband, enough money, so there is nothing more she could desire, the priest insists. 'There must be something more, there must be', Rose says. 'Why? Because Rosy Ryan wants it?', the priest asks. Rose pauses and then, in a moment of self-assertion, decides that yes, her wanting something more is reason enough. In response, the priest slaps her face so hard she falls to her knees – an emphatic patriarchal denial of female desire – and issues her with a warning not to nurse her wishes.

Major Doryan's arrival just after that exchange makes his eventual relationship with Rose seem inevitable. The problem this presented for

FEMINISING THE EPIC 215

the filmmakers was to find a way of getting the couple together without wasting any time (and risking spectatorial boredom) but still maintaining credulity. Lean puzzled over this for days before hitting upon the solution at four in the morning.[178] Rose minds her father's pub, with Michael also in attendance, when Doryan comes in for a drink. The film intersperses shots from Rose's point of view, tilting down the body of the handsome young officer standing at the bar, with shots that track in closer on her face as she surreptitiously observes him, an object of furtive desire. All is well until the incessant thumping of Michael's boot against the seat precipitates a nervous attack in the shell-shocked solider. Christopher Jones's shaking might be overdone, and Maurice Jarre's musical accompaniment certainly is (Lean admitted a failure of nerve in trusting the images to do the work[179]), but the transition from the pub to the trenches is very cleverly achieved, as the sounds and images of shellfire suddenly intrude and transport a traumatised Doryan straight back to the front line. As he is huddled semi-foetally on his hands and knees in a dark shell-hole, a pale female hand suddenly extends up into the frame and reaches towards him. The hand belongs to Rose and they exchange longing looks before moving inexorably into a kiss. His distress makes Rose's response not only sexual but also 'an act of charity'.[180] Their meeting takes place in a true no-man's land, neither pub nor trench, but a shadowy indistinguishable location. But slowly, the naturalistic sounds of the village return to the soundtrack and the lights come back up (it is as bold a manipulation of lighting as Laura's isolation in *Brief Encounter*). What had been a fantasy oneiric realm turns back into the very real space of the pub, with villagers audible just a few yards away. In a panic, Rose tries to regain the calm equilibrium of a few moments before (unlike on her wedding night, a transformation really *has* taken place); just in time, because the pub is soon full of customers, noise, activity. Like Laura Jesson, Rose must hide her true feelings in a public space, must feign equanimity, pretend nothing has happened. She examines her reflection in a clouded mirror behind the bar, her face betraying a mixture of disbelief and pride, while Doryan endures her father's pontificating hospitality, then drinks up and leaves.

As the film tracks the escalating attraction between the lovers, a heightened stylised mode of filmmaking predominates. Lean had instructed Freddie Young to give the scenes detailing Rose's romantic obsessions, first with her teacher and later with the English major, 'the voluptuous quality of an erotic thought',[181] a phrase that perfectly describes moments such as the twinned shots of Rose and Doryan in their respective beds, separate but connected by their thoughts of each

15 The voluptuous quality of an erotic thought: Rose (Sarah Miles) among the lilies in *Ryan's Daughter* (1970)

other, their proximity suggested by the connecting sound of the garrison generator thumping away in the background like a heartbeat. Or Rose looking up towards the army camp, leaning against a stone obelisk and sighing, weighed down and weary with longing, then pictured in the midst of a patch of white lilies in the dusk, her white blouse and black skirt making her visually correspond to the swaying flowers as she walks among them. Akin to the daffodils in *Zhivago*, the camera tracks right into the centre of one, but this time their sexual symbolism is made more explicit by the smear of lily pollen staining her skirt. Her yearning look up towards the garrison is answered by Doryan's appearance in gothic silhouette on the crest of the hill, almost as though her imagination has brought him into existence (Plate 15).

The voluptuous tone reaches its height in the sequence detailing Rose and Doryan's first full sexual encounter. Cantering out on their horses, the couple reach a wood densely carpeted with bluebells, the ideal location for the sexual epiphany to come. Moving further into the woods, they encounter a richly detailed natural world, with close-ups of the horses' warm breath condensing in the cold air, and moss-covered logs on the forest floor. This had to be ingeniously reconstructed indoors by Eddie Fowlie when bad weather made outdoor filming impossible. Bolt had provisionally rewritten the scene to take place in a ruined tower but in the end a forest glade was faked by means of hot-housed foliage and flora, a cyclorama, and ingenious lighting.[182] Something else also had to be faked, according to Sarah Miles's hilarious account of filming the scene: any sense of chemistry between the lovers. Bolt had envisaged Doryan's passion for Rose as 'a last blaze of natural life',[183] and instead Jones was, in Miles's estimation, 'as vibrantly alive as suet pudding'.[184] The film's pressbook discussed Lean's direction of this moment in highly idealised terms: 'Instead of shouting instructions from a canvas chair, Lean stood beside them and simply stared into their eyes, each in turn. Then he took them aside separately, his hand on a shoulder, placed his mouth an inch from the actor's ear and whispered some private thought.'[185] However, the truth was more prosaic: the mutual antipathy of Sarah Miles and Christopher Jones meant that Lean 'had to behave like some awful schoolmaster, saying "now, look, you two. You've got to pull yourselves together. It doesn't matter what you think of each other".'[186] Perhaps due to Jones's allegedly tranquilised state, Doryan's act of unbuttoning Rose's red riding clothes is undertaken very slowly, inadvertently building a greater sense of erotic anticipation. Eventually their clothes are discarded and the couple lie naked (albeit discreetly framed) on the forest floor.

Two very different sexual experiences define Rose's coming of age. Her first was her disappointing wedding night with Charles. In this second very different sex scene, the cutaways are not to village revels but to sympathetic natural phenomena; a breeze working through ferns and tree branches, the swaying canopy of trees overhead with the sun intermittently glinting through (reminiscent of *Rashomon* (1950), a film Lean admired[187]) whose accelerating rhythm is used to connote Rose's first experience of orgasm. The sexual politics of this moment are complex. On the one hand, the film recognises and validates the importance of female sexual satisfaction, even seeing it as worthy of epic treatment. Sue Harper reads *Ryan's Daughter* as 'Lean's most sexually radical film, in which for the first time he celebrated female desire and charted its social interdictions'.[188] Rose's sexual discovery and self discovery drive the narrative for the first half of the film, and the two sequences detailing first her loss of virginity and then her first orgasm are pivotal privileged set-pieces. If, as Adrian Turner suggests, David Lean had really wanted *Doctor Zhivago* to be 'a film about fucking', then perhaps his wish came true not with that film but with *Ryan's Daughter*. The film's emphasis on female orgasm corresponded to the broader sexual culture of the time, as outlined by Linda Williams: 'Masters and Johnson's scientific "discovery" of the female orgasm in 1966 ... provided important political leverage against previous theories of the propriety and naturalness of female passivity in sexual relations.'[189] Rose's desire for sexual pleasure is important and legitimised in the film. But on the other hand, all the diffuse questions of female dissatisfaction raised earlier in the film ('how can I know what I want when I don't even know what there is?') have been answered with sex. It echoes Betty Friedan's observation in *The Feminine Mystique* about women being given 'an explicitly sexual answer to a question that was not sexual at all'.[190] Rose's proto-feminist quest for a vast indefinable 'something more' is effectively curtailed by her successful achievement of orgasm.

Rose and Doryan lie perfectly contented and satiated on the forest floor, creatures of nature. Rose scarcely moves at all, instead clinging onto a mossy branch as she appears to take in the transformation that has taken place. The composition's colour scheme is simplified to a striking and harmonious combination of the green wood, the flesh tones of the naked lovers, and finally the red drapery of Rose's discarded clothes wound around their bodies. Where before Rose was twitchy with guilt and disappointment, now she is the very image of slow, still contentment. The next episode of lovemaking between Rose and Doryan is even more lushly rendered, with the lovers visually linked to dancing intertwined gossamer threads, dandelion clocks scattering their seeds and fern fronds unfurling. These are moments of unapologetic, emphatic, near ludicrous, romanticism recalling *Summer Madness*'s firework display. Lean stated his intention to shift 'to a mood of wild romance' once Rose's affair begins: to go 'at it full tilt'.[191] But he later felt he'd made a mistake by not signposting more clearly that certain passages of the film were meant to be read ironically as springing from the bedazzled heroine's perspective, to 'have the priest say "Rosy, you're seeing everything through rose-coloured spectacles," and ... a good cut to something wildly romantic. If I'd told them what I was up to, it would have worked.'[192] But this may have been a partial retreat from a total commitment to romanticism and an attempt to ironise after the fact. When Lean went 'at it full tilt' for the lilies and bluebells sequences, he was not only replicating the heroine's enchantment, but his own: 'The critics all said "Oh, Lean's gone over the top. He's in love. He's seeing the world through rose-coloured glasses." Well so what? As a matter of fact I *was* in love, and I was seeing the world that way.'[193] Nervous of being seen as an over-beautifier anyway, Lean tried to remove himself from complete identification with the film's lush romanticism (and the heroine's rose-tinted perspective), motivated by a sense of embarrassment at going too far, no doubt made worse by critics' scornful attitude to the film's purple passages. He lost his confidence in these moments so attempted to distance himself from them.

After Rose and Doryan's magical transformative tryst in the woods, nothing will be the same. In the moments leading up to the film's intermission, we see Rose return back home to Charles. Whereas Laura Jesson could tell her husband lies while being 'trusted implicitly', Charles sees straight through Rose's feeble deceptions, asking her outright, 'you'd never be unfaithful to me, would you Rose?' The camera tracks in on a close-up of Rose's face, seen over Charles's shoulder, as the chug of the garrison generator thumps away in the background, a Poe-esque telltale heartbeat. The second part of *Ryan's Daughter* then follows the consequences of Rose's affair. It begins on the beach again, but with Charles now tracking Rose's footprints in the sand. Charles envisages the young lovers walking on the beach, Doryan in full dress uniform and Rose in a glamorous orange gown and elaborate white hat, accompanied by Beethoven's 'Eroica' symphony. In the frame but unseen by the lovers, Charles hides behind a rock while Doryan dreamily retrieves a shell from a saltwater pool for Rose. The hallucinatory style suggests that all this is a figment of Charles's imagination, but his fantasies prove strangely accurate. Back home in Rose's chest of drawers, hidden among her nightgowns, is exactly the perfect pale shell of Charles's imaginings; a vivid symbol of secret female sexuality.

Rose's adultery is soon public knowledge and she is shunned as a 'British soldier's whore'. She and Charles are conspicuously absent from the highly spectacular sequence in which all the villagers join forces to haul arms from the sea for the IRA during a ferocious storm. Where the previous set-piece, the love scene in the woods, had been lushly romantic in its evocation of the natural world, this next standalone sequence thrusts the viewer into the middle of violent natural forces. A Clear Screen device enabled the camera to film from right inside the storm without poor visibility from water-drops on the lens,[194] so the filmmakers could capture the most extreme meteorological phenomena, even managing to show 'a river pouring over a cliff and being blown back by the force of the wind'.[195] The benign coastline where Rose had previously wandered is suddenly transformed into a fiercely dangerous place. Given its divorcement from the film's main drama of adultery, a great deal of time and care is lavished on the storm, mainly for the purposes of creating stunning spectacle, which the sequence certainly achieves. Through their telling absence, the sequence also establishes Rose and Charles's alienation from everyone else in the village as they all act as one to help O'Leary and his men land their guns and ammunition. Some are there under sufferance, like Ryan, but most freely volunteer, including the priest and Michael, and through Jarre's jaunty positive music the film seems to celebrate their group mobilisation inspired by nationalist fervour. When Tim O'Leary is arrested by the British, the angry villagers naturally assume Rose is the informer. Rose has been guilty of adultery with a British soldier, and has driven her husband to despair by pursuing her affair, but she is not guilty of the crime for which she's tried and found guilty by the villagers' kangaroo court. Her father, the real culprit, flees the scene as the pack of villagers drag Rose and Charles outside to exact their revenge. There ensues a violent struggle between Rose and Maureen, her demotic alter ego, before Rose is swallowed up in the melee. Items of her clothing are thrown about, while the brandishing of a pair of scissors, and finally a hank of hair, give an indication of her punishment. The separate entrances for boys and girls on the school building are very prominent in the shot just after Rose has been divested of her hair and corsets, the markers of sexual difference. Inside we see Rose 'huddled in a blanket by the fire, naked and shorn and trembling',[196] deep scissor cuts and scratches marking her face and scalp. Casting off the final vestiges of femininity, she throws a recovered tress of hair onto the fire which then sizzles and smokes. As Lance Pettitt points out, this particular aspect of the film had inadvertently required a renewed relevance after British troops were sent into Northern Ireland in 1969, and the ritual shearing of Rosy for collusion with the enemy 'echoed the tarring and feathering of women in nationalist communities in Northern Ireland who had consorted with British soldiers deployed there'.[197]

When it came to the matter of the ultimate fates for Rose, Charles and Doryan, Robert Bolt felt strongly that *Ryan's Daughter* demanded 'the disastrous end which I feel is really in store for all three'.[198] However, the film departed from its Flaubertian template in letting its heroine live and instead Doryan's suicide substitutes for the heroine's. He takes his own life, by means of a discarded box of dynamite on the beach and a detonator unknowingly supplied by Michael. Despite his generally inexpressive performance, Christopher Jones manages to imbue with genuine poignancy Doryan's last moments, looking out to sea, waiting for the final disappearance of the setting sun. The film deliberately plays on the famous cut in *Lawrence of Arabia* in which a blown-out match inaugurates an Arabian sunrise. Here, a slowly sinking orange sunset cuts to an extreme close-up of a match being struck. It lights a lamp back at Rose's house but also appears to detonate the explosives on the beach, an event indicated through soundtrack: a huge distant boom followed by the cries of seagulls.

Charles and Rose end up departing for a new life in Dublin, possibly together, possibly apart. Still shunned by the villagers, with the exception of one of Charles's pupils who risks a beating to leave flowers for him, they wait for the bus that will take them away into urban exile. In the opening scenes Charles had suggested that Rose was meant for the wide world; the final scenes come good on his original prophesy. Rose's tentative optimism about the fine weather for their journey – 'a sign of good luck' – is immediately answered by a final instance of nature's cruelty, as the wind snatches away her hat and reveals the shorn head beneath. The previously haughty Rose has learnt humility, as symbolised by her kiss

FEMINISING THE EPIC   221

goodbye to Michael after she had previously shunned him (although for Pauline Kael this was 'the final cliché' in the film's predictable drama of 'losing one's uppitiness and finding redemption'[199]). The final notes upon which *Ryan's Daughter* ends emphasise uncertainty. The priest gives the couple a present of a holy relic of doubtful authenticity to take with them – 'a fragment of St Patrick's staff, I don't suppose it is though' – and a piece of advice to reconsider their decision to separate once they reach Dublin: 'And that's my parting gift to you, that doubt.' It's a deliberately inconclusive conclusion to this tale, told on an epic scale but coming back down to the very small private matter of whether or not a husband and wife stay together.

The attack upon Rose by an angry, jealous mob rather parallels the film's treatment at the hands of the critics. As Tony Sloman sums up: '*Ryan's Daughter* never deserved the scorn poured on her; not Rosy Ryan in the story, nor the film itself.'[200] Adopting the mantle of a romantic young woman left Lean dangerously exposed to the harshest of criticism, and I think the retirement from David Lean from the screen for several years after *Ryan's Daughter* can be understood partly in relation to that specific humiliation. He had gone out on a limb and responded to the sexual revolution with his own decorous but still explicit flower-powered love scene; the result was then held up to widespread public ridicule. Perhaps even more stinging than the mockery of his personal sexual fantasia was the fact that the means of its dramatisation was through wholesale alignment with a female perspective, totally identifying with a young girl undergoing a sexual awakening. As Sue Harper points out, Flaubert's declaration of empathy with his heroine can be re-appropriated for Lean's film: 'Rosy, *c'est moi.*'[201] *Ryan's Daughter* certainly has its flaws but it is also Lean's boldest and most personal attempt at feminising the epic and reconfiguring what constitutes epic subject matter.

A Passage to India (1984)

Lean had long cherished the idea of making a film in India, at least since the mid-1950s. After *Hobson's Choice*, Korda suggested a project about the Taj Mahal and sent Lean off on a recce; this was his first trip to India and when he met his fourth wife, Leila. Lean remembered feeling 'really knocked over by the first impact of the East' but also 'completely at home' there.[202] *Taj Mahal* never happened, and nor did *The Wind Cannot Read*, which was to be partly set and filmed in India. The closest he came in the 1950s was *Kwai*, using Ceylon to stand in for

Burma. After *Kwai*, there was also Lean's planned Gandhi biopic, which went as far as meetings with Nehru ('the most attractive man I've ever met in my life',[203] according to Lean) but was never realised by him, Gandhi's story instead being brought to the screen by Richard Attenborough in 1982. Lean had toyed with the idea of making his version of *Madame Bovary* in India – 'in which the glamorous hero would have been a young Maharajah'[204] – but as we have seen it ended up as the Ireland-set *Ryan's Daughter* instead. Back in the early 1960s, Lean had also made enquiries about the rights to E. M. Forster's *A Passage to India* after seeing Santha Rama Rau's gripping stage adaptation. However, Forster resisted almost all requests to film his novels, one rare exception being a television version of Rau's play broadcast by the BBC in 1965. After Forster's death in 1970, requests to film the novelist's work were handled by his literary executors and eventually they granted the film rights to *A Passage to India* to the producers John Brabourne and Richard Goodwin. David Lean was signed up to direct in 1981. And so Lean's long-awaited Indian film would finally come to pass, although not without further financial uncertainties and stop–start pre-production. It is somewhat ironic that Lean's final foray into epic storytelling, and indeed his final completed film, would be made financially possible partly because of the support offered by the television company HBO (along with Columbia and Thorn-EMI). Because of this, the director famed for his widescreen shots would have to adopt a new approach to composition, as cinematographer Ernest Day marked the camera viewfinder with 'two vertical side lines to indicate TV cut off'.[205]

Nonetheless, Lean's film aimed for large-scale visual spectacle and in that respect, as well as in its mobilisation of E. M. Forster, Lean's *A Passage to India* anticipated the heritage film boom of the 1980s, which began with *Chariots of Fire* and *Brideshead Revisited* back in 1981 but reached its apotheosis in the cycle of Forster adaptations by Merchant Ivory Productions inaugurated by *A Room with a View* (1985). Some even view David Lean, purveyor of middlebrow literate English cinema, as the unacknowledged 'grandfather of heritage film'.[206] Certainly, Lean's films have been subject to similar criticisms as heritage films about political and stylistic conservatism. Looking again at Pauline Kael's review of *Ryan's Daughter*, it is striking how many of her comments anticipate later critiques of the 'self-conscious visual perfectionism' and 'fetishisation of period details'[207] in heritage films: 'The painstakingly constructed streets, the antiquated houses ... They have a gleaming pictorial look, a prepared look – everything is posing for a photograph.'[208]

A Passage to India's depiction of British rule in India also raised critical heckles. When Salman Rushdie wrote his influential critique of the

FEMINISING THE EPIC 223

1980s fashion for returning to the days of the British Raj, David Lean was one of his primary targets. Rushdie saw *A Passage to India*, like its television peers *The Jewel in the Crown* and *The Far Pavilions* (both 1984), as largely recuperative in intention:

> Thatcherite Britain encourages many Britons to turn their eyes nostalgically to the lost hour of their precedence. The recrudescence of imperialist ideology and the popularity of Raj fictions put one in mind of the phantom twitchings of an amputated limb. Britain is in danger of entering a condition of cultural psychosis, in which it begins once again to strut and posture like a great power while in fact its power diminishes every year.[209]

Most unforgivably for Rushdie, the Raj cycle perpetuated 'the fantasy that the British Empire represented something "noble" or "great" about Britain; that it was, in spite of all its flaws and meannesses and bigotries, fundamentally glamorous.'[210] Some of Lean's statements around the time of making *A Passage to India* certainly seem to support Rushdie's suspicion that a nostalgic impulse underpinned the Raj revival. The director expressed his desire to present the British in a more positive light than Forster, who 'came down very hard against the English and very much for the Indians. I tried to balance it a bit more.'[211] One of Lean's letters to his producers evokes precisely that 'glamour' of empire that Rushdie so forcefully refutes: 'I find myself looking at those old photographs with affection and admiration. It's India designed for the English by Cecil Beaton.'[212] There was also Lean's assumption of representational pre-eminence when it came to India: he wrote, again to his producers, that aside from fellow European Jean Renoir's *The River* (1951) 'I don't think anyone has put India on the screen',[213] happily disregarding the distinguished work of countless Indian filmmakers, not least the globally celebrated Satyajit Ray. When *Sight and Sound* reiterated and upheld Lean's claims to originality, Paul Willemen decried it as 'an especially despicable example of the Anglocentrism besetting English discussions of cinema'.[214]

This attitude also extended to the casting of the film, and most controversially the decision to have Alec Guinness play the Hindu Brahmin Professor Godbole, partly because Lean couldn't conceive of an Indian actor equal to the task. Cross-racial casting had still been commonplace when Guinness played an Arab in *Lawrence of Arabia*, but by the 1980s the choice of a well-known white actor for an Indian role looked highly incongruous.[215] In addition, Lean's treatment of the Indian actors in his cast could also verge on the insensitive. Victor Banerjee resisted Lean's attempts to get him to play Aziz with an exaggerated accent complaining that 'playing one Englishman's idea of another Englishman's idea of an

Indian isn't my scene'[216] (Lean did at least have the presence of mind to observe, 'I don't blame Victor. I do understand. We were, as it were, an army of occupation').[217] Lean's single-minded pursuit of his cinematic vision resulted in other cultural insensitivities. Following on from having black rocks painted white in Cape Town for *Ryan's Daughter*, the director attained permission from the highest Indian authorities to create caves in a rock formation in order to realise his ideal Marabar. 'What would happen if an Indian film director decided he would like to rearrange Stonehenge or the Cheddar Gorge?'[218] asked Ian Jack in his provocative account of the film's production, going on to suggest that Lean had ordered the dynamiting of ancient holy rocks (others working on *A Passage to India* have since countered what they felt was unfair and inaccurate reportage).[219] But Ian Jack's description of Lean 'suit[ing] the role of viceroy rather well: silver-haired, curtly polite, slightly military'[220] is slightly harder to counter, and does seem to chime with a certain imperial tendency in Lean's epic mode of filmmaking, colonising foreign lands, building on them, commanding troops, marshalling impressive and imposing spectacles.

Although arch-traditionalist in some aspects of his filmmaking, in others Lean was deeply radical. Despite adapting a revered literary text, Lean's approach to E. M. Forster's novel was anything but faithful, to the consternation of many scholars and critics. Neil Sinyard brilliantly anatomises the 'ineffably patronising tone' adopted by many reviewers of Lean's *A Passage to India*, insisting upon the director's inability to deal with 'Forsterian subtleties'.[221] Lean was very much aware of the specific difficulties of transposing to the screen a novel he described – to his friend Katharine Hepburn – as 'a curious amble of a book about a set of four or five more or less equally balanced characters who almost drift through the story. They come and go, brush up against one another and pass on.'[222] In many respects, adapting Forster's novel posed similar problems to those caused by *Doctor Zhivago*. Back then, he and Bolt had despaired of Pasternak's digressions, and, twenty years later, Lean described in near identical terms how 'Forster doesn't – as you have to do in a film – have a well-defined thread going through it. One of the difficulties was not to be tempted by side-tracks. He is a wonderful side-tracker.'[223] The core of the film, for Lean, had to be the picnic at the Marabar caves; indeed, his first question on the phone to producer John Brabourne in relation to the film was 'what happened in the caves?'[224] Back when he made *Madeleine*, Lean had experienced the difficulties attendant on maintaining a sense of narrative ambiguity and understandably did not want to repeat that unhappy experience. In any case, Forster's rationale for leaving the events in the cave vague

FEMINISING THE EPIC 225

in his novel – 'a particular trick I felt justified in trying because my theme was India'[225] – is rather unconvincing and just as implicated in Orientalist assumptions (of Eastern enigma) as any subsequent direction taken by Lean in his adaptation. In the film, Forster's 'mystery' (or 'muddle') is solved: Adela Quested is not molested by anyone but experiences a kind of hallucination precipitated, it is strongly suggested, by her frustrated sexual desires.[226] This bold move befits a director whose wife, Sandy, spoke of his 'fearless innocence'[227] when adapting classics, an approach which had served him very well with his highly respected Dickens films back in the 1940s. What happened to Adela in the caves would be made definite in Lean's version rather than left ambiguous and would act as the narrative's fulcrum. The cross-cultural relationship between Aziz and Fielding, though still important, would now occupy secondary importance to Adela's trajectory; a marked departure from Forster's chosen emphasis. In *Lawrence of Arabia*, Lean had invoked the intense closeness and homoeroticism of an interracial male friendship with great sensitivity but in *A Passage to India* he chose to depart from this template in favour of a focus on another of his cherished themes: the woman in turmoil due to her erotic compulsions. Adela, a character that Lean felt 'Forster didn't care for' and whose sole function was 'as a somewhat tiresome tool in the plot'[228] moves centre stage, with Lean describing this process as 'upping' her character from the 'dry stick' of the book.[229] In Lean's version she becomes 'the best part in the picture'[230] and the character who, more than any other, is the key to his take on the story: 'this is going to be a very secret, sensual film. An eavesdrop on a respectable young English woman whose sexuality is aroused by her reactions to India.'[231]

This vision of the young white woman being awoken and overwhelmed by India is firmly entrenched in Orientalism, in which 'The East' is rendered Other, the site of all the West's abjected qualities such as the irrational, the erotic and the primitive. This resonates in one of Lean's letters to Santha Rama Rau: 'I've often wondered why Europeans first arriving in the East either like it or hate it. Lids tend to come off. Some become deeply disturbed ... It may be that India somehow reflects echoes out of our distant past where our inhabitants weren't so strong. In a sense we do walk down our aircraft steps into the past.'[232] Lean establishes the idea that the film will be what he called 'a walk in old places'[233] from the very beginning of the film. Its credits appear over images of rich golden-toned Indian murals flecked with the dilapidations of age. Their warmth contrasts sharply with the cold tones to follow in the film's opening sequence, set on the grey streets of London during a downpour. Sustained close-ups on the beguiling faces in the mural, especially the eyes, give way to the anonymity of umbrella-carrying pedestrians hurrying through the rain, the one exception being a young woman. She stops on the street to gaze at a window display of a large model steamer, drawn to its 'gleaming brass and spotless paintwork in glamorous contrast to the rain-swept street'.[234] This woman, we will soon discover, is Adela Quested (Judy Davis), who has come to book her passage to India on a real steamer. As the booking clerk suggests, she is seeking 'new horizons', making her a typical Lean protagonist. While filling out the necessary paperwork, Adela notices several framed pictures on the wall that give hints of the trip to come. One is of a ship on the Suez Canal, the boundary between West and East, and another is of the Taj Mahal, legendary monument to uxorious passion, suggesting what Adela hopes to find in India with her fiancé Ronny (Nigel Havers). But the third picture on the wall will prove the most portentous; an image of the Marabar caves. Just as Forster introduced the caves in the first sentence of his novel, Lean aims for a cinematic equivalent, making sure that they are immediately foregrounded as 'extraordinary'.

We see nothing of Adela's sea voyage; her purchase of the tickets is followed immediately by her arrival in Bombay, accompanied by Mrs Moore (Peggy Ashcroft), Ronny's mother. They arrive on the same ship as the viceroy, and so are met by imperial ceremony of the highest order, with red carpet rolled out and a full military band playing as his party make their way through the monumental Gateway to India (done with a complex matte shot[235]). The strictly linear and airily spacious compositions showing the viceroy's entry into Bombay clash with the chaotic and densely packed *mise en scène* showing Bombay's inhabitants, offering India as 'a cauldron of anarchic eros',[236] as Laura Donaldson suggests. A full set of Indian representational clichés is in evidence as Adela and Mrs Moore make their journey from Bombay to Ronny's home in Chandrapore: snake charmers, women cloaked in burqas, a busy market piled with multi-coloured fruits, flowers and spices, and the spectacle of a garlanded shrouded corpse being taken to burial. According to Lean, these scenes were 'rather a sort of copy of when I first landed in Bombay years and years ago. Tremendous noise, tremendous bustle.'[237] Not for the first time, Lean deploys the point of view of his female protagonists, Adela and Mrs Moore, to reanimate his own powerful feelings, this time his first encounter with India.

Both Adela and Mrs Moore express a desire to encounter 'the real India' and 'real Indians', sentiments which are perhaps treated as slightly naive but entirely laudable (they're rather more satirised in Forster's novel). The free-thinking Adela finds the suggestion that Ronny is becoming 'a proper sahib' disconcerting. Meanwhile, her fellow Englishmen and women feel quite differently about the country they inhabit and govern. Everywhere they attempt to replicate the culture of home, from the names given to stations and thoroughfares (Victoria, Wellington, Kitchener, Trafalgar) to the imported digestive biscuits and decanters of port available on the train, and the band playing 'Tea for Two' at the bridge party. Mrs Turton (Antonia Pemberton), the 'memsahib' wife of Chandrapore's chief administrator, covers her nose when walking past Indians on the street, and her husband's car races through the market's crowds, horn honking ceaselessly, union jack fluttering on the bonnet, forcing women to flatten themselves against the wall, and nearly knocking Aziz (Victor Banerjee) and his friend Ali (Art Malik) off their bicycles. Although Lean had mentioned making his depiction of the British in India more positive in tone, there is little evidence of it in the completed film, which does not stint from showing the colonisers as insensitive, blinkered and racist. We see Aziz having to drop everything when he is called to Major Callendar's house, but when he arrives there is nobody there to meet him and no message for him. His carriage is then taken by two memsahibs who deliberately ignore him, and the porch light is suddenly turned off, leaving him in darkness and with no means of transport home. This moment encapsulates the total lack of consideration for the Indians on the part of the British attitude. Even though Ronny is made more sympathetic than in Forster's book, he still shows the same blithe disregard for the Indians, demonstrated in the scene in which, as magistrate, he sentences one Indian man to two months' hard labour. A close-up of the convicted man's shocked reaction suggests the impact of his actions but Ronny has scarcely noticed, too preoccupied with his mother and Adela watching from the public gallery and looking over to them the second he completes his official duties with a proud boyish smile.

Women like Mrs Turton and Mrs Callender (Ann Firbank) exemplify the worst excesses of colonial arrogance in the film. But the main dissenting voices against empire's legitimacy are also those of women.[238] Mrs Moore directly criticises the British Raj as 'an exercise in power and the subtle pleasures in personal superiority'. She also participates in perhaps the only genuine moment of Anglo-Indian connection in the whole film, when she and Aziz first meet by chance. The location is a moonlit mosque overlooking the Ganges, its partitions hung with vines; a suitably magical space for this oneiric encounter. Aziz initially mistakes Mrs Moore's veiled white figure for a ghost; indeed, there is an un-reality to their meeting which then seems to prompt an unusual degree of candour in their discussions, temporarily free from the usual social barriers. Lean uses intimate close-ups of Aziz and Mrs Moore, showcasing their mutual kindliness (both have gentle sympathetic eyes). But this utopian moment of understanding is never recaptured in subsequent meetings.

In the build-up to the trip to the caves, *A Passage to India* takes pains to establish Adela's state of mind, particularly her awkward interactions with her fiancé. Handed a lace-edged posy and kissed primly on the cheek when she first arrived, Adela is disappointed when Ronny's knock on the door on her first night with him is followed only by a chaste 'goodnight dear' and retreating footsteps. Adela surveys her reflection in the mirror as if assessing her own attractiveness and finding it wanting (the same issue will be raised in the court case). She decides to break off her engagement, telling Ronny at the ultra-pukka setting of a polo match. Their split is amicable and Adela directly links the situation's emotional tepidity to national character: 'we're being awfully English about this, aren't we?' But a sudden unexpected encounter with 'the real India' changes her mind, in one of Lean's most contentious additions to Forster. He includes a sequence in which Adela, while out bicycling, notices an intriguing ruin just off the path and goes to explore it. A piece of broken statuary in the grass depicting a female torso piques her interest and she cycles further into the ruins, seemingly being watched by an assortment of imposing stone figures carved on the walls whose collective gaze the screenplay characterises as 'arrogant and scornful'.[239] Pushing past strange bulbous hanging vines, and by now bathed in a light sweat from her exertion, Adela finally reaches the threshold of an abandoned temple and goes inside. Worn by time and hung with creepers, she sees first a statue depicting a naked couple in the middle of what Mrs Moore had described in the preceding scene as 'carnal embracement'. Further statues of couples kissing and clasping each other, twisted into strange positions, the women with high round breasts and prominent outthrust buttocks, all seize her attention and the camera tracks into a tight close-up on Adela's face as she responds to their sexual imagery (Judy Davis plays this scene very effectively, neither over- nor under-doing it but definitely suggesting the spectacle's erotic impact on Adela). Maurice Jarre's score unusually pairs a theremin with a rising soprano voice to give the moment an air of the uncanny. This is when Adela is confronted with the eroticism of antiquity, when she walks down the plane steps into her primitive past, in Lean's phrase. And lest Adela might try to temper her intense response to the statuary by aestheticising it, any possibility of contemplation is then cut short by a sudden insistent linkage of carnality and feral animality. Adela is not alone in the temple; high above, a pack of monkeys notices her just as she notices them and they start scurrying down the statues towards her, 'little demons blending with the lovers' as Pauline Kael described them in her review.[240] Adela cycles away in fright as the monkeys pursue her, and the final shot of the sequence returns to the scornful look of the statue on the threshold of the temple, upbraiding her for her hubris in daring to enter a temple of love.

A shaken Adela immediately mends her broken engagement to Ronny upon arriving back at his bungalow. Perhaps in marriage to Ronny, she is seeking the kind of sexual fulfilment which she's momentarily glimpsed. Or, perhaps more likely, she is in flight from it, sensing that Ronny will subdue those yearnings, 'protect her from them'.[241] Mrs Moore's comment that 'India forces one to come face to face with oneself' suggests that Adela's brief glance into this metaphysical mirror has terrified her and pushed her back into the safe embrace of imperial wifedom. However, the music at the party subtly and impishly suggests Adela's continuing potential for waywardness: Gershwin's *Lady Be Good*. Rather like Rosy Ryan, Adela seems to hope for transformation through marriage, and expresses her disappointment at not feeling more excited by her engagement: 'I feel perfectly ordinary' she laments before the party to celebrate the occasion. But lying in bed afterwards, lightly veiled by a voile curtain and with the scent of abundant frangipani drifting over from the open window (Lean specifically directed Judy Davis to imagine inhaling its scent), Adela's thoughts return to the statues, now shown bathed in sensual moonlight rather than harsh daylight. The notes in the screenplay leave little doubt as to the erotic import of the moment: 'It is still hot. She lets out a little gasp and pulls down the sheet. She lies looking up at the ceiling.'[242] The gentle reprise of Jarre's temple music is suddenly interrupted by a loud boom of thunder, and a harsher wind moves through the flowers and the curtains making them disarrayed, echoing Adela's disturbed psyche. This image of a woman lying awake in bed lost in her thoughts (often romantic or sexual ones) recurs throughout Lean's films, appearing in *Brief Encounter*, *The Passionate Friends*, *Madeleine* and *Ryan's Daughter*. Such moments are always highly significant, marking the point when the heroine's secret feelings place her under the utmost pressure.

The day of the picnic finally dawns and a series of sequences show the party's slow ascent towards Marabar, first on narrow-gauge steam-train over vertiginous bridges, and then up onto the back of a painted elephant, and finally scaling a smooth stone incline up to the summit. There's a wonderful close-up of the elephant's feet, showing the simultaneous weight *and* delicacy of its tread, accompanied by the intermittent jingle of the tiny bells around its ankles. The sheer magnificence of the spectacle – and the film's marketing very cannily used it as the key image on its advertising posters – inspires a reverie from Aziz on his Moghul ancestors, to which Adela listens with interest as they approach their destination. Her own imaginings will have far less benign consequences.

Mrs Moore is the first of the two women to experience the caves' unearthly power. Crowded by the people packed into the dark low-ceilinged cave, her distress and anxiety are exacerbated by the echo. A baby's cry and the guide's single word cause a rolling reverberation which amplified by the cave's walls. It temporarily abates but then returns as pure noise, indistinguishable and inescapable; a very good approximation of Forster's 'boum'. Aziz's kindly meant but disastrous cry of 'Mrs Moore' terrifies her, causing her to flee the caves, just as Adela had fled the monkeys at the temple. Mrs Moore comes face to face with herself and discovers an inner abyss: 'I suppose like many old people I sometimes think we are only passing figures in a godless universe', she tells a concerned Adela. The last part of her sentence is accompanied by a close shot of the moon's surface, as seen through Mrs Moore's dark spectacles as she looks up at the sky. Moonlight's romantic dimensions are stripped away, replaced by a cold glare emanating from hard pitted rock. There had been images of foreboding previously connected with the Mrs Moore's perspective – the crocodile breaking the surface of the Ganges during the club's nightly rendition of 'God Save the King', the sad little gravestone of an empire wife that she fixes upon in the churchyard, her reactions to some of Godbole's penetrating looks – but what happens in the caves marks an absolute sea change in the character and presages her imminent death.[243]

16 A life-changing moment of physical contact: Aziz (Victor Banerjee) offers his hand to Adela (Judy Davis) as they climb up to the Marabar caves in *A Passage to India* (1984)

FEMINISING THE EPIC 231

If Mrs Moore's moment of reckoning disturbs her, it is nothing compared to Adela's equivalent crisis. She and Aziz, accompanied only by a local guide, climb to a higher set of caves, leaving behind the rest of the party. Their distance from Chandrapore, so far away it looks like 'a mirage', and her doubts about her forthcoming marriage combine in prompting Adela to ask Aziz about his own marriage, an arranged partnership. 'What about love?', Adela enquires. 'We were a man and woman and we were young' is Aziz's simple explanation, evidence of a natural unforced sexuality which seems to disquiet Adela, once again fearing herself lacking in that department. When they continue their steep ascent, there is a meaningful exchange of looks – just kindness or something more? – before Aziz offers an exhausted Adela his hand, and the camera focuses on their clasped hands, framing the point of physical contact in tight close-up (Plate 16). Still holding his hand, she asks 'did you have more than one wife?' and Aziz answers in the negative, slightly embarrassed by her naive Orientalist assumptions. We later see him steal away to have a smoke, looking quite shaken, while Adela waits outside the rectangular entrances to one of the caves, hot from the climb and the blazing midday sun, looking as though she is anticipating something. As she enters one of the caves the film cuts to Aziz stubbing out his cigarette. He tries to find her and calls out her name. Sequestered in her cave, Adela strikes a match and then blows it out, and even those tiny noises create an echo which begins to rise towards a deafening boom. A shot from Adela's point of view shows Aziz in silhouette in the entrance to the cave, still calling her name, which then joins the echo already reverberating around the interior; for both Adela and Mrs Moore, it is the sound of their names being called that seems to provoke their ultimate crisis. When the film returns to Adela in close-up, tears are forming in her red-rimmed eyes, and they fall down her cheeks as she looks downwards, the sound of the echo gathering force, growing as loud as a jet engine. All of this and Adela's jerky involuntary little head movements indicate that she is in the grip of something overwhelming; a seizure of orgasmic intensity. This is followed by a sudden cutaway to a pool of water overflowing onto a dry cleft rock, diegetically caused by the elephant bathing but metaphorically suggesting sudden female sexual arousal. It seems that just as in *Ryan's Daughter* a woman's orgasm will precipitate a whole series of dramatic narrative events, and Robert Bolt's description of Rosy Ryan experiencing 'the cataclysmic impact of primitive sexuality' applies equally well to Adela Quested.[244] 'What's happened?' asks Mrs Moore, suddenly waking from her sleep, and following hard comes a shot of a small boulder, hurtling down the mountainside, then match-cut with Adela's hat, also rolling down. As

Alexander Walker suggests, that hat is only 'the first bit of damning evidence that will dislodge an avalanche of courtroom accusations and bring social ruin' to the accused man.[245] We next see Adela running down the same mountainside, distressed and with her hands and chest marked with blood, while Aziz still calls after her. After she disappears into a motor car far below (Mrs Callender's vehicle), the only remnant of her presence at the caves is a pair of binoculars left behind, their leather strap broken; another piece of 'damning evidence' that will be used to accuse Aziz of sexual assault.

Aziz, Mrs Moore and the newly arrived Fielding (who had missed the morning train to Marabar) try to make sense of Adela's disappearance. Mrs Moore guesses that the caves may have affected Adela's mental state, deeming Marabar 'a dangerous place for new arrivals'. Upon those words, the film sharply cuts to Adela, her white shirt torn, bloody scratches up her arms, sobbing and panicking as she's helped into bed by the memsahibs and injected with tranquiliser. The subsequent scene of Aziz's arrest upon arriving back in Chandrapore follows as logically and inevitably as clockwork. As Ronny later observes, 'the machinery has started'. Adela has given voice to a sublimated but generally felt fear and is co-opted for the purposes of colonialist propaganda; not falling prey to just any hallucination but *the* perfect hallucination, the collective delusion of native onslaught.

The next section of the film moves into courtroom drama as Aziz faces charges of attempted rape. It pitches English colonial prejudice against Indian victimhood with Fielding trying to place himself in between. Mrs Moore's reaction is to absent herself, refusing to engage with 'such trifles'. Invoking destiny, she recalls Professor Godbole's non-interventionist stance and even directly repeats his words of non-committal: 'nothing I can say or do will make the least difference' (the phrase is strikingly similar to the one that Richard Dyer says epitomises narratives of English imperial crisis: 'there's nothing I can do, nothing!'[246]). Her final fraught exchange with Ronny before she leaves India is, for me, one of the understated highlights of the film. Pressure was put on Lean from potential backers for the film to 'cut the old dame' because 'young people are bored by old people'[247] but thankfully he was able to resist. Age seems to liberate Mrs Moore into being able to disregard the conventional pieties – 'love in a church, love in a cave, as if there were the least difference' – to the shock of her strait-laced son. Mrs Moore's mind is not fixed on the impending trial, or her son's marriage, but on the far horizon of death. Time is running out and she wants to escape 'fuss and muddle', to arrange her affairs and retreat 'into some cave of my own'. Critic David Denby complained that 'what could have been a philosophical drama of almost terrifying dimensions becomes a story of sudden crankiness in old age',[248] but I feel this criticism is misplaced. *A Passage to India* presents old age as a nihilistic state, a position helped enormously by an unsentimental performance from Peggy Ashcroft. Significantly, Lean was by now in his seventies, actually the same age as Ashcroft, and it would be surprising if questions pertaining to old age, and the necessity of getting things done before time runs out, were not also on Lean's mind while making the film. Certainly, Lean was viewed by many members of his crew and cast as being prey to the same kind of querulous awkwardness attendant upon old age as Mrs Moore. Cinematographer Ernest Day saw it as the root cause of Lean's frequently evil temper during the production: 'David committed the crime of getting old.'[249] Such extra-textual knowledge adds another level of meaning to the line given to Major Callender (Clive Swift) as a warning to Ronny: 'Old people never take things as one expects. They can cause a great deal of trouble.'

The farewell scene between mother and son speaks of their communicatory impasse as Ronny admits: 'I don't understand you. I've never understood you any more than you've understood me.' On the station platform, Ronny's low 'goodbye', inaudible to his mother and so uttered only to himself, underlines the sad finality of their parting, and their never-to-be-mended estrangement. But Mrs Moore's true goodbye to India is provided by Professor Godbole's strange salutation, stepping out of the shadows with his hands above his head in prayer as her train pulls away. Lean and Guinness repeatedly disagreed but Lean was moved to utter 'clever old bugger' when filming the actor's performance of this moment, providing a gesture imbued with his unmistakable 'authority and aura'.[250]

While Mrs Moore leaves India, Adela stays on to face the legal process she has set in motion. In comparison with the erotic statuary off the beaten track Adela had glimpsed earlier, her journey to court with the Turtons takes her past some very different statuary, new rather than ancient: a figure of Queen Victoria. The earlier temple scene is also recalled when a near-naked man in the crowd painted to look like a monkey leaps down from a tree onto the Turtons' car. He startles Adela before being pulled away and savagely beaten by police; the violently confrontational tone thus set for the trial ahead. Adela's accusation has behind it all the force of the British Empire's assumptions about native barbarity while Aziz has in his favour a very prestigious defence counsel, Indian nationalist lawyer Amritrao (Roshan Seth) working *pro bono*. An individual case is being tried but it also functions as a pretext for the marshalling of broader arguments for and against British rule in India. During his advocacy for Adela, Chief Superintendent McBryde (Michael Culver) will proclaim it 'a universal truth' that 'the darker races are attracted to the lighter but not vice versa'.[251] 'Even when the lady is less attractive than the gentleman?' counters Amritrao, a quietly cutting swipe at McBryde's colonial humbug meant to humiliate Adela and expose her to the court's ridicule. Much like *Madeleine*, another Lean film culminating in courtroom drama, femininity is on trial as much as any particular crime.[252] The situation inside and outside the court becomes increasingly volatile when Ali, Aziz's friend and the lawyer assisting on the case, angrily quits the court and incites the crowds outside to call for Mrs Moore, whom he believes has been banished by the British. Just as Lawrence became 'El Aurens', Mrs Moore becomes transfigured into 'Esmiss Esmoor', a kind of demi-goddess whose name becomes an incantation. But shortly after the cry goes up in Chandrapore for Mrs Moore, the film cuts to her burial at sea – she had correctly intuited her coming death – ensuring that she will never be able to testify either for or against Aziz. Her body is claimed as British by the Union Jack draped over it but it plunges down into the immense borderless, nation-less ocean, presented in one of the last and finest of Lean's many horizon shots.

When Adela finally takes the stand, Lean cleverly suggests her mental dislocation and isolation from everything around her through tight facial close-ups, shot in very shallow focus.[253] The film intermittently cuts away to shots from Adela's point of view – of McBryde, Amritrao, Aziz's shoes, and finally the Bible produced for her to swear upon – suggesting their strange disjointed appearance to her. As she takes the stand to testify, the camera circles around her with some unusually unsteady (for Lean) hand-held cinematography. The unsettling eerie motifs in Jarre's score are then supplemented by a very distant thunderous sound, subtly recalling the boom of the caves. When McBryde begins to question her, taking her back into the moment, she suddenly experiences a disconcerting, almost subliminally brief, flashback to Aziz clasping her hand. This interruption of past into present unsettles Adela and seems to begin the unravelling that follows. Adela recalls that during the ascent at Marabar she was thinking about her own engagement to Ronny. 'Seeing Chadrapore so far away', she suddenly admits, as much to herself as to the court, 'I realised I didn't love him.' At this point, the film cuts away to Ronny's reaction to this very public humiliation. Forster's novel had Ronny break from Adela after the trial had collapsed so as not to damage his career, but here he is presented much more sympathetically. Meanwhile, Adela looks up to the swaying punkah above her head, as if seeking a way out. The close-ups on Judy Davis grow ever tighter when Adela begins to narrate what occurred in the caves, her voice speaking over the recalled images. She enters, lights a match, hears Aziz calling her and blows out the match, as before. After Aziz appears in the entrance to the cave, the film returns to Adela no longer in the caves but back in the courtroom, framed in a choker-tight close-up. There is the same accelerating booming sound, the same downward look and narrowed eyes and the same slightly twisted bodily movement that accompanied her orgasmically intense moment in the caves. After a pause, her response to McBryde's next question is a stilted 'I'm not quite sure', with pauses between each words as if to show the difficulty of its articulation. The camera tracks into the tightest of its close-ups on Adela as the truth finally outs: 'I'm afraid I've made a mistake. Dr Aziz never followed me into the cave.' Finally, pressed by the judge Das (Rashid Karapiet), Adela relents. 'I withdraw everything', she says with an outward breath emphasising the last word, as though opening a floodgate. Judy Davis's performance is particularly fine during this scene and, despite their difficult working relationship during the making of the film, Lean was unstinting for his praise for her, rightly judging her 'absolutely marvelous in it'.[254]

Outside, the crowds of Aziz's supporters hear the news and cheer in celebration. Inside, Adela looks up through the skylight to see a huge swelling cloud, which releases a few isolated heavy raindrops onto the glass, followed fast by a deluge. As with the use of the same motif near the end of *Black Narcissus* (1947), the arrival of the monsoon indicates catharsis, relief from what had become unbearable tension. For Aziz, it means literal release, carried out of court on the shoulders of his supporters while Adela remains on the opposite side of the room, alone and dejected. Lean later wondered if he should have taken a similar adaptation route as Santha Rama Rau's play and also ended his version of *A Passage to India* after the collapse of the trial.[255] Instead he decided to follow events through to show Aziz's alienation from the British, his renewed embrace of his Muslim identity – Victor Banerjee very effectively enacts Aziz's total transformation in demeanour – and his relocation far away from Chandrapore. The film also explores the breach in Fielding and Aziz's friendship, although many Forsterians complained bitterly at Lean's removal of the final scene of the novel in which horses, rocks and all elements of the colonial landscape 'in their hundred voices'[256] conspire to prevent the two men from being friends. Michael Cowdy, the Bursar of Kings College, Cambridge, even wrote to John Brabourne to plead for its inclusion: 'For Forster', he claimed, it was 'the very heart of the novel'.[257] But despite its apparent visual dynamism, it looked to Lean like stale prophesy whereas it had been prescient back in 1922 when India was yet to gain its independence.

Rather than ending on fissure, Lean chose to end on a note of 'forgiveness, reconciliation and understanding'.[258] Fielding manages to re-establish contact with Aziz, who has moved to Kashmir, and introduces him to his new wife, who is not Adela as Aziz had mistakenly believed but Mrs Moore's daughter Stella (played silently and serenely by Lean's wife Sandy Hotz). The men part but having tentatively revived their friendship. Although John Hill suggests that 'it is the relationship between the two men that carries the greatest emotional weight in the film',[259] I believe that Adela fulfils that function to a greater extent, and the character was deliberately re-written into the story at the end for that reason, in contrast to her complete disappearance from the later part of the narrative of Forster's novel. Lean envisaged various ways of ending the film. An earlier version of the screenplay, dated 17 May 1983, gave Godbole the closing moments of the film, performing the dance enacting the wheel of life that he had alluded to earlier in the film. The draft script explains:

> GODBOLE is standing in the centre of a great WHEEL carved in the floor of a ruined TEMPLE. CAMERA cranes higher and higher.
> PEOPLE clapping their hands in time with the cymbals as GODBOLE turns, addressing himself to the different spokes of the wheel. The music builds to bring in the titles. Everyone joins in the dance. THE END[260]

Perhaps due to his well-documented disagreements with Alec Guinness, and the difficulties posed by trying to stage Godbole's dance, but also because he wanted to come back to Adela, Lean decided to amend his original concept. As Judy Davis recalled, she and Lean had managed to strike up a rapport during the later stages of the production making her 'suddenly the golden girl for a while.'[261] One day on set, Lean drew Davis aside and explained to her a number of important script changes: 'Dear. The last scene of the film. You're at the window. Fuck Alec Guinness.'[262]

The final words of *A Passage to India* belong to Aziz, from his letter to Adela granting her forgiveness and talking elegiacally about his final parting from Fielding and Stella: 'I do not think I will ever see them again.' But the final image is of Adela, who finishes the letter, replaces it in its envelope, and then goes to the window to look out at the pouring English rain, taking the film back to its cathartic courtroom scenes but also further back to its opening sequence on the rainy streets of London. Jay Cocks noticed the similarity of this film's 'last lingering image' to the ending of Lean's *Lawrence of Arabia* twenty years before: 'Lawrence is going home; the woman is already there. But both have been changed fundamentally, uprooted and unsettled forever.'[263] Male and female protagonists share a fate, but it is telling that the woman is already placed within the domestic sphere, a woman looking out from a window, whereas Lawrence is never shown reaching that 'home' his driver mentions, and he remains in transit. However, the last image of Lean's career is not of the questing man on the far horizon but a close-up of a woman's face: a fitting conclusion to a filmmaking career richly abundant in female-centred drama, from a director equally conversant in the epic *and* the intimate.

Notes

1. Vivian Sobchack, 'Surge and Splendor: A Phenomenology of the Hollywood Epic Film', *Representations*, Vol. 29, Winter 1990, p. 25.
2. Ibid.
3. Hall and Neale, *Epics, Spectacles and Blockbusters*, p. 6.
4. Constantine Santas, *The Epic in Film: From Myth to Blockbuster* (Lanham: Rowman & Littlefield, 2008), p. 116.
5. See Hall and Neale, *Epics, Spectacles and Blockbusters*, p. 166 for more on *Cleopatra*, including the irony that so spectacular a film 'ultimately went into profit not from its theatrical release but from a sale to television'.
6. This story is told in detail in Peter Biskind's *Easy Riders, Raging Bulls* (London: Bloomsbury, 1998).
7. Hall and Neale, *Epics, Spectacles and Blockbusters*, p. 191.
8. Ibid., p. 181.
9. Brownlow, *David Lean*, p. 586.
10. Ibid., p. 588.
11. Ibid.
12. Virginia Woolf, *A Room of One's Own* (London: Penguin, 1945), p. 74.
13. Lean quoted in David Lewin, *Daily Mail*, 12 November 1970.
14. *Kine Weekly*, 28 April 1966, p. 8.
15. Derek Malcolm, *Guardian*, 19 March 1985.
16. Fuller and Kent, 'Return Passage', p. 36.
17. Quoted in Silverman, *David Lean*, p. 190.
18. Silver and Ursini, *David Lean and His Films*, p. 211.
19. Boris Pasternak, *Doctor Zhivago*, translated by Max Hayward and Manya Harari (London: Collins and Harvill, 1958), p. 16.
20. Letter to Robert O'Brien dated 4 June 1964. UoR Spec Coll.
21. Sobchack, 'Surge and Splendor', p. 24.
22. Interviewed by Mary Blume in 1970, anthologised in Organ (ed.), *David Lean: Interviews*, p. 37.
23. Interviewed by Robert Stewart in 1965. Ibid., p. 23.
24. Letter from Bolt to Lean dated 24 October 1964. UoR Spec Coll.
25. Raymond Durgnat, *Films and Filming*, June 1966, p. 9.
26. Silverman, *David Lean*, p. 154.
27. Reproduced in Lean with Chattington, *David Lean*, pp. 26–7.
28. Brownlow, *David Lean*, p. 505.
29. Letter from Bolt to Lean dated 20 June 1964. UoR Spec Coll.
30. Turner, *Robert Bolt*, p. 237.
31. Lean with Chattington, *David Lean*, p. 26.
32. David Lewin, 'Shooting for an epic hat-trick', *Daily Mail*, 27 August 1965.

238 DAVID LEAN

33 Letter to Omar Sharif dated 18 October 1964. UoR Spec Coll.
34 Letter to Robert O'Brien dated 4 June 1964. UoR Spec Coll.
35 Ibid.
36 Alexander Walker, *Evening Standard*, 28 April 1966.
37 Arthur Knight, *Saturday Review*, 15 January 1966. Conversely, the film was criticised in other quarters for making Zhivago too active, against the spirit of the book: 'But Dr Z in the book was an onlooker who saw red Russia being born. The film tries to turn him into a hero.' *Daily Express*, 11 January 1966.
38 Nina Hibbin, *Morning Star*, 27 April 1966.
39 Durgnat, *Films and Filming*, p. 9.
40 Walker, *Evening Standard*.
41 Knight, *Saturday Review*.
42 Pasternak, *Doctor Zhivago*, p. 202.
43 Reproduced in Lean with Chattington, *David Lean*, p. 27.
44 Letter to Bolt dated 15 June 1964. UoR Spec Coll.
45 Quoted in Brownlow, *David Lean*, p. 504.
46 Letter to Robert O'Brien dated 4 June 1964. UoR Spec Coll.
47 Doctor Zhivago: notes on draft script, undated, p. 5. UoR Spec Coll.
48 Letter from Bolt to Lean dated 20 June 1964. UoR Spec Coll.
49 Ibid.
50 Letter to Bolt dated 2 July 1963. UoR Spec Coll.
51 Barry Norman, 'Somebody had to say it ... and Lean did!', *Daily Mail*, 19 January 1965.
52 Letter to Robert O'Brien dated 4 June 1964. UoR Spec Coll.
53 Helen Lawrenson, 'Letter Home', *Esquire*, December 1965, p. 132.
54 Turner, *Robert Bolt*, p. 274.
55 Walker, *Evening Standard*.
56 Knight, *Saturday Review*.
57 David Robinson, *The Times*, 29 April 1966.
58 Kenneth Tynan, *Observer*, 1 May 1966.
59 Durgnat, *Films and Filming*, p. 9.
60 Dilys Powell, *Sunday Times*, 1 May 1966.
61 Reproduced in Lean with Chattington, *David Lean*, p. 27.
62 Sobchack, 'Surge and Splendor', p. 31.
63 'The Lion's Roar' (MGM press release) dated 13 January 1966, *Doctor Zhivago* microfiche, BFI library.
64 Lawrenson, 'Letter Home', p. 132. The promotional strategies for the film outlined in its exhibitor's manuals also hinged on luxurious hyperbole with stunts and tie-ins involving fur coats, vodka and caviar.
65 Introduction to screenplay of *Doctor Zhivago*, cited in Turner, *Robert Bolt*, p. 232.
66 Ibid.
67 Letter to Alec Guinness dated 11 November 1964. UoR Spec Coll.
68 Bolt's summary 'An account of the intended script 2.2.64'. UoR Spec Coll.
69 Doctor Zhivago: notes on draft script, p. 5. UoR Spec Coll.
70 Ibid.
71 Howard Maxford, *David Lean* (London: Batsford, 2001), p. 128.
72 Clive Hirschhorn, *Sunday Express*, 1 May 1966.
73 The image's antecedence in the novel is notable: 'Had I touched you at that moment with so much as the tip of my finger, a spark would have lit up the room.' Pasternak, *Doctor Zhivago*, p. 383.
74 For more on this, see Ian Christie, *The Art of Film: John Box and Production Design* (New York: Columbia University Press, 2008) and Laurie Ede, *British Film Design* (London: I. B. Tauris, 2010), pp. 129–30.

FEMINISING THE EPIC 239

75 Letter to Robert O'Brien dated 4 June 1964. UoR Spec Coll.
76 Silverman, *David Lean*, p. 165.
77 Letter from Bolt, undated. UoR Spec Coll.
78 There's an intriguing parallel here with a much later 'feminine epic', James Cameron's *Titanic* (1997). Both films draw parallels between a young woman's loss of virginity and larger traumatic historical change: as Peter Kramer notes, the 'ship is on its maiden voyage and Rose is still a virgin; the Titanic's voyage comes to an end shortly after Rose has lost her virginity.' 'Women First: Titanic, Action-Adventure Films and Hollywood's Female Audience', *Historical Journal of Film, Radio and Television*, Vol. 18, No. 4, 1998, p. 617. Cameron was quite candid in admitting the influence of *Zhivago* on *Titanic*: 'I'd been looking for an opportunity to do an epic romance in the traditional vein of *Gone With the Wind* and *Doctor Zhivago*, where you're telling an intimate story on a very big canvas.' Quoted in Kramer, 'Women First', p. 614.
79 *Doctor Zhivago* pressbook, BFI microfiche. Dalton's original plan had been to go for an all-grey outfit, but Lean urged her to go all out for glamour, however unrealistic it might be. The foregrounding of a fabulous show-stopping outfit over dirty realism may also have had something to do with a promotional strategy that depended heavily on fashion.
80 Robert Bolt's 'account of the intended script' dated 2 February 1964, p. 6. UoR Spec Coll. In a letter to Rod Steiger dated 2 December 1964, Lean wrote of Komarovsky: 'I would like most women in the audience to understand his attraction for her – a piece of information they would not pass on to their husbands.' His recurrent reference point for the character was actually Sam Spiegel: 'Imagine S. S. for a moment in this situation...' *Doctor Zhivago*: notes on first draft script, p. 11. UoR Spec Coll.
81 Quoted in Brownlow, *David Lean*, p. 534.
82 Pasternak, *Doctor Zhivago*, p. 64.
83 Phillips, *Beyond the Epic*, p. 337.
84 Christie recalls Lean and Young being initially dissatisfied with the shot so covering her in more fake sweat and asking her to look directly to camera to get the desired impact of the moment. Brownlow, *David Lean*, p. 511.
85 *Time*, 31 December 1965.
86 Tynan, *Observer*.
87 Lawrenson, 'Letter Home', p. 140.
88 Norman, 'Somebody had to say it... and Lean did!'
89 Lean interviewed by Robert Stewart in 1965 in Organ (ed.), *David Lean: Interviews*, p. 24.
90 Bolt's 'An account of the intended script 2.2.64', p. 11. UoR Spec Coll.
91 *Doctor Zhivago*: notes on first draft script, p. 26. UoR Spec Coll.
92 The actress playing the woman, Lili Murati, nearly fell under the moving train and was lucky to sustain only minor injuries. See Brownlow, *David Lean*, p. 530.
93 Lean's 'Notes for discussion with Robert' dated 14 February 1964. UoR Spec Coll.
94 Hibbin, *Morning Star*.
95 Eddie Fowlie ingeniously etched the crystals using a feather. With regards to dourness of the scene prior to the daffodils, Lean's idea was that 'people will gasp because of the sudden advent of colour after three minutes of greyness'. Brownlow, *David Lean*, p. 774, p. 531.
96 *Doctor Zhivago*: notes on first draft script, p. 32. UoR Spec Coll.
97 Bolt letter to Lean dated 25 May 1963. UoR Spec Coll.
98 Notes in Lean with Chattington, *David Lean*, p. 28.
99 Durgnat, *Films and Filming*.
100 Notes in Lean with Chattington, *David Lean*, p. 27.

101 Doctor Zhivago: notes on first draft script, p. 6. UoR Spec Coll.
102 Brownlow, *David Lean*, pp. 527–8. In the absence of the expected Spanish snow, Box and Eddie Fowlie had to find another way of suggesting a snowy exterior and resorted to everything from whitewash to plastic sheeting to sackloads of marble dust strewn over the fields.
103 Doctor Zhivago: notes on first draft script, p. 2. UoR Spec Coll.
104 Ibid.
105 Ibid., p. 18. UoR Spec Coll.
106 Pasternak, *Doctor Zhivago*, p. 449.
107 Doctor Zhivago: notes on first draft script, p. 26. UoR Spec Coll.
108 'Months ago I remember you talking about a huge poster of Stalin. Do let's have it where Lara walks away down the street for the last time.' Lean's 'Notes for discussion with Robert' dated 14 February 1964. UoR Spec Coll.
109 Ibid.
110 Sinyard, 'Sir Alec Guinness: The Self-Effacing Star', p. 149.
111 Doctor Zhivago: notes on first draft script, p. 36. UoR Spec Coll.
112 Patrick Gibbs, *Daily Telegraph*, 28 April 1966.
113 Durgnat, *Films and Filming*, p. 9.
114 Lean's 'Notes for discussion with Robert' dated 14 February 1964. UoR Spec Coll.
115 Letter from Bolt to Lean dated 26 February 1966. UoR Spec Coll.
116 Lean interviewed by Harlan Kennedy in 1985 anthologised in Organ (ed.), *David Lean: Interviews*, p. 80.
117 Bosley Crowther, *New York Times*, 24 December 1965.
118 Letter from Alexandra Tolstoy dated 5 January 1966. DL/23/1, BFI Spec Coll.
119 Letter quoted in Turner, *Robert Bolt*, p. 277.
120 Ibid., p. 299.
121 Ibid.
122 Ibid., pp. 297–9.
123 Adrian Turner suggests that *Ryan's Daughter* rehearsed both Lean and Bolt's fears of being cuckolded, of not coming up to scratch for their nubile young brides (Bolt even changed the husband's profession from doctor, as in the original Flaubertian template, to schoolteacher, his own former job, implying a degree of biographical investment in the character of Charles). Ibid.
124 Brownlow, *David Lean*, p. 554.
125 Peter Miller quoted in ibid., p. 554.
126 Letter to Alec Guinness, ibid., p. 559.
127 Pratley, *The Cinema of David Lean*, p. 204. Eddie Fowlie recalled Lean inviting him to work on 'a little gem' and then revising his opinion: 'I don't think it's going to be a little gem, it might be a bit bigger.' Quoted in Brownlow, *David Lean*, p. 566.
128 Turner, *Robert Bolt*, p. 315.
129 Pauline Kael, *New Yorker*, 21 November 1970.
130 Gavin Millar, 'Rosy', *Listener*, 17 December 1970.
131 Microfiche for *Ryan's Daughter*, BFI Library.
132 *Daily Mail*, 12 November 1970.
133 Alexander Walker, *Evening Standard*, 10 December 1970.
134 Title of Kenneth Eastaugh's review in *The Sun*, 9 December 1970.
135 Herb A. Lightman, 'On location with Ryan's Daughter', *American Cinematographer*, August 1969, p. 788.
136 Quoted in Brownlow, *David Lean*, p. 583.
137 Hall and Neale, *Epics, Spectacles and Blockbusters*, p. 181 and Philips, *Beyond the Epic*, p. 394.

FEMINISING THE EPIC 241

138 William Grieves, 'Last of the Big Spenders?', *Daily Mirror*, 13 June 1970.
139 *Today's Cinema*, 17 November 1970. Privately he complained about 'a bunch of untrained, semi-talented whiz-kids stealing all the thunder with a half-arsed ill-lit amateur night at the Classic.' Letter to Freddie Young, quoted in Brownlow, *David Lean*, p. 565.
140 *Los Angeles Herald Examiner*, 8 November 1970.
141 Christopher Hudson, *Spectator*, 19 December 1970.
142 Ernest Betts, *People*, 13 December 1970. His is one of the few positive British reviews, in which he admits to finding the moment when Rose rushes out to her lover 'a moving, tender little scene [which] brings tears'. Dilys Powell was also pleased to be reviewing 'A story of love': 'a relief, that. After all the stories of simple bed.' *Sunday Times*, 13 December 1970.
143 The MPAA suggested its selection of this rating was due more to the film's sympathetic treatment of adultery than to its nude scene. *Variety*, 18 November 1970.
144 Letter to Robert O Brien dated 4 June 1964. UoR Spec Coll.
145 Trade press ad published in *Variety*, 14 February 1968, p. 12, reproduced in Hall and Neale, *Epics, Spectacles and Blockbusters*, p. 190.
146 *San Francisco Chronicle*, 29 August 1969.
147 Joseph Gelmis, *A Conversation with Robert Bolt*, transcript of a 'Sound on Film' broadcast, November 1970. BFI library.
148 Ibid.
149 Christopher Hudson, *Spectator*, 19 December 1970.
150 Pratley, *The Cinema of David Lean*, p. 204.
151 *Los Angeles Herald Examiner*, 8 November 1970.
152 *San Francisco Chronicle*, 29 August 1969, p. 48.
153 Silver and Ursini, *David Lean and His Films*, p. 203.
154 Margaret Hinxman, *Sunday Telegraph*, 13 December 1970, describes the film as a visual poem but wonders if that is enough these days. She also says 'I couldn't help feeling this is an intimate affair groaning under the weight of the epic proportions imposed on it.'
155 Molly Haskell, *From Reverence to Rape* (Chicago: University of Chicago Press, 1987), p. 362.
156 *Photoplay*, February 1971, p. 11. The huge success of *Love Story* at the end of 1970 and into 1971 also suggests that thirst for romance among certain sectors of the movie-going public.
157 A parallel could be drawn with reviewers' objections to Fox's three-hour Cinemascope film *The Diary of Anne Frank* (1959), which proved that 'even the most intimate of subjects could be turned into an epic', however inappropriate that might seem. Hall and Neale, *Epics, Spectacles and Blockbusters*, p. 177.
158 Kael, *New Yorker*.
159 Mark Goodman, *Time*, 10 November 1970.
160 John Simon, *New Leader*, November 1970, and Walker, *Evening Standard*.
161 Tom Milne, *Observer*, 13 December 1970.
162 Ibid.
163 Walker, *Evening Standard*.
164 Felix Barker, *Evening News*, 11 December 1970.
165 Ibid.
166 Pratley, *The Cinema of David Lean*, p. 204.
167 Ibid.
168 Brownlow, *David Lean*, p. 554.
169 Ruth Barton, *Irish National Cinema* (London: Routledge, 2004), p. 134. Similar analyses are made by John Hill, 'Images of Violence', in Kevin Rockett, Luke

Gibbons and John Hill (eds.), *Cinema and Ireland* (Syracuse, NY: Syracuse University Press, 1988), pp. 147–93, and Fidelma Farley, 'Ireland, the Past and British Cinema: *Ryan's Daughter*', in Claire Monk and Amy Sargent (eds.), *British Historical Cinema* (London: Routledge, 2002), pp. 129–43.
170 Walker, *Evening Standard*. Gavin Millar describes specific characters as fitting the stereotypes of 'stomping, eccentric priest, jerking village idiot, squinting shrewish gossip, ogling village bint.' Millar, *Listener*.
171 Farley, 'Ireland, the Past and British Cinema: *Ryan's Daughter*', p. 133.
172 E. Butler Cullingford, 'Gender, Sexuality and Englishness in Modern Irish Drama and Film', in A. Bradley and M. Gialanella Valiulis (eds.) *Gender and Sexuality in Modern Ireland* (Amherst: University of Massachusetts Press, 1997). The Irish National Film Institute objected to a British-scripted film showing 'Irish country girls in a disgustingly immoral light. Not content with putting on the screen the consummation of her marriage, we see her a few weeks later commit adultery in the woods with a British major.' Quoted in Mark Patrick Hederman, 'Far-Off, Most Secret and Inviolate Rose', *The Crane Bag*, Vol. 1, No. 2, 1977, p. 30.
173 Cited in Lance Pettitt, *Screening Ireland* (Manchester: Manchester University Press, 2000), p. 101.
174 Farley, 'Ireland, the Past and British Cinema: *Ryan's Daughter*', p. 136. There is also the vignette featuring Gerald Sim as the Yorkshire officer who has received his embarkation leave for France, and the front line, who shamefully admits to his replacement Doryan 'I'm a coward, you see', and foresees his own death and disgrace. Adrian Turner describes this scene as 'a little masterpiece, a short story tucked into an epic'. Turner, *Robert Bolt*, p. 316.
175 Interview with Gelmis in 1970 in Organ (ed.), *David Lean: Interviews*, p. 47.
176 These early parts of *Ryan's Daughter* are highly reminiscent of the 'Nausicaa' sequence in James Joyce's *Ulysses* in their depiction of a young Irish girl on a beach, togged up in her best gear (the pathetic ribbon trim on her battered hat), head full of elaborate romantic fantasies, seeing great things in an unremarkable middle-aged man. Gerty MacDowell, Rosy Ryan's intertextual sister, envisages herself as a romantic heroine and constructs an elaborate romantic persona for a passing man (Leopold Bloom) which bears little resemblance to reality: 'Here was that of which she had so often dreamed. It was he who mattered and there was joy on her face because she wanted him because she felt instinctively that he was like no-one else. The very heart of the girl-woman went out to him, her dreamhusband, because she knew on the instant it was him ... mayhap he would embrace her gently, like a real man, crushing her soft body to him, and love her, his ownest girlie, for herself alone.' James Joyce, *Ulysses* (London: Penguin, 2001 [1922]), pp. 465–6. Gerty's fixation on the distinguished older gentleman results in nothing more than the bathos of being the stimulus for his masturbation; Rosy is arguably less fortunate since her crush on an older man changes the course of her life irrevocably.
177 Bolt's direction in 'Coming of Age', early draft of *Ryan's Daughter* dated 1 March 1969, p. 28. DL/8/2. BFI Spec Coll.
178 Brownlow, *David Lean*, p. 564.
179 Interviewed by Steven Ross in 1972 in Organ (ed.), *David Lean: Interviews*, p. 56.
180 Silver and Ursini, *David Lean and His Films*, p. 205. Sue Harper describes Rose as having no choice but 'to succour him with her body'. *Women and British Cinema* (London: Continuum, 2000), p. 135.
181 Quoted in Brownlow, *David Lean*, p. 565.
182 Ibid., p. 573.
183 Ibid., p. 564.

184 Sarah Miles, *Serves Me Right* (London: Phoenix, 1996), p. 340.
185 *Ryan's Daughter* pressbook, BFI Library.
186 Brownlow, *David Lean*, p. 574.
187 Interviewed by Stewart in 1965 in Organ (ed.), *David Lean: Interviews*, p. 31.
188 Harper, *Women in British Cinema*, p. 135.
189 Linda Williams, *Hardcore: Power, Pleasure and the Frenzy of the Visible* (London: Pandora, 1990), p. 171.
190 Betty Friedan, *The Feminine Mystique* (London: Penguin, 1965), pp. 226–8.
191 Brownlow, *David Lean*, p. 584.
192 Ibid.
193 Silverman, *David Lean*, p. 178.
194 Brownlow, *David Lean*, pp. 576–7.
195 Ibid., p. 575.
196 Hederman, 'Far- off, most secret, and inviolate Rose', p. 31. He added that this image struck 'a far deeper and more familiar chord than other, perhaps, more flattering pictures' of Ireland and the Irish.
197 Pettitt, *Screening Ireland*, p. 101.
198 Letters from Bolt to Lean quoted in Brownlow, *David Lean*, p. 563.
199 Kael, *New Yorker*.
200 Tony Sloman, '*Ryan's Daughter* Revisited', *in70mm.com: The 70 mm Newsletter*, Issue 54, September 1998, www.in70mm.com/newsletter/1998/54/ryans/index.htm (accessed 11 December 2013).
201 Sue Harper, 'History and Representation: The Case of 1970s British Cinema', in James Chapman, Mark Glancy and Sue Harper (eds.), *The New Film History* (London: Palgrave, 2007), p. 33.
202 Brownlow, *David Lean*, p. 310.
203 Ibid., p. 397.
204 Ibid., p. 554.
205 Day, 'A Passage to India', p. 62.
206 Nick James, 'Empire's last gasp', *Sight and Sound*, August 2008, p. 46.
207 Andrew Higson, 'Re-Presenting the National Past: Nostalgia and Pastiche in the Heritage Film', in Lester Friedman (ed.), *Fires Were Started: British Cinema and Thatcherism* (London: UCL Press, 1993), p. 113.
208 Kael, *New Yorker*, 21 November 1970.
209 Salman Rushdie, 'Outside the Whale', *Granta*, No. 11, 1984, p. 125.
210 Ibid., p. 138.
211 Fuller and Kent, 'Return passage', p. 30.
212 Letter dated 31 December 1981. DL/10/18, BFI Spec Coll.
213 Letter dated 6 February 1983. DL/10/18, BFI Spec Coll.
214 Paul Willemen, 'An Introduction to Framework', www.frameworkonline.com/about2.htm (accessed 30 November 2012).
215 Guinness had expressed serious misgivings about taking the role, especially playing alongside Indian actors, but recognised it as a great part. In one single letter to Lean dated 10 April 1983, he first vows 'Godbole is not for me' but then a page later relents and partly agrees: 'Godbole would bring, so to speak, Herbert Pocket full circle.' DL/20/2, BFI Spec Coll. On seeing the finished film, Guinness wrote to Lean again to suggest that his first instincts to turn down Godbole may have been correct. However, the performance has won some support in unexpected quarters. Malaysian critic Stephen Teo mentions an Indian friend of his who was 'bowled over' by Guinness as Godbole. 'Under the noonday sun: David Lean's Asian epics', *Cinemaya*, Nos. 17–18, Autumn/Winter 1992–93, p. 23.
216 Quoted in Ian Jack, *Sunday Times Magazine*, 24 March 1985, p. 15. An example of

Lean's direction of Banerjee can be seen in the *South Bank Show* on Lean which shows the director advising the actor exactly how he should play the scene in which Aziz first meets Fielding, and playing it out himself for Banerjee to copy.
217 Fuller and Kent, 'Return Passage', p. 34.
218 Jack, *Sunday Times Magazine*, p. 37.
219 See Brownlow, *David Lean*, pp. 660–2.
220 Jack, *Sunday Times Magazine*, p. 15.
221 Neil Sinyard, 'Lids Tend to Come Off: David Lean's Film of E. M. Forster's *A Passage to India*', in Robert Giddings and Erica Sheen (eds.), *The Classic Novel: From Page to Screen* (Manchester: Manchester University Press, 2000), p. 149.
222 Letter dated 31 October 1982. DL/10/11, BFI Spec Coll. Lean initially proposed that Hepburn could play Mrs Moore but both agreed against the idea.
223 Fuller and Kent, 'Return Passage', p. 30.
224 Production notes for *A Passage to India*, BFI library.
225 Forster quoted in the introduction to *A Passage to India* (Harmondsworth: Penguin, 1986 [1924]), p. 26.
226 However, there are still those who read the caves incident differently. For example, T. Muraleedharan insists a rape has happened and that 'the ambiguity is only regarding the identity of the assailant' in the essay 'Imperial Migrations: Reading the Raj Cinema of the 1980s', in Claire Monk and Amy Sargeant (eds.), *British Historical Cinema* (London: Routledge, 2002), p. 157. This divergent reading suggests that Lean may have retained more ambiguity in his presentation of the events in the caves than he is usually given credit for.
227 Brownlow, *David Lean*, p. 656.
228 Letter from Lean to Santha Rama Rau, quoted in Brownlow, *David Lean*, p. 649.
229 Silverman, *David Lean*, p. 186, and Lean quoted in 'Return of a Film Knight', *Yorkshire Post*, 19 March 1985.
230 Letter to Rau, quoted in Brownlow, *David Lean*, p. 650.
231 Letter from Lean to Richard Goodwin and John Brabourne dated 31 December 1981. DL/10/18, BFI Spec Coll. Although the actress who eventually took the role of Adela, Judy Davis, would have many disagreements with Lean during the making of the film, her assessment of Adela's malaise is actually quite similar to his, albeit expressed in very different language: 'she's in the cave and she feels her blood starting to go; her whole body. She just freaks out. She can't cope with her own sexuality, so she tries to cover up, to lie to herself.' Production notes for *A Passage to India*, BFI Library.
232 Letter to Rau, quoted in Brownlow, *David Lean*, p. 649.
233 Lean interviewed by Harlan Kennedy in 1985 anthologised in Organ (ed.), *David Lean: Interviews*, p. 82.
234 Completed screenplay dated 4 September 1982, p. 1. DL/10/10, BFI Spec Coll.
235 See Fuller and Kent, 'Return Passage', p. 30.
236 Laura E. Donaldson, *Decolonizing Feminisms: Race, Gender and Empire-Building* (London: Routledge, 1993), p. 92.
237 Fuller and Kent, 'Return Passage', p. 32.
238 At least in this early stage of the film before the character of Fielding (James Fox) is introduced. He will take over as what Laura Kipnis calls the 'white male moral centre of the film, possessing anachronistically enlightened consciousness'. Laura Kipnis, 'The Phantom Twitchings of an Amputated Limb: Sexual Spectacle in the Post-Colonial Epic', *Wide Angle*, Vol. 11, No. 4 (October 1989), p. 50.
239 Completed screenplay dated 4 September 1982, p. 45. DL/10/10, BFI Spec Coll.
240 *New Yorker*, 14 June 1985. Kael, a former nemesis, filed a glowing review of Lean's final film, particularly praising the two female leads – 'Judy Davis's performance

FEMINISING THE EPIC   245

is close to perfection ... this Miss Quested is a heroically honest figure', 'Peggy Ashcroft breathes so much good sense into the role that Mrs Moore acquires a radiance, a spiritual glow' – but also highly appreciative of Lean's direction, as was Richard Schickel, who insisted in his review that Lean was emphatically not 'an empty pictorialist'. *Time*, 31 December 1984.

241   Sinyard, 'Lids Tend to Come Off', p. 157. Incidentally, the Lean phrase that Sinyard uses for the title of his essay is echoed in a comment on the film's monkey scene from reviewer Nigel Andrews: 'It's as if a simmering pot has overflowed, unlidding our heroine's self-control and her dainty preconceptions of India.' *Financial Times*, 22 March 1985, p. 21.

242   Screenplay dated 4 September 1982, p. 48. DL/10/10, BFI Spec Coll. An earlier draft also had the outline of her breast slightly visible in the darkness.

243   I have to say that Philip French's remarks of this scene and Peggy Ashcroft – 'You would think she was a daytripper who had an attack of the vapours in the Cheddar Gorge' – strike me not only as facetious but also totally inaccurate. Philip French, *Observer*, 24 March 1985, p. 25.

244   Silverman, *David Lean*, p. 171.

245   *Evening Standard*, 13 December 1984, p. 21.

246   Dyer, *White*, pp. 184–207.

247   Lean interviewed by David Ehrenstein in 1984 in Organ (ed.), *David Lean: Interviews*, p. 74.

248   David Denby, 'A Tale of Two Indias', *New York Times*, 7 January 1985, p. 69.

249   Brownlow, *David Lean*, p. 666.

250   Sinyard, 'Lids Tend to Come Off', p. 158.

251   An earlier draft of the script also had McBryde comment that 'Indian men are indecently obsessed by the female leg'. Draft script notes, DL/10/6d, BFI Spec Coll.

252   See also Kipnis, 'The Phantom Twitchings of an Amputated Limb', p. 47.

253   Lean changed of focal length of lenses during the courtroom scene, starting at 35 and going up to 150, blurring the background to isolate her. Aljean Harmetz, 'David Lean films a famed novel', *New York Times*, 7 December 1984, p. 21.

254   Fuller and Kent, 'Return Passage', p. 34.

255   Silverman, *David Lean*, p. 187.

256   Forster, *A Passage to India*, p. 316.

257   Letter from Michael Cowdy to John Brabourne dated 19 November 1982. DL/10/18. BFI Spec Coll.

258   French, *Observer*, p. 25.

259   John Hill, *British Cinema in the 1980s* (Oxford: Oxford University Press, 1999), p. 108.

260   Draft screenplay dated 17 May 1983. DL/10/6a, BFI Spec Coll.

261   Brownlow, *David Lean*, p. 675.

262   Ibid., p. 676.

263   Interviewed by Jay Cocks in 1984 in Organ (ed.), *David Lean: Interviews*, p. 66.

Filmography as director

In Which We Serve, 1942, 116 mins, b/w

Production company: Two Cities Films
Directors: Noël Coward, David Lean
Producer: Noël Coward
Associate Producer: Anthony Havelock-Allan
Screenplay: Noël Coward
Adaptation [uncredited]: David Lean, Anthony Havelock-Allan, Ronald Neame
Director of Photography: Ronald Neame
Art Director: David Rawsley
Sound: C. C. Stevens
Music: Noël Coward
Editors: [David Lean], Thelma Myers
Cast: Noël Coward (Captain Kinross), Bernard Miles (Walter Hardy), John Mills (Shorty Blake), Celia Johnson (Alix Kinross), Kay Walsh (Freda Lewis), Joyce Carey (Mrs Hardy), Richard Attenborough (Stoker)

This Happy Breed, 1944, 111 mins, colour (Technicolor)

Production company: Two Cities Films
Producer: Noël Coward
Screenplay: Noël Coward, from his play
Adaptation: David Lean, Ronald Neame, Anthony Havelock-Allan
Director of Photography: Ronald Neame
Art Director: C. P. Norman
Sound: C. C. Stevens, J. C. Cook, Desmond Dew
Music Supervisor: Muir Matheson
Editor: Jack Harris
Cast: Robert Newton (Frank Gibbons), Celia Johnson (Ethel Gibbons), John Mills (Billy Mitchell), Kay Walsh (Queenie Gibbons), Stanley Holloway (Bob Mitchell)

Blithe Spirit, 1945, 96 mins, colour (Technicolor)

Production company: Cineguild-Two Cities Films
Producer: Noël Coward
Screenplay: Noël Coward, from his play
Adaptation: David Lean, Ronald Neame, Anthony Havelock-Allan
Director of Photography: Ronald Neame
Art Director: C. P. Norman
Sound: J. C. Cook, Desmond Dew
Music: Richard Addinsell
Editor: Jack Harris
Cast: Rex Harrison (Charles Condomine), Constance Cummings (Ruth), Kay Hammond (Elvira), Margaret Rutherford (Madame Arcati), Joyce Carey (Mrs Bradman), Hugh Wakefield (Doctor Bradman), Jacqueline Clark (Edith)

Brief Encounter, 1945, 86 mins, b/w

Production company: Cineguild
Producer: Noël Coward
Screenplay: David Lean, Ronald Neame, Anthony Havelock-Allan, based on Noël Coward's play *Still Life*
Adaptation: Noël Coward
Director of Photography: Robert Krasker
Art Director: L. P. Williams
Sound: Stanley Lambourne, Desmond Dew
Music: Rachmaninov's 2nd Piano Concerto played by Eileen Joyce
Editor: Jack Harris
Cast: Celia Johnson (Laura Jesson), Trevor Howard (Dr Alec Harvey), Cyril Raymond (Fred Jesson), Joyce Carey (Myrtle Bagot), Stanley Holloway (Albert Godby), Valentine Dyall (Stephen Lynn), Everley Gregg (Dolly Messiter), Margaret Barton (Beryl)

Great Expectations, 1946, 118 mins, b/w

Production company: Cineguild
Producer: Ronald Neame
Executive Producer: Anthony Havelock-Allan
Screenplay: David Lean, Ronald Neame, Anthony Havelock-Allan with Kay Walsh and Cecil McGivern, based on the novel by Charles Dickens
Director of Photography: Guy Green
Production Designer: John Bryan
Sound: Stanley Lambourne, Gordon K. McCallum
Music: Walter Goehr and [uncredited] Kenneth Pakeman
Editor: Jack Harris
Cast: John Mills ('Pip'), Valerie Hobson (Estella), Bernard Miles (Joe Gargery),

Francis L. Sullivan (Jaggers), Finlay Currie (Magwitch), Martita Hunt (Miss Havisham), Anthony Wager ('Pip' as a boy), Jean Simmons (Estella as a girl), Alec Guinness (Herbert Pocket), Ivor Barnard (Wemmick), Freda Jackson (Mrs Joe Gargery), Torin Thatcher (Bentley Drummle)

Oliver Twist, 1948, 116 mins, b/w

Production company: Cineguild
Producer: Ronald Neame
Screenplay: David Lean and Stanley Haynes, from the novel by Charles Dickens
Director of Photography: Guy Green
Art Director: John Bryan
Sound: Stanley Lambourne, Gordon K. McCallum
Music: Sir Arnold Bax
Editor: Jack Harris
Cast: Robert Newton (Bill Sikes), Alec Guinness (Fagin), Fay Walsh (Nancy), John Howard Davies (Oliver), Francis L. Sullivan (Mr Bumble), Henry Stephenson (Mr Brownlow), Mary Clare (the Matron), Anthony Newley (the Artful Dodger)

The Passionate Friends, 1949, 91 mins, b/w

Production company: Cineguild
Producer: Ronald Neame
Screenplay: Eric Ambler, based on the novel by H. G. Wells
Adaptation: David Lean and Stanley Haynes
Director of Photography: Guy Green
Production Designer: John Bryan
Sound: Stanley Lambourne, Gordon K. McCallum
Music: Richard Addinsell
Editor: Jack Harris
Cast: Ann Todd (Mary Austin), Trevor Howard (Steven Stratton), Claude Rains (Howard Justin)

Madeleine, 1950, 114 mins, b/w

Production company: Cineguild
Producer: Stanley Haynes
Screenplay: Stanley Haynes and Nicholas Phipps
Director of Photography: Guy Green
Art Director: John Bryan
Sound: Gordon K. McCallum
Music: William Alwyn
Editor: Geoffrey Foot

Cast: Ann Todd (Madeleine Smith), Ivan Desny (Emile L'Angelier), Norman Woland (William Minnoch), Leslie Banks (Mr Smith), Barbara Everest (Mrs Smith), Ivor Barnard (Mr Murdoch)

The Sound Barrier, 1952, 118 mins, b/w

Production company: London Films
Producer: David Lean
Associate Producer: Norman Spencer
Screenplay: Terence Rattigan
Director of Photography: Jack Hildyard
Production Design: Vincent Korda
Sound: John Cox
Music: Malcolm Arnold
Editor: Geoffrey Foot
Cast: Ralph Richardson (Sir John Ridgefield), Ann Todd (Susan Ridgefield Garthwaite), Nigel Patrick (Tony Garthwaite), John Justin (Philip Peel), Dinah Sheridan (Jess Peel), Joseph Tomelty (Will Sparks), Denholm Elliott (Chris Ridgefield)

Hobson's Choice, 1954, 107 mins, b/w

Production company: London Films in Association with British Lion
Producer: David Lean
Associate Producer: Norman Spencer
Screenplay: David Lean, Norman Spencer and Wynyard Browne, based on the play by Harold Brighouse
Director of Photography: Jack Hildyard
Art Directed by Wilfred Shingleton
Sound: John Cox
Music: Malcolm Arnold
Cast: Charles Laughton (Henry Hobson), Brenda de Banzie (Maggie), John Mills (Will Mossop), Daphne Anderson (Alice Hobson), Prunella Scales (Vicky Hobson), Richard Wattis (Albert Prosser)

Summer Madness, 1955, 99 mins, colour (Eastmancolor)

Production company: Lopert Films/London Films
Producer: Ilya Lopert
Associate Producer: Norman Spencer
Screenplay: David Lean, H. E. Bates, based on the play *Time of the Cuckoo* by Arthur Laurents
Director of Photography: Jack Hildyard
Art Director: Vincent Korda
Sound: Peter Handford

Music: Alessandro Cicognini; *La gazza ladra* by Giacomo Rossini
Editor: Peter Taylor
Cast: Katharine Hepburn (Jane Hudson), Rossano Brazzi (Renato Di Rossi), Isa Miranda (Signora Fiorina), Darren McGavin (Eddie Jaeger), Mari Aldon (Phyl Jaeger), Jane Rose (Edith McIlhenny), MacDonald Parke (Lloyd McIlhenny), Gaetano Autiero (Mauro)

The Bridge on the River Kwai, 1957, 160 mins, colour (Technicolor)

Production company: Horizon Pictures
Producer: Sam Spiegel
Screenplay: Pierre Boulle and [uncredited] Carl Foreman, Calder Willingham, Michael Wilson, and David Lean, based on Boulle's novel. Due to blacklisting, neither Foreman nor Wilson received script credit, which was given to author Boulle, who had nothing to do with scripting the film.
Director of Photography: Jack Hildyard
Art Director: Donald M. Ashton
Sound: John Cox, John Mitchell
Music: Malcolm Arnold; 'Colonel Bogey March' by Kenneth J. Alford
Editor: Peter Taylor
Cast: Alec Guinness (Colonel Nicholson), William Holden (Shears), Jack Hawkins (Major Warden), Sessue Hayakawa (Colonel Saito), James Donald (Dr Clipton), Geoffrey Horne (Lieutenant Joyce), Andre Morell (Colonel Green), Percy Herbert (Grogan)

Lawrence of Arabia, 1962, 207 mins, colour (Technicolor)

Production company: Horizon Films
Producer: Sam Spiegel
Screenplay: Robert Bolt (draft screenplay by Michael Wilson)
Director of Photography: Freddie Young
Production Designer: John Box
Sound: Paddy Cunningham
Music: Maurice Jarre; 'The Voice of the Guns' by Kenneth J. Alford
Editor: Anne V. Coates
Cast: Peter O'Toole (Thomas Edward Lawrence), Alec Guinness (Prince Feisal), Anthony Quinn (Auda), Jack Hawkins (General Allenby), Omar Sharif (Sherif Ali), Anthony Quayle (Colonel Brighton), Claude Rains (Mr Dryden), Arthur Kennedy (Jackson Bentley), José Ferrer (Turkish Bey), Donald Wolfit (General Murray)

FILMOGRAPHY AS DIRECTOR 251

Doctor Zhivago, 1965, 193 mins, colour (Metrocolor)

Production company: Carlo Ponti/MGM
Producer: Carlo Ponti
Executive Producer: Arvid L. Griffen
Screenplay: Robert Bolt, based on the novel by Boris Pasternak
Director of Photography: Freddie Young
Production Designer: John Box
Sound: Paddy Cunningham
Music: Maurice Jarre
Editor: Norman Savage
Cast: Omar Sharif (Yuri Zhivago), Julie Christie (Lara), Geraldine Chaplin (Tonya Gromeko Zhivago), Tom Courtenay (Pasha/Strelnikov), Alec Guinness (General Yegraf Zhivago), Siobhan McKenna (Anna Gromeko), Ralph Richardson (Alexander Gromeko), Rod Steiger (Komarovsky), Rita Tushingham (Tonya), Klaus Kinski (Kostoyed)

Ryan's Daughter, 1970, 206 mins, colour (Metrocolor)

Production company: Faraway Productions/MGM
Producer: Anthony Havelock-Allan
Associate Producer: Roy Stevens
Screenplay: Robert Bolt
Director of Photography: Freddie Young
Production Designer: Stephen Grimes
Sound: John Bramwell
Music: Maurice Jarre
Editor: Norman Savage
Cast: Sarah Miles (Rosy Ryan), Robert Mitchum (Charles Shaughnessy), Trevor Howard (Father Hugh Collins), Christopher Jones (Major Randolph Doryan), John Mills (Michael), Leo McKern (Tom Ryan), Barry Foster (Tim O'Leary)

Lost and Found: The Story of Cook's Anchor (TV), 1979, 40 mins, colour

Production company: South Pacific TV/Faraway Productions
Producers: George Andrews, Wayne Tourell
Teleplay: Robert Bolt, David Lean, Wayne Tourell
Photography: Ken Dorman, Lynton Diggle, Eddie Fowlie
Editor: David Reed

252 FILMOGRAPHY AS DIRECTOR

A Passage to India, 1984, 163 mins, colour (Technicolor)

Production company: G. W. Films, John Heyman, Edward Sands, Home Box Office
Producers: John Brabourne, Richard B. Goodwin
Executive Producers: John Heyman, Edward Sands
Screenplay: David Lean, based on the novel by E. M. Forster and the play by Santha Rama Rau
Director of Photography: Ernest Day
Production Designer: John Box
Sound: Graham V. Hartstone, Nicolas Le Messurier, Michael A. Carter and John W. Mitchell
Music: Maurice Jarre; 'Freely Maisie' by John Dalby
Editor: David Lean
Cast: Judy Davis (Adela Quested), Victor Banerjee (Dr Aziz), Peggy Ashcroft (Mrs Moore), James Fox (Fielding), Alec Guinness (Godbole), Nigel Havers (Ronny Heaslop), Richard Wilson (Turton), Michael Culver (McBryde), Art Malik (Mahmoud Ali), Saeed Jaffrey (Hamidullah)

Bibliography

Primary sources

David Lean Papers, University of Reading Special Collections, MS 3874 (UoR Spec Coll)
David Lean Papers, British Film Institute Special Collections (BFI Spec Coll)
Microfiche collection, BFI Library

Secondary sources

Ackroyd, Peter, *Introduction to Dickens* (London: Sinclair-Stevenson, 1991)
Aldgate, Anthony and Jeffrey Richards, *Britain Can Take It: The British Cinema in the Second World War*, 2nd edition (Edinburgh: Edinburgh University Press, 1994)
Anderegg, Michael, *David Lean* (Boston: Twayne, 1985)
Ashby, Justine, 'It's Been Emotional: Reassessing the Contemporary British Woman's Film', in Melanie Bell and Melanie Williams (eds.), *British Women's Cinema* (London: Routledge, 2010)
Balcon, Michael, 'Ten Years of British Films', *Films in 1951: A Special Publication on British Films and Film-Makers for the Festival of Britain* (London: BFI, 1951)
Barr, Charles, 'Madness, Madness!: The Brief Stardom of James Donald', in Bruce Babington (ed.), *British Stars and Stardom* (Manchester: Manchester University Press, 2001)
Barton, Ruth, *Irish National Cinema* (London: Routledge, 2004)
Basinger, Jeanine, *A Woman's View: How Hollywood Spoke to Women, 1930–1960* (New York: Knopf, 1993)
Bazin, André, *What Is Cinema? Volume 2*, translated by Hugh Gray (Berkeley: University of California Press, 2005)
Bazin, André, *Bazin at Work: Major Essays and Reviews from the Forties and Fifties*, translated by Alain Piette and Bert Cardullo (London: Routledge, 1997)
Bell, Melanie and Melanie Williams, 'The Hour of the Cuckoo: Reclaiming

the British Woman's Film', in Melanie Bell and Melanie Williams (eds.), *British Women's Cinema* (London: Routledge, 2010)

Benedict, Ruth, *Patterns of Culture* (Boston: Houghton Mifflin, 1934)

Bhabha, Homi K., 'Of Mimicry and Man: The Ambivalence of Colonial Discourse', *The Location of Culture* (New York and London: Routledge, 1994)

Biskind, Peter, *Easy Riders, Raging Bulls* (London: Bloomsbury, 1998)

Boorman, John, *Adventures of a Suburban Boy* (London: Faber, 2003)

Boulle, Pierre, *The Bridge on the River Kwai*, translated by Xan Fielding (London: Fontana, 1957)

Bourne, Stephen, 'Secrets and Lies: Black Histories and British Historical Films', in Claire Monk and Amy Sargeant (eds.), *British Historical Cinema* (London: Routledge, 2002)

Boyd, Kelly and Rohan McWilliam, 'Introduction: Rethinking the Victorians', in Kelly Boyd and Rohan McWilliam (eds.), *The Victorian Studies Reader* (Abingdon: Routledge, 2007)

Briggs, Asa, *Victorian Things* (Harmondsworth: Penguin, 1990)

Briggs, Asa, *Victorian People* (Harmondsworth: Penguin, 1990 [1955])

Britton, Andrew, *Katharine Hepburn: Star as Feminist* (London: Studio Vista, 1995)

Brownlow, Kevin, *David Lean* (London: Faber, 1997)

Cardwell, Sarah, *Adaptation Revisited: Television and the Classic Novel* (Manchester: Manchester University Press, 2002)

Caton, Steven C., *Lawrence of Arabia: A Film's Anthropology* (Berkeley: University of California Press, 1999)

Chapman, James, *The British at War: Cinema, State and Propaganda, 1939–1945* (London: I. B. Tauris, 2000)

Chapman, James and Nicholas J. Cull, *Projecting Empire: Imperialism and Popular Cinema* (London: I. B. Tauris, 2009)

Christie, Ian, *The Art of Film: John Box and Production Design* (New York: Columbia University Press, 2008)

Coward, Noël, 'Shadow Play', *To-Night at 8.30* (London: Methuen, 2009 [1936])

Coward, Noël, *Future Indefinite* (London: Bloomsbury Methuen, 2004)

Coward, Noël, 'Introduction', *The Collected Plays of Noël Coward*, Vol. 5 (London: Heinemann, 1958)

Coward, Noël, *Present Indicative* (London: Heinemann, 1937)

Cullingford, E. Butler, 'Gender, Sexuality and Englishness in Modern Irish Drama and Film', in A. Bradley and M. Gialanella Valiulis (eds.), *Gender and Sexuality in Modern Ireland* (Amherst: University of Massachusetts Press, 1997)

Davies, Peter N., *The Man Behind the Bridge: Colonel Toosey and the River Kwai* (London: Athlone, 1991)

Day, Barry (ed.), *The Letters of Noël Coward* (London: Methuen, 2007)

Day, Ernest, 'A Passage to India', *American Cinematographer*, March 1985

Denby, David, 'A Tale of Two Indias', *New York Times*, 7 January 1985

Denby, David, 'A Romance in Venice', *Premiere*, March 1990, p. 30

Dickens, Charles, *Great Expectations* (Harmondsworth: Penguin, 1982 [1861])
Doane, Mary Ann, *The Desire to Desire: The Woman's Film of the 1940s* (Bloomington: Indiana University Press, 1987)
Donaldson, Laura E., *Decolonizing Feminisms: Race, Gender and Empire-Building* (London: Routledge, 1993)
Durgnat, Raymond, *A Mirror for England: British Movies from Austerity to Affluence* (London: Faber, 1971)
Dyer, Richard, *Stars*, 2nd edition (London: Routledge, 1998)
Dyer, Richard, *White* (London: Routledge, 1997)
Dyer, Richard, *Brief Encounter* (London: BFI, 1993)
Ede, Laurie, *British Film Design* (London: I. B. Tauris, 2010)
Eisenstein, Sergei, 'Dickens, Griffith, and the Film Today', in *Film Form* (London: Dennis Dobson, 1951), p. 195.
Ellis, John, 'The Quality Film Adventure: British Critics and the Cinema, 1942–1948', in Andrew Higson (ed.), *Dissolving Views: Key Writings on British Cinema* (London: Cassell, 1996)
Farley, Fidelma, 'Ireland, the Past and British Cinema: *Ryan's Daughter*', in Claire Monk and Amy Sargent (eds.), *British Historical Cinema* (London: Routledge, 2002)
Fielding, Steven, Peter Thompson and Nick Tiratsoo, *England Arise! The Labour Party and Popular Politics in 1940s Britain* (Manchester: Manchester University Press, 1995)
Forster, E. M., *A Passage to India* (Harmondsworth: Penguin, 1986 [1924])
Fraser-Cavassoni, Natasha, *Sam Spiegel* (London: Time Warner, 2004)
Freud, Sigmund and Josef Breuer, *Studies on Hysteria* [1893–95] (London: Pelican, 1974)
Friedan, Betty, *The Feminine Mystique* (London: Penguin, 1965)
Fuller, Graham and Nicholas Kent, 'Return Passage: Interview with David Lean', *Stills*, March 1985
Gaines, Jane, 'Costume and Narrative: How Dress Tells the Woman's Story', in Jane Gaines and Charlotte Herzog (eds.), *Fabrications: Costume and the Female Body* (New York and London: Routledge, 1990)
Gardiner, John, *The Victorians: An Age in Retrospect* (London: Hambledon and London, 2002)
Gelmis, Joseph, *A Conversation with Robert Bolt*, transcript of a 'Sound on Film' broadcast, November 1970. BFI library
Geraghty, Christine, *Now a Major Motion Picture: Film Adaptations of Literature and Drama* (Lanham MD: Rowman and Littlefield, 2008)
Geraghty, Christine, *British Cinema in the Fifties: Gender, Genre and the 'New Look'* (London: Routledge, 2000)
Giddings, Robert, Keith Selby and Chris Wensley (eds.), *Screening the Novel: The Theory and Practice of Literary Dramatisation* (Basingstoke: Macmillan, 1990)
Glancy, Mark, 'David Lean and Noël Coward: *In Which We Serve* and Authorship', unpublished paper, available at www.sllf.qmul.ac.uk/filmstudies/davidlean/index.html (accessed 23 July 2010)

256 BIBLIOGRAPHY

Gordon, Eleanor and Gwyneth Nair, *Murder and Morality in Victorian Britain: The Story of Madeleine Smith* (Manchester: Manchester University Press, 2009)

Granada TV Network, *Granada's Manchester Plays* (Manchester: Manchester University Press, 1962)

Gray, Frances, *Noël Coward* (Basingstoke: Macmillan, 1987)

Hall, Sheldon and Steve Neale, *Epics, Spectacles and Blockbusters* (Detroit, MI: Wayne State University Press, 2010)

Harmetz, Aljean, 'David Lean films a famed novel', *New York Times*, 7 December 1984

Harper, Sue, 'History and Representation: The Case of 1970s British Cinema', in James Chapman, Mark Glancy and Sue Harper (eds.), *The New Film History* (London: Palgrave, 2007)

Harper, Sue, *Women in British Cinema* (London: Continuum, 2000)

Harper, Sue, 'Historical Pleasures: Gainsborough Costume Melodramas', in Christine Gledhill (ed.), *Home Is Where the Heart Is: Studies in Melodrama and the Woman's Film* (London: BFI, 1987)

Harper, Sue and Vincent Porter, *British Cinema of the 1950s: The Decline of Deference* (Oxford: Oxford University Press, 2003)

Hartman, Mary S., 'Murder for Respectability: The Case of Madeleine Smith', *Victorian Studies*, Vol. 16, No. 4, June 1973

Haskell, Molly, *From Reverence to Rape* (Chicago: University of Chicago Press, 1987)

Hawley, Michelle, 'Quiller-Couch, the Function of Victorian Literature and Modernism, 1890–1930', in Miles Taylor and Michael Wolff (eds.), *The Victorians since 1901: Histories, Representations and Revisions* (Manchester: Manchester University Press, 2004)

Hederman, Mark Patrick, 'Far-Off, Most Secret and Inviolate Rose', *The Crane Bag*, Vol. 1, No. 2, 1977

Higson, Andrew, 'Space, Place, Spectacle: Landscape and Townscape in the "Kitchen Sink" Film', in Higson (ed.), *Dissolving Views: Key Writings on British Cinema* (London: Cassell, 1996)

Higson, Andrew, *Waving the Flag: Constructing a National Cinema in Britain* (Oxford: Clarendon, 1995)

Higson, Andrew, 'Re-Presenting the National Past: Nostalgia and Pastiche in the Heritage Film', in Lester Friedman (ed.), *Fires Were Started: British Cinema and Thatcherism* (London: UCL Press, 1993)

Hill, John, *British Cinema in the 1980s* (Oxford: Oxford University Press, 1999)

Hill, John, 'Images of Violence', in Kevin Rockett, Luke Gibbons and John Hill (eds.), *Cinema and Ireland* (Syracuse, NY: Syracuse University Press, 1988)

Hoare, Philip, *Noël Coward: A Biography* (London: Sinclair-Stevenson, 1995)

Hopkins, Harry, *The New Look: A Social History of the Forties and Fifties* (London: Secker and Warburg, 1963)

Horton, Robert, 'Jungle Fever: A David Lean Joint', *Film Comment*, September/October 1991

Hutchings, Peter, *Dracula* (London: I. B. Tauris, 2003)
Jackson, Kevin, *Lawrence of Arabia* (London: BFI, 2007)
James, Nick, 'Empire's last gasp', *Sight and Sound*, August 2008
James, Nick, 'David Lean', *Sight and Sound*, July 2008
Johnston, Claire, 'Dorothy Arzner: Critical Strategies' (first published 1975), in Constance Penley (ed.), *Feminism and Film Theory* (London: Routledge, 1988)
Joyce, James, *Ulysses* (London: Penguin, 2001 [1922])
Kaye, Linda, 'David Lean and the Newsreels', paper presented at the David Lean centenary conference, Queen Mary, University of London, July 2008
Kent, Howard, *Single Bed for Three: A Lawrence of Arabia Notebook* (London: Hutchinson, 1963)
Kipnis, Laura, 'The Phantom Twitchings of an Amputated Limb: Sexual Spectacle in the Post-Colonial Epic', *Wide Angle*, Vol. 11, No. 4, October 1989
Kramer, Peter, 'Women First: Titanic, Action-Adventure Films and Hollywood's Female Audience', *Historical Journal of Film, Radio and Television*, Vol. 18, No. 4, 1998
Kynaston, David, *Family Britain, 1951–57* (London: Bloomsbury, 2009)
Lant, Antonia, *Blackout: Reinventing Women for Wartime British Cinema* (Princeton, NJ: Princeton University Press, 1991)
Lahr, John, *Coward the Playwright* (London: Methuen, 1982)
LaPlace, Maria, 'Producing and Consuming the Woman's Film: Discursive Struggle in *Now, Voyager*', in Christine Gledhill (ed.), *Home is Where the Heart Is: Studies in Melodrama and the Woman's Film* (London: BFI, 1987)
Lawrence, T. E., *Seven Pillars of Wisdom* (London: Jonathan Cape, 1935)
Lean, David, 'The Film Director', in Oswell Blakeston (ed.), *Working for the Films* (London: Focal, 1947)
Lean, David, 'Brief Encounter', *Penguin Film Review*, Vol. 4, 1947
Lean, Sandra with Barry Chattington, *David Lean: An Intimate Portrait* (London: Universe, 2001)
Light, Alison, 'What larks, Pip', *Guardian* (Review), 21 September 2002
Lightman, Herb A., 'On location with Ryan's Daughter', *American Cinematographer*, August 1969
Lomax, Eric, *The Railway Man* (London: Vintage, 1996)
McFarlane, Brian, *An Autobiography of British Cinema* (London: Methuen, 1997)
McFarlane, Brian, *Novel to Film: An Introduction to the Theory of Adaptation* (Oxford: Clarendon, 1996)
McKee, Al, 'Art or outrage? *Oliver Twist* and the flap over Fagin', *Film Comment*, January 2000
Mack, John, *A Prince of Our Disorder* (New York: Little, Brown and Company, 1976)
Manvell, Roger, 'Brief Encounter', in *Masterworks of the British Cinema* (London: Faber, 1990)

BIBLIOGRAPHY

Marcus, Steven, *The Other Victorians: A Study of Sexuality and Pornography in Mid-Nineteenth-Century England* (London: Weidenfeld & Nicolson, 1966)

Martin, Adrian, 'Incursions', in Alex Clayton and Andrew Klevan (eds.), *The Language and Style of Film Criticism* (London: Routledge, 2011)

Maxford, Howard, *David Lean* (London: Batsford, 2001)

Mayer, J. P., *British Cinemas and their Audiences* (London: Dennis Dobson, 1948)

Medhurst, Andy, 'That Special Thrill: *Brief Encounter*, Homosexuality and Authorship', *Screen*, Vol. 32, No. 2, Summer 1991

Miles, Sarah, *Serves Me Right* (London: Phoenix, 1996)

Modleski, Tania, *The Women Who Knew too Much: Hitchcock and Feminist Theory* (London: Methuen, 1988)

Morley, Sheridan, *Noël Coward* (London: Haus Publishing, 2005)

Muraleedharan, T., 'Imperial Migrations: Reading the Raj Cinema of the 1980s', in Claire Monk and Amy Sargeant (eds.), *British Historical Cinema* (London: Routledge, 2002)

Neame, Ronald, *Straight from the Horse's Mouth* (Lanham MD: Scarecrow, 2003)

Organ, Steven (ed.), *David Lean: Interviews* (Jackson: University of Mississippi Press, 2009)

Orr, John, 'David Lean: The Troubled Romantic and the End of Empire', *Romantics and Modernists in British Cinema* (Edinburgh: Edinburgh University Press, 2010)

Paglia, Camille, *Sexual Personae* (London: Penguin, 1992)

Pasternak, Boris, *Doctor Zhivago*, translated by Max Hayward and Manya Harari (London: Collins and Harvill, 1958)

Paxman, Jeremy, *The English: A Portrait of a People* (London: Penguin, 1999)

Payn, Graham and Sheridan Morley (eds.), *The Noël Coward Diaries* (London: Weidenfeld & Nicolson, 1982)

Perkins, V. F., 'Must We Say What They Mean? Film Criticism and Interpretation', *Movie*, Vol. 34, No. 5, 1990

Pettitt, Lance, *Screening Ireland* (Manchester: Manchester University Press, 2000)

Phillips, Gene D., *Beyond the Epic: The Life and Films of David Lean* (Lexington: University of Kentucky Press, 2006)

Plain, Gill, *John Mills and British Cinema* (Edinburgh: Edinburgh University Press, 2006)

Pratley, Gerald, *The Cinema of David Lean* (London: Tantivy: 1974)

Pulver, Andrew, 'Adaptation of the week: *Oliver Twist*', *Guardian* (Review), 10 April 2004, p. 19

Rance, Nick, '"Victorian Values" and "Fast Young Ladies": From Madeleine Smith to Ruth Rendell', in Gary Day (ed.), *Varieties of Victorianism: The Uses of a Past* (Basingstoke: Macmillan, 1998)

Rattigan, Neil, *This Is England: British Film and the People's War, 1939–1945* (Madison, WI: Fairleigh Dickinson University Press, 2001)

Reisz, Karel and Gavin Millar, *The Technique of Film Editing* (London: Focal Press, 1953)

BIBLIOGRAPHY 259

Richards, Jeffrey and Dorothy Sheridan (eds.), *Mass-Observation at the Movies* (London: Routledge, 1987)
Ross, Steven, 'In Defence of David Lean', *Take One*, July/August 1972
Rushdie, Salman, 'Outside the Whale', *Granta*, No. 11, 1984
Ruskin, John, *Sesame and Lilies* (London: George Allen, 1865)
Rutherford, Jonathan, *Forever England: Reflections on Masculinity and Empire* (London: Lawrence & Wishart, 1997)
Rutherford, Jonathan, 'Who's that Man?', in Rowena Chapman and Jonathan Rutherford (eds.), *Male Order: Unwrapping Masculinity* (London: Lawrence & Wishart, 1988)
Said, Edward, *Orientalism* (Harmondsworth: Penguin, 1991)
Samuel, Raphael, *Theatres of Memory Vol. 1* (London: Verso, 1994)
Santas, Constantine, *The Epic in Film: From Myth to Blockbuster* (Lanham: Rowman & Littlefield, 2008)
Sarris, Andrew, *The American Cinema: Directors and Directions 1929–1968* (New York: E. P. Dutton, 1968)
Shohat, Ella, 'Gender and Culture of Empire: Toward a Feminist Ethnography of Cinema', *Quarterly Review of Film and Video*, Vol. 13, Nos. 1–3, 1991
Silver, Alain and James Ursini, *David Lean and His Films* (Los Angeles: Silman-James Press, 1992)
Silverman, Kaja, *The Acoustic Mirror: The Female Voice in Psychoanalysis and Film* (Bloomington and Indianapolis: Indiana University Press, 1988)
Silverman, Kaja, 'Lost Objects and Mistaken Subjects: Film Theory's Structuring Lack', *Wide Angle*, Vol. 7, Nos. 1–2, 1985
Silverman, Steven M., *David Lean* (London: Andre Deutsch, 1998)
Sinyard, Neil, 'Sir Alec Guinness: The Self-Effacing Star', in Bruce Babington (ed.), *British Stars and Stardom* (Manchester: Manchester University Press, 2001)
Sinyard, Neil, 'Lids Tend to Come Off: David Lean's Film of E. M. Forster's *A Passage to India*', in Robert Giddings and Erica Sheen (eds.), *The Classic Novel: From Page to Screen* (Manchester: Manchester University Press, 2000)
Sinyard, Neil, *Jack Clayton* (Manchester: Manchester University Press, 2000)
Sinyard, Neil, 'David Lean: home and the concept of Englishness', unpublished paper, 1998
Sloman, Tony, '*Ryan's Daughter* Revisited', *in70mm.com: the 70 mm Newsletter*, Issue 54, September 1998, www.in70mm.com/newsletter/1998/54/ryans/index.htm (accessed 10 December 2013)
Smith, Adrian, 'The Dawn of the Jet Age in Austerity Britain: David Lean's *The Sound Barrier* (1952)', *Historical Journal of Film, Radio and Television*, Vol. 30, No. 4, 2010
Smith, Grahame, *Dickens and the Dream of Cinema* (Manchester: Manchester University Press, 2003)
Sobchack, Vivian, 'Surge and Splendor: A Phenomenology of the Hollywood Epic Film', *Representations*, Vol. 29, Winter 1990

Spada, James, *Hepburn: Her Life in Pictures* (London: Columbus Books, 1986)
Stam, Robert, 'Beyond Fidelity: The Dialogics of Adaptation', in James Naremore (ed.), *Film Adaptation* (London: Athlone Press, 2000)
Stern, Lesley and George Kouvaros (eds.) *Falling for You: Essays on Cinema and Performance* (Sydney: Power Publications, 1999)
Stevens, George Jr. (ed.), *Conversations with the Great Moviemakers of Hollywood's Golden Age* (New York: Knopf, 2006)
Street, Sarah, '"In Blushing Technicolor": Colour in *Blithe Spirit*', *Journal of British Cinema and Television*, Vol. 7, No. 1, 2010
Sweet, Matthew, *Inventing the Victorians* (London: Faber, 2001)
Tabachnick, Stephen E. and Christopher Matheson, *Images of Lawrence* (London: Jonathan Cape, 1988)
Tasker, Yvonne (ed.), *Action and Adventure Cinema* (London: Routledge, 2004)
Taves, Brian, *The Romance of Adventure: The Genre of Historical Adventure Movies* (Jackson: University Press of Mississippi, 1993)
Taylor, Miles, 'G. M. Young and the Early Victorian Revival', in Miles Taylor and Michael Wolff (eds.), *The Victorians since 1901: Histories, Representations and Revisions* (Manchester: Manchester University Press, 2004)
Taylor, Miles, 'Introduction', in Miles Taylor and Michael Wolff (eds.), *The Victorians since 1901: Histories, Representations and Revisions* (Manchester: Manchester University Press, 2004)
Teo, Stephen, 'Under the Noonday Sun: David Lean's Asian Epics', *Cinemaya*, Nos. 17–18, Autumn/Winter 1992–93
Thompson, James, 'The BBC and the Victorians', in Miles Taylor and Michael Wolff (eds.), *The Victorians since 1901: Histories, Representations and Revisions* (Manchester: Manchester University Press, 2004)
Thomson, David, 'Unhealed wounds', *Guardian* (Review section), 10 May 2008
Todd, Ann, *The Eighth Veil* (London: William Kimber, 1980)
Tomalin, Claire, *Charles Dickens: A Life* (London: Viking: 2011)
Turner, Adrian, *Robert Bolt: Scenes from Two Lives* (London: Vintage, 1999)
Turner, Adrian, *The Making of David Lean's Lawrence of Arabia* (London: Dragon's World, 1994)
Watt, Ian, 'Talking of Films', BBC broadcast, recorded Monday 23 March 1959, transcript on BFI microfiche for *The Bridge on the River Kwai*
Waymark, Peter, 'Portents of an Indian Summer', *The Times*, 16 March 1985.
Waugh, Evelyn, *Brideshead Revisited* (London: Penguin, 2000 [1945])
Weintraub, Stanley and Rodelle Weintraub, *Lawrence of Arabia: The Literary Impulse* (Baton Rouge: Louisiana State University Press, 1975)
Wells, H. G., *The Passionate Friends* (New York: Harper, 1913)
Willemen, Paul, 'An Introduction to Framework', www.frameworkonline.com/about2.htm (accessed 30 November 2012)
Williams, Linda, *Hardcore: Power, Pleasure and the Frenzy of the Visible* (London: Pandora, 1990)

Wintour, Eleanor, 'Do women really want this?', *Tribune*, 7 October 1955
Wollen, Peter, 'Riff-Raff Realism', *Sight and Sound*, April 1998
Wood, E. R., 'Introduction', *Hobson's Choice* (London: Heinemann, 1964)
Woolf, Virginia, *A Room of One's Own* (London: Penguin, 1945)

Index

Note: page numbers in *italic* refer to illustrations

Ackroyd, Peter 41, *43*
African Queen, The (1951) 113, 120
Aldgate, Anthony 20, 21
Aldington, Richard 163
Alexander Nevsky (1938) 197
All Quiet on the Western Front (1930) 153
Alpert, Hollis 4
Ambler, Eric 8, 101, 103, 104
Anderegg, Michael 10, 32, 63, 103, 108, 140, 152, 156
Anderson, Lindsay 24, 153
Anstley, Edgar 29
Arnold, Malcolm 73, 74, *137*, *147*
Ashby, Justine 85
Ashcroft, Peggy 226, 233
Ashly, Iris 140–1
Asquith, Anthony 16
Astruc, Alexandre 6
Atonement (2007) 88
Attenborough, Richard 20, 21, 222
Austen, Jane 203
Autiero, Gaetano 119

Bahrenberg, Bruce 205
Baldwin, Stanley 28
Banerjee, Victor 223–4, 227, 230, *235*
Banks, Leslie 64
Barker, Felix 134, 209
Barr, Charles 153
Barretts of Wimpole Street, The (1934) 64

Bart, Lionel 59
Barton, Margaret 90
Barton, Ruth 209–10
Basinger, Jeanine 84
Bates, H. E. 112, 127
Battleship Potemkin (1925) 188
Bax, Arnold 54
Bazin, Andre 89, 151
BBC, The 42, 43, 86, 222
Beethoven, Ludwig van 212, 214, 219
Bells of St Mary's, The (1945) 52
Ben Hur (1959) 175
Benedict, Ruth 8, 133
Beraud-Villars, Jean 156
Bergner, Elisabeth 16
Berlin, Irving 35
Bhabha, Homi 160
Big Parade, The (1925) 48, 126
Billy Liar (1963) 183
Black Narcissus (1947) 48, 235
Blithe Spirit (1945) 33–6, 72, 73, 112, 247
Blixen, Karen 177
Blythe, John 26
Bolt, Robert 5, 85, 87, 123, 144, 160, 161, 165, 179–216 *passim*, 224, 231
Bonnie and Clyde (1967) 176
Boorman, John 9
Boulle, Pierre 133, 134, 145, 146, 148, 149, 150, 152, 154
Box, John 5, 166, 187, 198

INDEX 263

Boyd, Kelly 42
Brabourne, John 222, 224, 235
Braine, John 72
Brazzi, Rossano 86, 118, 122
Breuer, Josef 94
Brick Lane (2007) 88
Brideshead Revisted (TV, 1981) 222
Bridge on the River Kwai, The (1957) 2, 4, 7, 8, 9, 11, 84, 106, 124, 133, 134, 144–59, 176, 221–2, 250
Brief Encounter (1945) 1, 7, 8, 9, 10, 11, 12, 36, 45, 63, 64, 85, 86, 87, 88–101, 102, 103, 105, 107, 111–12, 115, 123–4, 125, 127–8, 139, 164, 185, 203, 212, 215, 229, 247
Briggs, Asa 42
Brighouse, Harold 71, 72, 73, 77–8
British Gaumont 16, 150
British Movietone News 16
Britton, Andrew 113, 125–6, 127
Brownlow, Kevin 3, 9, 17–18, 60, 76, 146, 152, 203
Bryan, John 5, 54
Burton, Richard 88, 176
Butler, Samuel 41

Calvert, Phyllis 106
Camelot (1967) 176
Cardwell, Sarah 40
Carey, Joyce 23, 90
Caton, Steven 156–7, 161, 165, 167
Cavalcade (play) 26, 27, 43
Chamberlain, Neville 21, 28
Chaplin, Charlie 15, 183
Chaplin, Geraldine 183, 189
Chapman, James 161
Chariots of Fire (1981) 222
Christie, Julie 179, 183, 184, 191, 198, 199
Christmas Carol, A 50
Cineguild 34, 36, 51–2, 56, 62, 101, 102
Citizen Kane (1941) 18, 21, 162
Cleopatra (1963) 175–6
Cocks, Jay 236
Cole, Barbara 5, 166

Colman, Ronald 145
Columbia 7, 155, 165, 222
Conquest of the Air (1936) 135
Convoy (1940) 20
Cook, William 101
Coronation Street (TV, 1960–) 155
Courtenay, Tom 183, 187
Coward, Noël 5, 11, 17–36 *passim*, 50, 72, 90–1, 92, 120, 154, 157
Cowdy, Michael 235
Crist, Judith 205
Crowley, Evin 210
Crowther, Bosley 203
Cruikshank, George 57, 60
Cukor, George 1, 84, 154
Cull, Nick 161
Cullingford, E. Butler 210
Culver, Michael 234
Cummings, Constance 33, 34
Currie, Finlay 44, 47

Dad's Army (TV, 1968–1977) 88
Dalton, Phyllis 157, 158, 189
Darling (1965) 184
Darwin, Charles 62
Davies, John Howard 54, 55, 57
Davies, Terence 27
Davis, John 7, 102
Davis, Judy 9, 84, 226, 228, 230, 235, 237
Day, Ernest 222, 233
de Banzie, Brenda 71, 75
De Laurentiis, Dino 177
Deckers, Eugene 67
Dehn, Paul 164
del Guidice, Filippo 17
Demi-Paradise, The (1943) 25
Denby, David 126, 178, 232–3
Design for Living (play) 33
Desny, Ivan 64
Diary for Timothy, A (1945) 30
Dickens, Charles 4, 41, 43–4, 49, 50, 53, 57, 58, 60, 72, 76, 78, 196, 225
Dixon, Campbell 75
Doane, Mary Ann 85

264 INDEX

Doctor Doolittle (1967) 176
Doctor Zhivago (1965) 5, 9, 11, 12, 48, 176, 177, 178, 179–203, 205, 216, 217, 224, 250–1
Documentary News Letter 19
Donald, James 145
Donaldson, Linda 226
Donat, Robert 30, 74
Dors, Diana 55
Drew, Bernard 205
du Maurier, Daphne 87
Durgnat, Raymond 89, 100, 106, 109, 180, 184, 186, 202
Dyall, Valentine 97
Dyer, Richard 8, 85, 86, 89, 93, 96, 101, 113, 232

Earhart, Amelia 32
Easy Rider (1969) 176
Eisenstein, Sergei 43, 188, 197
El Cid (1961) 175
Elliott, Denholm 137
Emma (novel) 203
Erskine, Eileen 27, 47
Escape Me Never (1935) 16

Fallen Idol, The (1948) 56
Far Pavilions, The (TV, 1984) 223
Farley, Fidelma 210
Feminine Mystique, The 217
Ferrer, José 159
Firbank, Ann 227
Flaherty, Robert 151
Flames of Passion (1989) 90
Flare Path (play) 135
Flaubert, Gustave 204, 221
For Whom the Bell Tolls (1943) 25
Foreman, Carl 146
Forrest, John 49
Forster, E. M. 178, 222, 224–5, 226, 234, 236
49th Parallel (1941) 16
Foster, Barry 212
Fowlie, Eddie 5, 145, 147, 191, 216
Frears, Stephen 155
French, Philip 154, 164

Freud, Sigmund 94, 104
Friedan, Betty 217
Fuller, Graham 1, 3
Furse, Margaret 70

Gaines, Jane 157
Gandhi, Mohandas 177, 222
Gardiner, John 41, 49
Gaumont Sound News 16
Genevieve (1953) 142
Geraghty, Christine 40, 56
Gershwin, George 229
Gibbs, Patrick 202
Gilbert and Sullivan 42
Glancy, Mark 17
Godard, Jean Luc 154
Goldman, William 1
Gone With the Wind (1939) 175
Good Old Days, The (TV, 1953–83) 43
Goodwin, Richard 222
Gordon, Charles 41
Gorris, Marleen 69
Gosse, Edmund 41
Graduate, The (1967) 176
Grant, Elspeth 140
Great Expectations (novel) 43–4, 46, 47, 49, 50–1
Great Expectations (1946) 7, 11, 40, 41, 42, 43–52, 53, 54, 56, 60, 186, 197–8, 247
Green, Guy 5, 44, 60
Greene, Graham 34
Gregg, Everly 91
Guinness, Alec 49, 55, 57, 84, 145, 147, 148, 149, 150, 160, 183, 185, 201, 223, 233, 236

Hall, Sheldon 176
Hammond, Kay 33, 34, 35
Harman, Jympson 78
Harper, Sue 7, 217, 221
Harrison, Kathleen 24
Harrison, Rex 33, 34, 36
Hartman, Mary S. 61
Haskell, Molly 208

Hatari! (1962) 154
Hatter's Castle (1942) 64
Havelock-Allan, Anthony 5, 9, 18, 33, 34, 62, 102
Havers, Nigel 226
Hawkins, Jack 145, 161
Hawks, Howard 154
Hayakawa, Sessue 145, 148, *150*
Haynes, Stanley 8, 101, 103
Hayworth, Rita 63
HBO (Home Box Office) 222
Hello Dolly! (1969) 176
Hepburn, Katharine 84–5, 86, 112–14, 117, *119*, 120, 125–6, 127, 224
Hibbin, Nina 195
Higson, Andrew 28
Hildyard, Jack 5, 117, 124, 151
Hill, Derek 151
Hill, John 236
Hindle Wakes (play) 72
Hinxman, Margaret 208
Hitchcock, Alfred 2, 67, 86–7, 111, 123
HMS Bounty 9, 177
Hoare, Philip 32
Hobson, Valerie 46, 52
Hobson's Choice (1954) 11, 40, 41, 71–8, 144, 221, 249
Hoffer, Willi 103
Holden, William 145, 150, 151
Holloway, Stanley 27, 90, 91
Hopkins, Harry 136, 139
Horne, Geoffrey 151
Horniman, Annie 72
Horton, Robert 2, 7
Hotz, Sandy 236
Houghton, Stanley 72
Hound of the Baskervilles, The (1922) 15
Hovat, Ted 175
Howard, Trevor 17, 89, 97, 98, 103, 108, 208
Hudson, Christopher 207
Hunt, Martita 45, *46*, 47
Hunted (1952) 56

Huston, John 203
Hutchings, Peter 3–4

In Which We Serve (1942) 5, 11, 17–25, 26, 50, 246
Ingram, Rex 15
Iron Petticoat, The (1956) 113
Irvine, Andrew 135

Jack, Ian 224
Jackson, Freda 44
Jackson, Kevin 3, 161
James, Nick 3
Jarre, Maurice 5, 166, 168, 186, 196, 199, 212, 215, 219, 228
Jaws (1975) 153
Jewel in the Crown, The (TV, 1984) 223
Johns, Mervyn 64
Johnson, Celia 21, 23–4, 26, 29, 84–5, 86, 89, 91, 93, 94, *96*, 97, *98*
Jones, Christopher 208, 215, 216–17, 220
Joyce, Eileen 92
Justin, John 137

Kael, Pauline 177, 204, 208, 221, 222, 229
Karapiet, Rashid 235
Kay, Bernard 192
Keats, John 94, 105
Kelly, Grace 123
Kennedy, Arthur 162
King Lear (play) 75
Kinski, Klaus 193–4
Knight, Arthur 182, 184
Kolodyaznaya, Vera 25
Korda, Alexander, 7, 72, 74, 115, 123, 135, 136, 139, 221
Krasker, Robert 99
Krish, John 72
Kwietniowski, Richard 90

Lady from Shanghai, The (1948) 63
Lambert, Gavin 20, 90

266 INDEX

Lant, Antonia 101
LaPlace, Maria 84
Last Year in Marienbad (1961) 105
Laughton, Charles 64, 71, 74, 75
Laurent, Arthur 112
Laurie, John 68
Lawbreakers, The (see also *HMS Bounty*) 177
Lawrence, A. W. 146
Lawrence, T. E. 155–6, 157, 158, 160, 162, 163, 164, 165
Lawrence of Arabia (1962) 1, 2, 8, 9, 10, 11, 71, 84, 85, 87, 123, 133, 134, 137, 144, 154–68, 179, 196, 200, 201, 203, 210, 220, 225, 236–7, 250
Lawrenson, Helen 185
Lawson, Tony 205
Lean, Edward 15
Leaves of Grass (poem) 162
Leggatt, Alison 27, 29
Lejeune, C. A. 26, 28, 34, 68, 91, 121
Lennon, Peter 46
Lester, Joan 101
Light, Alison 46
Lindbergh, Charles 135
Lion Has Wings, The (1939) 135
Lockwood, Margaret 106
Lomax, Eric 99, 147
Loneliness of the Long Distance Runner, The (1962) 183
Long Arm, The (see also *HMS Bounty*) 177
Loren, Sophia 88, 183
Lost and Found: The Story of Cook's Anchor (TV, 1979) 251
Lubitsch, Ernst 16
Lugosi, Bela 104
Lytton, Edward Bulwer 50

MacDonald, Ramsay 28
MacGowran, Jack 195
McFarlane, Brian 44
McGrath, Robert J. 184
McKee, Al 57, 59
McKern, Leo 208
McWilliam, Rohan 42
Madame Bovary (novel) 204, 222
Madeleine (1950) 9, 11, 40, 41, 59, 61–71, 102, 103, 135, 142, 213, 224, 229, 234, 248–9
Magnet, The (1950) 56
Magnificent Ambersons, The (1942) 73
Maher, Kevin 97
Majdalany, Fred 72
Major Barbara (1941) 16
Malcolm, Derek 178
Malik, Art 227
Mallory, George 135
Mann, Pamela 86
Manvell, Roger 99
Mare Nostrum (1926) 15
Martin, Adrian 6
Mary Broome (play) 72
Maslin, Janet 156–7
Mason, Richard 144
Mass Observation 19, 25
May, Elaine 88
Mayer, J. P. 26
Medhurst, Andy 90
Merchant Ivory Productions 222
MGM 7, 176, 179, 181, 184
Miles, Bernard 20, 45
Miles, Sarah 203, 207, 214, 216, 217
Milius, John 145
Mill, John Stuart 61–2
Miller, Gavin 107, 204
Millions Like Us (1943) 25
Mills, John 20, 22, 43, 47, 71, 208
Milne, Tom 209
Milton, John 22
Ministry of Information 18, 19
Mint, The (memoir) 156, 168
Miranda, Isa 116
Mitchum, Robert 4, 208, 212
Modleski, Tania 86–7
Monkhouse, Allan 72
Morley, Sheridan 28
Mountbatten, Louis 18, 22
Mousetrap, The (play) 34

Nash, Robin 75
National Federation of Far Eastern Prisoners of War 147–8
National Society of Film Critics 177, 204
Neale, Steve 176
Neame, Ronald 5, 8, 9, 18, 27, 33, 35, 36, 56, 101–2, 147
Nehru, Jawaharlal 222
New York Film Critics Circle 204
Newley, Anthony 55
Newman, Paul 181
Newton, Robert 26, 29, 57, 64
Nichols, Mike 88
Nietzsche, Friedrich 8
Nightingale, Florence 41, 42, 68
Notorious (1946) 67, 110
Now, Voyager (1942) 157

O'Brien, Robert 179
Oliver Twist (novel) 41, 53
Oliver Twist (1948) 11, 40, 41, 49, 51, 53–60, 68, 103, 186, 248
On Liberty (book) 62
On the Origin of the Species (book) 62
Organ, Steven 9
Orr, John 67, 105, 106, 111
Orwell, George 25, 30
O'Toole, Peter 84, 156–7, 158, 159, 164
Out of Africa (memoir) 177

Paglia, Camille 133–4
Paradine Case, The (1947) 111
Parke, MacDonald 114
Pascal, Gabriel 16
Passage to India, A (1984) 1982, 8, 9, 12, 17, 68, 127, 177, 221–37, 251–2
Passionate Friends, The (1949) 5, 8, 9, 11, 62, 63, 84, 85, 86, 101–12, 125, 135, 142, 229, 248
Pasternak, Boris 179, 180, 190, 196, 224
Patmore, Coventry 62

Patrick, Nigel 137, 138
Paxman, Jeremy 88–9
Paxton, Joseph 61
Peek, Ian Denys 147
Pemberton, Antonia 227
Perkins, V. F. 6–7
Pettitt, Lance 220
Philadelphia Story, The (1939) 113
Philips, Gene 16, 143
Piccadilly Incident (1946) 90
Pink String and Sealing Wax (1945) 64
Plain, Gill 20
Ponti, Carlo 7, 180, 183
Porter, Vincent 7
Powell, Dilys 35, 73, 115–16, 117, 137, 166, 184
Powell, Michael 16–17, 48
Pratley, Gerald 60
Pressburger, Emeric 48
Priestley, J. B. 25
Private Life of Henry VIII, The (1933) 74
Private Lives (play) 33
Pudovkin, Vsevolod 24
Puttnam, David 177
Pygmalion (1938) 16

Q Planes (1939) 135
Quayle, Anthony 159, 162
Question of Silence, A (1982) 69
Quigly, Isabel 151–2, 153
Quinn, Anthony 158, 160

Rachmaninov, Sergei 91, 92, 94, 99, 100, 102
Radford, Basil 100
Rainmaker, The (1956) 113
Rains, Claude 104, 108, 110, 159
Ramsay, Peggy 202
Random Harvest (1942) 19
Rank, J. Arthur 7, 102
Rank Organisation 144
Rashomon (1950) 217
Rattigan, Terrence 135, 139
Rau, Santha Rama 222, 225, 235

Ray, Satyajit 223
Raymond, Cyril 93, 100
Rear Window (1954) 190
Rebecca (1940) 87
Reed, Carol 59
Reed, Rex 205
Règle du jeu, La (1939) 89
Reisz, Karel 107
Renoir, Jean 89, 223
Resnais, Alain 105
Rest is Silence, The (play) 62
Richards, Jeffrey 20, 21
Richardson, Ralph 137, 138, 145, 183
River, The (1951) 223
RKO 17
Robinson, David 157, 184
Roeg, Nicolas 6, 177
Room at the Top (novel) 72
Room at the Top (1959) 72
Room with a View (1985) 222
Roots (play) 78
Rose, Jane 113
Roses of Picardy (1927) 150
Rossini, Gioachino 121, 125
Rushdie, Salman 222-3
Ruskin, John 60
Rutherford, Jonathan 155-6
Rutherford, Margaret 33, 36
Ryan's Daughter (1970) 2, 7, 9, 11, 12, 59, 65, 68, 85, 123-4, 176-7, 178, 203-21, 224, 229, 231, 251

Said, Edward 160
Samuel, Raphael 49-50, 51, 58, 59
Sarris, Andrew 1-2
Schickel, Richard 177
Scott, Robert Falcon 135, 198
Searle, Ronald 147
Sears, Ann 150-1
Seth, Roshan 233
Seven Pillars of Wisdom 155, 156, 160, 164, 165
Seven Year Itch, The (1955) 88
Seventh Veil, The (1945) 90, 106, 111
Shadow Play (play) 95
Sharif, Omar 9, 84, 157, 164, 179, 181-2, 184, 188, 198, 200
Shaw, George Bernard 16, 76
Sheed, Maisie 148
Sheridan, Dinah 142
Shingleton, Wilfred 73
Shipley, Margaret 141
Ships with Wings (1941) 20
Shulman, Milton 103, 124
Sight and Sound 1, 3, 89, 223
Silver, Alain 9, 53, 76, 100, 143, 178, 208
Silverman, Kaja 88
Silverman, Stephen 115
Simmons, Jean 45, 46, 47
Sinyard, Neil 149, 201, 224
Sloman, Tony 221
Smiles, Samuel 75
Smith, Grahame 47, 49, 53
Sobchack, Vivian 175, 179, 184
Sound Barrier, The (1952) 11, 72, 102, 112, 133, 134, 135-44, 150, 186, 249
Sound of Music, The (1965) 176
South Pacific (1958) 122
Spartacus (1960) 175
Spencer, Norman 62, 73, 77, 136, 137, 146, 151
Spielberg, Steven 1, 153, 154
Spiegel, Sam 5, 7, 144-6, 148, 152, 162, 166
Stam, Robert 40
Steiger, Rod 5, 183, 187, 191
Stephenson, Henry 55
Stevens Jr, George 4
Still Life (play) 91, 100
Strachey, Lytton 41
Street, Sarah 36
Sullivan, Francis L. 49
Summer Madness (1955) 9, 10, 11, 85, 86, 87, 112-28, 145, 218, 249-50
Summertime (1955) 112, 125, see *Summer Madness*
Sweet, Matthew 41, 68
Swift, Clive 233

Tasker, Yvonne 134
Taste of Honey, A (1961) 183

Taylor, Elizabeth 176
Taylor, Miles 41, 42
This Happy Breed (1944) 8, 9, 19, 25–33, 50, 73, 87, 112, 246
Thomas, Lowell 162
Thomas, Ralph 144
Thomson, David 11
Thorn-EMI 222
Three Coins in the Fountain (1954) 118
Time of the Cuckoo, The (play) 112
Titfield Thunderbolt, The (1953) 142
To Catch a Thief (1955) 123
Todd, Ann 62, 63, 70, 71, 85, 86, 102, 106, 108, 109, 111, 136, 137, 139, 140, 141–2, 150
Toland, Gregg 18
Tolstoy, Alexandra 203
Tomalin, Claire 50–1, 59
Tomelty, Joseph 138
Tonight at 8.30 (play) 91, 95
Touch of Class, A (1973) 88
Tracy, Spencer 113
Trainspotting (1996) 58
Tringham, David 155
Turner, Adrian 180, 204, 217
Tushingham, Rita 183, 186
20th Century Fox 176
2001: A Space Odyssey (1968) 176
Tynan, Kenneth 184, 192
Typically British (TV, 1995) 155

Unsworth, Maggie 5
Ursini, James 9, 53, 76, 100, 143, 178, 208

Van Dyke, W. S. 151
Veness, Amy 27, 55
Verney, Guy 28
Vidor, King 154
Visconti, Luchino 203
Vivre sa vie (1962) 154
Von Braun, Wernher 144

Wager, Anthony 44, 46
Walker, Alexander 167, 181, 184, 205, 209, 210, 232
Walsh, Kay 9, 22, 23, 26, 32, 53, 57, 59, 103
Watt, Ian 147, 152
Waugh, Evelyn 42
Way to the Stars, The (1945) 135
Welles, Orson 17, 18, 21, 27, 63, 73, 162
Wells, H. G. 101, 102, 103, 105, 111
Wesker, Arnold 78
West, Rebecca 105
White, Merrill 16
White Shadows of the South Seas (1928) 151
Whitebait, William 26, 36
Whitley, Reg 141
Whitman, Walt 162
Whittle, Frank 135
Wicked Lady, The (1945) 52, 90
Wilcox, Herbert 42
Wilder, Billy 1, 154
Willeman, Paul 223
Willey, Basil 42
Williams, L. P. 101
Williams, Linda 217
Willingham, Calder 146
Wilman, Noel 195
Wilson, Michael 146, 160, 161–2, 166
Wilson-Apperson, John 158
Wind Cannot Read, The (novel) 144, 151, 221
Winnington, Richard 28, 33, 47
Wiseman, Tom 166
Wollen, Peter 4
Wood, E. R. 76
Wood, Victoria 88
Wooland, Norman 64
Woolf, Virginia 177–8
Wyler, William 1, 10

Yellow Balloon, The (1953) 56
Young, Freddie 5, 166, 190, 215
Young, G. M. 42, 61

Zinnemann, Fred 154